SEX AND CONQUEST

SEX AND CONQUEST

Gendered Violence, Political Order, and the European Conquest of the Americas

Richard C. Trexler

Cornell University Press
Ithaca, New York

Copyright © Richard C. Trexler 1995

The right of Richard C. Trexler to be identified as
author of this work has been asserted in accordance with the
Copyright, Designs and Patents Act 1988.

First published in 1995 by Polity Press
in association with Blackwell Publishers Ltd.

ISBN 8014–3224–3

A CIP catalogue record for this book is available
from the Library of Congress.

Typeset in 10½ on 12 pt Sabon
by CentraCet
Printed in Great Britain by T.J. Press, Padstow, Ltd

This book is printed on acid-free paper.

For the children

Contents

List of Illustrations   ix
Acknowledgments   xi

Introduction   1

1 Backgrounds   12

2 Iberian Experiences   38

3 The Military and Diplomatic Berdache   64

4 The Domestic Berdache: Becoming   82

5 The Religious Berdache   102

6 On the Ground   118

7 Attitudes and Assessments   141

8 Yesterday and Today   173

Notes   181
Bibliography   266
Index   286

List of Illustrations

1 Attic red-figure vase (R1155), after 460 BC, with the inscription: 'I am Eurymedon. I stand bent over.' Museum für Kunst und Gewerbe, Hamburg.　　15

2 Heap of Libyan penises and hands, from Medinet Habu, Egypt. Reproduced from H. Nelson et al., *Later Historical Records of Ramses III: Medinet Habu*, vol. 2 (Chicago, 1932), pl. 75; Bodleian Library, Oxford.　　16

3 Penile evisceration of enemies by the soldiers of Outina. Reproduced from T. de Bry, *America*, pt 2, fig. XV, in the account of Jacques Le Moyne; Bodleian Library, Oxford.　　69

4 *Martirio del Bendito Pe. Fray Diego Ortiz en Vilcabamba*, engraving by Petrus de Jode after Erasmus Quellin, page 782–3 of *Coronica moralizada del Orden de San Augustin en el Perú*, 1638, reproduced by permission of Boston Athenaeum.　　70

5 An Andean, tied to a *picota*, is beaten by a Spaniard and a black slave. Reproduced from Felipe Guaman Poma de Ayala, *Nueva crónica y buen gobierno*, ed. J. Murra, R. Adorno and J. Urioste, vol. 2 (Madrid, 1987), 511; The Royal Library, Copenhagen.　　75

6 Balboa's mastiffs attack the Panamanians. Reproduced from T. de Bry, *America*, pt 4, fig. XXII, in the *Historia* of Girolamo Benzoni; Bodleian Library, Oxford.　　83

7 Homosexual anal intercourse, Moche Culture. National Museum of Archaeology, Anthropology and History, Lima.　　112

8 Hetero- or homosexual anal intercourse, Coastal Inca Culture. National Museum of Archaeology, Anthropology and History, Lima.　　113

9 George Catlin, *Dance to the Berdash*, oil on canvas, 49.6 × 70.0 cms, reproduced by permission of National Museum of American Art, Smithsonian Institution, gift of Mrs Joseph Harrison, Jr.　　119

10 *Wewa Zuni, Man-Woman Priestess*, reproduced by permission of National Anthropological Archives, Smithsonian Institution.　　120

11 *St Michael destroys the Sodomitic Giant*, reproduced from Pedro de Cieza de León, *La chronica del Perú, nuevamente escrita, por Pedro de Cieca de Leon, vezino de Sevilla*, 1554, c. 104r © Berlin – Preußischer Kulturbesitz/ Handschriftenabteilung.　　144

Acknowledgments

In fifteenth-century Florence, Italy, fathers worried that their sons, whom they feared, had become soft. A decade ago, when I switched from studying Florence to the Americas, I found the same anxieties at work in the so-called New World, from the time of the Iberian conquests almost until the present day. Having just completed their conquest of the allegedly 'effeminate' Moors, Iberian warriors now an ocean away faced feathered warriors and, fearing them, called them women.

Yet both in Florence and America, those who were feared ultimately had to be regendered male. It seems that a central paradox involved in transgendering male enemies is that, to rule them, erstwhile 'sissies' must be converted to worthy male adversaries. How do gender and conquest intermix? Thereby lies a story: of Iberians, themselves vulnerable, seeking to dominate by understanding the different sexual cultures of the Americas; of native Americans, themselves accustomed to gendering enemies, attempting to survive the conquerors' ridicule.

Many friends and colleagues have nourished my interest in this topic and contributed to the story, both through their knowledge of the subject, and by sensitizing me to the ideological import today of this early modern reality. Such awareness, I feel, has significantly refined my understanding of the historical realities. Without that sense of the present, I have learned, there can be no 'feeling into' the past. I am especially grateful to William A. Christian, Jr., Ramón

Gutiérrez, Cecelia F. Klein, Sabine G. MacCormack, Catharine A. MacKinnon, Randy McGuire and Michael J. Rocke for critically reading various drafts. Thomas Africa, Peter J. Arnade, Judith C. Brown, Jane Collins, K. J. Dover, David F. Greenberg, John Hollister, Christiane Klapisch-Zuber, Jeffrey Masson, Eugene F. Rice and Norman Stillman are but a few of many colleagues who have contributed to my understanding of the theme of sex and conquest; many others are acknowledged at particular points in the notes. Discussions on the subject I conducted at Stanford and Cornell universities, and at the Centre de Recherche Historique in Paris, proved invaluable to my understanding. The John Simon Guggenheim Foundation and the Wissenschaftskolleg in Berlin helped materially. Finally, the gay and lesbian movements, and the women's movement more generally, provided moral inspiration, the best institutional backing there is.

Introduction

This abomination is better forgotten than placed in memory. But I wanted to mention it.[1]

Homosexuality becomes an instrument for establishing rank and status, validating masculinity, and creating protective-dependent relationships.[2]

In 1519, the year the Spaniards settled on the North American mainland, the council of the new town of Veracruz wrote to Charles V about the natives the Spaniards had encountered. The council urged the Catholic monarchs to obtain permission from the pope to punish 'evil and rebellious' natives as enemies of the holy faith:

> Such punishment [might] serve as a further occasion of warning and dread to those who still rebel, and thus dissuade them from such great evils as those which they work in the service of the devil. For in addition to ... children and men and women [being] killed and offered in sacrifice, we have learned and have been informed that they are doubtless all sodomites and engage in that abominable sin.[3]

There is more to this characterization than the inveterate male habit of gendering enemies female or effeminate. As they had from their earliest contacts with Americans, the Iberians on this occasion claimed the right to conquer native American males once they demonstrated that the latter practiced 'sodomy,' by which they usually meant homosexual behavior, among themselves. This 'nefarious,' 'unmentionable' and 'abominable sin' was, it was said, 'against nature.'[4] Soon such denunciations appeared in a literary format. In 1526, the Spanish royal historian Gonzalo Fernández de Oviedo began to publish his multi-volume *General History of the Indies*, and it contains many first-hand reports claiming that homosexual

practices were common in both hemispheres.[5] Thus a few years after
permanent settlements of whites were established on the American
mainland, a body of information on the sexual proclivities of
Americans began to appear in print. It forms the basic resource for
the following work, whose first and primary purpose is to describe
and analyze American homosexual practices and the male transvestism often associated with them, as the Iberians heard of these
practices during their original contacts with the many peoples of
what would come to be called Latin America.

Yet how much can we learn about the Americans when the Iberians
who are our primary informers often stood to gain by accusing them
of sodomy? Not much, claimed the Dominican Bartolomé de Las
Casas. He told the emperor in 1540 that the Spaniards' denunciations
of sodomy (*los pecados nefandos*) served 'only their temporal
interest.'[6] The very richness of the sources, which stretch, with the
conquests themselves, from the late fifteenth through the eighteenth
centuries,[7] stems in part from the personal gain involved. Still, my
view is that there is much to learn from this mountain of (exclusively
male) sources, and even a way to approach the topic so as to allow
us to discount some of the sloganeering indulged in by the Iberians.
And that is to begin by surveying the Mediterranean sexual scene on
the eve of the conquests. In this way, we may encounter American
sexuality against the background of the European experiences and
interests of those conquerors who are usually our only sources on the
subject. This is not Eurocentric in character, but merely prudent. As
is well known, inattention to the character of these Iberian sources
often has led to serious misapprehensions of the meaning of these
sources.

Let us not conceal the fact that all discourse about sexuality and
gender, whether in Europe about Europeans, within an American
tribe, or by Iberians conquering New World males, as they see it, is
among other things about hierarchy, about dominion and subordination. Sexuality defines gender, a discourse that is about power
relations. Some may claim that the interpretations native American
sexualities assigned to such markers as hair length, paint, clothing
and gestures were so much at variance with those of the conquerors
as to make any comparative view of American gender practices
impossible.[8] I disagree. We can learn a good deal about American
sexual practices if we keep in mind that the Iberians were the
conquerors and that their descriptions of sexual practices are discourses about power no less than were indigenous sexual practices.
Sexuality was, in Foucault's words, less a drive opposed to power

than 'an especially dense transfer point for relations of power: between men and women, young people and old people, parents and offspring, teachers and students, priests and laity, an administration and a population.'[9] Thus a second purpose of this work is to explore the relation between conquest and eros both within Amerindian societies and in the Iberian mind.

A third purpose will be to explore where, on the basis of their observations of native American life, the Iberians thought sodomy fit into a theory of cultural development. To achieve this goal, the changes over time and the different intentions of the Iberian sources have to be well understood. The original conquerors were, alas, not only biased but downright dull in their reporting as regards politically charged matters such as homosexual behavior. As the Veracruz letter shows, 'the enemy' being one, conquerors tended to repeat sweeping generalizations. It was another matter with the politicians who came after the conquerors. They had to administer subjects, not enemies, and so warrior writers were soon balanced by bureaucratic intellectuals such as Alonso de Zorita in Mexico and Pedro de Cieza de León in Peru. These men knew that the Aztec and Inca empires could not be made to serve as a basis for Spanish imperial structures if the Europeans indiscriminately denounced all tribes great and small as sodomitic. An ideological counterwave arose which argued that, while lesser nations might be sissy, the Aztecs and Incas were macho.

Missionaries added mightily to the data provided by lay conquerors and administrators, and the main reason for their often thick descriptions is obvious. The European clergy needed reliable information on native sexual institutions if they were to conquer the devil and convert these gentiles. Of course, each religious order had its own reasons to over- or underestimate the extent of native homosexual behavior: an order that thought of the Americans as close to nature might, for instance, decide that their 'unnatural' sexuality was minimal, while another order that viewed the natives as fallen might espy homosexual acts everywhere.

Yet just as lay institutions affected lay reporting, so did European clerical institutions influence the way missionaries described native sexual practices. First, the monastic subordination of young novices to father-monks and friars within a male ambience, a subordination that often had a sexual component, was bound to influence the ways in which the missionary fathers judged and suppressed, or tolerated, native sexual practices.[10] One example may suffice at this point. We will see that, while European laymen, and the native Americans, were most offended by adult males who played the so-called passive homosexual role, usually through anal reception, clerks here as in Europe were more outraged by so-called active homosexual partners, for whom the term 'sodomite' was usually reserved. Clearly, not only the Europeans' sexual conceptions of cultural development, but the status of the authors of the European sources as well, must be carefully weighed when describing what they have to say about the Americas.

We feel the need to relate the European to the native sexual experience, but not one of our sources would have any of it. They showed an overwhelming preference for talking about the natives without reference to their own sexual world, which one might naively conclude was untouched by such 'crimes.' Freed from the necessity of comparing America with Europe, by the mid-sixteenth century authors used certain rhetorical markers to identify whose side they were on as regarded the central question of how extensive American homosexual behavior was. There were still many who believed that sodomy among Americans was widespread, and even that it had deep psychological roots. The reason for this conviction had changed, however. Instead of sodomites being effeminate losers in battle, the specter of native revolt was introduced as evidence of sodomy. As early as 1525, we find a missionary furious with native boys for just this reason. He had interned the sons of the local chiefs in the Dominican friary in Chiribichi (Venezuela) to save their souls through indoctrination. Ungratefully, the boys soon revolted. The friar promptly denounced these 'stupid and silly' natives as being 'more sodomitic than any other nation.'[11]

Yet quite as many other writers now denied that homosexual practices were widespread, tending to play down sodomy's political or cultural implications even among the natives. At the mid-sixteenth century, one of them, the Dominican friar and bishop Bartolomé de Las Casas, became the most persistent critic of Oviedo on this as on other matters. Las Casas, who compared American sexual practices not with those of Europeans, but with those of the Roman and Greek 'gentiles,' went so far as to deny that a single American people condoned homosexual practices. Further to the south, the authoritative ethnographer of the Andes, Pedro de Cieza de León, might admit that the Mantan tribes in modern Ecuador had accepted male homosexual behavior. But elsewhere in the Inca realm, Cieza continued significantly, only single individuals, from one to ten in any village, practiced the 'evil,' 'just as sinners did everywhere.'[12]

Here was a formulation that remained rare enough. Cieza distinguished between socially condoned sodomy – a 'political sin,' whose extent he radically circumscribed but which another contemporary found 'almost permitted' in most areas of New Spain[13] – and an individual practice without social approbation that he implied was no more at home in the Andes than in Europe, for example. Cieza was almost, but not quite, alone. While discussing America, the Dominican theologian Francisco de Vitoria had divided up Europe in similar fashion as early as 1537. He denounced the notion that American sodomy gave Spaniards a right of conquest, because by the same logic, he said, 'it would follow that the French king could make war on the Italians because they commit sins against nature.'[14]

With these exceptions, Iberian sources strictly avoid comparing American sexual practices with European, let alone Iberian, ones, even with those of the Moors whose history was so bound up with that of Spain. Vitoria himself made no reference to Spain, but only to France and Italy. The habit has persisted: to this day there is little serious literature on either Iberian or North African homosexual behavior.[15] In his *The Pre-Columbian Mind* (1971), the physician Francisco Guerra proved to his own satisfaction that, since they were a nation of warriors, Spaniards could not have introduced any homosexuality into the Americas. In the one possible case of homosexual 'contagion,' in which a trio from a Spanish galley was executed for sodomy, Guerra gratifyingly found no Spaniards: two of the sodomites were Italians and the third was a German. The extensive sodomy in the New World had obviously spread from tribe to tribe, and not across the ocean.[16] Or if it had, as some later 'enlightened' authors would have it, it spread to the Americas not from Europe but from black Africa.[17] What need to study the sexual habits of the Europeans?

Thus almost all sources, whether they thought sodomy was extensive or limited, describe American homosexual practices as unheard of (*nunca oída*), exotic practices. But we should lay aside all such ideological claptrap: both the view that native souls were and are incomparable with European ones, and the cliché that Europeans were rational and Americans exotic, or European sexuality repressive, Amerindian folkways liberating.

This book can study the relations between eros and power at the time of the conquests with a more or less free hand because the massive recent literature on homosexual behavior has often been in denial, uncomfortable with questions of power. Thus some scholars have been so determined to find adult same-age, consenting homosexual subcultures in medieval and early modern European sources that they have denied that homosexual behavior involving power could even be called 'homosexuality.' Instead, it was 'pederasty.'[18] Perhaps perversely, however, this book avoids using the word 'homosexuals' or 'homosexuality' altogether, because we now know that, while power certainly existed in this age, 'homosexuality' and 'homosexuals' in the modern sense did not.[19]

In American studies, the absence of power in the discourse on homosexuality has been particularly marked in discussing the 'berdache' or permanently transvested male who, when he was sexually involved, always assumed the passive role in homosexual relations. As recently surveyed by Walter Williams, these important figures are seen more as forerunners of modern liberated gays than as emblems of tribal power and authority, genial artistic types rather than the embodiments of dependence they prove to be in the period of the conquests.[20] The present book, on the other hand, is less about desire or 'homosexual love,' those hallmarks of the struggling individual, and more about seduction, that eros of the political collectivity.[21]

Yet even as power has been neglected as a component of homosexual behavior in Europe and America, research in two other areas of the world and of science has made the problem of power in sexual relations one that will not go away. First, differences of age in homosexual practices have emerged as crucial in the study of the politics of tribal life in Papua New Guinea and Melanesia.[22] The emphasis of these tribes on cohorts has helped me to distinguish between homosexual relations as a periodic activity of pre-nuptial celibates, in which the youngest play the passive role and elders the active role, and homosexual behavior as a lifelong experience of many transvested passives, usually if not always with elder males. As we shall see, the second type predominated in pre-Conquest America, and in Europe.[23]

Second, Gerda Lerner's *Creation of Patriarchy*, which concentrates on the ancient Near East, has proved helpful because it forced me to view male hierarchical relations, concerned predominantly with power, in the light of the historical subordination of women, concerned in the first place with property. To be sure, the present work would have benefited from monographs on female homosexual behavior, or on the so-called female berdache, which are almost non-existent due to the dearth of information in the sources. Surely, I do not intend to downplay violence against past women through this discourse about men. To the contrary, what I describe as the treatment of the male berdache will throw light on the more obscure topic of the treatment of women. In this sense, Lerner's attention to the rape of women offered me a springboard for understanding the rape of men by judicial authority, as has, *mutatis mutandis*, the work of Irene Silverblatt on Inca women.[24]

Thus, interested from the start in the relation between force and sex, this book begins with the European and Mediterranean backgrounds of our sources. Its purpose is to categorize a framework of forces at work in antiquity that will to some extent persist throughout the early history of Iberian America. First, it argues that, in much of antiquity, males as well as females were born into a world of penetrative penality. That is, men as well as women were sometimes punished through sexual means. To understand such a violent context, it is best to subdivide. The desire to control and increase property required that owners punish other males who endangered their possession of slaves, women, and the like. The desire to accumulate power, on the other hand, required that strong men show a flashy retinue of usually younger males who were effeminized, *mutatis mutandis*, often by the sexual punishments I will here pass in review. This overview concludes by clarifying two concepts that are a key to much of what follows. First, the specifically ancient and medieval notion of 'effeminacy' is examined. Then a primary paradox is laid on the table. Why is it that, while homosexual 'actives,' that is, those who penetrate, were generally admired or at least tolerated by traditional cultures, precisely such 'sodomites' might be more harshly legislated against than were the pathics or 'passives' who received these penetrators?

With this general background and question-posing on the table, Chapter 2 turns its specific gaze to Moorish and Christian Iberia. The aim is to furnish the most detailed background on sexual mores possible in an Iberian culture whose historians have notoriously neglected or trivialized this aspect of their past. The overview begins with evidence that Moorish Spain was a fulcrum for commerce in eunuchs and young boys between Europe and North Africa during the central Middle Ages, creating strong reason to suppose that Moorish, or perhaps Mediterranean, sexual institutions remained a part of re-Christianized Iberia. Then this chapter passes in review peninsular legislation on the matter from the Visigoths to the sixteenth century, with particular attention being given to differences between passive and active roles as they surface from this legislation. This is followed by an analysis of three notional complexes related to homosexual activity: monasticism, the role of women in increasing or decreasing male homosexual activity, and, finally, the key role of Spanish military life in determining the culture's attitude toward homosexual acts. The analysis then turns to a description of the surviving information on actual punishments of this 'crime.' For all their alleged harshness, the conclusion of this chapter shows that, like the rest of Europe, Spain's move toward court 'civilization' meant an increasing effeminization of its macho soldiers, bringing them more in line with the courts of far-off India and Persia, of which they were learning at just the moment they discovered and conquered America.

Chapter 3 enters the native American sexual universe where Europeans first encountered it: in the field of war and diplomacy. Outside their own towns and villages, native American warriors used certain sexual behaviors to gender outsiders, and these deserve our primary attention. It is true that scholars usually conceive of warrior actions as projections from a group's domestic institutions, but a better way to understand a culture's homosexual practices may be first to study gendering not inside but outside, in the insults and games associated with victory and defeat. This chapter looks at gendering among warriors and camp followers, and then the sexual roles that such behavior forced upon living and dead prisoners. Postures of gendered dominance and submission in the diplomatic realm also require our attention, as does the gendering of the lesser partner after an 'equal' diplomatic treaty.

In Chapter 4, the warriors return home, so to speak, to create civil institutions, among which none is more important to this book than the social constructions that were the berdaches or adult males who played women – not a third or fourth sex – within most native American tribes, and usually assumed the receptive sexual position. Here I sketch the social and political forces which produced the institution of the berdache, dismissing romantic notions according to which individual Amerindians merely allowed innate sexual proclivities to come to the surface. The chapter then shows that there were three life stages at which males might become berdaches: during childhood, at puberty, and – something largely ignored by earlier literature – when a senior. I then show that these transitions had a familial context on the one hand, and a political one on the other. Finally, an absolutely fundamental difference between European and American practice is driven home: Europeans might easily practice homosexually without transvesting and, even if they did, they changed back easily. When an American boy was dressed as a woman, he took on that dress for life.

Chapter 4 had the task of demonstrating that society and culture produced berdaches. Chapter 5 begins to locate the berdache and his

homosexual practices within that social and cultural field. It concentrates on working out their religious role in Amerindian society, not
because that role is more important than life at ground zero (reserved
for Chapter 6) but because the functions of the berdaches appear
most transparently in their services on the mountains. In different
parts of Mexico and the Andes we encounter young men forced to
dress as women, who serve as offerings to the gods when, in religious
rites, they were anally raped by the tribal big men or priests.
Articulators of power, class and status, such males were, perhaps
especially in the Andes, a central tribal religious resource. This having
been said, however, I then stress what the berdaches of our period
were not. They were not soothsayers or doctors, as they later became,
nor, before the seventeenth century, do we find the counsel of these
figures to have been a tribal capital good. A picture of the berdaches
emerges that was, at the time of the conquests and in these first
centuries of colonialism, one of degradation, if with an occasional
silver lining.

Our account now turns to summarizing the few social facts we
possess about the berdaches, to come as close as possible to the
homosexual experiences of these transvestites. As a matter of fact, it
seems that berdaches were to be found in almost all American tribes,
North and South, but, as a matter of stereotype, Iberians had their
own ideas where homosexual behavior was most pronounced, which
they assiduously tried to map. We come away from this chapter with
some idea of the number of berdaches found in each tribe or
settlement, and of their ages. I give extensive attention to their
appearance, both in dress and gesture, and to the occupations they
were expected to fulfill, both sexual and domestic. In conclusion, the
chapter turns its attention to the alleged first appearance in the
seventeenth century of heterosexual anal intercourse and to lesbian
practices, both the product, it is said, of the desire of the native
Americans to avoid conceiving children in the hellhole to which the
Iberian exploitations exposed them. Some contemporaries believed
that, as Iberian repression took root, the so-called deviant behaviors
of the past only increased.

In Chapter 7, the attitudes of both Iberians and Americans toward
transvestism and homosexual behaviors are finally laid on the table;
their description has been delayed till now to avoid the notion that
the behaviors we have now described were the products of such
attitudes, rather than their causes. The problem of such attitudes is
first addressed by analyzing what natives and Iberians had to say
about the sexual history of the Americas. The legend of the giants

who in days past had come ashore in present-day Ecuador and fallen to uncontrolled penetrations of the natives leads to a survey of the principle of homosexual infection as it was understood by the Spaniards. Then our attention is turned to the rise and decline of civilization understood as a history of sexuality, in which we pursue the Iberians' notion that sodomy was characteristic of a lower level of civilization.

At this point in the chapter, we turn to native and Iberian attitudes regarding fundamental questions of native comportment. One such question is whether the Americans, North or South, had laws against homosexual behavior, an important test case for judging the objectivity of our European sources. A second query to be raised is that of women's attitudes toward male homosexual comportment. In the midst of this examination we find that, as a general rule in these cultures, insults directed against those involved in homosexual undertakings were usually turned by women and men against passives, and not against actives.

The chapter concludes by showing that such native resentment against passives was shared not ony by contemporary Spanish culture – in the persons of peninsular missionaries – but by much of today's Latin America as well. To this day in many areas of the continent, the passive, and only the passive, is called a 'homosexual.' The active is an *hombre*. That is, to be sexually active over and against a lesser is what a man *is*.

The eighth and concluding chapter of this book begins with a summation of the main points of the work, both points I have made and arguments I have assuredly *not* put forward. In concluding, the reader will also be told what information – and it is substantial – has not been forthcoming from the sources. Much of the mystery will remain; no European visitor to the New World came away thinking that sex among the natives was just one damned thing after another, nor shall we. Yes, there were tribes whose sexual division of labor was partially the reverse of the Iberian one! No easy matter to understand! Not to mention earrings, long hair, and the absence of facial hair. And yet, if American males, in Cieza's words, 't[ook] care of their faces and other effeminate offices' in a way still strange to European men in 1500, the latter's bewilderment would not last long in the new European world of wigs, paints, and odors.[25] In many ways, the Iberians and the native Americans were definitely worlds apart. To descry both the apartness and the solidarity seductively has been the challenge.

In the end, however, there is the violence to be accounted for, and the concluding pages of this book will explain the historical and psychological models of Sigmund Freud that have helped me along the way, especially since the harem complex, so important to Freud, was a rooted part of the social orders of the Mediterranean and of the main cultures of the Americas. It is baffling to realize that Freud, but not just Freud, was convinced at the beginning of the twentieth century that the harsh ways of sexual behavior were a thing of the past. An honest conclusion to this book requires us to draw the connection between the ancient treatment of the berdaches and the present problem of child abuse. We shall remind the reader that at the end of the twentieth century we are in the midst of breaking down the last tabu, that which forbids us from talking about the widespread child abuse that has been, and is, part of our 'civilization.'

1
Backgrounds

If a man has intercourse with the hindquarters of his equal, that man will be foremost among his brothers and colleagues.
—Babylonian divination manual.[1]

Wherever, on the contrary, they submitted readily and without a struggle, he inscribed on the pillars ... female genitalia to mark that they were a nation of women, that is, unwarlike and effeminate.
—Herodotus on Pharaoh Sesostris.[2]

A century ago the orientalist Richard Burton determined that there was a particular region of the globe, which he called the Sotadic Zone, where male homosexual behavior was common and condoned.[3] Burton's attempt to localize such practices has not fared well. Parameters to simplify the study of homoeroticism well up, only to shift away in the sands of time. Beginning an overview of homosexual behavior in the millennium before the European discovery of the New World, it is well to emphasize how quickly certainties become dubious. Are we sure in contrasting, for example, the tolerance which traditional China appears to have shown for male homosexual behavior with the dislike much of Indian culture is said to have harbored for it? Or, further west, are we at ease with the acceptance accorded this activity which experts find among several early Mesopotamian cultures and the intolerance others ascribe to the Israelites and the Egyptians? Are we ready to accept, in short, stereotypes of the ilk of the Sibylline Oracle, who reportedly said of the Jews:

They have no unholy intercourse with boys as do the Phoenicians and Egyptians, the Latins and the Hellenes, the Persians and Galatians, and all the nations of Asia.[4]

Differences not only in space but in time can be massive: fifth-century Greeks had a positive attitude toward the male body, yet in the Hellenistic period that attitude is said to have been superseded by an ascetic, even negative disposition toward the flesh. According to one recent scholar, Christianity itself may have shifted in the high Middle Ages away from early tolerance to intolerance of homosexual acts.[5]

There is no denying enormous variety. To do so would be tantamount to constructing a faulty polarity of Europe with America, whereas the purpose of this chapter is to provide readers with a comparative background in Europe to those sexual structures the Iberians will later describe across the Atlantic. Thus our first task is to search out some general problems of sex and gender that each social order must solve, and only secondly to account for the differences and changes shown by the nations and eras. The present chapter emphasizes structures. I will first sketch three fundamental fields or paradigms of sexuality, three problematics of social organization through gendering, to which, I believe, the Spanish conquerors were heirs. Property comes first, and subsequent pages will describe those sexual behaviors which create, represent and enforce patriarchal property rights over women and other dependents. Power is second, and so the following section will explore the behavior of older males which, in ancient times, gendered younger ones as types akin to dependent women. The phenomenon of adult effeminacy stands third and last. Always a minority phenomenon among adult populations, it nonetheless has always been a powerful metaphor for the larger society ordering power relations between adults.

Property

Searching for the roots of inequality among the sexes, the historian Gerda Lerner drew attention to the fate of the losing side in the interstate conflicts of the ancient Near East. According to her sources, in early times vanquished males were not imprisoned, but killed on the spot. Captured women, on the other hand, were raped and then, along with the children, for whose sex Lerner shows no interest, enslaved. The institution of slavery originated in the conquest of women, Lerner argues: slavery was suggested to the conquerors by existing civil disabilities under which the conquerors' own women already existed.[6]

The causal relation between the institution of private property and the legal and comportmental disabling of the female sex has long been a matter of dispute among social thinkers. In the present context, however, Lerner's information will serve a practical more than a theoretical use. Her view that, among other humiliations imposed upon these prisoners, rape in this context served as a legal procedure for claiming property provides me with an important tool for organizing the following exposition.

In the first place, I hope to show that violence certainly accompanied most homosexual acts mentioned by early sources, in part because homosexual violence in war is mentioned more often than is homosexual domestic rape. Second, it appears that, in the early sources, more often than it is encountered as a domestic tort, homosexual rape is found as a punishment which authorities used to defame male criminals as if they were propertied slaves. Third, I want to show that male homosexual rape was but one in a class of legal punishments, called by Meulengracht Sørensen the political use of sexual punishments, intended to brand other males as akin to women – that is, as possessing that set of characteristics males associated with females.[7] Finally, this section argues that the most representative crime punished in this sexual way was theft, and specifically theft of the female property of the punishers.

Thus, searching for early evidence of homosexual *institutions*, I begin not at home but in the field, relating male homosexual institutions to patriarchal property rights in women. As an example, a powerful triumphal vase (see figure 1) shows a fleeing, bent-over Persian pursued by a victorious Greek who thrusts his erect penis toward the Persian. 'I am Eurymedon,' the easterner says, 'I stand bent over.' This as much as proclaims for the Hellenes: 'We've fucked the Womanish Persians!'[8] To then insure the ensuing peace, the defeated fathers often bequeathed their sons to the victors as hostages; they would be raped if the peace was broken.[9] According to Livy, young male hostages were in just such danger, for they were 'of an age which particularly exposed them to injury.'[10] And so, most important, I will argue that, far more than intimacy in microrelationships, the primary and preordaining social fact regarding male homosexual behaviors in the societies under review was the threat of *punitive* gendering of foreign and domestic enemies to show them as akin to women.

Let us begin, then, by reviewing the ways victorious early Near Eastern cultures disposed of the male enemy. For even if we were to assume with Lerner that all losing adult males were executed, that would not mean that the modes of their executions were irrelevant. Some means of execution had the effect of insulting fallen victims, thus manipulating their family and communal statuses.

We begin with acts practiced on cadavers, especially because killing

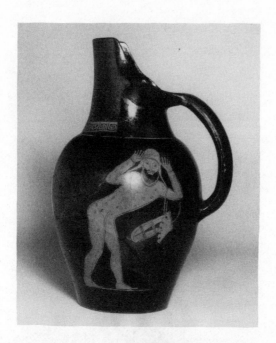

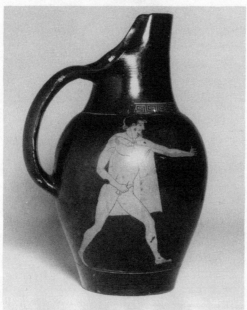

Figure 1   Attic red-figure vase (R1155), after 460 BC, with the
inscription: 'I am Eurymedon. I stand bent over.'

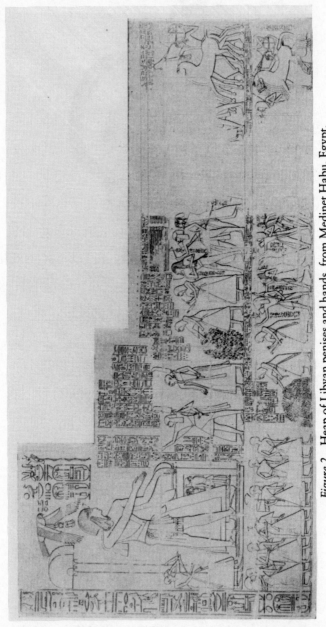

Figure 2   Heap of Libyan penises and hands, from Medinet Habu, Egypt.

able-bodied men may have been the usual disposition of those taken
in battle. The ancient practice of the quartering or decimation of a
corpse is, conceptually at least, the punishment that best helps us
understand that sexual punishments commonly fit within a larger
body of insults that treat a victim 'as if' it was something or someone
else. That is, a cadaver is 'gutted the way a pig is gutted,' assertedly,
when not actually to the end of devouring its parts, comparable to
the way in which one might use butcher's language to describe a
man's intercourse with a woman, whose very identity might rest on
her penetrability.[11] Indeed, Walter Burkert speaks of the *'military*
metaphors for sexual organs and activity.'[12] 'Let his body be cut in
pieces on the third marked day,' the Twelve Tables of republican
Rome said of a bankrupt, that is, of a man who had 'stolen' one's
property; 'it may be cut into more or fewer pieces with impunity. Or,
if his creditors consent to it, let him be sold to foreigners beyond the
Tiber.'[13] Such slaughterhouse vocabulary and practice is part of a
broad human tendency first to emasculate or desexualize, conse-
quently to dehumanize, and thus finally to treat our enemies as dirt.
We may complete this loop of associations by noting that, even
today, many legal codes make no distinction between anal intercourse
practiced with males, females or animals. It is all 'bestial.'[14]

The reasoning in this world of executions is that a punitive agent
may butcher a dead loser the way animals are butchered, comparable
to the right any powerful male has to have intercourse with a less
powerful warrior who has assumed the posture or 'mode of an
animal' (*more animalium*) or 'dog' (*canino more*). Such rites may
have a sacrificial character, of course.[15] In short, from an early point
in our sources, and to take only one such insult, homosexual rape
was viewed in this part of the world as the violation of an outsider,
like a foreigner, like an animal and, indeed, like a woman. The notion
that passive homosexual behavior was 'against nature' was a subset
of the larger view that one could butcher other, less 'natural,'
natures.[16] The logic extended into the civil world, where, according
to Aristotle, followed by Thomas Aquinas, a bad man was more
harmful than an animal, and one could, according to the theologian,
butcher a sinner as one would a beast.[17]

Among the various means of butchering corpses, none seems to
have been so widely practiced as castration. Such behavior began
with the living: Shang armies practiced it on the Chiang people they
conquered around 1300 BC, and the historian Herodotus describes
how, on conquering the Ionian cities, the Persian king had all the
'best favored boys' emasculated (but also how a Greek merchant of

Chios castrated good-looking boys to then sell them in the markets of Sardis and Ephesus). In ancient Norse society as well, castration was the common humiliation inflicted on losers.[18] In Burkert's words, castration appears to be a basic element in man's fighting instinct.[19] Why was this practice so widespread? Part of the answer certainly lies in the fact that, in several ancient cultures, castration produced the required proof that one had indeed slain or maimed an enemy. The most striking visual evidence of such castration in antiquity comes from the military life of ancient Egypt. Several of the great friezes documenting pharaonic triumph show heaps of penises as part of the booty displayed before the pharaoh (see figure 2), and another such frieze shows the actual castration of prisoners proceeding apace. Not surprisingly, Egyptian written records include inventories of Libyan penises gathered to the same end.[20] Yet the fact that warriors used these penises to vaunt their own triumphs only rubbed in the humiliation of the losers – whether they lay in the field or eternally shamed on the friezes – or of their gods. In Midrashic lore, the Amalekites cut off the circumcised members of the Israelites (both from prisoners and corpses). They tossed them into the air, shouting obscene curses at Yahweh: 'This is what you like, so take what you have chosen!'[21]

Circumcising fallen victims, still another type of military humiliation, often had the same purpose of allowing a victor to prove to his lord that he had slain a given number of foes. These foreskins, in turn, became in Israel the currency that permitted lord and vassal themselves to pact with each other, and both to unite with their god. To cite but one example from the Old Testament: Saul required 100 foreskins of enemies from David for the hand of his daughter; the latter magnanimously provided twice that number. Then, in Jerusalem, a Hill of Foreskins bore witness to the covenant with Yahweh himself.[22]

The fear of such mutilation remains to this day. For most of the Middle Ages, Christian boys were told that they would be circumcised if captured by Jews or Muslims, and still today Moroccan boys hear that they will be circumcised a second time if they misbehave.[23] And in fact, the practice of circumcision was still standard in the military life of Ethiopia in the eighteenth century. Infant or childhood circumcision, which Freud regarded as symbolic castration or as a vestige of an earlier practice of castration, is still widely practiced on boys and girls in many parts of the world today,[24] and castration remains a standard means of dishonoring the fallen.[25]

In summary, in the Near East and elsewhere in the Mediterranean world, ancient peoples humiliated cadavers by making them appear either mere boys or women: like a powerless boy or woman unable to protest, the dead spirit was violated from behind or circumcised, or like a helpless child was castrated so as to look like a woman in perpetuity, if indeed the child survived.[26] Lerner may be right that women were enslaved before males. Still, it is clear that, even in death, men were violated in war; that is, they were eternally changed into dependents. And the fate that befell them in turn affected the status of the male relatives who were spared, for, to their eternal shame, they could not defend their fallen. These sexual practices were used in the first place to represent the power of one group of men over another.

A second type of sexual punishment brought certain death to its victim in its application. I have in mind evisceration, of course, which, especially when practiced through the anus, was understood as none other than the anal rape of a victim, the spear or whatever other lance substituting for the penis. The practice was far from unknown in the ancient world – 'And he struck his enemies in the behind,' sang the Psalm, 'giving them eternal shame'[27] – and it extended into later times as well, as we shall see in the next chapter. Thus in 1327 the quasi-official executioners of Edward II of England put a red-hot poker 'thro the secret place posteriale.'[28] And still, in modern times, the Zulus are said to have executed adulterers by pushing lances up their rectums.[29]

Yet most sexual punishments practiced on the living belong to a third type of punishment, one which allowed the victim to survive and thus carry the insult on his body or in memory. In one European tradition, it is true, criminals did not long survive: having first been sexually punished, they were subsequently executed. That double punishment may represent a historical overlap of a type, for the thirteenth-century English jurisprudent Bracton believed that survivable sexual punishments had replaced earlier sentences of death for certain crimes.[30] Indeed that liberality can already be traced in antiquity. In Imperial Rome, for instance, the Golden Ass heard his master tell the young boy who had cuckolded him by sleeping with his wife that he was not a barbarian, and would not call for the boy's execution, as the law required. Instead, he humbled both wife and boy by sleeping with the latter.[31] It seems clear, therefore, that sexual punishments in antiquity and in traditional Europe often aimed at branding living males as dependent and thus not fully male: either as defenseless, passive males, or as women. Needless to say, castration and circumcision were sexual punishments that, when they did not bring on death, branded the shamed body of offenders permanently.[32]

Other sexual punishments left a temporary mark of shame on the body. Perhaps the most important of these was depilation, especially the burning off of anal and pubic hair. The practice was known to the ancient Jews – Isaiah prophesied that they would be humiliated in this way[33] – and to the Athenians. In both cases the insult lay in part in the fact that only women singed their pubic hair. But since pathics themselves often removed their pubic hair to preserve their appeal to older men, the punishment doubtless also bore this association.[34]

Once pubic hair grew back in, the physical mark of shame vanished, and memory took over; the punitive event itself, the world-historical happening that had turned man akin to woman, might defy all attempts to suppress recollections of shame. This is the third group of sexual punishments aimed at regendering or pacifying victims that draws our attention, and for the purposes of this book certainly of the greatest importance. I only mention the insult of forcing losers to parade with their bottoms bare, that of force-masturbating naked enemies in public to maintain them erect, and come at once to the anal rape of male captives, a practice notoriously rife in the ancient world and, as Edwardes has pointed out, often justified by divine example.[35]

Let me pass in quick review two Jewish legends that highlight the inherent political import of the practice. According to the Babylonian Talmud, the Babylonian Nebuchadnezzar systematically sodomized all the captive chieftains of Judah – proof, if such were needed, of the representational linkage between gender and humiliation in warfare.[36] Then, in a majestically pure tale driving home the role of sexual humiliation as a backdrop to civil order, the traditions of the Babylonian Captivity claim that four different kings, enemies of Yahweh, claimed to be god: Hiram of Tyre, the same Nebuchadnezzar, Sheshonk of Egypt, and Joash of Judah. They each shared the same terrible fate, the story-teller savors, each being sexually abused – that is, his integrity violated, as if he were a woman. Thus those who would play gods were anally raped.[37] Needless to say, symbolic substitutes for actual anal rape – forcing any type of object into the anus of a victim – were manifold, and Aristophanes furnishes us with one in the domestic sphere: the insertion of a radish into the anus of a victim.[38]

Doubtless, each of these and other sexual punishments are different, and on the surface might seem worlds apart. Castration permanently brands a victim, anal rape may mark the victim for only a short time, if memory is merciful. But the common feature of all these sexual punishments used against males, to which – can we doubt it? – fathers took sons to impress on their memory – cannot be ignored: they showed military and domestic losers as despised dependents, as passive boys akin to women; they were all cultural representations produced to similar ends. As Aristophanes said, forcing a radish into a rectum changed a virile male into a passive.[39] It was a lesson one learned soon enough.

Impressive as was the range of sexual punishments inflicted on males, the *domestic* crimes to which such punishments were applied in early Mediterranean, European and Near Eastern cultures are of equal interest and importance. What were they? The image of the Greek God Priapus provides a succinct, memorable answer. On hundreds of columns and city walls, statues of Priapus, penis erect and thus threatening rape, guarded towns against unwanted foreign entrants, while within the cities the godly figure, affixed to residences, threatened thieves with the same punishment.[40] Theft, in all its variations, was the major precipitant for sexual punishments in domestic affairs.

Loss of property provoked victims to show their power by representing their despoilers as women or boys, and human property, especially in women, children and slaves, was obviously the most cherished. In what follows, I hope to show that men's homosexual legal acts against other men, whether these acts were official or private, were in fact closely tied to the violation of property rights and perhaps especially to the female property Lerner's dialectic emphasizes. Students of sexual punishments have tended to see them as related to sexual crimes, as resulting, that is, from the *lex talionis*. I demur. I can document many thefts absent a sexual character that were punished sexually, and as a result I do not believe that the private criminal act deserves such eminence in explaining the public reaction. The politics of gender are more important than any individual sexual relation in antiquity. Already in ancient polities, there existed a powerful superego that punished individual males by making them 'womanish.'

Browe, for instance, provides substantial evidence that Roman and some Germanic laws permitted husbands to apply the customary punishment of castration to males found *in flagrantis* with their wives, and thirteenth-century English law still permitted it to the husband. Browe did cite one case of a medieval public authority applying the punishment directly, but in general he saw castration as a surviving private right, underestimating its public relevance.[41]

Though he too stressed the sexual character of the crimes in question, in his study of punitive anal rape (*Strafvergewaltigung*) Fehling recognized that theft of property was at the bottom of the matter. We saw earlier that, for adultery – the theft of a husband's property – Athens permitted a husband to force a radish up the violator male's anus – a substitute for anal rape. The several Roman pieces of evidence, so substantial that they cannot be laid out here, are, to be sure, largely literary rather than documentary in character, but after much study Fehling came away convinced not only that the threat was ever present, but that anal rape was indeed used at times to punish such malefactors.[42] On one occasion referred to earlier, the narrator in the *Golden Ass* has the husband himself raping a boy who had cuckolded him, and this story resonated throughout the Middle Ages.[43] But it was perhaps more common, and certainly more insulting, for the husband to order one's servants or slaves to rape the fornicator.[44]

Such punishments were not, of course, levied only against those who made off with female property. An ancient Assyrian code, for example, prescribed first anal rape, and then castration for a male who forced anal intercourse upon any other male.[45] That is, the violation of a free adolescent was experienced as a terrible violation of the father's, and perhaps of the collectivity's, rights of property.[46] That property emphasis is clearly evident in regulations that permitted such sexual punishments to be applied against men who sexually violated another's slaves, whether they were male or female.[47] In effect, since an owner had the right to traffic sexually with his male slaves, violating the cuckolder made the latter symbolically the slave of the abused husband or owner.

In trying to grasp the punitive character of such actions, it is wise not to construct false barriers between public and private. Usually, these sexual violations were not standard punishments of the civil authority itself. Yet no less than the time-honored anal rape of prisoners in war, the private law rights discussed here were public as well. There are graffiti at Pompeii, for instance, telling how a gang of men pinned down and violated a male who had fornicated with another man's woman, presumably a quasi-public act at least.[48] Neither has the rape of male adulterers, as well as their castration, been foreign to the public squares of the later European world.[49] If the collectivity does not punish those who exercise popular justice of this type, it is effectively a party to that justice.

Finally, my view that the condition or identity of women in several ancient cultures helps explain the male homosexual behaviors in those cultures brings us to a consideration of what students of Islam call harem culture,[50] a phenomenon by no means limited to Islam. That is, the nature and depth of relations between men depend in part upon men's access to women; males kept from women through war as well as through domestic 'asylums' such as harems or prisons or nunneries will often cultivate homosexual relations.[51] Biased Westerners may have no difficulty envisioning male guardians of a Near Eastern harem anally raping other males who attempted to gain illegal entry to women's quarters,[52] but in fact the harem is only a subset of a larger category, the Priapian practice of violating outsiders who dare seek entry to cities that, among other things, possess cloistered females. And in the story of the men of Sodom who, wishing to have intercourse with presumed male visitors, were bought off by an offer of virgin females, that category has impeccable Judeo-Christian credentials.[53]

Let me summarize this first glance at the structural foundations of ancient homosexual practice. First, our evidence intimates that it is vain to dwell on individual homosexual relations or practices before positioning them within a structural context. Other documentation yet to be presented will further solidify this position. Second, that context is the latent and often terrible power of the sovereign to use homosexual acts as a punitive threat: I will portray a commonweal that was often feared as an active – what the Middle Ages usually called a sodomite – that practiced homosexual acts for the purpose of keeping men boys, or 'making them women,' that is, to the end of making a state.[54] Finally, the prominence of property, and especially female property, as a factor in state homosexual activities that brought force to bear on male subjects cannot be ignored. To protest violations of property by mutilating the bodies of males was to create power. Property was at the roots of power in later European and Mediterranean society.

Power

In his *Anabasis*, Xenophon says that, in order to satisfy their sexual needs, sixth-century Greek soldiers either brought boys along from home who were below fighting age or captured them in the field. To the same end, they 'castrated' women slaves so that men could practice on them with no fear they would conceive.[55] Such arrangements were common in antiquity. Though in her model of the origins of patriarchy Lerner did not specify the sex of the ancient Near

Eastern children who, according to this author, shared primacy along with women in the origins of slavery, certainly young males were indeed spared, and then recruited, for such paramilitary duty. And these practices have remained familiar until fairly recently in the Far East as well. The 'charioteers of the soul' of Hellenic society were, after all, not totally different from the so-called Samurai Lovers of traditional Japanese society.[56]

Let us not forget that, to limit ourselves to Indo-European and Semitic languages, the words for 'boy' and for 'slave' or 'servant' were and often are one and the same; the American connotations of the word 'boy' are a case in point. For centuries, youngsters in many *Gefolgschaftswesen* provided masters with sexual services in the hope they would find occasion to kill enemies on the field of battle and thus become 'men.' Perhaps that practice was modeled on hunting custom. According to Ammianus Marcellinus, young Germanic Tai-fali remained at the sexual disposition of male elders until they killed a bear or a boar.[57]

I showed earlier that male homosexual activity was a punishment ancient Mediterranean and European men might inflict on those who violated their female property. In the typical telling, the punisher is older or socially superior, the cuckold younger or inferior. A second fundamental cause of male homosexual activity soon appears: quite apart from the stimulus of property, older males competed for and manifested their power by homosexually dominating younger ones. They built their estates, so to speak, for, as Cantarella pithily notes, it was the relationship between males, and not that between men and women, that lay at the center of Greek social organization.[58] What we today negatively call pederasty might in antiquity, however, be positively linked to pedagogy or *paideia*, that is, to the imparting of obedience, respectfulness and self-control to young males. 'I think I ought to say something also about intimacy with boys,' said Xenophon in describing the Spartans, 'since this matter also has a bearing on education.'[59]

Sparta was of course famous for military pederasty – astutely defined by Dover as 'the quite deliberate withdrawal of authority from fathers of families and its transference to the oldest male age-group'[60] – but it was not alone. To begin with, it is arguable that, both in the domestic and military realms, the earliest forms of profound male solidarity were generated in gangs or in the ranks, a type of collective bonding without any determinant patron–client relation, so that it cannot be defined as a 'marriage.' I shall shortly return to this matter. So I begin by describing the relations between particular older and younger males in ancient cultures, when they did arise, as types of homosexual marriages. These one-on-one homosexual unions emerge as fundamental parts of the process of creating, articulating and maintaining political power in ancient society, just as the later heterosexual marriages helped articulate institutions of property. In this homosexual marriage, the adolescent might emphasize his masculinity and even be repulsed by any hint that he assume the dress, voice or other habits of a woman, or he might not, and play the effeminate. But sexually, there was no ambiguity: all hypocrisy once laid aside, in fact he assumed the so-called passive role and was generally scorned as akin to a woman for doing so.[61] In my view, the ancient evidence demonstrates that this genderization of the relations between males was a central foundation for patriarchal politics. It informs the early, and perhaps even our contemporary, notion of the state.

In the majority, these domestic homosexual institutions seem to have been of two types, depending on whether castration had been practiced upon the passive party or not. It is true that, in the military context, I have described both those boys seized in battle and those brought out from the homeland to serve warriors – the former presumably more often castrated than the latter – as employed to the same passive sexual ends and even to similar non-sexual ends in war, such as porting, burying, cooking and the like; after all, as youngsters they all lacked citizen status and thus could be considered 'fair game.' But though they both served the same sexual function, dependent on their physical condition these boys found different social roles awaiting them on their return home.

On the one hand, since antiquity young enemy boys who had been castrated grew up servicing older males not only sexually, but also socially and politically. Such impotents fulfilled a series of functions within ancient societies that may best be characterized as maintaining separation between social groups. The best-known task of this type involved the supervision of harems, be they of wives or nuns, in ancient and medieval Mediterranean societies: since they could not usually consummate a heterosexual relationship with residents, eunuchs made ideal guards at harems, keeping out other men from those spaces reserved for the owner and his women. There being little fear of a eunuch producing heirs, rulers in antiquity and in the Middle Ages used them to a second important end: as high secular and ecclesiastical administrators whose power and influence perforce began and ended in their persons.[62] Doubtless degrees of castration might depend upon domestic function, and such functions might be racially determined. And certainly already in antiquity trade and not just war played a role in generating eunuchs.[63] For now, however, it is enough to insist that, from early times, eunuchs have been used to maintain social separation, and not lastly a separation between nubile girls of powerful patriarchs and the young men who would wish to possess them.[64]

The second fate for such boys did not involve castration but rather only the anal intercourse imposed on them by their masters. The boy mentioned in the Code of Hammurabi (ca. 1725 BC) may have been typical: a youth from home and not a captive, the *girsequ* or young war charioteer of Mesopotamian astronomy (passive to his active warrior master) emerges later as one of many palace domestics offering passive homosexual service at the royal court.[65] Along with eunuchs, if only for the time being, such boys often formed the basic, and so highly genderized, retinue of ancient men of power.

In what may functionally be characterized as a period of initiation, these boys began in their early teens by choosing a master to imitate – the key to the Greco-Roman educational ideal of *paideia* – not uncommonly in exchange for sexually servicing those masters; already in antiquity, the notion was in place that the intellectual and moral contents of learning were best passed on with semen.[66] Such passivity as part of a formal rite of passage is usually associated with certain New Guinea tribes, but traces of male initiation through sexual subordination in Indo-European cultures has also long interested scholars. And even in cultures where no traces of formal sexual initiation can be found, a practical sexual submission of young adolescents to adult males is a historical matter of fact.[67]

Different from the eunuch, in Mediterranean antiquity the passive's period of sexual dependence usually ended once, having abandoned shaving and depilation, he sprouted a beard.[68] At that point, the youth, usually about 18 years old, did indeed become an inserting active, but sometimes by inserting in a boy, rather than heterosexually, within the context of a second homosexual marriage. Since, generally speaking, a Mediterranean youth of 18 was not yet of an age for heterosexual marriage, his elders, so as to steer him away from legitimate nubile women, might encourage their boy to take up relations with female prostitutes, of course, but also with another, younger boy. Thus, in such relations, the sexually active partner (whether referring to anal intercourse roles or to fellation, where the [older] insertor was considered active) was always older than the passive one; sexual roles were rarely switched, as they sometimes are in modern relationships. But for all the macho he might now demonstrate – over this (and other) boy(s) – the active partner remained in passage from the homosexual to the other, heterosexual type of marriage. Bearded warrior though he might now be, he still did not possess much of the property and thus the authority of his father.[69]

In the processions of antiquity, as in the modern victory parade, power and authority were manifested by the presence of a queue of dependents. Eunuchs, handsome young passives and, yes, macho 20-year-olds who were not fathers joined such queues, for one had to be seen to be part of a master's retinue before one could form one's own.[70] It is as much the rule today as then that, the more powerful the master at the head of the procession, the more polygamous he was, the more 'marriages' he supported. Some would go on to form their own queues, others would hold back. Young age in itself was not the only constraint; rather, the absence of hair, of property, even of will, stood in the way. At stake in this world of domestic celibates were authority, rule, power. Still today, how many males recover from the violence of adolescence to fit the stereotype of macho most societies demand of young adult males?[71]

At least at the symbolic level, what could better express the role sexual dominance played in the building of Mediterranean states than the story of Seth and Horus, an allegory for the unification of upper and lower Egypt? 'How beautiful are thy buttocks,' the artful old warrior-god Seth flatters the divine young Horus before mounting him. 'I have done a man's deed to him,' he later boasts to all who will listen, thinking he has impregnated Horus when in fact, through the wiliness of Horus's mother Isis, it is Seth who has eaten the seed of Horus – and ends up castrated! Scholars have been quick, too quick, to insist that there is no evidence of actual anal rape in Egypt, yet, for all that, there can be little doubt that this is a conquest fable of some political import.[72]

Though of later date, a Cretan ritual practice shows a relationship between rape and state building that is all but symbolic. This is the practice of institutionalized homosexual rape described by Ephoros about 400 BC. The rite begins when an adult male kidnaps a boy, with the connivance of the boy's parents *and* of his cohort of friends. A battle ensues between the latter and the kidnapper, but if the adult is socially desirable as a patron, the friends just feign to prevent the abduction, fighting in earnest only if he is not. Upward social mobility is, therefore, a consideration for the boy. Once the abduction is effected, the couple remains in seclusion for two months, after which both return to the community and the active sets about honoring his youthful lover publicly. He ostentatiously bestows gifts on his passive, including fine clothes that bear witness to the fact that the boy has been penetrated. For it was an honor, Ephoros intimates, to be chosen by a desirable adult to submit oneself to. Finally, the relationship between the two is sealed when the active introduces his passive into his common mess – one of the conditions of citizenship and thus a key to the polis. Cartledge may go too far in designating this whole procedure as 'recruiting the political elite.'[73] But the political character of abducting and mounting these Cretan boys is obvious.

Another body of evidence allows us to pinpoint a similar sexual aggressiveness confronting young adolescents in Athens. Attic vases in overflow of the sixth and fifth centuries BC show Athenian men seducing adolescents for sexual intercourse by offering them gifts ranging from animals to money, while with their other hand they reach for the boys' genitals.[74] Koch-Harnack's study of these images shows that such behavior with boys was construed as a representation of the hunt, in which the active adult was the hunter (associated, for example, with a leopard), and the passive boy the hunted ('fishes' or 'birds,' in Plutarch's words), the latter thereby learning life skills from the former.[75] But Koch-Harnack does not lose herself in such symbolism. She identifies many such vase images in which the gifts obviously were meant to provide meals for the boys. The evidence that the animal gifts were pay for sexual servicing is so ubiquitous, the author concludes, that they no longer have the character of being gifts.[76] The author does not characterize these transactions as rape. But not for a minute does she neglect to remind us that this whole world of images is one of aggression, from the older, toward the younger, male.[77]

Dover had already published his masterful book on *Greek Homosexuality* when Koch-Harnack set to work. But as regards the Cretan abductions, even as he describes comparable rites in the Hellenic world, he prefers to view the sexual kidnappings as all but unique, thereby underestimating the significance of such homosexual violence. It is a Grecophile prejudice he shares with Cantarella – that of the gentle Athenians versus the barbarous Romans – one well rooted among our historical commonplaces.[78] His most telling comparison is based on Plutarch's insistence that, in Sparta, heterosexual marriage between the sexes was also formalized as a ravishment or kidnapping. Yet Dover pulls back, if not without a clever wink. 'It would be perverse,' he says, 'to suppose that [heterosexual abduction] emerged from a homosexual practice of the Cretan type, rather than the reverse.'[79] But things look different if equal importance is accorded to military as to domestic matters for, clearly, in war men in this age kidnapped boys as well as women. They also look different if this kidnapping is viewed as a first marriage, setting the tone and forms for a later, heterosexual one. Finally, things look different once youth groups, and not just couples, become part of the discourse about homosexual behavior, as Ephoros insists they be. It is time to recognize that an adolescent gang, though a more collective experience, may also be seen as a type of marriage.

To drive this point home, some comparison must be made of abduction within the medieval European charivari, where, as in Ephoros' Cretan tale, bachelors in a youth group also feigned threats against those who would 'kidnap' one of their numbers. That is, the medieval charivari also facilitated the move from one type of union to another.[80] Of course, the partner in the charivari 'marriage' or bond was a female, not a male, but that should not obscure the larger point that kidnapping or rape could be a central factor in moving from one type of primary social 'marriage' or bond – in this case the gang – to another. Thus such marriages might be conventionally distinguished according to the sex of the partner, but in behavioral terms they could as well be classified according to the dominance or submission of the sexual postures employed in them by the male.

From this perspective, a first set of 'marriages' is passively homosexual. It may begin with abusive domination by a father or by upperclassmen when one matriculates into a juvenile gang or fraternity. Just thirty years ago, gangs could be found in modern France in which the leader anally penetrated all other members of the gang as a sign of dominance, and in any case it is still common for one male gang to view other gangs as based on homosexual submission.[81] Nor is such a bonding mechanism still practiced only in fraternal halls, or prisons, or military barracks. In today's United States, gangs use homosexual rape in the streets to construct and maintain male hierarchies.[82] In antiquity, a group bond of this type often yielded to what I have called the first homosexual marriage, a union between that adolescent and a single dominant older youth or adult, a kidnapper of the type described by Ephoros.

Then, usually in one's late teens, the erstwhile passive becomes active with a new, younger boy in a second homosexual marriage. For a while, he may maintain plural relationships, a passive one with an older boy and an active one with a younger one, until usually only the active role remains. Thus the young man continues in that active role both before and after he takes a wife,[83] in which second marriage he eventually limits himself to heterosexual activity.

Not surprisingly, women in some ancient cultures were forced to play a significant role in facilitating what must have been a tense transformation from passive to active for these males. In certain Greek cultures, for instance, female slaves were first 'castrated,' that is, made incapable of reproducing, and then (presumably) mounted ('like eunuchs') by males, a procedure that for all the world looks like it was meant to introduce passive boys to heterosexual activity, if of an anal type. That motivation is patent in a Spartan institution, described by Devereux as part of the behavioral grammar of 'sliding' from one social status to another, in which brides were made to look masculine by dressing like males to the end of making it easier for grooms to become heterosexually active.[84]

It has long been a truism that the family is the foundation of the state, but, in fact, reflecting on the developments sketched above persuades us that those relations between males that begin in gangs and continue in these first homosexual marriages already provide a foundation of the state – that is, that set of relations between males that peaks in the power of the male sovereign. Only once power relations between men are established in these first homosexual marriages is property addressed in a later heterosexual marriage.

Once placed in this larger context, the Cretan rapes, rather than being dismissable as an isolated phenomenon, appear to be emblematic of state building. Dover saw that the Spartan heterosexual marriage was comparable with the Cretan homosexual union because both involved abduction, but they were also comparable because both involved the establishment of dominion. Long before Dover, Bethe had excellently compared the Cretan rapes to a case in which a Spartan governor killed a local Euboean boy who resisted being raped. And had not the very founder of Syracuse been resisted by a cohort of friends when he too attempted to kidnap a boy for himself? These were no mere brawls for desirable passives, as Dover thought,[85] but political acts, by which rulers sought to increase their public retinues. Certainly they prove the arrogance of empire but, as in the tale of Seth and Horus, they show as well political power being founded upon lords' sexual subordination of male servants.

Whether we are dealing with the homoeroticism of the Japanese Samurai, the Sacred Band of Thebes, or one of many other comparable institutions, the gendered character of male political organizations is a reality that might seem impossible for scholars to ignore.[86] The sexual subordination of young males may yet prove to be of comparable importance to the origins of patriarchy as is the rape of women, or even a reverse metal. To be sure, no one would deny that the active might 'truly love' 'the charioteer of [his] soul,' or vice versa: it would be foolhardy to judge that. Only add that Achilles loved his charioteer Patroclus in a society where power relations were mediated in part by homosexual relations. Greeks might indulge, even codify, the self-serving notion that one citizen never forced another, but, as Dover notes, even their gods kidnapped and raped passives in homosexual as well as in their heterosexual relations, and he might have added as well that temple prostitution in the ancient eastern Mediterranean and Mesopotamian world encompassed the submission not only of females, but of males as well.[87] Even among mortals, Dover adds, 'the virtues admired in a [passive male] are the virtues which the ruling element in a society approves in the ruled.' Homosexual relations, he concludes, were 'regarded as the product . . . of the pursuit of those of lower status by those of higher status.'[88]

Effeminacy

Although social historians become confident of their sexual facts only upon studying the fifteenth century, even before this age most males probably ended their homosexual behaviors soon after they married. If fifteenth-century statistics in Florence are any indication of older patterns, neither an individual's passive role as an adolescent nor his active role as a celibate young man predisposed him to homosexual preference in later life, and there is no evidence that ancients blamed a statistically uncommon adult passivity on adolescent experiences. So much for the persistent modern notion that exposure to a homosexual life style in adolescence predisposes male children to that sexual preference for life!

Another stereotype brings us directly to the central problem of effeminacy as a component of homosexual behavior: this is the modern view that a relation between the two necessarily exists. In fact, ancient European and Mediterranean sources often tell another story. First of all, apart from commenting on sexual intercourse, they rarely claim that 'effeminates' acted like women at all. That is particularly true for the active party, who in intercourse only did what men do – penetrate.[89] But it was often no less true of passives, whom actives often preferred to be macho: then, as now, actives wanting to demonstrate dominance in their sexual relations might choose as lovers athletic types who at least played at resisting their advances.[90] Thus, in antiquity, contemporaries rarely if ever thought of the active parties to homosexual relations as effeminate, but rather as macho or even supermacho, while outside the sexual realm, or just short of sexual submission, neither were passives commonly said to act like females. Thus, in this bisexual world, assuming different sexual roles at various ages did not necessarily correspond to assuming contrasting gender behaviors in one's everyday actions.[91]

All this does not mean that effeminacy is unimportant to a book on homoeroticism: the universal identification of sexual receptivity with womanhood, that is, the mere posture ascribed to the passive in the sexual act, at once excludes that notion. Thus it is important to back up and pin down what ancients meant by effeminacy. First, 'effeminates' in antiquity were often so defined because of certain physical movements – such as moving one's hands and wrists or speaking softly – in ways that were thought proper to women and not to males. Second, one might be defined as effeminate if one wore certain types of clothing thought to be proper only to women or defined, in cultural-historical terms, as clothing traditionally worn by effeminates.[92]

Needless to say, such categorizations were in large part cultural rather than biological in origin. Or they were sociologically comprehensible, as is the case where such 'effeminates' are found within groups of women. In a pathfinding study of the effeminates (*mukhannathün*) of Medina, Rowson found that, till the eighth century, this word referred only to males who sang with women, because singing was an occupation identified with females: the word does identify males who had no sexual interest in women, but not necessarily males who had a homoerotic interest. At a later point in this work we shall see that, in America as well, certain males' transgressions of the occupational division of labor between males and females may have preceded, rather than followed, gestural 'effeminacy.'[93]

Beyond the gestural and occupational aspects of effeminacy – neither of which, be it remembered, necessarily invoked sexual associations – Mediterranean antiquity produced a third notion of effeminacy in males that is psychological in character. Departing from the assumption that females shared a given characterology, ancient and medieval writers often stamped a male as effeminate less because of his behavior than because of an alleged character flaw. A male who seemed impulsive or 'irrational,' who fell hopelessly in love with a man *or woman* – or both at the same time – or, perhaps most damning, who was a coward, all risked being branded effeminates.[94] Again, a male of this type, who lacked the virtue of gravity, might be labelled 'effeminate' in ancient sources with no direct implication of sexual or even behavioral deviance.

Thus it is clear that, to avoid misunderstanding, the historian must handle the traditional term effeminacy with care and not automatically associate it with sexual deviance. Yet that having been said, I would insist that this age all but universally branded any male an effeminate who was an anal and perhaps an oral recipient, which of course did *not* preclude such reception being seen as a step on the road to masculinity.[95] Seen from another angle, all the previous, seemingly non-sexual notions of what it was to be effeminate have this in common, that they were aspects of dependency, neatly brought out by Halperin's discovery that poverty too was thought effeminate in the ancient Greek world.[96] Now the premier sign of male dependence was to be anally or orally penetrated by another male without, at least fictively, being able to resist. Whether deservedly or not, the non-sexual 'effeminate' was in fact easily denounced as a sexual passive. 'Effeminacy' always latently connoted *sexual* dependence.

From the foregoing it will be clear that effeminacy, though it might be cast in individual psychological terms, was a notion with strong sociological implications; one author, in fact, has found in ancient Athens a 'submerged association' between effeminacy and the poor as a group![97] On examination it indeed appears that several social groups were not denounced as 'effeminate,' and that, in fact, usually only free adult males earned what was so commonly an insult hurled at one's enemies. Obviously it made no sense to refer to women or girls as effeminates, and, slaves being dependents, their effeminacy was taken for granted but rarely enunciated. It may be more surprising that the slur of effeminacy was age-specific in character, but in fact boys too were dependents and, as such, the term was usually not wasted on them. True, if they went beyond merely suffering penetration and actually enjoyed it, they might be presumed to have a proclivity toward 'irrational' passivity in the presence of free adults, but usually the epithet was first used against young men old enough to wear the toga[98] – men, that is, such as Cleisthenes and Demosthenes, who passed the rites of passage without the expected signs of physical maturity appearing.[99] The 'effeminate' was a male adult who stayed 'delicate' even as his cohort moved toward a macho life style. For the Romans – and they were not alone – adults who continued to play the passive role in homosexual relations were 'unnatural' and effeminate.[100]

The strong association between particular social groups and so-called effeminacy also implicates political groups: as a general rule,

not only was one's military enemy automatically denounced as
effeminate, but, the lower one went in one's own social hierarchy,
the stronger its upper crusts found their effeminate traits to be.
Seneca must have had lower-ranking enemies and soldiers in mind
when he declared that 'bad army officers and wicked tyrants are the
main source of rapes of young men.'[101] Thus military history is
studded not only with dandified captured prisoners, but with gor-
geously dressed domestic soldiers who attended the likes of rulers
such as Darius III, William Rufus of England and Henry III of
France.[102] The ambivalence in the ancient record is clear. On the one
hand, effeminates would, it was feared, prostitute the civil order by
selling its secrets to the enemy.[103] On the other, to project power,
many rulers have needed gender gradations in their armies and other
representative institutions. For Machiavelli, that meant that com-
manding generals had to be decisive males with no hint of effeminacy.
The great Florentine writer had learned a lesson from Roman
antiquity where it was said that a military officer lost all pretension
to authority over his troops once it was known he was a passive.[104]

As a cultural stereotype, therefore, 'effeminates' were usually adult
males who were enemies and dependents: either lower-status males
in one's own polity, or opponents in other polities who were expected
to prove their dependence by losing. This overlap between subjection
and effeminacy was not, however, absolute, as the following remarks
will demonstrate. First comes the striking evidence from the early
Roman Empire onward that several of its rulers not only preferred
the pathic role, but, as Richlin and Barton have noted, even used it
to express political domination.[105] Second, there are the Roman
cinaedos, who, like the later Medinan *mukhannathün*, seem to have
been bands of (presumably) young males who performed cultural
acts that lay on the female side of the division of labor, such as
playing musical instruments or dancing, or passive sexual service:
'These girls,' Apuleius said in referring ironically to a group of boys
playing and singing away, 'were a band of *cinaedos*.'[106] Importantly,
the *cinaedos*'s passivity seems to have been blended with a commen-
surate activity: it appears that, as on the opposite side of the
Mediterranean at a later point, the *cinaedos* played the passive so as
to earn the money for subsequent activity with males or females.[107]

Although these two evidences of a 'positive passivity' certainly
caution us against an automatic identification of passivity with
sociopolitical subjection, the mass of evidence shows that, in general,
for a free adult male to be denounced as a sexual passive was the
most common slur in all of antiquity, and that such evidence of

revulsion fell most easily upon those who showed traits of 'effeminacy,' historically understood. Indeed, writers such as Suetonius who
tell us that the emperors engaged in passive sex do so at times as
evidence of the decadence of Rome. The scorn directed against
passives did not, of course, mean that they were excluded from
flattery, and Dover is profoundly right to note that 'a liking for
dalliance with a handsome adolescent boy did nothing to diminish
the seducer's contempt for the seduced.'[108] For only a woman, men
said, willingly submitted herself to the dishonor of anal penetration,
or the gesture necessary to such penetration.

Society and Culture

The English word 'bad' probably derives from an Old English word
for effeminate,[109] so culturally rooted was the degradation which
ancient penetrators ascribed to those suspected of being penetratable!
It cannot be stressed enough that these cultural traditions all but
uniformly ridiculed the latter and not the former. Yet a perplexing
conflict between this cultural tradition and ancient political traditions
cannot be ignored, for that conflict endures in some measure even to
the present day: while penetration was culturally appreciated, it was
often politically denounced. Certainly there must have been times
when adult passives were punished by popular fiat, reflecting the
repugnance these cultures felt for passivity. Yet when we encounter
the sovereign legislating in these matters, we find him threatening
sooner the active and only rarely the passive! Athens' laws already
seem to reflect this emphasis on the active, but the most studied
ancient law on the subject is the Roman *lex Scantinia*, which, while
it did threaten those who enjoyed submitting to penetration, was
aimed mainly at actives who took advantage of younger and unwilling adolescents.[110]

Surely the prevalence of pederasty explains this to some extent –
older actives could pay stiffer fines than dependent boys – but there
are other parts to this story, which need to be outlined at this point,
for this seeming chasm between cultural tabus and political penality
– penetrating is culturally positive but politically suspect – already
evident in some ancient polities, emerges often in the following pages.
The following factors, properly fleshed out, will ultimately lead to an
understanding of this deep-rooted paradox.

The first factor is political: like the tyrants of Seneca mentioned
above, those males who wished politically to dominate others might

seek to represent their authority sexually; a sovereign was no exception, nor was ancient Mediterranean society the sole focus of this *modus operandi*. Into the late Middle Ages, there was a large northern complex across Scandinavia where, to cite Vanggaard, 'it was not considered in the least shameful to be able to force another man into that [anal receptive] position – on the contrary, it was something to brag about.'[111] Precisely! Fear of conspiracy certainly then led early rulers to punish their cohorts' *active* homosexual behavior because it challenged their own plenitude of power. Conspirators, in turn, were known to engender loyalty by obtaining their followers' voluntary sexual submission.[112]

A second factor is pedagogic in character: the claim of certain groups of adult males to monopolize the protection and education of free young males, which is one possible type of claim to statehood or polity, made it predictable that such monopolistic groups, rather than admit that their boys might wish to be penetrated by outsiders, would denounce any older males who tried to seduce these boys away to their own flag, and thus penetrate them. This factor might explain why the organized priesthoods of the Mediterranean world, charged with the education of boys, prove to have been still more vociferously opposed in their legislation to activity than were secular lawgivers.[113] Thus the quest for political authority, which existed not least in one's claim to protect free boys from kidnapping and rape, involved a type of harem competition for boys between powerful men, one outlawing the sexual activity of the other.

A third clue to understanding this profound contradiction between cultural approval and political condemnation of penetration is the recognition that, even though activity was most seriously condemned by the law, ridiculing a subject or enemy as passive was a standard means of exerting power. That is, the sovereign not only suffered the timeless defamation that he was feminine because he could not defend the public against enemies.[114] He exploited the cultural order's privileging of activity by denouncing all others' alleged passivity. An early Christian case is as explicit as one could wish, making use of the fabled effeminacy of clergy. In Gregory of Tours' sixth-century *History of the Franks*, Count Palladius, in the presence of the king, hurls this insult against the 'passive and effeminate' Parthenius, bishop of Gévaudan: 'Where are your husbands, with whom you cohabit in lechery and turpidity?'[115] This was as much as to claim that the celibate bishop had patrons in the *saeculum* who had active homosexual rights over him. Thus a prelate's subordination was being defined sexually. In truth, the age, and the specific sexual role of each historical actor, is a matter of central concern as is the gendering of political organisms.

I hope some of the basic principles of sexuality that informed general life in this part of the world in antiquity are now in place. First, males were born into a universe of penetrative penality: a context in which the male threat to penetrate other males was as much a part of the cultural superstructure as was heterosexual rape. Such homosexual activity was viewed as one means of punishing those who had violated property rights, usually in women. Second, power among males was conceptualized in part as the rule of active adult men over passive adolescents or 'boys.' Third, passive homosexual behavior, if continued far into adulthood, was violently scorned in these ages, even when, along with the *castrati*, adult passives might provide important social and political services.[116] Fourth, even though one might be called an effeminate with no direct implication of homosexual behavior, passive homosexual behavior, and especially anal receptivity, everywhere defined a person as effeminate. Finally, though cultures seemingly universally despised and ridiculed adult passives, political rulers tended to punish and churchmen tended to condemn active rather than passive partners. From the beginning to the end of the ancient world, the worlds of sex and of political power were never far apart.

2

Iberian Experiences

You wander about, with your wavy hair glistening;
I have stubborn Spanish hair.
You are smooth from your daily depilatory;
I have shaggy shins and cheeks. Your lips are lisping, your tongue is weak . . .
So stop calling me 'brother,' lest I call you, Charmenion, 'sister.'[1]

Neither passives nor actives . . . will inherit the kingdom of God.[2]

Gendered notions of property and power, a complex concept of effeminacy inexorably linked to dependence, and finally authority's fear of the macho even as it accepts its culture's ridicule of the effeminate: these general facts, as well as the body of behaviors that derives from them, remain part of European and Anglo-American sexual experience. Harsh actions like male rape have not, that is, yielded to so-called civilization, as some claim.[3] These basic practices of Western sexual experience, and the fear of such practices, are arguably as powerful today as in the past. Does not at least the language of sexuality remain in modern society a key way of talking about property and power? The practices, and the language, were certainly alive and well in the Iberian peninsula at the time Europe discovered what it called the New World and began to explore its sexual universe.

Yet such assertions remain to be demonstrated by a closer study of Iberian sexuality at the time of the Conquests. Easier said than done, for there is a critical absence of serious studies on Iberian sexuality before the late sixteenth century. Still, the following pages can provide enough Iberian background to allow us to make sense of the Iberians' reactions to American sexuality after 1492. Throughout, the ensuing survey aims to determine how multiracial Iberia claimed property and built power by representing its sexuality.

Commerce

In the mid-tenth century, the knowledgeable imperial ambassador Liutprand of Cremona described an international market in boys that had Spain as its terminus. *Carzimania* (cf. French *garçon?*), Liutprand explained, was a Greek word for eunuchs who had lost both testicles and the penis. Because of the enormous profits, merchants in Verdun were ready to perform such castrations, and then ship the eunuchs to Spain for sale.[4] Thus, according to Liutprand, Islamic Spaniards bought eunuchs who had been castrated in Christian Verdun, though their Koran prohibited castration.

Meanwhile, the contemporary African travel writer Al-Muqaddasî (b. ca. 946) described a variant routing of the eunuch traffic. To be castrated, slaves from Uzbek were brought to a Jewish town beyond Pechina (arabic: *Bajjâna*), which lay just north of Almería in south-eastern Spain. Those who survived the castration were then shipped from Spain to Egypt for sale.[5] In this reading, the operation remained non-Islamic, but it was performed within Islamic Spain.

In the course of his account, Al-Muqaddasî also says he was told by some eunuchs that Byzantine Christians ('Romans') – implicitly different from Islamic peoples – 'castrate their [own] children, and then intern them in monasteries so they won't get involved with girls and so they would not be involved in sex,' a report replicated by a ninth-century Western source that shows boys in Benevento, Italy, who were destined for the clergy, being castrated at an early age.[6] It is hardly surprising that Byzantium also had its castration specialists, since eunuchs were widely used in Constantinople's imperial administration, including two patriarchs in that same century.[7] Presumably Jesus's alleged praise for those 'who have made themselves eunuchs for the kingdom of heaven' (Matthew 19.12) was cited to justify castration for internal Christian consumption. But like so many other sexual matters, the practice of castration in Byzantium remains to be studied.

Nor did Mediterranean Africa lack castration specialists in the time of Al-Muqaddasî, for North Africans dealt with factories to the south that castrated captured blacks and then sold them as domestic servants in Egypt.[8] At least in the later Ottoman period, black eunuchs more regularly underwent complete castration than did white servants, especially if they were to guard harems.[9]

Three centuries after Al-Muqaddasî, the Dominican William of Tripoli documented a comparable African market in males, but this one was in boys who were not eunuchs. William described how Egyptian merchants first developed such boys' corporeal attractiveness, bathing them in perfumes and dressing them in soft rich clothes to seduce Islamic buyers. These slaves were in fact being sold not just as domestics but as male prostitutes (one Arabic word for which was *bardadj* or berdache) who would sexually service their new masters. Indeed, the Dominican pointed out that in Islamic societies, presumably including southern Spain, men lived with such boys as husband with wife.[10] From the thirteenth century onward such descriptions of North African markets specializing in boys are common in the sources, and it would be surprising if they had been absent across the Straits in Islamic Spain. They existed in the Jebala area of Morocco into the twentieth century.[11]

Christians proved no less ready to participate in the boy traffic than they had been prepared to deal in the eunuch trade, as another Dominican, William of Adam, made clear in 1317. It being assumed by Christian merchants that Islamic men were sexually attracted to boys, they bought up attractive young boys (*pueri*) and prepared them for sale to the Saracens, William complained. 'Like dogs' in their sensuality, the latter snatched them up at premium prices.[12] Our sources make clear that the crusaders were not thought impervious to such seductions. Some brought back 'effeminate ways' from the Crusader States, while others stayed in the Near East and succumbed to the 'soft' life style.[13]

William of Adam furnishes us one further, precious bit of information about Muslim sexuality at this time when he informs us that the North African unions arranged through such commerce were not exclusively pederastic of character. He informs us that the Saracens:

> ... have effeminate men in great number who shave their beards, paint their faces, put on women's clothing, wear bracelets on their arms and legs and gold necklaces around their necks as women do, and adorn their chests with jewels ... The Saracens, oblivious of human dignity, freely resort to these effeminates or live with them as among us men and women live together openly.[14]

Thus the adult transvestite passives who in the Americas would be labelled berdaches existed if not in Antiquity, then surely in the fourteenth-century southern Mediterranean world.[15]

From this survey of the available information on human commerce it would appear there was a substantial difference in such sexual practices between the northern and southern, as well as the eastern and western flanks of the Mediterranean Sea. Eunuchs appear to have played a limited role in Western Europe in comparison with the one they assumed in Byzantium and Islam; they might have been produced in Verdun but I have yet to find a hint that they entered public life there. And though males comparable with berdaches might pop up in Northern Europe on occasion, in the present state of the evidence it seems improbable that effeminized male prostitutes were as prominent public figures in trans-Pyrenean Europe as they were in North Africa.

But given the small amount of study done for either area, such affirmations are as hazardous as they are unnecessary. For instance, can one exclude the possibility of commercial castration in Christian Spain *after* the expulsion of the Moors, given the existence of the famous Spanish falsettists, forerunners of the operatic *castrati* who, from the time of their first appearance in the sixteenth century, have been suspected of in fact being *castrati*? It seems one cannot.[16] Should one dismiss as anomalous and suspect the evidence that at least one Christian Spaniard was still selling the foreskins and penises of his fellows to Islamic enemies in the mid-fifteenth century? Perhaps.[17] But doubtless, rather than assertions, many more scraps of evidence are needed at this point.

It being our intent only to contextualize the Iberian sexual universe on the eve of the geographic conquests, what is of consummate importance at this point is to insist that an essential part of general Iberian culture remained Moorish in inspiration at the time of the discovery of America.[18] It is not so that the historian can ignore cultural mix once Christian knights had conquered some given part of Spain. Rather, the existence of customs on one side of the Straits of Gibraltar in these centuries cannot be excluded on the other side simply because of different hegemonic religious rhetorics. As our documentation will show, a broad range of sexual practices was still shared across both sides of the Mediterranean at the end of the fifteenth century.

As indicative as the commerce in young men is of the role of Spain in Mediterranean sexual exchange, so is a set of surviving poems revealing of Spain's role in the intellectual discourse regarding eros during this epoch. I refer to a body of Hebrew love poetry penned in Islamic Spain from the eleventh to the fourteenth centuries. In all probability the majority of this verse is homosexual in nature, the courtly speaker uniformly being an older active yearning for his young passive. One such group of poems, for example, called *barbiponiente*, idealizes boys in the moment they first show signs of a beard.[19] From dozens of erotic motifs, I cite one that links prayer and anal intercourse in a fashion we shall re-encounter:

> I saw a shapely youth in the mosque,
>   beautiful as the moon when it comes out.
> Those who see him bending to pray say:
>   'All my desires are that he prostrate himself.'[20]

The themes are many, and they certainly moved easily through the contemporary Mediterranean. One tenth-century Hebrew poem written in Southern Italy – within the later Catalan sphere of influence – speaks to the international character of erotic exchange. It begins by averring that the buyer paid too much for a shipload of beautiful girls. Then it continues:

> Behold ships, behold ships, coming into the port,
> Go and see what merchandise they bring.
> Handsome boys, finer than gold.
> Go and see what they were sold for.
> For a barrel of gold and gems.
> Ah, captain, you have been paid too little.[21]

Read in their entirety, these poems demonstrate that the Spanish culture of this time was one in which young boys were important objects of force, possession and love. Alone the number of prominent figures known for pederastic expression is significant: besides the Murcian chancellor Muhammad Ibn Malike, there was the famous grammarian Ahmad Ibn Kulayb (d. 1035), and many others.[22] Nor was such homosexual expression limited to Muslims. Practitioners of Islam obviously interacted with Christians. Thus the tenth-century poet Al-Ramadī was so in love with a boy from the Christian minority that he converted, while king Al-Mu'tamin of Saragossa was known for love of his Christian page.[23] And inversely, the usual percentage of Christian eminences, including Alfonso I of Aragon (1104–34), is said to have preferred homosexual partners.[24]

Yet such anecdotes should not miss the forest for the trees. Boswell has rightly noted that, for two centuries before a European-wide anti-sodomy campaign began in the thirteenth century, Spanish Christians warring with Spanish Muslims bypassed most opportunities to denounce the hated Muslims as 'sodomites.'[25] In short, because of their close cultural and social affinities with North Africa, the rebounding culture of Christian Spain, including its clergy, probably saw nothing particularly objectionable about the alleged homosexual actions of their Muslim compatriots. They did not use Moorish homosexual behavior as a rallying point against them.

And when in song and story a protest is heard, what that story tells us must be clearly understood. For example, one cannot deny the anti-Islamic import of the legend of St Pelayo or Pelagius, the teenage Asturian boy said to have been killed by the Córdoban caliph 'Abd al-Rahman (912–61) when he refused the latter's advances. What is being asserted is first, that Christian boys could choose 'honor' and avoid falling prey to the many seductions of cosmopolitan Islamic society, and second, that young Christian boys usually in fact chose Islamic refinements of this type.[26]

Norms

According to Boswell, before the Muslim invasion of 711, Iberian secular and ecclesiastical legislation regarding homosexual behavior was stricter than similar legislation north of the Pyrenees.[27] Indeed even before Constantine, the church Council of Elvira near Granada had excommunicated for life any man who violated boys.[28]

Then about 650 the Visigoth king, obviously more concerned by those who kept males (masculorum concubitores) than by the concubines themselves, moved decisively against the former, and those passives who consented. Castration was the prescribed punishment for the laity, a penalty that implicitly favored clerks because, as was traditional, they were to be handed over to ecclesiastical fora for punishments which excluded the shedding of blood.[29] When then a generation later it became evident that the ecclesiastics were not prepared to enforce the royal law against their own, a subsequent monarch took new action. In a call to action directed to the Council of Toledo, King Egica addressed himself specifically to 'the crime of those who keep males': such men – not the passives themselves – 'defiled the grace of a decent life and provoked the ireful heavens to vindication.'[30]

Does the monarch here bemoan the loss of boys' virginity, or was he concerned about other matters as well? An answer requires a broader, pedagogic context: the clergy, in fact, had charge of the education and often the boarding of boys of school age; the victims of such 'keepers' could, therefore, have been the sons of the nobility who consigned them. In any case, in 693 the Council of Toledo acceded to the King's demand and in its synodal decrees sentenced to ecclesiastical destitution those homosexual actives among the clergy – and 'those who allowed themselves to be involved' – whether they were bishops, priests or deacons; for their part, guilty laity were to be shaven bald and then excommunicated. All the emphasis is upon actives.[31]

That was still not enough for the king. This time drawing exclusive attention to actives, Egica modified the mid-century law of his predecessor by specifying that, while all those clergy 'who acted against other men' were to be destituted as the Council foresaw, all actives, whether lay or ecclesiastic and of whatever status or age, were to be castrated.[32] It would be fruitless to speculate on the motives of this fascinating moment in early Christian law. One can only be confident that it was the power that actives exercised over passives, whether the former were small businessmen pimps or nobles, that concerned Visigothic kings, who were, of course, seeking to strengthen their own power.[33] Next, the secular clergy definitely provided a particular institutional focus for that concern, the documents drawing attention to the power of prelates over the young who were attached to these clerical institutions. It appears that pre-Muslim Spanish law regarding homosexual behavior was concerned in some measure with challenges to royal and ecclesiastical authority.

By that time as well, and during the coming centuries, the central church was hardening its case against the homosexual active. In the immediate wake of the church uniting with the Roman state under Constantine, Lactantius had defined the active as a parricide, in the sense that birth-control was being practiced by the 'wasting' of the seed.[34] Now in the twelfth century, Peter Chanter again attacked the active, by stating that 'intercourse with a male incurs the same penalty – death – as intercourse with an animal.'[35] Bestiality was, of course, usually the crime of a penetrator and not a passive and, as we saw earlier, most of the animals in question were females.[36] Thus, while the general society may have considered the active role as 'natural,' the sexual object in question now made any penetration of an animal the antithesis of 'natural,' especially for the urban populations repulsed by rural habits.

From the end of the seventh century until the mid-thirteenth century, that is, in the long period when Islamic culture dominated much of Iberia, many Europeans did not doubt that the Christian warriors' ongoing humiliations were due in part to their 'sodomitic luxury': who would doubt that it was because of this crime that the soldiers' manly virility had failed them? Or that the homosexual passives among them were outright traitors because they would not fight for their country?[37] Yet, in these centuries, no further Christian legislation against homosexual behavior is known from Iberia.[38] Only in the thirteenth century does a normative harshness toward homosexual behavior become apparent, as it did in Europe at large.

The new regulations latch onto the Visigothic law for inspiration, even as they revise it. Thus the collection of various local Spanish laws called the *Fuera Real*, brought together in the mid-thirteenth century, includes the old punishment of castration, this time in public, but now, without limit, it is applied to both actives *and* passives. To that is added a provision that this castration was to be publicly meted out before the whole populace, that three days later the victims were to be hung upside down until dead, and that their bodies were never to be taken down.[39] This combined castration and death sentence would remain standard fare well into modern times in Spain.

A section of Alfonso X's *Siete Partidas* (ca. 1265), which became law throughout the kingdom of Castile in 1348, completes the general medieval secular law on the matter. Once sodomy was proven in court, the active party should be castrated and then stoned to death – an element of popular justice being thus introduced into the procedure.[40] Alfonso's treatment of passives was more refined. An age division of 14 having been established, those below that point were to be left unpunished because 'minors do not understand how serious a crime they have committed.' Passives 14 years or older, on the other hand, would only be punished – with the same penalty as that meted out to actives – if they consented to the act, 'because those who are forced are not guilty.' It has already been hinted that this was an open invitation for teenagers to come forward, claim that they had been raped, and inform on their sexual masters.[41]

Later fifteenth- and sixteenth century Iberian laws on the subject are not especially original, but they are important as background to the situation on the eve of the Conquests. Thus in 1446 the Portuguese King Afonso (1439–46), son of King Pedro, weighed in with what may be the earliest independent royal edict from that kingdom regarding homosexual behavior. Sodomites were to be burned. Afonso, himself suspect of sodomy (as was his near contemporary, Henry the Impotent of Castile), justified this punishment by referring, unsurprisingly, to the penalty Sodom and Gomorrah were said to have paid for their sins. But he gave a second justification for the law that was remarkable indeed: 'for committing this sin,' he said, 'the Order of Templars was destroyed throughout Christianity in one day.' [42] In his law of 1521, King Manuel of Portugal added confiscation of goods to the penalty of burning that his predecessor had established.[43]

In Spain, the one known national secular law of this period is Ferdinand and Isabella's Medina del Campo ordinance of August 22, 1497. The Catholic monarchs dropped the castration that had preceded execution at least since the *Siete Partidas*, and changed the death penalty for sodomy (and bestiality) from stoning or hanging to burning on the spot of the crime. Proof was sufficient if it matched that necessary to convict someone of *lèse-majesté* or heresy; thus on the eve of the settlements in the Americas, the old association of treason and sodomy was again invoked.[44] The monarchs' ordinance also slightly anticipated Manuel of Portugal in ordaining the confiscation of sodomites' goods. Philip II's 1593 pragmatic on sodomy, which was published in Portugal in 1603, did little more than diminish the burden of proof that had been established earlier.[45]

How difficult it is in the present state of research to determine who the Iberians thought these sodomites and their passives were, that is, who it was who made these laws necessary! Being the only law of the age whose text actually assesses the extent of homosexual behavior – burning being necessary, the monarchs say, because previous penalties had not extirpated the crime – the Medina del Campo law of 1497 is especially interesting because it at least implies that the Christian Spaniards themselves were the problem, and that sodomy was home grown.[46]

Yet the notion that infection – the contagion referring only to passives, be it well understood – from outside was responsible was certainly present in other sources. Thus a Franciscan preacher in Valencia in July 1519 blamed a perceived increase of sodomy on foreign merchants moving to that city.[47] Curiously, the source of infection of which the reader is most prepared to hear hardly occurs at all: despite the fact that the Christians conquered Granada in 1492, the last Muslim outpost in Europe, thus causing a mass of conversions of Muslims (and Jews) to Christianity, contemporary laws do not caution that sodomy might spread from Mohammedan to Christian. The concern is rather the fear of infection of Moor by Moor! Thus a bull of Pope Clement VII dated February 24, 1524, which allowed the Aragonese Inquisition to prosecute for sodomy not just Christians but also unconverted Muslims, mentions infection, but only between converted and unconverted Moors. Writing as if Old Christians were not part of the equation, Clement notes that sodomy had begun to spread among the unconverted *mudejares*. If such gross men were not socially isolated, he continued, they would 'spread their filth' among the converted *morisques*.[48]

While the legal penalties were at least as harsh here as in other areas of Europe, the laws in Christian Iberia obviously tell us little about the extent or dynamics of sodomy either in relation to the rest of Europe, or in relation to Mediterranean Islam. A comparable wariness is called for in evaluating Islamic norms, not to mention the jaundiced eye that should be applied to European slogans about Muslim sexuality. To repeat, the Koran is comparable with the Christian Bible in its dislike of homosexual practices, and the condemnations of active as well as passive homosexual behavior found in the writings of Western Mediterranean Muslim scholars, including jurisprudents, can be quite as firm in their own way as are the written laws of Christian Iberia.[49] Nor did Spanish Islam's normative tradition shy away from condemning specific homosexual contexts and personages. We know, for example, of one Islamic attempt to rid Andalusia's capital of passives. In early twelfth-century Seville, Ibn 'Abdun demanded that

> ... the mignons be expelled from the city. Those who are found after this measure has been put into effect should be punished. They should not be allowed to circulate among Muslims nor participate in the festivals, for they are vile and debauched persons, despised by Allah and the whole world.[50]

Yet reality was as different in Islam as in Christianity. Norms tell us little about the character of homosexual behavior in these cultures, indeed contemporary notions about the sexual identity of certain social groups may bring us closer to that reality than the norms themselves. These notions will also enable us to relate Iberian sexual experiences to their foundations in property and power. We turn to some contemporary notions about churchmen, women and soldiers.

Notions

When a critical social history of Iberia is finally written, the medieval Christian clergy will perforce be viewed in tandem with the Muslim clergy of the peninsula: both were charged with *cura animarum* across this land mass. Yet as similar as their duties might seem at times – both, we have stressed, denounced homosexual relations – their social differences cannot be ignored, and none less than this: the

Muslim clergy married during the high and late Middle Ages, but the Christian clergy did not.

Not surprisingly, the Christian clergy's sexual identity was suspect: like so many passive 'cowards,' they were forbidden to shed blood in battles, and quite as surely the circumstances of their celibacy were not reassuring. Such a note might be expected to be heard from Islam – the Sevillian Ibn 'Abdun, for instance, denouncing the Christian clergy as being peculiarly prone to sodomy[51] – but the same tone was at home in the Christian community as well. I earlier cited one example from Gregory of Tours, where a warrior asked a bishop about his 'husbands.' Byzantine bishops might suffer a terrible punishment if found guilty of sodomy: one was castrated then dragged through the street in an insult procession.[52] Half a millennium later, in tales from Scandinavia, that land of continuingly straightforward abuse of passives, bishops are often represented as women, one for example said to be the mother of nine children by a boastful male.[53] Like tales of lecherous clerks pursuing women, this suspicion that European clerks, especially when women were off-limits to them, practiced homosexual acts was a staple of story-telling in late medieval and early modern Europe.[54]

This stereotype about the secular clergy must, however, yield pride of ancestry to that which accuses monks of the same behavior. Once again, Muslim writers say what might be expected: I have already cited Al-Muqaddasî's flat conviction that children in Christian monasteries were castrated. But again, a similar presumption about monastic homosexual behavior was at home in Christianity as well. Leaving to the side the early Christian complaints about homosexual behavior in the monasteries, we may cite as an appropriate example in time an 802 capitulary in which Charlemagne, outraged that some monks were sodomites, warned that he would punish not only them, 'but others who consent to the same.'[55] Boswell indeed has made a persuasive case that monastic homosexual behavior was widespread well into the twelfth century, even if he mistook a pederastic reality – that is, a relation between active choir monks or instructors and novices or oblates – for a consenting behavior between cohorts.[56]

It is not enough to state that many medieval people shared the notion that church prelates, whether bishops or abbots, behaved passively toward powerful active outsiders, but actively with their own oblates and novices. We need rather to grasp the range of the social networks within which these sexual exchanges, real or metaphoric, occurred. Surely the pedagogic dependence of cathedral school or monastic novices upon their masters is a key to pederasty where it did exist – the ancient saw that semen helped pass the wisdom of the Book from teacher to student was certainly not unknown in Christianity – [57] but whence these boys hailed is quite as central to our understanding. Cathedral schools, chapters and monasteries not only provided permanent livings for some healthy legitimate sons; these ecclesiastical institutions commonly served as temporary billeting for children during their early schooldays,[58] and, of course, especially monasteries served as asylums for bastards and disabled children.[59]

There can be little doubt that, when it accompanied such 'vocations,' parental guilt fostered the disputes between patrons and prelates regarding the treatment of boys that mark medieval records. Avoiding child abuse was thus a parental consideration. Boswell cleverly notes, for instance, that from the fourth century on the Christian clergy attacked sodomy – that is, men taking the active role – as a means of halting the abandonment of unwanted children into slavery, where *Herr* almost inevitably used *Knecht* sexually;[60] the oblation of children into monasteries in those days was but another form of abandonment, so that, by decrying sodomy, churchmen were indirectly recruiting some of those same children.

Inevitably, then, the prelates of the monasteries and cathedral schools that warehoused children competed with the blood parents, both as 'fathers' of the boys, for their control.[61] In her study of the Ganymede theme in Christian art, Forsyth pointed to this hidden reality when she interpreted the sculpted theme at Vézelay of the eagle carrying off a terrified young Ganymede as a criticism of the sexual abuse of oblate children in monasteries.[62] Child abuse is indeed represented. Still, I think it just as probable that the monks were directing their criticism outward as well, against those outsiders who carried boys off to rape them, and even against the fathers who sealed such a fate!

A struggle between ecclesiastical and secular 'fathers' was also involved in those many cases in which parish rectors not only lived with female 'concubines,' as church authorities called the common-law wives of rectors, but were indeed themselves *concubitores masculorum*, that is, living with young boys alongside them. In the former case, a married clergyman might produce an heir to his ecclesiastical benefice, but on the other, as well, the benefice might pass from the 'father' to his male concubine. Thus the central thrust of the ecclesiastical reform movement of the eleventh and twelfth centuries, which was to regain the 'lands of Christ,' was certainly involved in the heightened clerical opposition to homosexual activity during this age.

Here then are some of the reasons why not just sovereigns, but prelates as well have historically condemned less the passive than the active partners in homosexual behaviors, even though Mediterranean societies almost uniformly directed their revulsion against passives.[63] Sharply put, they were trying to protect not only their tender boys from being abducted, but the institutions of monasticism and of the secular clergy, which outside males, who styled themselves macho, viewed as effeminate. Bynum is on the mark in claiming that medieval gender identities changed as clerical relations with the outside world changed, noting, for instance, that in the high Middle Ages Cistercian abbots started to think of themselves as mothers to their monks. 'Abbots were in fact increasingly called upon [by outside forces] to respond with qualities that medieval men considered feminine,' the author says, for these forces needed 'a new image of authority.'[64] The same gender dynamic was at work in the world of homosexual relations.

Recognizing the principle that gender was part of the rhetoric used to describe intra- and interecclesiastical power relations in Europe helps to throw light upon a gendered document of the late eleventh or early twelfth century urging a crusade, one of particular importance because it essentially began Europe's sexual stereotyping of Muslims. Though a forgery from the West, in this letter the Byzantine emperor paints for Western readers a horrible picture of Turkish behavior toward Christians in the course of their Western expansion. Not only do they rape any and all noble women, the emperor rails; the Turks mount them like animals! He continues: Not only do they circumcise both boys and youth; they go further and sodomize males of every age and rank,

> ... and what is worse and more wicked, [they sodomize] clerks and monks, and even – alas and for shame! something which from the beginning of time has never been spoken or heard of – bishops! They have already killed one bishop with this nefarious sin.[65]

Surely written by a bishop, this passage is important first of all as one of several examples we shall encounter of the European and Mediterranean theme that the rape of a man is more serious than that of a female.[66] But in the present context, what matters is that the writer was trying to shame Western warlords, who had not protected such adult dependents as the clergy obviously were. Thus gendering the prelacy as unwilling victims of anal penetration was one way of appealing to readers who themselves often gendered their clergy as passives.[67] Obviously the explorers and settlers of the Americas were entrusted with some deep-rooted notions about the gender of that division of labor that knelt and invoked the gods for a living. European men layered these social structures by gender.

Women provide a second notional complex central to the high and late medieval understanding of male homosexual relations, and specifically the relative access men had to them in any given social situation. In the medieval superstructure as in that of many societies, the crystalline myth of the Lady mediates our understanding of the power and property equations that associated king (who tried to control his underlings' sexuality, as we have seen), to noble male (who attempted to outdo his sovereign), to queen (who was the instrument of the game). Marchello-Nizia shows that in prose adaptations of the Tristan and Lancelot stories, the king, in allowing his beautiful knight and competitor to lie with his woman, makes him active with her but passive toward him.[68] Such was the literary dynamic that intermeshed women at the top of the pyramid of power with sexually constrained claimants to the throne. At lower, operational levels of society, the same holds true: there seems to have existed in fact an inverse ratio between male homosexual behavior and the availability of women. Nor was this so-called harem complex, in which relatively few men within any given class or status monopolized a large number of its nubile women, limited to North Africa, even if medieval moralists denounced a court full of women as the 'Mohammedan fashion.'[69] It was increasingly visible in parts of continental Europe as well: in late medieval Italy, for example, the fewer the available nubile women or prostitutes, the more male homosexual behavior seems to have occurred.[70]

Whatever the facts of the matter, however, that relationship between female availability and male sexual behavior was an article of faith at this time. This can be seen in the 'irrationalism' Europeans attributed to Muslims. Thus in the mid-thirteenth century the theologian William of Auvergne claimed that, despite the multitudes of wives Muslims were said to have, Mohammed's prohibition of sodomy had failed miserably. Other writers judged that this easy access to women made these husbands' homosexual behavior not only less explicable, but more grievous.[71] And in the fifteenth century, the Florentine government made female prostitutes available to young men because, without them, they thought, the males would consort with each other.[72]

Islamic traditions are not dissimilar. Other reasons for male relations were cited, to be sure. The eleventh-century author Al-

Katib, for example, knew that it was 'to avoid scandalous pregnancies' that the preferred form of homosexual contact, anal intercourse, was commonly employed in heterosexual, but also in homosexual fornication.[73] And in the fourteenth century Ibn Khaldūn explained pederasty itself (*liwât*) as the product of big-city decadence.[74] But male homosexual behavior was commonly explained by the scarcity of women. Indeed the ninth-century savant Al-Jahiz claimed that homosexual behavior was unknown in Islam until, tragically, the Abbasid Abū Muslim refused to allow his army to have any contact with women. That isolation, said Al-Jahiz, caused the fighting men to seek out boys and, once that practice was established, it became a cultural avocation. Later Islamic tradition assumed that pederasty was general in Islam by the tenth century.[75]

The Muslim myth that soldiers brought sodomy home in their knapsacks, so to speak, has a particular interest for us because, different from Islam, a society of men at arms was at the heart of Castilian culture, and it is the sexual universe of these conquerors that we hope to understand. Soldiering provides the third central background for understanding homosexual behavior in Iberia. Still, at the root of this profession in Iberia, I will argue, lay a male notion that women, easily available women, played a central role in military society by providing both domestic services such as cooking, sewing and portage, and ongoing sexual services.[76]

Women themselves set the tone. At least from the First Crusade forward, they joined armies for all imaginable reasons, dressing like men to fit in.[77] Then, to avoid the aforementioned 'mistake' of the Muslims, late medieval and early modern Spanish armies gained renown by taking great numbers of women into the field, and we shall later encounter a Spanish expedition in Peru where each soldier is said to have had 150 servants in his personal train, no small part being native women for sexual needs.[78] The habit was then old hat. Sancho IV (1284–95) was famous in the early fourteenth century for having expelled no fewer than 5,000 prostitutes from his military train, and one moralist urged a later Castilian monarch to emulate Sancho and clean house again, brushing aside the claim that lots of female prostitutes prevented males from sinning with each other.[79] In the early sixteenth century, the number of prostitutes accompanying the Spanish army was notorious. For example, in 1532 the Ferrarese chronicler Bianchi praised the Iberians for their many prostitutes by referring to the evils that arose because they were absent from other armies.[80] Thus a group of men released from general criminal sanctions for homicide at war was furnished with large numbers of peninsular women with whom, presumably, they could do what they wanted, much as they could do what they wanted with women vanquished beyond the peninsula.

The obvious advantages of bringing one's own females were clear to contemporaries such as Bianchi: even with the Spanish army in town, burghers' daughters were safe, because, unlike the French, the Spaniards had their own women.[81] Other Italian chroniclers spoke out for burghers' sons, who were also at risk. In 1512, for instance, the Spanish army was accused of raping the boys of Prato during the sack of that town, and in 1529, the inhabitants of nearby Florence were terrified of such homosexual rape – the supreme fear of civic degradation – if the Spanish armies entered the city.[82] Lastly, a plethora of women camp followers, it was said, kept males away from each other.[83]

So the advantages to armies and to civil populations of a large corps of one's own women was clear. Yet the great disadvantage was just as apparent: the endless battles within the army over who had a right to the sexual services of such women. The single officer might try to avoid a prohibition against bringing a prostitute by claiming that he brought his own 'wife.' In general, European governments of this age sought to avoid conflicts over women said to be the property of individual men by hiring a limited number of prostitutes, either from home or on the road, who served all the troops in common. The Spanish women outdid all others in their numbers.[84]

At this juncture, in the context of discussing how military discipline over women was maintained in camp, a particular institution documented in these years at Fez, across the Straits of Gibraltar from Iberia, takes on great importance because through it one can see how urban and military functions were closely interwoven with sexual ones. In his description (ca. 1520) of the hostels in this Moroccan city where he had grown up, the Granadan-born *morisque* Leo the African describes certain of Fez's inhabitants as follows:

> They are of a certain type called *el cheua*. They dress in women's clothes and ornament their persons the way women do. They shave their beards and try to imitate [women] right down to their manner of speaking. No, they go even further. They spin! Each of these infame men keeps a concubine, and has sex with him no differently than a wife has with a husband.[85]

Here again are our adult passives, this time definitely transvested and, significantly, described as if they were in charge of their 'husbands.' Indeed they may have been, for it transpires that these transvestites were in fact entrepreneurs in their own right. Leo continues:

> [*Elcheua*] also keep women who have the customs of the whores in the alleys of Europe ... And in the said hostelries, which are protected by the court, one can find all the males of evil life. Some are there to become inebriated, others to satisfy their libido with women who charge, still others for recourse to those other illicit and vituperous means it is best to remain silent about. Hostelers of this type have their own consul and they pay a certain tribute to the castellan and city governor.

How marvelously fascinating! Males dressed and acting as 'madams' supervise women and males selling sex, including the 'unmentionable sin' it was best to keep quiet about – sodomy – all the while supporting their own males gendered male who actively serviced them. But the most interesting revelation, the links of these brothels to military life, still lies ahead. Now the 'madams' send the working girls off to war. Leo continues:

> When called upon, [*elcheua*] are obliged to give a large number of their group to the army of the king or princes to do the cooking for the soldiers, since few others are proficient in this trade.

Leo concludes by apologizing to his readers. The best people don't associate with these brothel prostitutes, to be sure; only 'ribalds and those of vile blood' do. Still, our author pleads for understanding: 'The lords,' he notes, 'allow [*elcheua* and the prostitutes] to remain in this indecent and evil life because, as I have said, they use them for the needs of the camp.'[86]

If not perhaps as brothel 'madams,' men who dressed like women both for their own sexual needs and better to supervise subordinate females await us in the Americas as well. What is significant about this remarkable document in the Mediterranean context, however, is that it presents a major urban institution, the brothel, staffed by and completely dependent upon male transvestite entrepreneurs, being maintained by the authorities because women were often needed in the field for military purposes, and it shows this directly across the Straits from Spain, practiced by a people that had, until yesterday so to speak, controlled the society and culture of Granada and indeed much of southern Spain.

In the current state of Iberian social history, it is admittedly imposs-

ible to determine how close or distant Spanish or Portuguese practice
was from the traditions of Fez.[87] It is almost incredible, for instance,
to read that a favorite of Henry IV of Castile stood accused of
maintaining a lucrative trade with the Moors in the foreskins of
Christian children![88] But were male hostelers dressed as women
known in Christian Spain or elsewhere in Europe? That remains to be
determined. Yet in one area we can confirm a similarity by looking to
the north. In neighboring France, the official who supervised brothel
prostitutes in the cities – the King of the Ribalds – is the same who led
them off to war.[89] I suspect that it was little different in Iberia.

This institutionalization within urban society of a group needed
outside by lawless men at war best demonstrates the role armies
played in contextualizing male homosexual activity. As recently as
1970, it has been claimed that, the Spaniards being a soldierly people,
homosexuality remained foreign to them.[90] Of course this is non-
sense. But if through future comparative research it should transpire
that homosexual relations in the military society of Spain were less
frequent than in other areas of Europe, the omnipresence of women
in the Spanish camp might help explain that fact.[91] Doubtless, young
male pages must have served in the Iberian as well as in other armies
as attractive passives.[92] But by creating in the field the mirror image
of the harem or the Christian nunnery, that is, one in which a large
number of women belonging to no particular warrior could be
violated by all, just as enemy women might be, Spain and Portugal
may in fact have avoided 'worse.'

Praxis and Punishment

Of all possible approaches to understanding the Iberian attitude
toward homosexual acts at the time of the discovery of the Americas,
none deserves more attention than the actual punishments Iberian
authorities meted out for such violations in the late Middle Ages.
And yet it must be said up front that, at this point, the serious study
of Iberian sexual penology begins only in the late sixteenth century,
when the Spanish Inquisition began to prosecute homosexual acts in
earnest in Aragon.[93]

Alas, with the possible exception of two works whose interpretive
or documentary failures have compromised their usefulness in this
area, no scientific studies have been done on homosexual traditions
in Iberia during the Middle Ages. There is much of interest in the
work of Luis Mott on the Portuguese background, but his documen-

tation, where it exists, is shoddy.[94] More serious yet no more helpful, Boswell in his dissertation says he reviewed more than 2,000 registers of the crown of Aragon dating from 1355 to 1366 without finding one case of sodomy, even though these records are replete with other sexual matters. The detailed trial records of the same kingdom have no sodomy cases before 1500, Boswell hastily assures us.[95] The author seems to think this indicates that homosexual practices were at a minimum in Aragon; it of course only shows that, often in exchange for payment to judges, sodomy was often not prosecuted in those fora.[96]

In the absence of any competent studies based on serial records in Iberia, one is thrown back on largely anecdotal evidence from these centuries. That evidence is not, however, uninteresting. Certainly most tantalizing is Rossello's pamphlet on some fifteenth-century volumes in the royal archives of Palma de Mallorca: they include judicial sources that do, in turn, contain many prosecutions of homosexual practices.[97] In his impressionistic run-through, Rossello found that as a rule at least one person was executed for sodomy each year. The normal punishment imposed in these volumes was running the gauntlet, the second most common being burning at the stake. The author found no prosecution for sodomy of anyone from the upper classes; rather, those accused in this commercial center of Palma seem to have been predominantly outsiders, Catalans, Moors and Jews being especially noteworthy.[98]

The cases cited by Rossello show some significant differences in punishment. Most interesting are those between older and younger, that is, between active and passive partners. Rare indeed, the ages of the passive partners are often given: one meets an occasional boy 'of tender age,' but most are between ten and twelve years, and are often said to have been raped. Punishments meted out to passives who in the minds of the judges bore some of the responsibility, on the other hand, are also alluded to. Thus in 1498 one boy had his buttocks burned with a torch – a depilatory punishment we have already encountered in Antiquity. Again in 1504, 'considering his minority and tender age, and considering he was the passive, one Francisco [was] to be given three strokes with a blazing torch,' and then exiled from the kingdom.[99] There are several other related crimes of bestiality punished in these records, as well as details on a woman who had to run the gauntlet in 1455 (without being whipped), 'who went about like a man, both in the cut of her hair and in the type of hat, so as to provoke men to sin.'[100] Clearly, these Majorcan archival volumes deserve serious study.

While Rossello does not claim that the cases he selected were representative of those in the files, they do at least furnish a basis for some hypotheses about Iberian judicial practice that may be tested in future research. Outsiders and those of artisanal and lower status may have been particularly threatened with prosecution. Next, the rape of young boys may have been fairly common. Indeed, in his study of Inquisition records of the late sixteenth century, Bennassar found rape very common indeed.[101] Apparently, passives were punished less severely than actives. And finally, public humiliation and burning at the stake were seemingly common punishments.

Anecdotal information coming from the mainland in this period does not confound these hypotheses. It is clear, for example, that, in crisis, those known for homosexual practices were easy choices for public scapegoating, both in Christian and in Muslim culture. Thus during a crisis in 1149 or 1150, Moroccan Fez witnessed the sudden execution of 'eighty persons, between effeminates and members of the populace.'[102] Foreigners were particularly open to such public humiliations in Christian Spain. When the traveller Thomas Münzer stopped at Almería on October 19, 1494, he saw six persons first castrated, then hung by the neck, and then by the feet, with their testicles hanging from their necks. All six were Italians, Münzer noted, their undoing being that 'Spaniards hate this vice and especially watch out for it.' On the following January 25, the same Münzer saw two other men identically punished outside the gates of Madrid.[103]

To foreigners, the natives might seem just as guilty of sodomy. Visiting the royal city of Olmedo in July 1466, the Czech Rozmital assures us that the so-called Old Christians were worse than the Moors, their sodomitic life style defying description.[104] But in the event, foreigners and especially Italians were the ones who paid the price during crisis. Thus on the feast of the Magdalene in 1519, with Valencia hungry and infected with plague, a Franciscan preacher warned that sodomy was increasing, brought in by foreign merchants. The faithful promptly rushed out, rounded up a group of four 'sodomites' and burned them alive on July 29 to cries of 'Viva la justicia!' Before they died, these victims implicated two local clerks, one of whom, seized from church authorities, was given over to the crowd, which suffocated and burned him because 'the church shouldn't protect male prostitutes and sodomites.'[105] The so-called Germania uprising in Valencia the following March also featured popular justice: its leaders gave over to the crowd for incineration another young clerk who was accused of prostitution.[106] The burning of four more foreign men is recorded in Seville on January 29, 1521,[107] and in the detailed records of the Jesuit Pedro de León in late sixteenth-century Seville, the prejudice against Italians, if not their inordinate punishment, is pronounced.[108] A historian of seventeenth-century Valencia has documented actual persecution and not just prejudice against the Italians – some 13.5 per cent of all those the Inquisition executed for sodomy being Italians, and mostly poor soldiers and sailors to boot.[109]

Scattered as the evidence is on the eve of the Conquests, it does seem clear that castrations cum executions were not uncommon public spectacles in Iberia at the time of the discoveries. State building through violent sexuality was alive and well. This topos was not of course limited to the peninsula, and ranges across the centuries. Thus when the Earl of Leicester, Simon de Montfort, fell at Evesham in 1265, the victors, like butchers, decapitated him and cut off his hands, feet and genitalia; they then hung his testicles from either side of his nose before parading his head on a lance.[110] And in Metz on the eve of Epiphany 1492, a man accused of treason was hung after being totally castrated; many other European cases of the type could doubtless be gathered.[111] But there is no gainsaying the Spaniards' reputation for ruthlessness in punishing sodomy, any more than one can doubt the Italians' reputation for tolerating the practice. In one sixteenth-century case, in fact, we encounter a comparative note: in Rome, Diego de Simancas of the Spanish Inquisition told the Italians he knew how to stop their sodomy: children had to be terrified. A law was needed that required any boy who had been violated to inform officials of the event within four days. Otherwise he too would be burned when the facts became known.[112]

Yet for all the Spanish bravado and Europeans' presumptions about national sexualities, neither the records of such gruesome executions nor any other evidence demonstrates that sodomy was any less extensive in Iberia than elsewhere. As Rocke has shown persuasively in an Italian context, Florentine officials in the fifteenth century realized that the harsher the penalties, the fewer people would report the crime. Thus the Iberian evidence of harsh executions might suggest, as comparable evidence did in Tuscany, that sodomitic practice was actually widespread. Recall that Ferdinand and Isabella – half-sister of Henry the Impotent – justified their 1497 anti-sodomy law by noting the persistence of what sounds like homegrown, endemic sodomy.

One simply must expect certain sexual practices within certain social formations. Pederastic violence, for example, did not appear and vanish on certain days; it was to be expected in a social order that disadvantaged children. Bennassar found evidence in the Aragonese Inquisition records that the sexual abuse of young boys was part and parcel of much homosexual activity in the later sixteenth and seventeenth centuries; we also found it common in fifteenth-century Majorca.[113] How could it be otherwise, given the fundamentals of social organization in the Iberian peninsula during these centuries?

In the early seventeenth century, the court of Philip IV was famous for its luxury and sexual experimentation. Chronicles of the period are filled with talk of sodomy, both at court and in Madrid.[114] Now doubtless it would not be wise to argue that Spanish sexual culture in 1500 was little different from that of the court of Philip IV. But it would be just as silly to argue that a decadent king was responsible for the morality of his court — as biographical historians often do — or to claim that the structures underlying this now overt homosexual behavior at court were new in the seventeenth century.

Two documents of this later age clarify the kinds of structures that do not appear, or vanish, overnight. In 1623, a law took effect that rewarded men who married at 18 years and punished men who were still single at 28.[115] The law was clearly aimed in part against homosexual acts in a society where marriages were thought to be falling. Then in 1635, Fray Francisco de León, prior of Guadalupe, denounced 'men converted into women, soldiers into effeminates, who are haughty and full of airs, sport toupées, and for all I know wear women's cosmetics.'[116]

Such behaviors and sentiments cannot ignore the fact, however, that this was an age of royal absolutism, a system that forced a certain type of dependency upon courtiers, whose expression was gendered female, and the gendering of political structures was a customary reality. Thus when in the early seventeenth century the Portuguese thanked the king or *quiteve* of Sofali in East Africa for bestowing upon them the title 'wives of the king,' or the English and French at about the same time encountered a tribe in Pennsylvania that was a 'woman' to the 'male' tribe that ruled it,[117] they were not ignorant of the political realities that underlay such gender metaphors.

Notions of gender were simply built into concepts of power and dependence. An early chronicler of the discoveries, the Italian Peter Martyr d'Anghiera, wrote back to his Sforza patron in Milan in 1516 with a characterization of the conquering Spaniards that made that point well enough, and we may take it as a fundamental gender statement about all civil polities. Spanish males, whether burghers or nobles, were masculine indeed, the writer intimated; they make fun of men who wear rings and gems and don 'the perfumes of Arabia.' Burghers avoided such 'effeminacies,' Peter continued, because their use would have been out of character for those in their humble station. Nobles on the other hand avoided these effeminacies because 'effeminized' persons were suspected of complicity in *obscoena Venere* – that is, taking the passive role in homosexual liaisons. But all in all, Peter insisted, Spanish men were men!

Yet Peter knew one exception to his rule, which he described even at the risk that his soft and sweet words on such matters 'make for effeminacy more than good morals.' At marriages or at regal pomps, he admitted, Spanish nobles did after all like to wear objects Peter elsewhere categorically identified as 'feminine.'[118] In Old World public performances, in short, Spanish men assumed the effeminacies necessary to a political game of seduction. Each age chooses a different vocabulary to describe the relation between gender and power, and even in this age, the age of the massive princely codpiece, Peter Martyr might trip over himself proving the macho of the Spanish lords.[119] Like other reporters, Peter d'Anghiera would denounce the native American berdaches who dressed like women; and, with the exception of short-term male transvestism during festivals, such a type is indeed rarely enough documented in European Antiquity or in the European, if not the Islamic, Middle Ages.[120] But men's seduction of men was not at all foreign to the Old World.

Eastern Revelations

In the half-century preceding their discovery and conquest of the American mainlands, Europeans became increasingly well informed about the exotic worlds of Africa and the Middle East by way of an exploding number of travel reports. Not the least of their interest in such orientalia dealt with the sexual practices travellers encountered, including of course homosexual practices. To be sure, because of their own history and because of their proximity to Islamic culture, which dominated the newly explored areas, Iberians would have been less struck, perhaps, by such exotica than, say, the Germans. Still, certain of these reports deserve attention because they will help fix in our minds, on the eve of the American Conquests, the gender aspect of notions of power and property which is one basis for our study of homosexual behavior in the pre-Conquest Mediterranean.

A first selection from this travel literature comes from the famous *Viaggi* of Nicolò de' Conti, a Venetian who wrote up his travel experiences for the church fathers at the Council of Florence in 1439 – a council, it will be recalled, that also heard a great deal from princely Iberians about that peninsula's efforts at exploration.[121] In describing subcontinental India, Conti all but recommended the skills of India's public prostitutes to his European readers: these women, who had no peers at seducing men to enjoy themselves, were marvelously skilled at caressing men each according to his age. Conti's punch line drove home the utility of such behavior: 'From this it happens that the Indians do not know what the abominable vice is.'[122] Conti's concern can be traced to his origins: Venice itself officially encouraged its prostitutes to do those things that would entice men away from homosexual behavior, as the explorer certainly knew.[123] Here was a whole culture, Conti seems to say, where men did not caress each other because public women knew how to attract men away from dangerous male liaisons.

A second travel account comes from the Portuguese Tomé Pires's description of Persia, written about 1513–15. According to Pires, everyone in the area of Hormuz enjoyed the 'abominable vice.' Indeed there were brothels with male prostitutes, 'who are beardless and always dress as women.' Not only did the locals find no fault with sodomy; the Persians actually ridiculed the Portuguese for being repulsed by it.[124] Let us guard against assuming from this report that male brothels did not exist in Europe; we shall regularly verify that practices said to be *nunca oida* in Europe were in fact at home there.[125] But it is fair to say that, generally speaking, Europeans did not openly claim that, like female prostitution, institutionalized male prostitution might help preserve the established patriarchal power. To judge by modern authorities on Islamic sexuality, on the other hand, it appears that the determination of the patriarchy to maintain their Islamic women within harems caused them to tolerate male prostitution for the young men, who found themselves excluded from women.[126] It could have been no secret to Pires, who grew up across the Straits of Gibraltar from a thriving Islamic culture, that this 'repulsive' institution depended for its vitality in part upon the cloistering of women.

Finally, the record of Duarte Barbosa, another Portuguese traveller, requires our attention because it mentions the role of eunuchs in the same region of Hormuz. Writing about 1517–18, Barbosa noted that, for purposes of pomp, every gentleman of Hormuz was accompanied in his peregrinations by a page, and most of these pages in turn had a retinue 'of young eunuch slaves, with whom they slept.' Again, one is tempted to see this practice in relation to the status of women, precisely because Barbosa places this processional fact of retinue formation in the customary European discourse of whether women liked or disliked sodomites, that is, homosexual actors. Because these pages took the active role with eunuchs, said Barbosa, they were disliked by women[127] – obviously because they did not make love to them as much as they might have.

Without realizing it, many a curious conquistador lapping up these travel reports was forming his own sexual consciousness for an eventual meeting with the Americans. These soldiers grew up in a culture where sexuality was encountered in the political authority's public humiliation of lawbreakers before it surfaced in one's own individual development. They matured in a military culture whose own sexuality, whether hetero- or homosexual, had once been closely linked to cloistered young boys in monasteries and cathedral schools, and was now intimately coupled to the position of women – both to those cloistered ones who could not be used and to those prostitutes who were. And, even when they stemmed from the Extremadura as did so many, most of these future conquistadors breathed the continuing influence of Islamic culture.

Thus if on the eve of the settlement of America the Iberians had some vague notions of different Western and Eastern sexualities – especially of a greater African and Asian tolerance for male prostitution in which males wore female clothing and acted like women – they had no reason to be ignorant of the sexual practices they were about to encounter in the Americas. They knew of men who dressed as women for life, they knew that homosexual activities were common when women were unavailable and, whatever their ideologies might require them to say, they knew that homosexual activity was spread out across Iberia among the natives, and not just among foreign visitors.[128] For all the undoubted exoticism they were about to encounter, the Iberians did not arrive in the Americas straight.

Perhaps least arguable is that they recognized the link between the prayer mode of prostration – itself a figure of sodomy – and political domination. The story of Mehmet the conqueror and the son of Lucas Notaras, former megadux of Constantinople, was well known. On conquering Byzantium in 1453, Mehmet thought to appoint Notaras head of the city, but, so as to first test his loyalty, he demanded from Notaras his 14-year-old son 'to lustful ends.'[129]

It was but one more variant on an ancient theme: domination expressed itself through sexuality, which here gendered males female. It had long been so in Europe, the conquerors would find it in the Americas.

3

The Military and Diplomatic Berdache

[The Spaniards] seized two local boats and put fifty Indians in them with their bows and spears. And they sent them out to the [French] ship, giving them to understand that the people in it were sodomites, and if they did not kill them, they would land and seize many of them and use them as they would women.[1]

[The Hispaniolan] feared to fall into the hands of the Spaniards. Once before he had been taken by them and, as he showed us, they had cut out his genitalia.[2]

Europeans made their first contacts with native Americans – dogs, they called them – as soldiers prepared for battle, not in a domestic context. Marching through the American countryside, each soldier accompanied by a retinue of some 150 native *piezas de servicio, entre machos y hembras amorosas*, they encountered native sexuality in the midst of conflict before they studied it in the subordinated village.[3] Just as surely, natives had developed a military order in the field as a preface to constructing their civil life at home. The traditional habit of describing outside conflict as produced by inside civility is problematic. Military formations inspire domestic arrangements rather than vice versa.

This study of American sexual practices before the European Conquests begins outside, in the seeming chaos of war. My goals in this chapter, a first approach to native sexual life, are two. First, by listening to what Iberians say about sodomy and associated practices in native warfare, I aim to unearth the military information which will throw light on the characteristic American institution of the berdache. To repeat: a berdache is a biological male who dressed, gestured and spoke as an 'effeminate,' that is, as individual cultures said women did and expected women or effeminates to act; over the long rather than the short term, the berdache served macho males by assuming the female division of labor, often including the sexual servicing of males.[4] I aim in short to reconstruct the ways in which indigenous peoples gendered their armies.

Secondly, I wish to record the gendered insults which native armies used against each other. Perforce, that means an emphasis on males exchanging insults at war, the losing males having the accusation of effeminacy stick to them as a result of defeat. As an important ancillary goal, I want to present an image of the victors' females ridiculing these effeminized losers, so as to describe the ultimate character of the genderization of warfare as one of dependence mirrored in humiliation.

The earliest references to sodomy in the New World are found in descriptions of the military activities of the Caribs. In a letter of 1494, Columbus's doctor, Diego Alvarez Chanca, claims that, on capturing young boys from the islands of Guadeloupe, Maria Galante and Santa Cruz, these fierce natives – the word Carib is the source of our word cannibal – first castrated them, then used them sexually until they grew to adulthood, at which point they were killed and eaten.[5] Then in 1495, the Italian Michele di Cuneo wrote in a letter that the same Caribs and the more sedentary Arawaks were 'largely sodomites,' though they were probably unaware that homoerotic behavior was a vice. In the first application to the Americas of the old notion that homosexuality spread by contagion, Michele opined that sodomy may have passed from the Caribs to the Arawaks:

> For these [Caribs] . . . are wilder men. When conquering and eating those [Arawak] Indians, they may have committed that extreme offence [of sodomy] out of spite. Proceeding thence, it may have been transmitted from one to the other.[6]

We know that, to this day, homosexual as well as heterosexual rape remains an established insult among peoples beyond the tribal stage of organization, and that in Michele's own lifetime Europeans feared the wartime rape of boys by other Europeans.[7] Thus in this very first of the many European sources that will describe native American mores as exotic, we are cautioned that Michele di Cuneo knew well enough that homosexual rape was used as a military insult in the Old World.

These letters of 1494 and 1495 both link prisoners' castration to their subsequent homosexual rape, which might lead some to think that castrated prisoners of war bear no relation to native American berdaches, who will rarely be described as eunuchs, or even as impotent, in the following pages. That would be wrong, for our true interests are, first, the fact of homosexual intercourse, which is common to both berdache and eunuch, and, second, the value of dependence associated with such activity, again linking eunuch and berdache. But on closer reflection, the link was also physical. Eunuchs of the type described in Michele di Cuneo's letters – ones devoid of testicles *and* penises – had begun to look something like, taken on the 'clothing' of, contemporary American women. Distinct from the eunuch, the American berdache is usually described as having his roots in domestic affairs. It is time to follow him back to military violence.

Following this path, we quickly find one field of battle where eunuchs were said to be dressed as women, a standard characteristic of the berdache. I refer to peoples of the northeast coast of today's Texas, in what was called at the time 'Florida.' In a work published in 1542, Nuñez Cabeza de Vaca introduces us to the theme of the division of military labor among native Americans. He claims to have seen in this area a man who had 'married' (*casado*) another male, one who belonged to a class of 'impotent effeminates' (*unos hombres amarionados impotentes*). These males dressed like and performed the offices of women. They did not use the bow and arrow; being taller and stronger than other men, however, they did carry the heavy loads, especially but not only into battles.[8]

Nuñez Cabeza de Vaca may have been hinting that these trans-vested tribesmen were indeed armed, but in a fashion different from bow and arrow. This phenomenon of gendered arms must be addressed before proceeding. The Spaniards tended simply to identify femininity with a total absence of arms. Thus Lopez de Gómara, writing his history of the Conquests from Spain and without benefit of a residence in America, described Panamanian men (*hombres*) of fighting age who lived in brothels and 'shamelessly offered themselves and dressed like common bawds, in this way avoiding going to war.'[9] But other early Spanish sources hinted that arms were variously gendered. Thus in the 1520s Oviedo generalized that berdaches 'did not occupy themselves with using arms,' but, more narrowly, he meant that, in warfare, these transvestites or berdaches 'did not do the things that men do.'[10] A century later the Jesuit Pérez de Ribas again emphasized that the transvestites he knew could not bear a specific weapon, saying that the Sinaloans 'do not use the bow and arrow; rather, some of them dress like women.'[11] Another century on, Marquette in his account of the Illinois tribes of the 1660s insisted upon the arms-specific character of that tribes' berdaches: transvestites made war, he said, 'but they can use only clubs and not bows and arrows, which are the weapons proper to men.'[12] Thus, while it is commonly asserted that berdaches avoided arms, these transvestites do at times have an arms-bearing profile, one which prohibited them from bearing specific arms that were gendered male.

Let us return now to the Núñez Cabeza de Vaca documentation, which may hint at a division of arms while claiming with certainty that a division of labor also existed, one assigning load-bearing to transvestites who appear to have been eunuchs. In 1552 López de Gómara glossed Núñez Cabeza's text in his own work. While he omitted the latter's reference to load-bearing, he did correctly state that the same natives did *not* use the bow and arrow, and he did repeat the first part of Núñez's account, referring to the *impotentes*. However, he interpreted the meaning of the term, taking 'impotents' to mean eunuchs (*impotentes o capados*). There is, therefore, reason to believe that, in certain parts of 'Florida,' eunuchs dressed as women played a significant role in warfare. This would explain why precisely these men were of such size and vigor. Gómara was probably right in assuming that Núñez Cabeza was referring to eunuchs for, when castrated at an early age, eunuchs may indeed grow to be 'taller and stronger than other men.'[13]

One then finds the same load-bearing males among the Tumucua tribe of northeastern Florida, this time, however, without any reference to castration. Among the accounts of the Huguenots' experiences there in 1564, the French draftsman Le Moyne de Morgues and his captain Laudonnière paid special attention to certain persons they called 'hermaphrodites'; these men were transvestites as well, as can be seen from their long hair and skirts, shown in Le Moyne's drawings.[14] According to his caption, these men, whom we must in fact call berdaches, were 'considered odious by the Indians.' Still, 'when the kings set out to war,' the so-called hermaphrodites 'transport the supplies . . ., and carry their dead to the place of burial.'[15]

With some reason, Michael Alexander has speculated that these load-bearing berdaches were also the homosexually passive 'boys' of the Tumucua priests, since, in his account, Laudonnière says that some of these priests were 'sodomites.' Finally, the same Laudonnière notes that these 'hermaphrodites' wore war paint and feathers to appear more terrible.[16] How easy it must have been for Europeans, who conventionally associated such cosmetics with women, to think that all Indians were sodomites!

Berdaches, that is, biological males who appeared to be women and who performed women's tasks, were thus to be found in warlike settings in 'Florida,' possibly alongside eunuchs. They were despised members of the Tumucua tribe, whose warriors, in facing off against enemy tribes, in turn sexually defamed these outsiders. According to

Le Moyne, the Tumucua took no male prisoners, but before leaving the field of battle they symbolically sodomized, if not castrated, those they killed. 'What astonished me,' Le Moyne writes, 'was that [the Tumucua] never left the place of battle without piercing the mutilated corpses of their enemies right through the anus with an arrow' (see figure 3).[17] Different from evisceration through the stomach, spearing corpses from behind has a symbolic relation to penetrating passives: in the Valley of Mexico itself, the Texcocans are said to have punished precisely passives by 'removing the entrails through the lower parts.'[18] In Michoacán to the west of the valley, that punishment is indeed illustrated.[19] And the Incas will be found using the same action against a hated missionary, the Iberian source's use of the term 'nefandous sacrilege' leaving no doubt that it was considered a type of sodomy (see figure 4).[20]

Thus, after finding sodomitic rape but not forced transvestism among the military activities of the Carib to the south, we have located the transvested berdache and at least symbolic rape to the north, among the Tumucua of Florida and their dead enemies. Continuing the search for such information in central Mexico, we are rewarded with evidence if not of unarmed berdaches – unlike the Tumucua load-bearers, the famous Aztec *tamemes* left no evidence of their sexuality – then of berdaches as indubitable warriors. A so-called Chichimeca, so brave he was the last one captured by the Spaniards in 1530, made a great impression on the conquistador Nuño de Guzmán: 'Everyone was amazed to see such heart and force in a woman, since we thought he was [a woman] because of the clothes he wore.'[21] On finding out the native was a man, the Spaniards of course killed him.

The Aztec practice of sacrificing male war prisoners in their temples rather than killing them in the field is well known. Perhaps it is not surprising, therefore, that one searches in vain for evidence that the nations of central Mexico behaved in the insulting homosexual fashion we described among the Tumucua. True, the judicial punishment for passive homosexuality the Texcocans are said to have applied in the domestic sphere, to which we return later, turns out to be the same sodomitic penetration the Floridian Tumucua used on enemy corpses in the military realm – as if a method for punishing foreigners in war was imported to punish sodomitic domestic enemies – but the trail in the Valley of Mexico leads no further as concerns actual military behavior.

Evidence from much later sources that American tribesmen to the north raped or otherwise violated their prisoners is, of course, not

Figure 3 Penile evisceration of enemies by the soldiers of Outina.

Figure 4 Martirio del Bendito Pe. Fray Diego Ortiz en Vilcabamba,
engraving by Petrus de Jode after Erasmus Quellin.

wanting. The Winnebago are said to have done so, and the Osage especially should be mentioned.[22] But evidence is yet to be found that the ancient Mexicans in war, like their Caribbean counterparts, inflicted anal intercourse, or even castration or evisceration upon enemies.[23]

It would be unwise, however, to conclude from this that the Mexicans did not punish foreign enemies in homosexual fashion. Cecelia Klein has, after all, assembled powerful evidence showing that Aztec warmaking on the road to empire was conceived and mythologized, in effect, as a war of their god Huitzilopochtli against his sister Cihuacoatl: a war of the Toltec north against the south, authority against witchery, male against female principle.[24] Klein further shows that this historical experience of war was indeed preserved at the heart of imperial domestic ritual. The second of the two supreme male authorities in the Aztec Empire, called the Cihuacoatl, actually cross-dressed so as to represent Cihuacoatl as Huitzilopochtli's prisoner, to show, in short, the Mexican war god's male military dominance over its female 'people.'[25] The image of homosexual subordination in this conquest imagery could not have been absent, since obviously the warriors who had in fact been conquered by the Aztecs, if rhetorically womanized, had in fact been quite male.

Indeed, according to Seler, the Nahuatl word for a powerful warrior (tecuilónti) means 'I make someone into a passive.'[26] So the Cihuacoatl's domestic ritual reassertion of the enemy as female suggests that, at the behavioral level, the Aztecs also employed gender to make war. At the level of battlefield action, Aztec officers attempted to rally their troops by calling them sissies or effeminates, and inversely, during the famous Noche Triste, they cried 'Cuilon!', the Nahuatl word for a passive, at the Spanish soldiers fleeing Tenochtitlan. Then, turning back to self-recrimination, the Mexican overlords heaped intimations of homosexual softness upon their soldiers after they had lost a battle.[27]

This gendered humiliation of one's own soldiers among native peoples is in turn encountered in the far-off Andes. Here too, as in Florida, there is evidence that the soldiers of the Incas entered battle with boys who had never known women in their train, to then themselves be ridiculed as women if they lost.[28] On the eve of the Spanish Conquest, the Inca Huascar, angered at the chiefs who had lost a crucial battle to his competitor Atahualpa, sent them certain women's clothes and 'ordered them to immediately put them on and enter Cuzco dressed in that way.'[29] From this sixteenth-century source it is clear not just that Andean war was gendered, but that the military entry, whether triumphant or humiliating, was a crucial locus for ritually gendering one's comprehension of spatial organization.

In his dated yet unsuperseded study of the treatment of prisoners of war, Friederici took note of an important behavioral structure triggered in the immediate aftermath of battle among native peoples. As far as I know, it remains unstudied. Here it is not a question of male soldiers triumphantly shaming the women of the vanquished, like the Spaniards celebrating their victory over the Pueblos in 1598, or the troop of North American soldiers under Colonel Chivington who entered Denver triumphantly in 1864, with a woman's heart hoisted on a lance and wearing the genitalia of Indian women as hatbands.[30] Instead, the behavioral structure to which I refer involves the entry of women and children into the triumph, the social context or explanation usually being that these peculiar 'warriors,' the wives and children of warriors who had fallen or been wounded in battle, now took vengeance for their loss. First, there are descriptions of these dependents appearing on the field of battle and ritually humiliating prisoners and corpses; this practice is also well documented in Europe.[31] Soon thereafter, the American version of the triumphal entry – when warriors returned to their settlements – sometimes featured precisely the women and children heaping insults upon the losers, whether they were enemies or their own warriors.[32] Unfortunately, our best evidence comes from a later period, but that does not weaken the potential importance of this behavioral complex. Thus a triumphal entry of 1776 into a Pueblo village describes the scalp dance of certain Pueblo women. They touched their private parts to the scalps of the losers; they bared their buttocks to them. Then, playing as if the skeletons of the vanquished belonged to their second or third husband, they lay down on top of them in pretended intercourse. 'All of this was to take power away from the enemy,' one witness explains.[33]

If one is confident that such triumphs were practiced by earlier tribes as well, there is no reason to believe that they would have been formally identical with those of later American nations; one thinks again of the Aztecs, who seem to have fictionally flattered and not frontally humiliated at least those entering prisoners who would later be sacrificed. But the point I am making is that, in the triumphal entry, gender probably always played a role in remodeling and reconceptualizing the civil, military, and even the diplomatic order and space that emerged from the war. In the cases above, we see women and other dependents in such cases effectively effeminizing the enemy. The very dependents of the winners were seen to be more masculine than the humiliated enemy males.[34]

Now, however, the battle is behind us. A winner and loser exist, and history, having been made, must now be recorded. The demands of memory step to the forefront, and the winner soon realizes that, while calling or representing the enemy as women or effeminates might be effective during war and the ensuing triumph, there was a price to be paid if one continued to brand one's enemy a loser after peace was made. For, on reflection, what is the triumph in having defeated 'women'? And, even more important, how is one to retain the loyalty of the losers if they are not made to feel that they too had been winners of a kind?

The process of bridging this gap between the tactics of war and a strategy for imperial peace varied with different nations, but gendering was present in most attempts. We see it in the realm of mythology. In the Zuni story of Cha'kwena, the conquering Kia'nakwe people prepare a thanksgiving dance in which the imprisoned enemy gods were supposed to take part in celebrating their own capture. But being macho, the god Kolhamana refused, until, that is, the Cha'kwena forced him to dress up as a woman and dance, saying: 'You will now perhaps be less angry.' According to the Zuni, this instant of time in which the genders of outside losers and inside winners were reconfigured was the first time in history that a man had dressed as a woman.[35] In this myth, the loser in becoming woman entered the society of the winner.

The practice of changing gender as one moves from war to peace was obviously effected by the Spaniards as well. In a chapter of his *Crónica Indiana* entitled 'The valor of the Americans was not inferior; rather, their type of warfare was not equal,' Juan Ginés de Sepúlveda incorporated gender into his reflections on the Spanish conquests:

> In that battle, our men came to realize that these were not men with a feminine spirit, but rather a strong people, capable of despising death . . .[36]

And thus, in this European solution to the problem, the enemy nations 'became male' so that the virtues of the victors might be vaunted. Needless to say, the Spaniards as victors wanted to believe that, in turn, the most fearsome of their enemies regarded them, and not their usual enemies among the native tribes, as true men. Fray Benavides in describing his encounter with certain Apaches in 1630 states the matter with disarming naiveté:

> This entire nation is so warlike that it has proved to be the crucible of Spanish valor, and for this reason they have high regard for the Spaniards. They say that only the Spaniards, and not the nations of settled Indians, deserve the title of men (*gente*).[37]

In this reading, the Apaches flattered themselves that, as nomads, they were masculine, while sedentary peoples were feminine. But for the Spaniards' ears more gratifying and important, the Apaches regarded the peninsular conquerors, also sedentary, as macho. Thus the Apache, who had been effeminized by defeat, became macho again as brothers in warrior skills. Certainly from the point of view of many victims, the humiliation endured, as one can see in the spatial organization of native pictures such as those in the work of Guaman Poma de Ayala (see figure 5). However, from the peninsular angle, it was possible in an empire for subordinates to regain and be macho.

Thus through the haze and cries of war and triumph, a gendered image of peoples and of the spaces they inhabit emerges. This military organization of what becomes a peaceful diplomatic order was brought by the Iberians to the Americas and applied to their new enemies. Yet, as we have seen, such gendering sophistication was quite at home among the natives, being rooted in the very mythology of at least one American people, the Zuni. Now pushing our inquiry still further along in time, we encounter gender at work in the ongoing historical representations native peoples made of their past military victories. The phenomenon of taking hostages as tribute is one such representation. Locals told the historian Torquemada that, on conquering the area of Guatemala, the ancient Olmecs had not only seized its women, but also required each village to give up at any time, on demand, two boys (*niños*), perhaps for sexual purposes.[38] Further, one finds in middle America victors marking space in enduring gendered terms, for example at the Chontal Maya village of Cuylonemiquia, which means 'where we killed the [Mexican] queers.'[39] But perhaps most interesting of all is the evidence, slim but significant none the less, that in middle America military victors were known to 'put underskirts on' losers.[40]

True, the most striking evidence of indigenous nations and their spaces being gendered in the wake of warfare comes much later and at a distance, but it demands our attention because the practice in question graphically presents an institutionalization of the gendering impulses we have located in earlier history to the south. I refer to the practice in the eastern part of the present-day United States, before

Figure 5 An Andean, tied to a *picota*, is beaten by a Spaniard and a black slave.

all among the Iroquois Confederacy, of conceiving of and executing war as a battle, and peace as a pact, between men and women. At the outset, let it be said that, like most aboriginal nations, the tribes of the Iroquois Confederacy probably possessed berdaches.[41] Now, during the late seventeenth and eighteenth centuries, the Mahican nation, originally from present-day Connecticut, the Nanticokes, whose origins lay in the Delmarva peninsula, and the Tutelos, who came from present-day Virginia, came to be called 'women' by the Iroquois once the latter let them settle in their lands along the Susquehanna River in present-day Pennsylvania. They were *not* considered members of the Confederacy, but that is not to say that those tribes that were members were all 'men.' The Iroquois in fact designated the Tuscaroras, originally from today's North Carolina, as 'women' despite the fact that in 1713, they became the 'Sixth Nation' of the Confederacy itself upon settling in today's New York State.[42]

This usage certainly originated in war, not peace. In 1744, for example, when the European colonists tried to get the Iroquois and the Catawbas to make peace, the Confederacy responded that the latter had refused: 'The Catawbas refused to come, and sent us word that we were but women, that they were men and double men, for they had two p[enise]s; that they would make women of us, and would always be at war with us.'[43] Thus, if this Iroquois source is to be trusted, the systematic if not in this case demonstrably institutionalized gendering of belligerencies was not limited to the northeast of today's United States, but was to be encountered among the Catawbas, from what is today South Carolina. As is evident in their statement, in their conception waging war involved at least symbolically castrating the loser, so that from then on the loser would look like a woman while the winner would sport a double penis. In this tradition, tribes were conceived as two sexes in a state of war.

The origin in warfare of what became a gendered diplomatic institution is certainly best observed, however, in the relations of the Iroquois Confederation with the Delaware (Lenape) tribe. The story begins in the late seventeenth or early eighteenth century, by the terms of a pact this vanquished tribe entered into with the victorious Iroquois, 'when you first conquered us and made woman of us,' in the words of the Delaware (the very phrase would seem to indicate sexual conquest).[44] The first document referring to the institution is in a Delaware tribute payment of 1712. It was presented to the Iroquois, apparently by 24 actual women and six boys, because, our source says, 'the Indians reckon[ed] the paying of tribute becomes none but women and children.'[45] We again encounter a gendering of the fundamental military–diplomatic institution of tribute.

But was actual behavior, or only metaphor, at work in this institution? Once the rich documentation of mid-century is on the table, it becomes clear that indeed more was involved in the Delaware–Iroquois institution than words, such as those of the Mohawks: 'We the Mohawks are men,' they proclaimed. 'We are made so from above. But the Delawares are women and under our protection, and of too low a kind to be men . . .'[46] In 1744, the Iroquois asserted that the Delaware, who lived within the boundaries of the Mohawks, were 'women' who could not sell land or make war. That is, the actual disabilities of dependents – they were also labelled children – infringed on their sovereignty. Clearly, like the other tribes mentioned above, the conquered Delaware were not referred to as women in part because they lived within Iroquois lands.[47] Thus, as among the tribes of middle America, nations at war were at times construed to be of the opposite sex, but that was then carried over to tribes at peace, that is, to the diplomatic order. They became institutionally genderized, a phenomenon that in all the ramifications we shall sketch remains to be documented in middle America.

In the mid-1750s, the Delaware, in part because some of their numbers had migrated outside Confederacy lands to present-day Ohio, made the move to recover their manhood, and in the process revealed that this gendered institution involved factual transvestism, for in certain diplomatic contexts their men dressed as women and sported conventional signs of womanhood. In these mid-century documents, it now appears that, when the Delaware had first accepted their subordination to the Iroquois, as well as in later ceremonial reaffirmations of that original act of servitude, the Iroquois, clearly orating a vocal accompaniment to a solemn ceremonial transvestition, proclaimed:

> We dress you in a woman's long habit reaching down to your feet and adorn you with earrings . . . We hang a calabash filled with oil and medicine on your arms . . . We deliver unto your hands a plant of Indian corn and a hoe.[48]

This gendered subordination began to erode during a political crisis of the mid-century. In 1754, the Delaware first complained to the Confederation that they were not being protected from the 'French, your fathers,' and so they begged the Iroquois 'to take off our petticoat that we may fight for ourselves, our wives and children.'⁴⁹ After they came to an arrangement with the French in the following year, the Delaware responded to an Iroquois solicitation to cease this collaboration with the enemy by affirming that 'we are men and are determined not to be ruled any longer by you as women.' The Delaware sachem Teedyuscung proclaimed to the Seneca that he had thrown away the petticoat and put on 'my proper dress; the corn hoe and pounder I have exchanged for these firearms and I declare that I am a man.'⁵⁰ In thoroughly sexual terms, the Delaware proclaimed that they would finish off the established colonial rulers: they would castrate any Englishman who did not escape by ship, and do the same to the Iroquois if they did not let up on them. Beware, they said, 'lest we cut off your private parts and make women of you as you have done to us.'⁵¹

By 1756, at the beginning of the French–Indian War, the Iroquois were ready to compromise, and wrote to the Delaware that, if they would remain women, the Iroquois would train them to be men!

> Cousins, the Delaware Indians: You will remember that you are our women; our forefathers made you so, and put a petticoat on you and charged you to be true to us and lie with no other man. But of late you have suffered the string that tied your petticoat to be cut loose by the French and you lay with them and so became a common bawd, in which you did wrong and deserve chastisement. But notwithstanding this, we will still esteem you, and as you have thrown off the cover of your modesty and become stark naked, which is a shame for a woman, we now give you a little prick and put it into your private parts, and so let it grow there till you shall be a compleat man. We advise you to act as a woman yet, but be first instructed by us, and do as we bid you, and you will become a noted man.⁵²

But the solicitations of the Iroquois were unsuccessful, for soon after, in council, the Delaware Teedyuscung referred to his 'woman-hood' as a thing past:

> Now you may remember I was stiled by my uncles the Six Nations as a woman in former years and had no hatchet in my hand, but a pestle or hominy pounder.⁵³

There can be little doubt that the sachem was imaging, recalling to the mind's eye, a reality he had indeed experienced, a time when he had not been allowed into council precisely because he carried a pestle and hominy pounder in his hands on such ceremonial occasions.

The evidence for such a gendered institution apparently ends with the French–Indian War. And yet the stunning image of a 'woman' fitted out with a tiny penis so as to grow slowly into a notable, 'compleat man,' calls us back to the reality that these Delaware were actually biological males who were labelled 'women' because they lacked the sovereign force of other men. Indeed, to be the Confederacy's woman meant, as the Iroquois made clear in that above quote, to be loyal, and not to 'sleep with other men.' The Delaware were, as the sources proclaim repeatedly, 'effeminates,' even 'half-men,' because of their war-induced dependency.[54]

Henceforth, when the Iroquois 'man' and his dependent 'women' met, that is, on diplomatic occasions, both had to manifest their gender through the differential use of hatchets (males), earrings, pestles, pounders (females), and the like. Anthony Wallace indeed asserts that such an 'even context' evokes diplomatic activity in a simple, original form:

Technically, being 'women' [originally] meant only that they were expected to entertain official emissaries from the Great Council with food and lodging, a 'feminine' obligation in a society where women were responsible for the cultivation of maize, the preparation of food, and the maintenance of the household economy.[55]

With this insight – that these men become 'women' were fundamentally agents charged with hospitality in a diplomatic context – we return to Central America, whence we departed in an effort to show that the concept of the enemy as female did in other venues, if less demonstrably in middle America, end in an institutionalization of such gender paradigms.[56] Recall the figure of Cihuacoatl, that member of the ruling Aztec diarchy who, according to Klein, in dressing as a woman, referred in some way to the 'womanly' character of those people whom the Aztecs had absorbed into their empire. Those people were not, as far as is presently known, gendered female as a function of their dependent status within the empire, nor, as far as is perceived, did such props of the empire assume in diplomatic ceremonies the dress and accoutrements of women, as did the 'props of the [Iroquois] Confederacy.'[57]

At this stage of research, it is enough to have argued that it was in war that we first document these gender procedures – we recall the Inca Huascar forcing his losing general to dress as a woman for his shameful re-entry into Cuzco. And it must be just as sufficient to document that the Aztecs, who knew all about denouncing enemies as queers and women in military affairs, were also quite as well informed about gender in the formulation of diplomacy. According to two sources, certain fourteenth-century ambassadors sent by lord Itzcoatl of Tenochtitlan to the Tepaneca lord of Coyohuacan were forced by the latter, who sought war with Tenochtitlan, to don women's clothes and return to the Aztec court thus 'shamefully' attired; thereupon the inevitable war of revenge ensued.[58]

In earlier chapters, we saw that circumcision, castration, and sodomization have been conquest behaviors in many cultures aimed at leaving losers 'effeminate and subject.'[59] Now we have reviewed the American record to gain similar insights from the inception of war, through the triumphal return of warriors both losers and winners, finally to the evidence of diplomatic and imperial designing by gender resulting from such wars. There was evidence of such sexual practices in American wars, to be sure.[60] Yet, just as important, substantial evidence for dressing 'losers' as women has surfaced, both one's own non-belligerents and the enemy vanquished. These insults, rooted in the violence of war, came to inform diplomatic parlance as well, and among the distant Iroquois, at least, were a rhetorical basis for the organization of empire. In all these areas, the genderization of conflict and its resolution was always near the surface.

Thus while most theorists of the state move institutions from the intra- to the extramural, the opposite dynamic is worth contemplating. Military and diplomatic practices offered a model for creating domestic social orders, as at the beginning of this chapter our original authority, Michele di Cuneo, well opined. Not without a certain veracity, the Zuni myth, we recall, insisted that the first time in history that a man had dressed as a woman was when their god first forced cross-dressing and then dancing precisely on the victim of war. The roots of, the inspiration for, the American berdache are to be sought in the cauldron of warrior violence.

Yet the Zuni myth leaves little doubt that, as with the Delaware and other tribes, what lies beneath such stories is the primary social problem of gendering the outsider and insider, whether winner or loser, so as to integrate violent military history into future social realities. Thomas Zuidema has brought the results of such labors to the surface in an especially clear manner. In his survey of Andean languages, he isolated certain terms of kinship that are expressed as passive and active homosexual relations. In the Aymara tongue of Lake Titicaca, for instance, the word *ipa*, meaning 'father's sister,' also connotes 'the man who in a homosexual relationship is in the female position.'[61] The logic of such linkages is, in fact, that as a general rule a younger brother is a 'sister' to his older brother.[62] In Zuidema's view, the strong homosexual overtones employed by the Andean languages in describing relations between males of different ages can, then, be faultlessly transferred to a general master–servant language of artificial kinships. One hears these tones the more emphatically when in the background those sacerdotal berdaches sing falsetto who sexually service Andean lords.

Much in keeping with the general tenor of this work, therefore, Zuidema views gendering as constitutive of political hierarchization. But is he right in considering such linkages of homosexual pairs of rulers–servants, older–younger brothers and the like as endogamic, that is, built up from within domestic society? Further: is he correct in stressing that this system is 'symbolic,' presumably meaning that no actual homosexual activity was implied?

In the light of what has been presented above, that may be doubted. Whatever the consciousness of the user of the language at any moment in time, such words and phrases reach back to ancient force. Perhaps a definite link exists in fact between the Delaware, whom the foreign Iroquois 'made women,' and the Central and South American nations, who domestically called their younger brothers and sons-in-law passives. For high was male and low female. I shall argue that the homosexual activity described in our sources was commonly violent and abusive: already in the military field it converted prisoners into 'women' and retinue so as to construct states or statuses. 'Older brother' and 'younger brother' were political quanta, as one Maya Book of Chilam Balam shows so well. First the Itzá subordinated the Maya; the conquerors, the writer says, became older brother. Then the Spaniards came and conquered, and the writer repeats the same message: in submitting, 'showing their rear ends,' the Yucatec became younger brother to the penetrator.[63]

4

The Domestic Berdache: Becoming

Thrice weighed down is their strength, the younger brothers native to the land.[1]

Saw, astonished, necklaces bedeck Hercules' sturdy, sky-supporting neck . . .[2]

After Alvarez Chanca's mere hint of a military berdache in his letter of 1494, the American domestic berdache appears clearly for the first time in the accounts of Balboa's discovery of the Pacific in 1513. In the third decade of his *De orbe novo*, published in 1516, the Italian Peter Martyr d'Anghiera tells how, in his trek across Panama, Balboa found the brother of the cacique of Quaraca and some of his men dressed as women and practicing sodomy (*nefanda . . . Venere*). The conquistador quickly threw some forty of these transvestites (though apparently not their active partners!) to the dogs, the first record of Spanish punishment of sodomy on the American continent (see figure 6). According to Peter Martyr, it all happened to the applause of the native subjects, 'for the contagion was confined to the courtiers and had not yet spread to the people.' Sounding like the post-Justinian Christian he was, Peter has the people blaming their lords' sodomy for the famine and sickness, lightning, thunder and inundations they had suffered.[3] With this record, the berdache as a domestic institution entered the Hispanic-American historical record.

Iberians entering native American villages and cities in the early sixteenth century certainly acted shocked by much of what they saw, not least the sight of men dressed as women. Some of them had doubtless seen it before, either through their experiences in Granada or North Africa, or, at least in festivals, certainly in Christian parts of Iberia and elsewhere in Europe. For a man to dress as a woman was certainly a sin and actionable. However, it still did not give the Iberians the right

Figure 6 Balboa's mastiffs attack the Panamanians.

to conquer the natives; in the contemporary legal view, transvestism was not a 'just title of conquest.' Sodomy or male homosexual behavior, however, did bestow a right to conquer, if it could be demonstrated that it was widespread and tolerated by the indigenous civil authority. And, coterminously, the missionaries proclaimed to the Aztecs, the Maya and the Incas that sodomy was their downfall: the wrathful Christian god had decided to send the Iberians to conquer the Americans because they had engaged in homosexual behavior.[4]

The question of a linkage between transvestism and sodomy must be borne in mind to understand one of the crucial debates of the early colonial period, between the royal historian Gonzalo Fernández de Oviedo and the famed 'defender of the Indians,' Bartolomé de Las Casas. Neither denied that cross-dressing and some other cross-gender behaviors were widespread everywhere they went, but the two men diverged on the crucial political question of sodomy: Oviedo tended to find it everywhere, while Las Casas argued that it was minimal.

From the close reading to be made of these sources in the following chapter, it will become evident that Oviedo assumed that transvestites who behaved like women were passive sodomites, while Las Casas denied that these transvestites were engaging in homosexual relations. As we shall see, evidence from elsewhere in the Americas at a later time makes one suspect that these two men were actually describing berdaches of different ages – Oviedo ones of an earlier age associated with extensive sexual acitivity, Las Casas ones of a more advanced age linked to a decline in sexual activity. For patently political reasons, Oviedo and Las Casas were talking past each other, comparing berdaches who were apples and oranges.

Yet, in the meantime, the agreement of the two antagonists on the ubiquity of cross-dressing and -acting dictates our own approach to understanding pre-Columbian same-sex sexuality in what is today called Latin America. Because the berdache was often the representation *par excellence* that native males made of their females, we must begin by understanding the origins of the berdache in the Amerindians' own life experiences. A close study of that question will yield no small payoff: the institution of the berdache in the Americas overlaps the institutions of the natives' life cycle.

The Child

The debate over the nature of the Amerindian berdache has suffered from two ideological tenets; by beginning with the infant and moving on to berdaches of greater age, I will indeed tolerate these tenets, if only temporarily. The first is that of dependence: by constantly emphasizing the dependent status of these berdaches, as they did that of their own peninsular passives (who usually did not cross-dress), the Iberians perforce usually draw our attention to the young berdache, youth being the indisputable age of dependence. Much of the mystery about the berdache, however, rests with the elder ones. A second, more modern ideological tenet can prove no less misleading: convinced that there has always been a timeless essence to 'homosexuality,' many scholars have dwelled on the moments males 'freely' became and become involved in homosexual relations, and for them that often means adolescence. And yet, despite these problems of ideology, we shall tolerate them in the short run, and begin at birth, to find out soon enough that the berdache in 1500 did not originate as many have imagined.

In the mid-sixteenth century, an Aztec elder described for the Franciscan missionary-ethnographer Bernardino de Sahagún a decisive moment in the life of a young male. Nothing less was involved at this moment than what the parent 'should make of him,' the emphasis being upon the artisanal role of the parent. One possibility ran as follows: 'Is he perchance a woman? Shall I place, perchance, a spindle, a batten, in his hand?'[5] Sahagún's passage makes excellent evidence for those who view 'homosexuality' as innate, for it can be construed to mean that parents began to gender their sons as female only if and when the children themselves revealed 'feminine' mannerisms. And there is, of course, no reason to doubt that the so-called sissy syndrome, in which a limited number of young male children manifest and then tenaciously hold to culturally defined female behaviors, was found in earlier American societies as it is found in modern ones.[6]

In the historical record, alas, such boys are rarely met with, and to entertain the notion that parents usually waited to observe gendered behavior in their offspring amounts to a distortion of the evidence we do possess. In fact, there is substantial proof that parental gendering of males as female, and occasionally vice versa, began soon after birth, when not indeed before, and thus had nothing to do with the personality or behavior of the offspring. To the dismay of those who believe in 'homosexuality's' innateness, which often, if confusingly, amounts to a claim that native American children were 'free' to choose their sexuality, the evidence overwhelmingly supports the view that collectivities, with the parents in the lead, gendered children because of social and cultural imperatives.

The mid-seventeenth century report by Fernández de Piedrahita on the Laches of Colombia provides the model and is the most incisive document for such parental shaping of infantile gender. According to this writer, once a mother without daughters had given birth to five consecutive males, tribal law allowed one of them, on reaching one year of age, to be made a berdache, that is, to be transvested and made to act as a woman. The explanation for this action is banal yet incisive. According to the author, lazy Laches males wanted to be waited upon (*ambición que tienen de estar bien servidos*), and that was better done by females. The text does not specify if sexual service was also foreseen; rather, the emphasis is simply upon servility or dependence. But even if they were not fated in later years to be sexually 'used' by their fathers, such *cusmos*, as the Laches called their berdaches, could expect passive sexual usage by other tribal males. As Piedrahita explained, these people soon 'exercised the offices of women with the robustness of men,' and, for men looking for wives, the *cusmos* were considered better catches than were females.[7] Thus even in the small-scale social context of the Lache family, not so much internal family considerations as the prestige and wealth of the father among his tribal fellows seem to have been involved. While the future berdache was still an infant, parents were already looking down the road to her exchange value as a young adult.

In the later Kaska culture far to the north, one encounters the identical phenomenon of parents distributing gender among their infant children, with the difference being that a boy, not a girl, was engendered. A family having all female children but wanting a son to hunt for them would select a daughter to be 'like a man'; when the girl was five years old, her parents tied bear ovaries to her belt to prevent her conceiving her life long.[8] Certainly the so-called female berdache is still rarely enough encountered in the literature, and in the same culture area we find Kodiak mothers choosing their handsomest boy to raise as a girl.[9] But the Kaska case does show that a principle was at work, namely that parents in certain tribes routinely forced a particular gender upon their infant children quite apart from any quality of the child. Indeed, Westermarck found that, in the Chukchi nation of Alaska, a husband might be a biological female, a wife a biological male.[10]

The force of society was never far to seek. Returning to our time and culture area, we can find if we seek other explanations of the making of a berdache, for example, Las Casas' suggestion that natives thought the gods were pleased if young boys were prettified

as girls before they were sacrificed.[11] But the evidence of social and
political constraint in the creation of berdaches abounds. In 1541 we
find Hernando de Alarcón transcribing an experience he had had the
year before among the tribe of the lower Colorado while searching
for the cities of Cibola. A chief showed Alarcón his son: he was
dressed like a woman and 'exercising his office.' Alarcón asked the
father how many men of this kind there were among them:

> He replied that there were four of them, and when one died, a search was
> made for all the pregnant women in the land, and the first male born was
> chosen to exercise the function of women. The women dressed them in
> their clothes, saying that if they were to act as such they should wear their
> clothes. These men could not have carnal relations with women at all, but
> they themselves could be used by all marriageable youths of the land. They
> received no compensation for this work of prostitution from the people in
> the region, although they were free to take from any house what they
> needed for their living.[12]

What is so evident in this and other accounts is that, at least
according to the Spaniards, parents committed their young, or even
unborn, male children to an effeminate or 'female' way of life years
before their envisaged entrance into the tribal exchange system.[13]
Latin American sources do not allow us to follow these steps with
full clarity, and we are constrained to cite later sources to evoke
perhaps some idea of this progression. Thus in her study of the Zuni
llamana or berdache at the beginning of the twentieth century,
Parsons confirms the resilience of the ancient practice of 'making
girls,' noting that, 'if a household was short on women workers a
boy would be more readily allowed to become a *la'mana*,' without
any compulsion, her sources predictably assured her. Parsons then
carefully notes that the youngest of that tribe's four berdaches was
only six years old. As such, he was still dressed as a male, but his
shirt had a longer cut and was not tucked into his trousers – signs of
his impending femininity. Among the Zuni at this date, the age when
the berdache definitively assumed all-female dress was about 12
years.[14]

If we stick strictly with the evidence from middle America, we
cannot proffer more evidence that refers discretely to the assumption
of female clothes at a young age. However, three primary sources
from these early years do want us to believe that, even as children,
native Americans were introduced to homosexual behavior, presumably anal penetration but perhaps fellation as well, and usually in

conjunction with their assumption of female clothing. First, we have the word of the earliest mainland missionary, the Franciscan lay brother Peter of Ghent, who lived in the valley of Mexico from 1523 on and has preserved an unrivalled reputation for reliability based on his intimate knowledge of Mexican institutions. On June 27, 1529, he wrote his Flemish co-religionists about Aztec ecclesiastics as follows:

> Some of these priests do not have wives. Instead of them, [they have] *muchachos*, whom they abuse. This sin is so common in these regions that not just the young but the old commit it. And children six years old find themselves infested with it. But now they have begun to follow the natural order, thanks be to God. Already converted to Christianity, they ask to be baptised with great anxiety, and they confess their sins.[15]

The assumption that Peter was indeed referring to homosexual intercourse, rather than using the term 'sodomy' more loosely, is confirmed by the report of Nuño de Guzmán filed in 1530 describing the heroic warrior berdache mentioned earlier. On being asked why he dressed as a woman, this captive 'Chichimeca' said that he had been a passive berdache from the time he was *chequito*, and that he had long earned his living that way, that is, by dressing as a woman.[16] It was much the same with two Andean berdaches taken prisoner by the Spaniards, who let it be known that they had been dressed that way *and* had been forced to assume the passive position 'from the time they were boys.'[17] Again, the sources suggest that the full assumption of female clothing and the first reception of a penis were more or less simultaneous.

Puberty

In the teeth of Peter of Ghent's assertion, but congruent with Parsons' later information on the Zuni, I am inclined to believe, mostly for physical reasons, that anal reception, if not necessarily fellative passivity, usually began at about 12 years of age or shortly before.[18] However, in the later nineteenth century, Holder found that, among the Crow, the berdaches (*bote*), who were mostly fellators in this tribe, transvested at an early age, but only became sexually involved at puberty.[19] Just as important, I also think that, while it is probable that middle Americans who had begun earlier finished their transition to women's clothes when they were about 12, as did the later Zunis, it is probable that a new wave of youngsters first assumed female dress and homosexual passivity at this age. To use the language of the sources, some boys 'married' for the first time at about this time.

The European ethnographic record gives some impetus for us to hold to this latter age. In a pathfinding article on what he called 'pseudo-homosexuality' in ancient Greece, George Devereux made a sharp distinction between those young boys who at two and three years of age began to act and then dress like females (so-called sissies) and those who became passives only at puberty. The first were engaged in 'genuine perversion,' to use Devereux's freighted and frightening words, and remained so their lives long, while the second were 'pseudo-homosexuals,' who after some years usually 'slid' from passivity to activity in their late teens, to become exclusively heterosexual in their twenties.[20] This categorization does concur with the ancient, but also with some medieval European, evidence as well. For example, only at age 12 do substantial numbers of passives begin to appear in fifteenth-century Florentine judicial records.[21]

This book will prove that there was one decisive difference between European passive homosexual behavior and that of the Americas, and it needs to be stated clearly at this point. Those who look about in European records will have no difficulty finding men dressed as women, as we have seen, and probably some significant number of them were involved in passive homosexuality. There is, however, no significant evidence either in Greece, in Rome, in Florence, or in any other medieval European city that the typical adolescent passive transvested, and the relative absence of such cross-dressing has to have had a major impact on homosexual dynamics in Europe. In America, the link between homosexual behavior and cross-dressing is much more apparent. None the less, in the following pages I will show that, in America as in Europe and Islam, for sundry reasons, it was at about age 12, and linked to transvestism, that young boys through their sexuality became potent factors in native exchange systems. The onset of puberty was a significant passage in young boys' sexual history.

By referring to the relative absence of transvestism as a factor in the onset of homosexual behavior in Europe, I do not mean to imply that all American passives who engaged in homosexual behavior did transvest. Perhaps as few as three-fifths of the times that our sources allege sodomy do they make specific mention of transvestism, although it makes sense that sodomy was mentioned more often because it was the deadlier Christian sin. Still, the inverse linkage, that is, from cross-dressing to *passive* homosexual behavior, is a striking and almost uniform feature of our sources. Oviedo, for instance, the influential early historian of the Indies, explained that, once a boy engaged in sodomy, his masters had him dressed as a woman; the 'sin' was in essence the origin and cause of cross-dressing. Oviedo assumed, therefore, that any transvested male, that is, anyone who wore the *nagua* or woman's skirt, was a practicing homosexual receptor.[22]

Clearly the task at hand is to determine, in the absence of hard chronological data, the approximate age to which known vestimentary and homosexual practices can be assigned. Oviedo is not alone in describing situations where passive homosexuality came first, the native authorities then either punishing the malefactors by dressing them as girls or stating that such ought to be their punishment.[23] This quite Christian approach, which appears to emphasize individual decision-making and responsibility, is also found in the no less frequent view that entrepreneurial boys first assumed the dress of a woman so that they could then make a living by attracting active homosexual clients. The earliest person of this type we know of is the heroic 'Chichimeca' the Spaniards captured and executed in 1530: on being asked by the peninsulars 'why he wore a woman's clothes ... [he] confessed that he had done so from childhood and earned his living off of men in the office [of women].'[24] Several observers believed that in such an assertedly free choice of women's clothes lay the origins of male prostitution. Thus the conquistador Bernal Díaz del Castillo claimed that the coastal natives of the torrid zones were mostly sodomites who 'went about dressed in women's clothes so as to profit from that diabolical and abominable office,'[25] while, far to the south, the viceroy Toledo around 1570 described the rumor that those living around Lake Titicaca 'dress like women and use cosmetics in order to execute this sin' of sodomy.[26] I would suggest that 12 years is approximately the age at which such young entrepreneurs might have set out.

However, the human, but here specifically Christian, tendency to make the weak responsible for the 'sins' of the strong provides ample warning about accepting such dynamics at face value. Thus it is easy to imagine the actives being the ones to dress their partners as women before indulging themselves, even if this practice is not mentioned in the sources. Just as important, the sources, beginning with Oviedo, do provide evidence of another reality at odds with seeming. It might appear that boys who had already engaged in homosexual behavior were at times then punished by having to wear female dress, but the more characteristic reality was that their lords first raped these boys, and then 'punished' them, at least in Christian eyes, by dressing them as women. Oviedo's already mentioned assertion – that a master dressed a boy as a woman after the boy had been penetrated – is complete only when we know that it was the master who penetrated him.[27] This eye-witness 1526 description of the berdache is indeed the earliest actually to get past merely noting the institution's existence, and deserves extensive citation. We shall return to it often:

> The Indians who are lords and chieftains and who sin [against nature] keep young men [*tienen mozos*] publicly with whom they consort in this infamous sin. And once they fall into this guilt [of sodomy], these passive *mozos* then put on skirts like women . . ., and the other things that women wear. And they do not bear arms, nor do they do anything that men do. Rather, they involve themselves in common household services, like sweeping and mopping and other customary tasks of women. Such people are hated by women in the extreme, but since they are so subject to their husbands, [women] only rarely dare mention it to the Christians. In the language of Cueva, these passives are called *camayoa*. So when among them one Indian wants to insult another or vituperatively to deride him as effeminate and mean, he is called *camayoa*.[28]

In this passage, Oviedo does not, it is true, provide the most detailed description of the sodomitic dynamics between *Herr* und *Knecht*. There is help elsewhere. In the midst of an outraged description of sexual mores at the court of the Inca, in which women also allowed men to sodomize them, the late sixteenth-century friar Martín de Murúa asserts that the Cuzceñans appointed males to be women, then dressed them as such, and then fornicated with them; 'The one among them who got the job of being a woman or doing [a woman's] task in that bestial and excommunicated act was then put in women's dress, and was thereafter treated like one.'[29]

While Spanish claims that native lords practiced sodomy are not above suspicion, furthering as they did the peninsulars' right to conquer, the evidence to be presented in the course of this book makes this particular claim plausible. Nor was the problem limited to 'natural' rulers, like fathers and lords. Older boys, or brothers, merely as a function of their greater strength, often raped their juniors, including their younger brothers (and sisters). Fifteenth-century Italian boy confraternities had to be divided between older and younger groups because of this reality,[30] and so it is not surprising that in the Americas Las Casas was sensitive to the notion that older students might take advantage of younger ones in the native temple schools.[31] Then recall the linguistic link mentioned at the end of the last chapter between the older brother as active and the younger brother as passive in some Andean vocabularies. Finally, in the twentieth century, Devereux found such attacks of older on younger boys happening among the Mohave. Indeed, moderns are only now ready to recognize how widespread such violent incest is in today's post-industrial societies.[32]

There is no evidence from the conquest period, to be sure, that boys who were penetrated specifically by relatives also had to don female clothing; if the crime of child abuse remains little studied even in our own age, one can imagine how successfully ignored it has been in history. At this point, it is important to appreciate only that Oviedo, and Las Casas, understood from the beginning that it was a mark of status in the Tierra Firme and Islands for adults and up-and-coming young men to control young boys. Power consisted in part in being accompanied in public by coteries of (strong) boys dressed as girls.

Peter Martyr tells how during the Spaniards' first days on the North American continent a cacique gifted the conquistador Grijalva with a 12-year-old boy, whom the Spaniard rejected.[33] Clearly, this is the age when boys became commodities, and we must now proceed to outline first the familial and then the political content of this exchange system. Our task is to understand that system as it was articulated by the Spaniards. In the following pages, a preponderance of the evidence will show that the constraints exercised upon young boys by adults surely provided the normal means by which these juveniles became 'women' in dress and sexuality.

A first piece of familial evidence for the exchange of youngsters has already been introduced, even if it appears to be suprafamilial in character. I refer to Alarcón's 1541 documentation that the Yuma tribe appointed an infant to fill the post of fourth tribal berdache. Presumably upon growing up, this boy became a sexual resource or passive, not for all males but precisely for the nubile boys in the tribe. Thus the tribal institution of the presumably adolescent male berdache fulfilled the needs of young men, just as in other tribes females filled that need. In ancient Guatemala, for instance, fathers who promised pre-pubescent daughters in marriage customarily furnished the grooms with female slaves to lie with until their wives reached sexual maturity.[34]

In such cases tribal fathers clearly sought to prevent their young men from raping other tribal females in the interval. In other words, we see fathers trying to control their male heirs even as they began the process of empowering them. The process is clearly evident in two passages of Las Casas describing homosexual behavior among the same Guatemalan Maya. At one time these people had been free of sodomy, says Las Casas, and they were still unaware that it was sinful. The 'error' was introduced not by another tribe, as in Michele di Cuneo's account of the Caribs, or by a social class, as in the Balboa story, but by a divinity. Dressed up as a native, this spirit, named Chan, showed the local men that, since male divinities had intercourse together, so could they.[35] Now local fathers, on seeing the divinities performing homosexual acts, followed that example in arranging their sons' lives:

> They gave . . . to those who were young men (mozos) a boy (niño) so they would treat him as a wife (mujer). And if someone else got to the boy, they commanded that he pay what, in [the law regarding women], a male had to pay for violating a woman other than his own. As corrupt as [the whole arrangement] was, anyone who forced a resisting boy was castigated with the [same] penalty levied on someone who forced a wife.[36]

The parental practice of assigning youth passive boys for their sexual enjoyment during the period before the consummation of a heterosexual marriage is documented in the ethnographic record of other societies.[37] That record makes clear, however, that much more than enjoyment might be involved. In certain parts of Australia, for instance, penurious youth who could not afford wives were given five to ten-year-old boys to marry (chookadoo), their material want thus triggering this homosexual arrangement. Further, that need was particularly great in polygynous societies, where the richest men hoarded large numbers of women.[38] Now, though Las Casas does not say so at this juncture, polygyny was indeed widespread and troublesome in American societies, so much so that missionaries appealed to male commoners or macehuales to help bury polygynous 'paganism' so that they could finally find wives.[39]

At this point in his exposition, Las Casas was merely trying to defend the natives against claims of sexual impropriety, at another juncture claiming that fathers even married their sons when they were very young so as to remove them from this 'most vile corruption' – referring obviously to the very homosexual liaison the fathers had themselves established for their sons before the latters' marriage.[40] Despite his attempt to rationalize the natives' behavior, however, the friar does reveal that, as with the Yuma far to the north, so here in Central America the provision of sexual solace was one among other essential purposes of the young, unmarried berdache. Now we too can be confident that the creation of *young* berdaches was necessitated by young men's need for passive sexual partners. Oviedo and Las Casas both agree on this point.

Las Casas's just-cited passage is particularly revealing for what it implies about the arrangement's exchange procedures. Needless to say, in a society such as the one he describes, in which the father procures an individual boy for what amounts to a temporary marriage with his son rather than that son having access to a berdache prostitute who served all nubile males, as in a brothel, a market for such boys or some mechanism for gifting them in exchange for patronal protection had to exist here, as it did in Europe.[41] But there is also the technical matter of the payment to the 'husband' by all those who used the son's male 'wife.' How could this fine not have functioned among these Maya as a payment, perhaps disguised but perhaps straightforward as well, for contractual services rendered? The young man earned an income of sorts by renting out his 'wife.' In this way, the same virile bachelor began to assemble a retinue of male subjects, attracted by his 'wife.' Such strategies were too well known to our European sources for us to fail to recognize their discourse about American natives.[42] In the midst of the 'family,' future political orders were being created. The complex described by Las Casas is, in turn, too close to the more recent ceremonial heterosexual intercourse practiced by hierarchical superiors of some northern Plains nations with the wives of inferior males, which also passed power up from underling to superior, as not to justify this emphasis upon social exchange.[43]

From a familial exchange process, it is but one big step up to the political process, where lords are found building the state, that is, transindividual status, through a similar merchandizing of male youth. Where did the chief get the handsome 12-year-old whom he tried to offer to the explorer Grijalva if not from his brothel? What can we imagine to have been the context within which Oviedo's 'lords' first raped and then dressed young boys as females, if not in a boys' harem? The sources suggest that several caciques in this area did indeed maintain what, for want of a better term, I call brothels. From them came not only the human gifts which rulers could bestow, but the retinues, which to this day remain one of the most tangible evidences of a lord's status. From them, as we shall see in the following chapter, finally came religion, the ultimate manifestation of rulers' solemn authority over their 'women.'

The evidence for this notion of state or status organization is not decisive, but persuasive. We begin with the existence of brothels.

From apparently independent reports, early sources claim that brothels of young passive males were to be found at Pánuco near present-day Tampico, in the village of Darién in Panama, and along the northern coast of South America.[44] All three sources say not only that local lords kept (tenian) such boys, but that they did so in order to profit from them either in the brothels, or when the boys went abroad dressed as women to attract men. In short, the Spaniards paint a picture of political rulers using boys to political-economic, as well as sexual ends. Díaz del Castillo also, who commented elsewhere on berdaches as sexual entrepreneurs, could not be more clear than he is in providing an institutional significance for such practices. In his pages, Cortés warns the Zempoalan caciques in 1519 not just to break their images, but:

> ... that also, they had to be pure of sodomy. Because they keep [tenian] muchachos in women's clothes who go about profiting in that infamous office.[45]

Such evidence is far from decisive, but, combined with the information from the temples to be presented in the following chapter, I hypothesize social complexes in which certain rulers pimped rather than merely being pimped for. Obviously, this was an arrangement that was not foreign to Renaissance Europe, as must have occurred to our sources.[46] Further, this arrangement between powerful men and berdaches has by no means remained foreign to more modern visitors to native American tribes. They have claimed that chiefs still use the berdaches for their pleasure and status, but, just as interesting, these anthropologists and physicians, authority figures from outside, repeatedly tell how berdaches have tried to become their servants.[47]

Here in the Americas at the time of the Conquests, I see the mechanism as follows: the domestic berdache was a projection of military actions, in which young vanquished were taken. Domestically, while enjoying the boys themselves and benefiting from the protection they afforded, some caciques made them available to others in exchange for some price or service, even as they certainly used other men's dependents as 'payment' for various services.[48] Owning large numbers of women was one way rulers built their property base, as Silverblatt has described for the Andean context.[49] But male passives were stronger than women. Controlling the physical strength of gangs of male adolescents was, and is, a basis for executive power.

Seniority

In almost all studies of the North American berdache, the emphasis has been on origins, for reasons already stated. That has made for an almost exclusive attention to the process by which children and adolescents first transvested. Researchers have been uniformly curious about the connection of the transvestism of the young with their sexual practices. This has been for good reason: not only did many early authorities, Oviedo in the lead, presume that, simply because s/he was dressed like a woman, a berdache was a practicing passive sexually. In our own research, we have found tribes at either end of middle America making young boys into berdaches to fulfill specific sexual functions for the family and the tribe. There can be little doubt that sexuality was a fundamental causal factor in the creation of very young, and adolescent, berdaches.

Yet, as the following pages will demonstrate, native American tribes produced still another, understated, informal rite of passage in which some males became berdaches. This third generation of male berdaches were seniors, adults who by their own or by their tribe's decision left their erstwhile warrior status behind and assumed the skirt. Coming to grips with what their body was telling them, they realized that they could no longer defend themselves as they had once been known to do, and so they drew the vestimentary consequences from this insight. They had become 'defenseless women,' and now showed it.

This overview, linking berdache and life cycle, was by no means clear to the present writer when I began my work. Indeed, comprehension that before the Iberians arrived a discrete group of native American men made themselves berdaches only later in life dawned on me only while reading reports on nineteenth- and early twentieth-century North American berdaches. Most crucially, the institution of the senior berdache was also not clear to Bartolomé de Las Casas, the primary source upon whom we shall rely in these pages. This missionary-ethnographer did not realize that, to some extent, he and Gonzalo Oviedo were talking about two different age groups, his opponent about the young, he about elders. Convinced against Oviedo that homosexual behavior was *not* practiced by most berdaches, Las Casas, defender of the Indians, was driven by insatiable curiosity and determined to imagine, imagine anew, and imagine once again the form and content of a non-sexual berdache. Given the location and state of the documentation, our procedure is clear. We shall first describe Las Casas's speculations, and then fill in some blanks with ethnographic evidence, mainly from the North American tribes.

Las Casas repeatedly denounced the Spaniards' reasoning. Referring to explorers in Central America who found three men dressed as women, he objected that, 'on that account alone, they decided that they were corrupted by that sin [of sodomy].'[50] In fact, he says in a section on Honduras, men who were not eunuchs dressed as women and then lived with them not for any 'dirty' reason, 'but rather for some other reasonable or at least not ignoble cause.'[51] But what was this 'other thing'? Las Casas was able to say that he did not know. Thus while he was ready to admit that natives could be found who did indeed dress up as women and assume 'women's duties' (*oficios*), he was not ready to admit that they practiced sodomy. 'I said "duties,"' he once insisted, 'not the nefandous vices.'[52]

It is at this point that Las Casas's imagination came into play. Fleetingly, he considered the evidence for quite young berdaches (*mozos*). Since they were so young, the author clearly implied, it would not do to explain their cross-dressing as being for sexual purposes, as some of his thoughtless countrymen had done. The boys were dressed this way, he decided, because they were to be sacrificed and, prettily dressed, such sacrifices would please the gods.[53]

But Las Casas's attention was drawn mainly to the older berdaches, as his other explanations for the phenomenon make clear. He was convinced that the berdaches were impotent, that is, that they could not copulate with women. He was not alone among his contemporaries in holding this opinion, and still in modern times there are stories, not sufficiently grounded, that even the new young berdache in certain tribes was endlessly masturbated until he became impotent.[54] Las Casas did not raise such a possibility, and so he sought to explain by other means how that had happened, as he claimed. Classicist that he was, he referenced Galen to the effect that endless horseback riding had in effect crushed the berdaches' testicles. Some ancient Scythians were 'like eunuchs, incapable of being married. Because of this they take on all the practices of women, in speech and in works. They call them *afeminados*.'[55] Las Casas preferred this explanation to one offered by Herodotus, to the effect that Venus made Scythian men hereditarily like women after they had sacked her temple at Ascalon.[56]

Yet neither of these stories could explain the American berdaches, who were horseless. Again referencing Galen (the actual source being Hippocrates), Las Casas pointed out that the Scythians had lost blood to their genitalia not only by horseback riding, but by bloodletting their ears. Bloodletting the ears 'and other parts,' Las Casas noted, was also done by the American berdaches, perhaps causing impotence.[57] The last link in Las Casas's rationalizing chain was the actual transvestition, whose sole purpose, in this scholar-activist's view, was in fact only to announce one's impotence to others. Unable to fornicate with the women, 'they put on female clothes to announce their defect.'[58] That is, unable to carry out a man's office, they now 'dedicate, offer, and occupy themselves with the offices that women carry out.'[59]

Though unsure what to make of this social category of berdaches, Las Casas was obviously describing a class of men who became berdaches in their adult or advanced years, and not as children or adolescents. As Las Casas himself realized, however, the historical record was not devoid of other nations with transvestites, and, besides the Scythians, he described at length those Romans who worshipped the earth mother, with whom we have earlier become acquainted as *cinaedos*.[60] Let us also turn now to other ethnographic information to get a better sense of the motivation for this dramatic change in life style of the senior berdache. We might mention first the Nogia Tatars, that is, a people in the same general area inhabited by the ancient Scythians. According to their early ethnographer Reineggs, when such a Tatar man becomes old, sick and sterile, he takes on the appearance of a woman and, in this condition, begins to avoid the company of men and to live with the women and dress like them; 'anyone seeing him would take him for an old and ugly woman.' Bottom line: the absence of effective sexuality is what drives such men to live with and as women.[61] Other cases in the literature of specifically older or at least childless men turning effeminate might be added, such as the *manang bali* among the Sea Dyak of Borneo, who come to dress as women and assume their division of labor.[62]

But it is more interesting and perhaps more relevant to draw on ethnographic data regarding the native inhabitants of nineteenth-century North America. In 1839 Tixier encountered an effeminate Osage living in the Head Chief's lodge. His name was *la Bredache*; a few years before he had been a warrior, but now he stayed at home when war was made.[63] There is the interesting case of a Kansan Indian in 1819–20 who, to fulfill a vow after recovering from an illness, depilated himself from head to toe, let his scalp hair grow, exchanged his clothes for those of a woman, and took up women's work; this was a berdache, it should be said, who also took up homosexual activity.[64] Then there is the case of a Sioux who became a berdache in 1835 'because he did not want to fight anymore.'[65] Doubtless a serious search in the literature would turn up many more such adult entrants into the ranks of berdaches, but these suffice to better contextualize Las Casas's decisive recognition that there were many elders among the berdaches the conquistadors encountered, that a goodly number had entered that status when they were far beyond childhood or adolescence, and that they apparently did so for other than sexual reasons. In fact, in Las Casas's and some others' view, these males became what contemporaries called 'women' when they could no longer produce offspring or satisfy women, as was said, or when they no longer were effective fighters. In the following chapter, we will see just how they related to women when they took up women's tools of labor.

This survey of the origins of the berdache has demonstrated that males became berdaches at three fairly distinct stages of life. It has argued that sexuality played a central role at all three stages, if in different modalities. Those who became berdaches at a very young age were destined by tribes and families, if not for sacrifice, then to become homosexual passives at a later age, while those who transvested at around 12 years of age took on that sexual role promptly; both these groups, I believe, were under strong familial and political constraints to assume these new roles.

Effectively, these constraints forever precluded heterosexual activity; that needs to be emphasized and rightly understood. First, there is practically no evidence for berdache bisexuality, and only one Christian advanced the thoroughly European view that these males only dressed as women so they could enter female society for heterosexual pleasures.[66]

A second consideration is just as relevant. We recall that, in his study of ancient Greek homosexual behavior, Devereux isolated as a period of 'pseudo-homosexuality' the behavior of teenagers between 12 and 18 years of age, after which boys 'slid' toward penetrating behavior, with either passive berdaches or female prostitutes, in preparation for heterosexual marriage. I emphasized at the time that, in such Mediterranean experiences, there was no significant amount of transvestism related to homosexual behavior. While the experience in North Africa may have been somewhat different, even there transvestism and sodomy were far from automatically linked.

This is precisely where the Amerindian experience, in which Devereux, as a student of the Mojave, was also an expert observer, is decisively different. Without wanting to maintain that all male homosexuality was linked to transvestism, I do not doubt that a very significant link did exist in America between the two in a way it did not in Europe. Amerindians often put on women's clothes in relation to their assuming a passive homosexual posture.

And they put those clothes on forever. The decisive point to be made is that I have been unable to find any evidence, in this early colonial period, that, once this female clothing was assumed, it was ever put aside and male clothing (which in some tribes meant nudity) reassumed. In short, precisely what the Delaware Nation accomplished in wresting itself free of the Iroquois Confederacy – the refusal of the petticoat, the pestle and the cornmasher – is absent in the ethnographic record as regards the individual berdache.[67] To quote Marquette describing the Illinois, 'once males, still at a young age, assumed women's dress, they wore them for the rest of their lives.'[68] As a result, these berdaches no longer had any prospect of heterosexual activity. There appears to be no ritual for laying aside the *nagua*, and thus no likelihood that, as in the Greek model, one turned at some point to penetrative heterosexual behavior. In Europe, the penetrated youngster did not dress as a woman and thus could change to an active penetrator. The Amerindian, once dressed like a woman, seems to have stayed 'a woman' evermore.

Among native American berdaches, there was doubtless a wealth of behavioral variety that was not recorded by early colonial sources; one has only to read work on the berdaches of the last two centuries to recognize that.[69] But in all this literature, there is no former berdache who had converted back to men's work. This conclusion has an important implication. If 'once a berdache, always a berdache,' was once a true observation, then it might seem to follow that the relative ages of the partners to a homosexual act would be irrelevant: in this reading, an older berdache might easily service a young warrior.[70] Our sources, however, without anywhere near the specificity we desire, always imply and assume that, as in Europe, the passive was always younger, and thus less powerful, than the active party. I could find no contradictory evidence on that score.

One may adduce from this that the older berdache, at no matter what age he entered that estate, was concerned with other aspects of women's 'offices' besides the sexual one. This does not mean that the older berdache was never sexually active with others, for, as we shall see in the coming chapter, Peter of Ghent, our earliest source on such matters in Tenochtitlan, expressed surprise that elders (*viejos*) were practicing sodomy. But certainly the collectivity that was so much a catalyst in the making of young berdaches is less evident in these sources when older males join their ranks. Further, though Las Casas imagined them to be impotent, nonsexual beings, there is no evidence that such older men became berdaches as part of a life change to homosexual behavior. However, in another sense, these men definitely did assume a new sexual role, by omission. They were now men, or rather called 'women,' who could no longer make babies.

But did the collectivity apply pressure to force some older men to become berdaches? Neither our sparse sources, nor more modern ones, give any information on that score, so we are inclined to speculate that their choice was indeed a more individual one. By turning now to the life experiences of the berdache, we can perhaps shed more light on this problem.

5

The Religious Berdache

A relationship between men symbolized by sexual ties entails a dimension that is more symmetrical and endogamous than any heterosexual relation.[1]

We put a *picota* in the square and a gibbet outside town.[2]

The religious role of the berdaches has scarcely been mentioned while describing the conditions under which males assumed that role. And yet, sixteenth-century Iberians often observed and reported on American berdaches in temples and shrines. This neglect has a history. In the eighteenth century, scholars commonly highlighted the religious role of the berdache as well as his homosexual comportment,[3] and well into the nineteenth century generalists such as the American physician William A. Hammond were still recording the public religious involvement of the berdache, far to the north, among Pueblos of the Rio Grande river valley.[4] Then a reaction set in, whose hallmark was silence. While many indigenous peoples themselves – subjected, they said, 'like women' – began to 'forget' their nations' berdaches or homosexual behaviors, the Victorian intelligentsia – some of whose missionaries and anthropologists, willy-nilly agents of white domination, had themselves imbued the native Americans with shame at these 'forgotten' histories – began to drop such specters of religious sexuality from their own reports to other whites about native mores.[5]

In the previous chapter I presented evidence that making berdaches was often linked to discrete political goals, such as the very creation of a 'state' or 'status,' that is, a forceful collectivity of males under another male. In this chapter I hope to elaborate that argument by showing the extent to which, at the time of the European conquests, church, curing, and counselling structures existed among some native peoples that reflected political arrangements based in part on sexual inequalities. These sexual inequalities did include the dependent status of women, most noticeably in the institution of the Andean *acllas* or nuns who so strikingly represented the Inca rulers as propertied individuals to the outside world. Yet males might represent a big man's power in a way women could and did not, and it is this bio-social reality of a sovereign's ability to overpower the more powerful of the sexes, and force it to join the royal retinue, that draws our interest.

Church

Where he is found, the American temple berdache was a significant figure in social exchange. So were his or her more earthbound colleagues, to be sure, but at the top of the mountain, so to speak, this exchange character was more transparent. At times, European sources limit the role of such temple boys to that of mundane caretakers, comparable with the *castrati* who were occasionally said to guard the harems or monasteries of the Andean *acllas*.[6] Next, berdaches, presumably performing 'female duties,' were occasionally said to be kept in the temples until they were sacrificed to the gods.[7] Yet without any doubt, the early conquerors encountered many other homosexually involved transvestites who were not sacrificed, but lived long lives at the heart of the religious undertaking, especially in the great temples of Mexico and Peru. Comparable with certain temple prostitutes of ancient Mesopotamia, during festivals the American berdaches furnished their owners the joy of solemn mountings and fellations. These temple behaviors, these *ritos sacros abominables*,[8] expressed, modified, and then perpetuated dominance for the faithful to see.

The evidence for temple sexual activity in the Aztec capital of Tenochtitlan is scarce, and, in part for ideological reasons yet to be examined, Spanish sources nowhere clearly position berdaches within temples. To attack the problem through circumstantial evidence, therefore, we begin with religious ideas. There is slim but disputed evidence that the Mexican high god, Tezcatlipoca, had a homosexual side: disappointed supplicants denounced one of his manifestations (Titlacauan) as an unreliable passive male whore (*puto*).[9] Again early in the conquest period, the Franciscan Motolinía and then his followers claimed that a native deity had introduced and legitimated homosexuality into Mexico and central America.[10]

Moving from this largely unyielding world of creed to that of representation, you should know that Mexican males in festivals dressed up as women gods to honor female divinities, in some cases donning a sacrificed woman's flayed skin to replicate visually that goddess.[11] Indeed, on closer examination it appears that Mexican priests, or perhaps temple berdaches, were precisely the persons who specialized in miming their female gods festively in this way. Sahagún states that such priests were tall and strong, while Durán notes that they were not young.[12] They were seen to throw themselves to the earth in sexual pose, with their arms and legs extended before the warrior god Huitzilopochtli. 'All these people,' says a commentator upon a similar rite, 'were sodomite priests who do not leave the temples.'[13] Were such priests berdaches in the conventional sense? Perhaps not, since the 'clothes' they assumed were in fact the skin of a woman. But at the very least, one is struck by the similarity to the temple berdache of the Andes.

In any case, there never was reason to doubt that the Aztec temples were associated with sexual practices of varied types. The renowned Peter of Ghent's 1529 description of sodomy in the valley of Mexico, we recall, specifically referred to *temple* sexuality, saying that some priests kept in the temples boys whom they abused.[14] Add to Ghent the witness of Bernal Díaz who, though he wrote half a century after Ghent, actually saw the Mexican temples four years before Peter arrived. In his *True History* he corroborates Ghent's testimony even while expanding it:

> According to what they say and what we came to know, those priests were the sons of the leaders. And they did not have wives, but they held the infamous office of sodomies.[15]

Such is the best and most direct, if not our only, evidence of Mexican temple homosexuality. The claim in mid-century of Cervantes de Salazar and others that God had sent the Spaniards against the native Americans because of the latter's sodomy sounds as if they are alluding to Aztec ecclesiastical approbation of same-sex behavior, but they do not say so.[16] Writing about 1569, however, Tomás López Medel was specific. This author claimed that, in the old days, the Guatemalans and the Mexicans had had great numbers of priests in the temples, who 'practiced such abominable lusts and sins that it is an abominable and disgraceful thing to describe.'[17] From Europe, Tommaso Bozio recorded such notions simply, perhaps all too simply. 'In most temples,' he said, 'they keep men who serve to satisfy the libido through the most nefandous practices. This they may do because of an official, yes even, as is imagined, a religious decree.'[18]

Thus some early sources do indicate that Mexican temple practices included homosexual behavior. At the same time, however, a generally opposed historiographic tradition was springing up that downplayed the amount of sodomy in the general population. This picture could not have been more different from the one sketched by Peter of Ghent. Only 'two or three provinces' had permitted sodomy, said the Franciscan Motolinía, and they were 'quite far from Mexico City.'[19] He continues: In places where male homosexuality was not actually illegal, it was condemned by community opinion, as indicated by the fact that to call a person a passive (*cuy lumpult*) was a grave insult.[20] Alas, these commentators address only the general extent of homosexual behavior in the Valley of Mexico, and not the specific question of the existence of homosexual action within native religious establishments.

Once again, Las Casas, though an apologist for the natives, breaks this silence, and assures us that, in fact, homosexual behavior was found in the temples. The subject arises when the Dominican tries to combat 'falsities and pernicious testimony' of some Spanish writers about the temple education of upper-class youth in New Spain, who claimed that the *mancebos* in the temples 'commit the nefandous sin with each other.' The question here is not, therefore, about pederastic intercourse between priests and underlings of the type Ghent mentions, but about actions within a student body. Now, Las Casas recognized that such contacts could occur: elsewhere, describing Guatemalan conditions, he noted that, although fathers hated sodomy, they sent their boys to live in the temples so that they could learn religious doctrines. There they were penetrated by the older boys, and Las Casas agreed with conventional thinking that, once this happened, it was hard to break the habit of homosexual behavior.[21] But in the Mexican case he dismissed the allegations out of hand, because he knew better: he had queried elders on the matter, and they assure him that they had never heard of such a thing.[22]

Yet at this juncture, Las Casas now put forward an alternate text, which in fact recognized that sodomy was practiced in some Mexican temple contexts. Perhaps such a thing did exist after all, even if 'not in all, but in some parts or provinces' of the empire, but the natives always condemned it, Bishop Las Casas insists. Indeed he asserted that, among the Mixtecs, near his own episcopal town of San Cristóbal, he found a public ritual that was used to humiliate such a temple boy before he was hung and burned. He has the judges cry out: 'Oh evil one, how dare you commit such a great sin in the house of the gods!'[23] In this case, the usually intransigent Las Casas had bent to what seemed indisputable: homosexual behavior was a rooted part of temple activity, at least in the temple schools.

Despite Las Casas's authority, a later writer, like Motolinía favorable to the Aztecs, reclaimed the view that the Aztec schools were truly innocent. The Franciscan Juan Torquemada certainly knew that, since European antiquity, isolating adolescent schoolboys with young men in educational or monastic contexts had afforded a favorable seedbed for homosexual practices, for the same problem was being widely discussed among contemporary Europeans.[24] But he would not have such uncertainty as regarded his beloved American 'children.' Glowingly contrasting Aztec with ancient Greek education, he insists that, in Tenochtitlan, the Aztecs 'rebuffed the vices of antiquity, which in the ancient polities were used by similar congregations.'[25] For ideological reasons that we shall later examine, Torquemada obviously protested too much. All in all, the Mexican evidence makes it almost certain that berdache transvestism in the temples was an ongoing matter, with homosexual intercourse practiced in the temples of Tenochtitlan.

Turning now to Peru, we shall find the berdache was well established in Andean temples long before the Spanish Conquest and perhaps even before the Inca. But again, before zeroing in on the temple evidence, let us begin with some feeling for the sources' assessments of general indigenous homosexual behavior. After Gómara's claim that Peruvians in general were guilty of sodomy,[26] most sixteenth- and early seventeenth-century authorities, including Pedro de Cieza de León (ca. 1550) and the mestizo Garcilaso de la Vega (ca. 1609), played down the extent of this 'bestial and excommunicated act.'[27] The soldier-historian Cieza de León, for instance, protested vigorously against 'those writers who have condemned the Indians in general, claiming that they are all sodomites,'[28] maintaining instead that even pre-Inca homosexual behavior was limited mostly to individual 'sinners.' Thus, Cieza, far and away the most reliable of the historians of the Andes, wished, like Las Casas, to delimit the extent of sodomy in the general population.

But Cieza was in this whole discourse speaking of sexual relations between laity, a category he kept separate in his mind from religiously sanctioned sexual activity by noting that the former were known to be sinful by their practitioners, while the latter, performed in temple areas, were assumed to be permissible. Now when Cieza turns his attention to this religious activity, specifically the festive practice of active lords copulating with passive priests,[29] it is clear that temple homosexual behavior in the Inca Empire was not at all limited to the coast. For example, as if it was ubiquitous, he refers in an offhand fashion to those practitioners of sodomy 'whom they kept in the temples' around Lake Titicaca, in the southern part of the Inca Empire.[30] Then, in a chapter dedicated to the subject of berdaches' religious activities, Cieza approvingly cites the following crucial statement of Fray Domingo de Santo Tomas, which indicates the broad scope of temple homosexual behavior the length and breath of the Inca Empire:

> It is true that, as a general thing among the mountaineers and the coastal dwellers [Yungas], the devil has introduced this vice under the pretense of sanctity. And in each important temple or house of worship, they have a man [hombre] or two, or more, depending on the idol, who go dressed in women's attire from the time they are children, and speak like them, and in manner, dress, and everything else they imitate women. With them especially the chiefs and headmen have carnal, foul intercourse on feast days and holidays, almost like a religious rite and ceremony.[31]

This is as close as we shall come to sensing the actual experience of such intercourse. Fray Domingo may have been suggesting, with other writers, that such sodomy accompanied states of ritual drunkenness. He was not hinting, nor does any source, that a ritual enema, itself a type of 'sodomy,' was associated with this sexual activity or with the berdache.[32] Still, Fray Domingo is not finished, and goes on to provide more information about two particular berdaches who resided in the temples. The one came from the Andes near Huánuco, the other from the province of Chincha near Lake Junín. They entered temples, perhaps those in their own locales, while still children. The friar does not state the 'Indians'' age when he met them, but they were presumably adults. Most helpful, while paraphrasing these berdaches' statements, Fray Domingo leaves little doubt that force was an inherent part of their having become berdaches in the temples:

> They answered me that it was not their fault, because from childhood they had been put there by the caciques to serve them in this cursed and abominable vice, and to act as priests and to guard the temples of their idols.[33]

Thus the circle closes: the boys' own lords had put them in the temples, so that, to follow Cieza, 'on feast days the lords [could] have intercourse with them.'[34]

Before proceeding, let us note that, according to one account, not all these boys had to be coerced to serve in the temple. In his narrative of approximately 1590, Blas Valera claimed that, in Inca times, many *muchachos* volunteered to serve in the temple and promised to remain virgins. So desirable were such posts, Valera said, that many of the boys underwent castration, either at their own hands if they were older or at those of others if still young.[35] So in addition to the berdaches, whose bodies remained integral, temples seem also to have housed willing eunuchs who, much like the contemporary *castrati* in Italy, were drawn to temples as career opportunities.

Perhaps different from Mexico, where Las Casas implies that the passives might have been young sons of the nobility, here in Peru Cieza suggests, at least, that the berdaches were commoners. The devil, he wrote, wanted the lords to sacrifice to him, so he made (common) Indians available to them, presumably as a combined object of sacrifice and pleasure. He wanted to keep the natives under his thumb, 'in the chains of their perdition':

> It is considered certain that, in the shrines and temples where conversation was held with [the devil], he let it be known that he would consider it a service if certain *mozos* were attached to the temples from childhood, so that, at the time of sacrifices and solemn feasts, the chieftains and other men of rank could indulge in the cursed sin of sodomy.[36]

With all the richness of these citations, which show the coerced Andean berdache or transvestite functioning as a central tribal religious resource, there admittedly remain questions these sources leave untouched. Had these natives already been violated by the local lords before they were dressed up as girls and assigned to the temples? And once there, did they serve for life or at term? Yet the value of these citations cannot be gainsaid, perhaps especially because of what they reveal about the Spaniards' own understanding of Andean ecclesiology. The Spaniards regarded the homosexual act in the temple as a religious offering on the altar of power, class and status. Witness for example the title of chapter 64 of part 1 of Cieza's *Crónica*, dedicated to the subject of religious homosexual behavior:

> How the devil made the Indians of these regions believe that it was an offering pleasing to their gods for them to have Indians as temple assistants so the chieftains could have carnal knowledge of them, thus committing the heinous sin of sodomy.[37]

Second, these sources show that the Spaniards were conscious of status, that is, of the chieftains' hierarchical power over the assistants, when they described this homosexual behavior. The same class and status awareness is even more clear in Garcilaso's account of the history of the great shrine of Pachacamac in the desert just south of Lima. Its divinity promised to converse with the faithful on the condition that only the Inca upper class or *orejones* address him; another shrine, that of Rimac or Lima, grew up nearby to accommodate the lower classes.[38]

It is thus established that ceremonial homosexual penetration, masked, so to speak, as a heterosexual copulation between a male lord and a 'female' dependent, was a fundamental aspect of certain Andean religions, as it had been, *mutatis mutandis*, in the ancient Near East. But striking as is this powerful evidence of a link between liturgical solemnity and sexual posturing, our Andean evidence takes us still more deeply, to show these native Americans professing reverence to the gods through gestures that are discretely sexual in character. In pursuing these leads, we are struck by the similarity between the kneelings of the berdache and the reverences of the devotee!

At the outset, let us not lose sight of the fact that, whatever its sacrificial or theological significance, a lord mounted upon a subject, or being fellated by him, had a definite social significance in this ecclesiastical context. In a helpful study of modern Cuzceñan brothel behavior, Arnold shows that communications flow less between coital partners than between patrons. First, fornicating males advertise their machismo to other males, and second, they prove to their cohort that their women will do anything they command by performing with them so-called unnatural acts.[39] Having intercourse with berdaches in a temple could not have been much different. Through their actions, mighty men proved their authority over their retinues of berdaches to those who watched these divine services.

Various cultures have used sexual signs and gestures of subordination to express reverence toward their gods and lords. Indeed, only those ready to avoid the topic will be surprised that some corporal expressions of religious reverence, such as kneeling, bowing and prostration, remain formally close to certain sexual postures. This is not the place to delve deeply into the matter, of course.[40] Here it suffices to present the evidence that, at Pachacamac itself, a specific prayer posture mirrored the passive posture in anal intercourse. To understand the words in what follows, note that Pachacamac was one of the relatively few shrines where the so-called devil 'gave response' to questioners. It was, in short, a temple of the type into which, as Cieza has said, the devil wanted temple berdaches installed. According to the Jesuit Acosta, the prayer posture at Pachacamac was:

> Stepping backwards, [with] the back turned to the idol. Then bending the body and inclining the head.

Acosta called this posture merely ugly (*fea*), but Bernabe Cobo, otherwise copying Acosta, added that it was indecent.[41] It appears, therefore, that these writers may in fact have been describing 'presentation,' the submissive position of the sexual recipient, as the prayer posture that 'increased adoration through sensuality,' in Calancha's words, the third source referring to this same act of reverence.[42] In Yucatan, but certainly not only there, passives were indeed referred to as 'those who are used to showing their buttocks,' and, indeed, this is a recognizable posture of reverence in many areas of the world.[43] In turn, this reverential posture may have been identical to that used by a subject on approaching his terrestrial lord. During Columbus's fourth voyage, it was recorded that 'the people of Veragua and the region around about, turn their backs when they converse with each other,' and soon after Oviedo says that subjects in the New Kingdom of Granada (Colombia) never approached their lords face to face. Rather, 'they enter where he is with their backs turned to him.'[44]

Almost certainly, the Pachacamac devotee was offering himself, either symbolically or in actuality, to God – that is, to his priest or cacique – for anal penetration. The Andean temple was a significant space in which the berdaches and their masters, comparable with the Peruvian *acllas* or nuns and their masters, could pompously show the power relationships they, and the areas and peoples they represented, entertained with each other.[45]

In addition to witnessing these reverential corporal representations of anal intercourse at Pachacamac and in Nueva Granada, while others documented the actuality of that intercourse in various other parts of the Inca Empire, early European explorers often also described religious art objects they had seen which featured representations of male homosexual acts. Oviedo for instance mentions a gold necklace he saw in the Tierra Firme, which showed the act of sodomy with 'one man on top of the other.' He then records that Christians in the Maya-Aztec region of Tabasco had found 'among the *zemis* or idols' one wood and another pottery figurine, the former featuring 'one knight riding the other,' the latter a man holding what appeared to be a circumcised penis.[46] Also recounting the early contact period, Bernal Díaz describes clay figurines at Cape Catoche off Yucatan: the action was sodomy among divinities.[47] Slightly later, Antonio de Herrera records paintings of both heterosexual and male homosexual activity in Sinaloa, far to the north, 'for [these peoples] are much involved in sodomy.'[48] All these reports used these figures as documention that sodomy was in fact widespread;[49] all but Herrera thought that the homosexual behavior shown in the figures was between divinities.

While I have been unable to find extant homoerotic figures from the conquest period, a substantial body of pottery with this theme from a much earlier time does survive. I refer to the famous Moche pottery of the northwestern coast of today's Peru, and, specifically, to a large group of bowls and cups that show two persons engaged in anal intercourse, the one in the dominant position, the other in the subordinate position. These figures seem to date from around 700 until about 750 AD, when Moche culture declined. They have only been retrieved in modern times, and, significantly, all from the so-called *huacas*, the funerary religious sites of Peru.[50] There has been much debate about the meaning of these figures. I am persuaded that many of them represent homosexual activity between rulers and berdaches of the type Domingo de Santo Tomas described in the sixteenth century or, to switch locations, the homosexual or at least anal reverences that indigenous people still paid the god at Pachacamac when the Spaniards arrived (see figures 7 and 8).[51]

These figures were intended to express dominion. That is clear from the rarity of face-to-face coital representations and the predominance of hierarchical representations, either of the majority type showing mounted intercourse or the occasional representations of fellation. This dominion is sterile, so to speak: it is apparently not meant to flaunt one's ability to reproduce oneself through sex. For measuring the relative positions of the two figures, Larco Hoyle found that at least 95 per cent of these figures require the presumption of anal, not uterine, penetration.[52] This dominion of sterile, hierarchical intercourse makes it all the more important to know the sex especially of the passive partners if we are to divine the meaning of these figures.

Seduced by nationalistic sentiments, and in the teeth of all the evidence we have reviewed, Larco dismissed suggestions that the figures in question showed homosexual intercourse, and that alleged absence gratified his feelings for the ancients.[53] All the identifiable

Figure 7   Homosexual anal intercourse, Moche Culture.

figures in the subordinate sexual position were women, he claimed; they wore women's clothes and styled their hair as did women.[54]

The reader of these pages will react quickly: we know that devotees at some shrines commonly bent over backwards to present themselves to priests playing gods fully seven hundred years after the Moche. Some of them were male transvestites who wore women's clothes and hair while performing the role of sexual subordinates. Yet Larco and most other students of these figures never consider the possibility that some of the subordinate figures in this Moche work were berdaches feigning women. They were supposed to replicate women. And in Gómara's words, such berdaches 'lacked only breasts and child-bearing to be fully women'![55]

The possibility that these Moche figures are the distant ancestors of the homosexual figures the Spanish conquerors encountered in the early sixteenth century is not diminished by an overview of the sexes represented in the figures of this corpus. Unsurprisingly, all the figures on top are male, because they are dressed as males, and women rarely

Figure 8   Hetero- or homosexual anal intercourse, Coastal Inca Culture.

appear to have dressed as men anywhere in the Americas. Also unsurprisingly, all the figures on bottom are dressed like women. Moving now to signs of their actual sex, we find only an occasional one of these subordinate figures clearly revealing their male sex. A few more show a vulva and thus reveal their female sex. The great majority, however, do not reveal their biological sex at all, only appearing women because of their hair and clothes. So uncertain is the matter that, after surveying several hypotheses of sex differentiations in this pottery, Donnan decided that it was best to identify the sex of a figure only where the genitals are clearly depicted.[56] Thus there is little in these objects to prevent me from hypothesizing that most of the figures in the subordinate position were understood by contemporaries to be transvested males. When one adds the literary evidence for mounted homosexual intercourse, it appears that, from the Moche culture into the Spanish period, mounted homosexual intercourse was among other things a religious activity between males of different social standings. This activity was a type of presentation posture for representing submission, one preserved in certain modern gestures of reverence.

Larco could not understand why these figures were found exclusively in the religious context of the *huacas*. Donnan took a decisive position in this matter, believing the postures in the figures to be 'ritual practices that occurred in ceremonial contexts.'[57] I believe that they show prayer, prayer for the maintenance of the political dominion of Moche rulers over their male subjects, reduced, as one said, to women. Thus the pictorial sources as well as the written ones indicate that, as a general behavioral phenomenon, temple homosexuality in ancient Peru expressed existing power relationships. Almost certainly, it also subverted and modified them, thus making new ones.

Cures

Having established the important role of berdaches in some American tribes' religious expression, we might seem but a step away from affirming the widely held view that pre-Columbian berdaches or passives were seers and thus healers.[58] There has been a common presumption of an association between shamans – priests who achieved occult knowledge through visions – and the berdache, a notion fostered by an incautious use of Mircia Eliade's classic work on *Shamanism*. My own less theological suspicion that, when the Iberians arrived, the transvestite might have been linked to occult knowledge and thus healing artistry has rested on their common use of falsetto voice: berdaches used women's voices, while Andean priests, hallucinating, spoke for the 'devil' by mimicking his very voice or voices.[59]

Doubtless, in the later seventeenth or eighteenth century, berdaches did come to have 'medicine,' did come to be associated with occult life, but this book cannot tell that later story. In the period of early contacts between the Iberians and the native Americans, however, my own suspicion and the presumptions of other scholars have come to naught: there is no evidence that berdaches or male passives were doctors or diviners, or, inversely, that healers and seers were berdaches or homosexual passives. The famous *piaches* of the Tierra Firme have most misled scholars on this score. The *piaches* did in fact get a good deal of attention from early reporters. They were healers and visionaries, and were occupationally identified as those who talked with the gods; they even helped the Christian priests converse with 'the demons' so that they too could know the future. At a very early point, Peter Martyr devoted a long passage to those in Chiribichi or Venezuela, and, in mid-century, Las Casas subsumed Peter's account into his own Apologetic History.[60] The pajes or piaches were repeatedly described as religious and medical specialists. Unfortunately, none of these sources associates the piaches with transvestism or with sodomy.[61]

Perhaps it was sometime in the later seventeenth century that things began to change, and the occult figures of the piache or the shamans began to resemble the berdaches. Like most scholars, Metraux is peremptory in claiming that the shamans of the Chilean Araucanians, for instance, were male berdaches.[62] His source, however, was both more precise and interesting. In his Cautiverio feliz of 1673, Núñez de Pineda distinguished two types of shamans (machis), the one made up of berdaches, that is, transvested homosexual passives (hueyes or weye), the other not. Though they disliked this passivity – activity did not phase them at all – the Araucanians tolerated such passive machis 'or curanderos,' who were terribly ugly, said Núñez, because it was they who had a pact with the devil.[63] Still, the link between shamanism and the berdache did not establish itself everywhere. The nineteenth-century scholar Park, for instance, in his work on Shamanism in Western North America, could find no case of a berdache who had become a shaman.[64]

This association of berdaches with the devil occurs here for the first time in the literature. As indicated earlier, the piaches or curanderos were a group who 'spoke to the devil,' and not at all berdaches or, seemingly, homosexual passives. Now they become that in this corner of the native American universe. Just as original is Núñez' implication that, because these religious berdaches were known to have a pact with the devil, they were thought to have an advantage at healing.

Is this truly the beginning of a new linkage between the berdache and occultism, or will further research reveal that there were after all close relations between the indigenous berdaches and the religious specialties of healing and seeing on the arrival of the Europeans? That remains to be determined. However, at this point, it would be hazardous to extend the Araucanian experience backwards in time. The American berdache was not a doctor or a visionary by profession when the peninsulars encountered him. Where he appears as a religious official, he is a subordinate being with no occult authority. Kneeling, he expresses the principle of hierarchy, or rather, of subordination.

Counsel

In the same year, 1673, that Núñez de Pineda published his description of berdache doctors, Father Marquette wrote down his experiences with Illinois berdaches:

> I do not know what superstition leads some Illinois as well as some Nadoüessi, while they are still young, to assume women's clothing for the rest of their lives. It is mysterious. For they never marry, and they are proud to abase themselves by doing all those things women do. They go to war, but they can only use a club rather than the bow and arrow which are the correct male arms. They participate in all the games and in the solemn dances which are performed in honor of Columet. They sing there but they cannot dance. They are summoned to councils, where nothing can be decided without their advice. Last, because they profess such an extraordinary life, they are considered big shots, that is, geniuses or persons of consequence.[65]

A later chapter of this work studies the reputation in which berdaches and homosexual activities were held. At this point, we address ourselves only to the question of whether earlier berdaches did in fact provide counsel of the type Marquette found among these northern tribes toward the end of the seventeenth century. Needless to say, in modern times many berdaches within the border of the present United States have provided such wisdom; one has only to recall the Zuni berdache We'wha (1849–96) in this regard.[66] But did they do so in the colonial past and before?

The answer is negative: I can find no evidence to support that notion. Nor is that surprising, for we have found little confirmation that berdaches, even those who took the female robe as an elder, were thought to have any particular knowledge or medicine that was applied in the religious sphere. Based on this absence of evidence alone, we would have to characterize the existence of berdaches as a degraded one. Yet my final view on this matter will have to await a review of the berdache in his or her quotidian secular life.

Thus while the berdache was in the temple when the Iberians arrived in the New World, he does not seem to have been in the halls of power. In this contact period, no evidence suggests that he looked into the future for his people, or sought to heal its members. Rather, the berdache seems to have been occupied mostly with guard duties, and presumably with other duties associated with women.

The most important of these tasks seems clearly to have been their sexual subordination to and intercourse with lords, which is documented in different parts of the Inca Empire and among different North American tribes including the Aztecs, the Pueblo nations, and perhaps even far northern agglomerations such as the Iroquois.[67] This action by the lord represented to one's equals and competitors the prowess he could exercise over powerful young males. Above one's subordinates, a master asserted their abasement to that authority in the person of the berdache, comparable to the way prayer gestures of abasement worked in European religions then and now. Finally, this action was a sacrifice to a god, who repaid the lord for that flesh with the sexual gratification itself. These lessons did not trickle down from the temple to everyday life. Rather, they had ascended the steps. But they tended always to reinforce, and vividly to represent, the principle of authority over all 'women,' to whom the very soldiers of the lord, because of such demonstrations, feared themselves reduced.

6

On the Ground

[The berdaches] performed the duties of women with the robustness of men.[1]

For extraordinary privileges which he is known to possess, he is driven to the most servile and degrading duties which he is not allowed to escape.[2]

Once descended from the sixteenth-century temple mountain, or once returned from the battlefield, the student in search of a charismatic berdache personality will be sorely disappointed. There is no outstanding persona documented in the historical record, no single colorful event that can be seized, contextualized, and re-presented to readers. Unlike that rare nineteenth-century Zuni berdache (*llamana*) We'wha (see figure 10), the Central American berdache of earlier times has no name attached.[3]

If the author had his wish, this chapter would describe the daily life of the berdache. It would draw on a trove of quotidian realities so as to make that (absent) charismatic berdache spring from the sources. That is not possible; instead, rather than re-creating that life itself, the materials at our disposal do allow us to shed light on some of the categories, or social facts, informing daily life, and that is the path we shall pursue.

I begin with the location and proceed with the population of these berdaches and of their homosexual behaviors. Then I continue with information about berdaches' occupations. The chapter concludes by considering the male berdache's interface with women during the late sixteenth and seventeenth centuries, when the native population largely collapsed from disease and alienation. I propose to limit myself in this chapter as much as possible to descriptions of observed realities. Native and Iberian attitudes toward berdache behavior will be taken up in the following chapter.

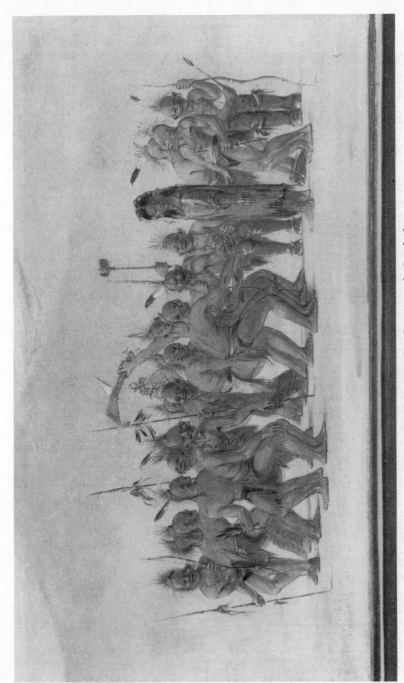

Figure 9 George Catlin, *Dance to the Berdash.*

Figure 10   *Wewa Zuni, Man-Woman Priestess.*

In that later chapter Iberian ideology will obviously impinge mightily upon any alleged truth claim about native American ideas. Has that problem of sources ever been far from the reader's mind? What needs emphasis here is that our present attempt to determine the social facts of the berdache and of homosexual behavior is not based on any statistics we, or the peninsulars, have compiled. Rather, the generalities I shall report are no more than those of the conquerors and missionaries themselves. That is to put it mildly. In fact, what I report often is nothing more than their stereotypes. I can only promise to comment on their truth value as we proceed.

Geography

Historians and anthropologists are still searching for a North American people that never knew the berdache as a part of its social organization, and there would be no difficulty demonstrating much the same historiographic pattern in middle and south America; the reader of the present work will, in fact, find single tribes said to have no, and then many or much, berdaches and sodomy. As a reaction to some early denunciations of all native peoples as being 'all sodomites,' which approximated a claim that all tribes possessed male transvestites, later historians claimed that, while an occasional tribe such as the Huayllas were 'infected' with homosexual behavior, numerous, nay most tribes were free of it, and thus of berdaches.[4] But on examination, the reality is that one would be hard put to identify one tribe in today's Latin America, or in the hemisphere as a whole, without the berdache having been part of its historical social organization.

Evidently, early modern Iberians came to America with the firm notion that certain geographical locations had a greater or lesser level of homosexual practices. Just as surely, they found what they expected. Perhaps the most routine presumption was climactic in nature, and was verbalized by an early conquistador, Bernal Díaz del Castillo. Most natives were sodomites, he said, but 'especially those who live along the coasts and in hot lands.' To the south, the thinking was much the same. At one point, the chronicler Cieza de León, being extremely careful, asserted that, while the island of Puna off today's Ecuadorian coast was full of sodomy, the mainland itself was clean.[5] Yet at another, he defined socially approved and institutionalized homosexuality as always having been limited to the coastal areas of present-day Ecuador,[6] where it flourished until early in the conquest. Captain Francisco Pacheco, and especially the resident Chief Justice Juan de Olmos, 'burned great numbers of these perverse Indians' at Puerto Viejo.[7] With that action, taken soon after the Spaniards landed, much of this localized sodomy diminished or vanished, according to Cieza. Garcilaso de la Vega followed, believing that 'especially coastal Indians' were given to sodomy.[8] The very Castilian feeling was that, the further inland and higher a culture lived, the less given it was to the 'nefarious sin.'

Writing shortly after Garcilaso, the Augustinian Calancha found that those in the valleys near the Pacific coast were much inclined to sodomy, while tribes in the sierras were mostly free of the crime.[9] Calancha extended the Peruvian homoerotic zone further south than Cieza, finding male homosexual behavior accepted in the plains and river valleys 'from Payta to Guarmey,' that is, south almost to Lima.[10] Of great significance, this stretch includes the area around Trujillo that has yielded such an abundance of erotic pottery from the Moche, Chimu and other pre-Inca cultures. Calancha says that the Augustinians 'purified' these valleys of their sodomy with the help of certain miraculous images of Mary.[11] Thus, by limiting the area of socially acceptable public homosexuality to the hot coastal areas and deserts, Cieza and Calancha, like Bernal Díaz in North America, seemed to confirm the idea that 'base passions' flourish in torrid zones.

The second geographical stereotype was that 'beyond the equator there is no sin' (*infra equinoxialem nihil peccari*), that is, that a notion of sin did not dissuade people in the southern hemisphere from 'immorality.' The essence of this view appears to be chromatic rather than climactic in nature. Thus Garcilaso described the sodomitic and incestuous Passau people as living (in the mountains) 'exactly on the equator,' while Zárate in 1555, in accepting the notion of sodomy as common south of the equator, blamed it for the ill-treatment of wives in this hemisphere.[12]

A third notion, rather than being racist, combines the coastal theory with fear of the unknown. Its best representative is the mid-sixteenth-century Jesuit Acosta, who thought the 'most shameful sins of lechery and sodomy' were to be found 'among the Moscas of the New Kingdom [Colombia], those of the area of Cartagena with its whole coast, those who inhabit the coasts of the Rio Paraguay, and those who live in the vast if little explored regions between the two oceans, the Atlantic and Pacific.'[13]

There are many reasons almost to dismiss the veracity of such generalizations, not the least of which is that, in general, explorers and missionaries usually believed that coastal peoples were at a lower point in cultural evolution than the interior tribes: if the Europeans found no incest tabu, little clothing, cannibalism and the like among such tropical coastal peoples, it was easy to find one more 'barbarism,' that of sodomy. Easier to find because such peoples lived more in the open, accessible to the conquerors, without the elaborate housing or administrative centers of some other tribes. Thus generalizations about the incidence of 'sodomy' are often rather measurements of the relative publicity of homosexual behavior. Cieza realized this: coastal peoples in tropical zones, especially south of the equator, were said to make homosexual liaisons in public, and this chronicler therefore distinguished between practitioners of public, and private, homosexual behaviors.[14]

The mapping of sodomitic practices or their absence is shown in paradigmatic fashion by the eye-witness account that Pedro Castañeda gave of Coronado's march to Cibola (Zuni pueblo) and beyond in the year 1540. Between the west coast of today's Mexico at Culiacan, Sinaloa, and the uninhabited areas of southern Arizona, this chronicler found men dressed as women among the Tahus, then determined that the 'barbarous' Pacaxes at the foot of the Sinaloan Sierras were also *grandes sométicos* and cannibals. After pausing to note that the 'savage, bestial, naked' men and women at the mouth of the Colorado River down along the eastern shore of Baja California 'copulated like animals, the female placing herself publicly on all fours,'[15] Castañeda then asserts that the natives around Petlatlan, Sinaloa, not far from the coast, had many sodomites. Turning north and inland, Castañeda found the people of the Suyo Valley, just short of or in today's Arizona, to be *grandes sométicos*.[16] But after crossing the desert and arriving at Cibola, the first of the fabled Seven Cities, Castañeda discovered that the rightly clothed and agricultural Zunis were another matter: among them there was 'no drunkenness or sodomy or sacrifices, nor do they eat human flesh or steal.'[17]

The Zunis had, in fact, many of the hallmarks of the Spaniards themselves, as Castañeda naively determined. Christians, he said, should settle inland Cibola and not coastal Sinaloa, because the aborigines of the two areas were different:

We see the differences between the one land and the other: It is [Cibola] that merits being populated by Spaniards, and not [Culiacan], the other way around. For in the former one finds human reasoning, while in the latter there is animal barbarity and worse.[18]

Population

It is clear: the Spanish sources are at best a flawed guide in constructing any valid geography of American homosexual practice. They are so often overpowered by ideological expectations – for example, that berdaches could be assumed to practice homosexually and that a homosexual passive sooner or later wore women's clothes – so concerned either to prove sodomy's presence or absence, and so unlikely to actually recognize what appeared to be a 'woman' as a berdache, or indeed to witness homosexual behavior, as to preclude many sound findings.

These sources are often quite as problematic in determining the actual number of berdaches within particular tribes and, as we have seen, even their ages. For lack of better data, in what follows I have been forced to combine the sparce early modern Iberian sources with information from nineteenth-century travelers, physicians and anthropologists in the (mostly southwestern) United States to give us some idea about the population of berdaches, even if it is only of anecdotal value.

About 1569, Tomás López Medel 'dared not describe' the homosexual acts of 'great numbers' of priests in the pre-conquest Mexican and Guatemalan temples, because they were of such variety and number.[19] Topping this to the contrary, Cieza de León, at one with Las Casas, claimed that public or notorious sodomy was so unusual in the old Inca Empire that those who had said otherwise owed the natives an apology.[20] But once we get beyond these generalities, we are left with just two sixteenth- or seventeenth-century sources that actually measure the occurrence of homosexual behavior or of transvestism in a given social body. The first is Ruíz de Arce, a member of the Pizarro expedition. Around Cape San Mateo along today's Ecuadorian coast, which was famous for its open homosexual comportment, Ruíz de Arce found that 'there was no chief who was not followed by four or five gallant [homosexually passive] pages whom he kept as boys.'[21] The second, and perhaps more representative source, is the already cited report of Hernando Alarcón from 1540 that a tribe (the Yuma) or one of its settlements on the lower Colorado River maintained four berdaches for the sexual pleasure of young men who had not yet married.[22]

From that point on, there is no further information of this type until the mid-eighteenth century, when the Franciscan missionary Junipero Serra's biographer described the discovery of a berdache (*joya*) serving as a wife in the Californian mission of San Antonio. He wrote that only at Santa Barbara were such berdaches to be found among the other missions of California. Speaking of the nearby Channel Islands, Palou states that, in the villages of that coastal region, two or three berdaches (*tamacsuma*) were normal.[23] At about the same time (1775), we encounter an identical figure of two or three per village from Fages' 1775 report on the Californian coastal villages between La Carpintería and Punta de los Pedernales, around San Luís Obispo, and further inland.[24]

The nineteenth century also brought occasional approximations for some tribes outside the Latin American area. For example, the traveller John Tanner believed that each Indian tribe had one berdache.[25] But certainly most helpful in this regard is the 1889 report by the physician A. B. Holder regarding berdaches (*bote*) among the Crow of the northern plains. This writer states that the berdaches formed a class within each tribe, and that berdaches from different tribes were friendly with each other. Taking his information from white doctors among the different tribes, and from a particular Crow berdache, he came up with the following figures for tribes in the western plains and in the Northwest: the Crow themselves had five; among the Lower Brulé Agency (Dakota), and among those in Klamath, Oregon, one each; among the Lower Gros Ventres, more than five; Flatheads, four; Nez Percés, two; Gros Ventres, six; Sioux, five; and Shoshonis, one.[26]

These are the best estimates available on the number of berdaches in any given settlement. An average of two or three berdaches per village may be a realistic approximation for earlier rural America, but it cannot serve as an approximation of the number of berdaches in the occasional urban complex of Central and South America. We have seen hints that sizable numbers of berdaches might live in the temple areas of urban complexes, and other indications that local rulers at times gathered numbers of young berdaches together to sell their services while building their own corteges. But once we get beyond what might be labelled officially employed berdaches in towns and villages, there is no way of even guessing at the number of 'private' berdaches, that is, those who were created by their parents for domestic purposes and those many berdaches who married and led a domestic life. I am only confident in saying that the berdache was a common figure in native American life before the arrival of the Spaniards.

Alas, much the same problem of uncommunicative sources is encountered when the ages of berdaches are in question, as became clear when we studied the ages at which one entered that estate. Indeed, the problem is stark, since not one primary source from the sixteenth or seventeenth century estimates the ages of the berdaches he encountered. This seriously hampers our ability to analyze the berdache: while the Spaniards or natives might repeatedly protest 'nefandous' sins, we can hardly pin down the source of their agitation if the ages of the passives remain in question. Recall that, in Europe, the most revolting type of homosexual behavior to 'decent people' was for a grown man to play the passive role. Here in the Americas, no similar native revulsion has come to light, although it bears repeating that berdaches, once transvested, remained in that costume for the rest of their lives. To put these documentary lacunae into perspective, however, other facts of omission that bear on the age relation between partners bear repeating. The weight of the evidence, we have insisted, assumes that passives were younger than their actives. There are few references to a passive of mature or advanced age being involved in sexual activity, though there are in modern North American sources occasional references to attempted seductions by such persons. And there is no reference to a passive older than an active, or to partners of comparable age.

Once again, modern North American information must be used to get any notion of the age spread among individual berdaches in single nations. The famous Zuni *llamana* We'wha died in 1896 at the age of 47; that apparently stimulated an 18-year-old named Kasinelu to become a berdache. Kasinelu died before 1946, in his late sixties, making him the oldest known berdache in my records; his closest competitor in that regard was a Chipewa berdache some 50 years of age.[27] But at Zuni, the elder *llamana* was not alone. In 1915, Parsons found the six-year-old boy Lasbeke, who was 'qualifying' for the status of berdache, plus three mature berdaches (Kasinelu, Tsalatitse and U'k) who were in their late thirties or early forties.[28] In the mid-nineteenth century in the eastern Pueblo region, Hammond had carefully examined a 35-year-old berdache at Laguna and one who was about 36 at nearby Acoma. The latter told Hammond that s/he had assumed her office at 26 or 27 years of age;[29] by way of comparison, a physician to the Crow tribe met a 33-year-old berdache who said s/he had become one at five years of age. Finally, another observer encountered an Osage berdache who was 25 years old.[30] If nothing else, these ages demonstrate that transvestites here, and presumably in Central and South America as well, were often people of mature or even advanced age. Of interest as well is the fact that young men assumed women's clothes not just at a young or advanced age, but in their later adolescence and even twenties.

Appearance

In the course of this study, I encountered one small group of American berdaches who bore certain deformities: in the Andes, some of them had mutilated noses and lips. On examination, however, it appeared that these mutilations were probably incurred because these berdaches' particular occupation was to guard female *acllas* or nuns: with such marks, they would not be attractive to those they guarded.[31] This may be a variant on another group of mutilated persons who when dressed could be mistaken for berdaches: the eunuchs. Sometimes after voluntary emasculation, they too were able to hire on as guards of the same Andean nuns.[32]

But with these rare exceptions, the American berdache, far from being easily discovered, usually passed well enough for a female that s/he might in everyday if not necessarily always in festive life be all but completely unrecognizable as a biological male.[33] As Gómara wrote in the mid-sixteenth century, sodomites in what is today Venezuela 'lacked only breasts and childbirth to be totally women.'[34] And, as mentioned earlier, the Franciscan missionary in California in the eighteenth-century was only convinced he had a *joya* on his hands after undressing the 'wife' and finding she did not indeed have the developed breasts proper to a woman of the berdache's age.[35] There are other examples of such successful feigning in our period, but certainly the most convincing account regards the Zuni berdache We'wha. A century ago, the anthropologist Matilda Cox Stevenson brought We'wha from Zuni to Washington, DC, to show her off. During We'wha's half-year stay, Stevenson at her Friday afternoon receptions billed her, completely innocently, as everything but a male: as a Zuni princess, a priestess, or even a maiden, precisely because the scholar, who had known her subject for some time in Zuni, believed that the physically imposing We'wha was indeed a woman! Not until some time after she and the berdache returned to Zuni did Stevenson discover the truth.[36]

Thus it is not surprising that the early modern Iberian sources characterize the berdache's appearance according to what any particular tribe or region considered to be women's clothing. Easily the most universal reference was to the so-called *nagua* or female skirt, which Oviedo from South America defined early on as 'certain short cotton cloths with which the Indian women cover themselves from their waist to the knees.'[37] In a variant, a late sixteenth-century observer of the Araucanians (Chile) noted that the berdaches did not wear male britches, but a small coat in front (*mantiçuela por delante*).[38]

Other sources specified that berdaches wore women's jewelry. Oviedo for instance said they wore 'strings of beads and bracelets and the other things used by women as adornment,' and Gómara followed, both describing the northern coast of South America.[39] The many berdaches of the Lake Titicaca area wore makeup so as to seduce other men, it was said,[40] while we have seen the Inca Huascar punish a losing general by forcing him and his officers to don 'women's clothes, belts and mirrors, of the type used by women.'[41]

Obviously, the berdaches wore their hair in the style of their own tribe, which for the Chonos meant high off the neck.[42] But elsewhere it was different. In one part of Tierra Firme passives (*putos*), besides wearing a necklace (to the god Priapus!), 'grew their hair and covered their shame as did women, for other [males] were tonsured like friars, and thus were called "the crowned." '[43] Just how universal or culturally specific depilation was for berdaches is difficult to say, since it is not often referred to. On recalling that, in Europe, denuding the body and all its orifices of hair kept one young in appearance and was de rigeur for passives, one suspects that native Americans would have done the like, though they were naturally less hairy than Caucasians. Indeed, I have already cited the case of the nineteenth-century Kansan Indian who, on becoming a berdache, systematically removed his chin, underarm, pubic and eye-brow hair, and there are occasional other references of this type.[44] On the other hand, at least one observer, the Moravian Loskiel, believed that all Iroquois men and not just the tribes' berdaches practiced self-depilation.[45]

As demonstrated earlier, the imitation of women extended far beyond hair, clothing and cosmetics, to include the gestural and vocal universes, to the point that Devereux found the modern Mohave berdache using a certain peculiarly feminine vocabulary.[46] This world of appearance certainly extended to still other spheres, for instance, food. Sahagún tells us that, while men and women in general chewed chicle in private for hygienic purposes, prostitutes and unmarried women did so in public, apparently to advertise their respective estates. Then, obviously continuing on to those he considered male prostitutes, Sahagún says that 'the chewing of chicle [is] the real privilege of the addicts termed "effeminates." [It is] as if it were their privilege, their birthright. And the men who publicly chew chicle achieve the status of sodomites: they equal the effeminates.'[47] It is quite possible, in short, that berdaches consumed alimentary items otherwise limited to women, and perhaps even avoided foods peculiar to active males.

A similarly precious contemporary document is not, as far as I can determine, available to show that berdaches carried with them in public some of the symbolic objects associated in art with women, such as the loom. Yet a hint that artistic representations of this type did carry over to the behavioral universe can be found in the military-diplomatic institution of tribal 'womanhood,' where at least in ceremonial interactions the Delaware, 'women' of the Iroquois, wore petticoats, earrings and the like, but also bore symbolic pestles, metates and other 'womanly' objects.[48] That type of documentation may yet surface in the Central and South American cultural areas.

In the context of studying how young boys were made berdaches, I have already developed one of the fundamental theses of this work, which is that, in several areas of today's Latin America, male children were often forced to transvest and were anally raped so as to create a retinue of dependents – perhaps the central representation of political power then and now – that inevitably took the form of a macho-effeminate polarity, a virile lord followed by a group of presenting, if also virile, fine young men. Spanish sources in fact automatically associated homosexual behavior with the existence of such retinues. That is why the conquistador Ruíz de Arce in 1545 first characterized the coastal natives of today's Peru or Ecuador as 'all sodomites,' then without breaking stride immediately explained that 'there is no lord who is not followed by four or five most gallant pages.'[49] And even earlier, Oviedo told of Chibcha-speaking (Muisca, northern Colombia) caciques returning from a temple with at least one small boy each whom they raised to puberty before sacrificing him to the sun. Oviedo implies that the boy was used homosexually in that period. In the meantime, the boy, as an orant, represented his master to the gods at temple.[50]

Thus an important role of these berdaches in some cultures was their appearance in public representations as signs of their masters' power and authority. The berdache was subordinate to his master, but in some cultures, through the sale of sex or indeed through its denial, s/he enriched that monopolistic master. A particular feature of Aztec festive life illuminates this politico-economic function of both female and male prostitutes, that is, the berdaches. Earlier I showed that one package of Aztec celebratory rituals was composed of males who, for the length of a festivity, masked and dressed themselves as women divinities and as the women who had been sacrificed to such divinities; there is indeed one small, precious phrase by Oviedo, who describes Nicaraguan men transvested during such formal dances.[51] However, in the autumn month of Quecholli, the month of the hunter, in which lovers were honored, berdaches seem to have played a role equal to all those others dedicated to love. At Tlaxcala during this festivity, berdaches were allowed openly to solicit business.[52] And in the Aztec capital as well, these professionals participated in the month's festival: 'the effeminate and woman-like men also entered this festival, wearing the habit and costume of women.'[53]

Whether or not such berdaches played a part in honoring the gods of the month is unknown. Nor does Torquemada imply any more than that these berdaches were in some way distinguishable from women. Indeed, their presence in the festival follows Torquemada's account of the 'bad women' or prostitutes' presence. These women were not, however, just any prostitutes, but army campfollowers! Their description deserves citation:

> In this month called Quecholli, the public, indecent women manifested themselves. And they offered themselves for sacrifice in a recognized, moderate dress. For they were the ones who went to the wars with the soldiery. They were called *maqui*, which means gossips. And they got involved in battles, many of them throwing themselves to death in them. Such women were very indecent and shameless: when they went to their deaths, they cursed themselves and hurled many insults against good, retired and respected women.[54]

Ignored by the existent literature, these Aztec women, understood by Torquemada as brothel prostitutes transplanted to the field of battle as ribalds or shock troops (but certainly as cooks and sexual servants as well), were apparently a functional part of Aztec society, and the suspicion arises that, at least emblematically, the berdaches were too.[55] I noted earlier the absence of direct evidence that the Aztecs employed these institutional 'cowards' in their armies, as did other nations. But in the light of this document it would be hazardous indeed to dismiss the possibility that the berdaches, retinue *par excellence* in a patriarchal society – though strong, they played women to virile lords – are represented here, with their female campfollowers, as a type of military unit.

Occupations

To inquire into those occupations of the berdaches that were generally unrelated to military life and to religious service, I have followed
three guidelines. First, while the sources do make occasional references to homosexual behavior without alluding to transvestism, the
peninsulars rarely refer to a transvestite without assuming that s/he
engaged in 'sodomy' as a passive. Second, throughout this discussion
of the berdache at work, I assume that, like a member of any other
social group, the berdache was a product of his or her environment.
Thus at the point s/he assumed that status, the berdache was a
dependent both of the cultural past and of the social present. Third,
the nature of this dependency was related to the age of the berdache.
Age especially must be kept in mind as a qualifier, and its determination as a desideratum of the merely pragmatic division I now make
between the sexual and non-sexual occupations of the berdache.

Sexual services

When the Andean or Mexican overlord at temple mounted his
berdache, his supernal posture emblematized a world of domination
and submission gestures that suffused the world below the temple.

On entering that quotidian world, a link to sacerdotal postures
might not be apparent. Entrepreneurs always disclaim any dependence on larger contexts, and a rare Iberian observer in the first years
of the conquests did report that certain berdaches operated as private
entrepreneurs, making a living by selling sex to all comers. Bernal
Díaz speaks in that vein, as does Nuño de Guzmán in his description
of the entrepreneurial warrior berdache of Patzquaro.[56] Yet, on
reflection, these sparse references to berdaches operating on their
own are more first impressions than the basis of a binding analysis of
the genre of male prostitutes. In fact, whatever their moral stance,
our authorities usually say enough to allow us to recognize that,
whether male or female, natives presented themselves for sexual
penetration because they wanted and needed to be protected, or at
least not to be harmed, by their penetrators. In short, these outsiders
sought inclusion.[57] In keeping with that view, our Iberian sources
describe male prostitutes as they do female ones: as embedded within
broader social institutions and thus beneath the canopy of temple
sacrality. Even the entrepreneurs, meeting their marks at the sweat-

baths, might take them back to something like a brothel, that is, to an institution also profitable to others.

According to Gregorio García, writing in 1606, there were only two or three provinces in the Aztec heartland that possessed male brothels,[58] and our sources mention only one such area: *mancebías* existed in the province of Pánuco, to the north of Veracruz, Gómara said, facilities 'where thousands of [men] resort at night.'[59] There was, as we shall later see, reason for such denial. To the south, however, other brothels are mentioned. Thus in the province of Darién (Panama), Gómara told of 'female and even male brothels.'[60] And from today's Brazil came Soares's report that, in Tupinamba villages, 'there are certain of them who keep public shop (*tienda*) for those who wish to make use of them as public women.'[61]

I earlier presented evidence for the hypothesis that powerful men sometimes created these brothels to house the young males they sexually dominated, and market them to their profit. Whatever the brothel dynamics, however, there is no doubt that the peninsulars believed that such men did instrumentalize male brothel prostitutes. This is clear not only from evidence already presented, but from the fact that the Iberians themselves instrumentalized female houses of prostitution to similar ends. In the early years of the conquest, the royal historian Oviedo, while echoing conventional European repulsion with male homosexual behavior, did approve the female brothels of Nicaragua because they obviated copulation between males.[62] And Landa provided the evidence in practice: the Maya loved female prostitutes and patronized their brothels so much, he said, that there was little homosexual behavior.[63]

The same notion of 'preventing worse' in turn influenced ethnographic reporting in America. Thus, writing at the turn of the sixteenth century, Antonio de Herrera credited the scarcity of male homosexual activity among the Nicaraguans to the existence of a caste of female prostitutes.[64] Finally, Garcilaso de la Vega says the Incas tolerated female prostitutes because they prevented worse.[65] As we shall see, the Iberians understood that a competition for protection was at the heart of 'preventing worse.'

Yet what if this evidence for preventing male sodomy with female brothels were stood on its head, as seems occasionally to have been the case outside the brothel? As in Europe, the reason often emerging in the sources as a native justification for establishing female brothels is to prevent the rape not so much of men as of women.[66] But to the same end of protecting women (and perhaps males as well), the authorities also are said to have established male brothels. Thus, just as in Guatemala young husbands were given female prostitutes to keep them from raping other women, so Alarcón found among the Yuma along the Colorado River four transvested male prostitutes maintained by the community, presumably in community, to that same end.[67] Most directly to the point, there came reports that in Collasuyu, around Lake Titicaca, communities posted transvested male prostitutes at the borders and elsewhere for the specific purpose of preventing the rape of females by strangers and visitors.[68] We can be confident, I think, that male prostitutes often stood alongside female ones, but with the obvious advantage for clients that they did not become pregnant. To repeat, their advantage for the powerful men who pimped for the male prostitutes was that passive males remained physically stronger than females; they not only helped power their lords' authority, but facilitated the construction of male networks of power through using their sexuality with other men.

We are woefully underinformed on the question of the type of sexual activity these berdaches engaged in, and can only be confident that individual participants in homosexual encounters rarely if ever exchanged sexual roles with each other.[69] In the absence of direct evidence, one would assume from the silence of the literature that anal penetration was the usual mode of intercourse, and signally so in public homosexual activity. Still, let us not jump to conclusions. We are informed by Oviedo, for example, that several wives of certain powerful caciques in the Tierra Firme specialized in 'viper copulation' or fellation of their masters, and it would be surprising if the male prostitutes of powerful men did not have the same range of professional specialties at this time.[70]

There is indeed modern evidence that the berdaches of some tribes in the northern plains and in the Northwestern United States were not penetrated rectally, but only orally. Holder, who served as physician to the Crow for two years in the 1880s, went so far as to distinguish the fellating 'bote' type from the passive anal receptor berdaches he knew from another physician, Hammond, to be usual among the Pueblo nations.[71] Interestingly, Holder implies that the berdache as fellator might be on the average older than the anal-receptive berdache of other nations, which is of some interest given my earlier distinction between those who became berdaches when young and those who assumed that status at an older age – at an age, that is, when at least in the European experience passive males lost their sexual attractiveness to actives. Perhaps in some tribes fellatio was the assigned task of berdaches too young to undergo anal penetration without damage, and it may have been the customary form of berdache sexual comportment in whole tribes. It would be wise to keep all our options open when we know so little.

Domestic services

When the Mexican temple priests span and wove cloth as did women, and when on the feasts of Ochpaniztli and Xochiquetzal male impersonators bore not only the flayed skins of sacrificed women, but those women's instruments of spinning and weaving,[72] their gestures of dominance over earthly women spoke to the world of submissives below the temple.

While every source at our disposal says that berdaches performed the 'offices of women,' these were thought to be so self-explanatory that only two of them state what they were. In 1526 Oviedo cites sweeping and washing to exemplify 'women's offices,'[73] and in 1601 Herrera says that the duties of Nicaraguan women included grinding corn, spinning and cooking.[74]

Clearly, these were occupations the Iberians themselves assumed to be female in character, yet our sources, especially Cieza de León, are alert to some important differences between the peninsular and the native divisions of labor. Speaking of those living near Quito, for instance, Cieza noted that 'it is the women who till the fields and care for the plantings and the harvests, and the husbands who spin and weave and occupy themselves in making clothing *and other women's work.*' Cieza uses much the same language to describe the genders of work in the province of Cañari.[75] This presented the Iberians with a problem and a paradox. The problem was that, quite apart from their sexual behavior, some of their new male subjects 'unnaturally' did what the Iberians *knew* to be female things. Though not reported, a paradox certainly existed in that, among such tribes, the berdaches, though said to be unnatural in their sexual expression, given their transvestism as women, had 'natural' work habits as far as the Europeans were concerned.

The American berdaches performed these 'domestic services' in two distinct contexts. The first was the marital estate (*casado*), in which the berdache lived with a single other man, the second was the company of women. First, marriages: in a late nineteenth-century report by an erstwhile prisoner of the Chipewa, John Tanner tells of being (unsuccessfully) seduced by a 50-year-old berdache who, he said, 'had lived with several husbands.'[76] The implication of that remark bears emphasis: the active partner in homosexual liaisons might, as an active, move from passive to passive. As Las Casas and others emphasize, fathers procured passives to live or at least copulate with their sons in temporary marriage, until such a time as those sons began sexual relations with their wives.[77] But what was a temporary matter for the active male was never so for the passive one. As the Jesuits Marquette and Lafitau knew three centuries ago, a fundamental characteristic of the berdaches was that, once they assumed women's attire, they bore it for the rest of their lives, and 'they never [heterosexually] married.'[78] Thus, much as with a woman, from the moment a boy or a young man assumed the *nagua* until he died, a reliable and durable 'marriage' of some type afforded the berdache his only hope of survival, security and protection. It was the passive and not the active who was constantly abandoned and widowed, the transvested passive and not the active party to homosexual liaisons who performed the services 'of a woman.'

Without doubt, an important number of berdaches across the Americas were 'married' to, or lived with, active male husbands, to whom they provided domestic services. The earliest reference to this arrangement may come from Núñez Cabeza de Vaca, who told of seeing 'a man married to another man' in his 1534 trek across today's eastern Texas. Recall that Núñez Cabeza thought the 'effeminate' partner to this marriage was a eunuch, and that Lopez de Gómara essentially repeated this information in his 1552 *Historia*.[79] In the meantime, in 1540 Pedro Castañeda saw 'men dressed like women who marry other men and serve as their wives' in Sinaloa, along the Gulf of California.[80] Contemporaneously, the mid-sixteenth-century Jesuit Nóbrega already found the custom of berdache marriages widespread among the Portuguese settlers of coastal Brazil, who were taking native berdaches as wives 'according to the custom of the land.'[81] Next, we may recall that marriageable males among the Laches of the western Andes (Colombia) were said to show a preference for berdache wives. Finally, eighteenth-century Franciscan missionaries still encountered unions of this type among native Californians.[82] The institution of homosexual marriages or common domicile was apparently found in many different areas of today's Latin America.

From the aforesaid, the marriage hearth appears the obvious place in which the berdache would perform women's work, or at least the stated tasks of sweeping, washing, corn grinding and cooking. According to this model, the active male in these agrarian and hunting-gathering societies followed his interest, which was to have a strong 'wife' as his partner. As Piedrahita said of the Laches, their active males knew, perhaps first from their days as warriors, that berdaches 'performed the duties of women with the robustness of men,' and so 'married them as if they were women and preferred them to actual women.'[83] Nor was he alone in this sentiment. In his description of the Acagchemem tribe (San Juan Capistrano, California) about 1822, Fray Gerónimo Boscana wrote that, 'being more robust than the women, [berdaches, who had been selected as infants] were better able to perform the arduous duties of the wife, and for this reason they were often selected *by the chiefs* and others ...'[84] Thus potential husbands, and not only those who were too poor to afford wives, but also those who were in the best financial position to practice polygyny, certainly looked on berdaches as valuable economic assets because they were biological males; and, vice versa, the berdaches certainly looked on such 'husbands' as guarantors of their well-being. In East Africa, in fact, Shepherd has found the economic character of such unions much more fundamental than the sexual tie.[85]

As is already evident in Núñez Cabeza de Vaca's report, an occasional source does indeed link a report of homosexual marriage to the statement that the 'wife' in question performed 'female offices.' But truth be told, the berdache marriage is fairly uncommon when compared with the innumerable times our sources simply call attention to the berdache's 'womanly' character. In fact, only indirect information surfaces on where berdaches bedded, and even less on where they spent their waking hours. Enough is known, however, to make it unwise indeed to think that the berdache's function in native society was either inside a homosexual marriage or outside, one way or the other. A century ago, Holder warned against simplification when he noted that, though a Crow berdache might live constantly in a marital partnership, s/he still was 'ready to accommodate any male desiring his services,' like any female member of the tribe.[86]

Retreating to our own time period, we must again take an example from the woman's world to demonstrate exactly what I mean. Cieza de León notes at a certain point that Cañari men 'gave us a large number of women to carry our luggage.'[87] Can one doubt that the berdaches of this same tribe were also objects of gifting and exchange, perhaps especially for load-bearing, a task that belonged to their division of labor among other native peoples, as we have seen? In conversation with the Europeans, native men indeed often dismissed the significance of their berdaches precisely because they did the same things women did.

We are now confronted with a fundamental native, as well as Iberian, ambivalence about where these males belonged once they assumed the clothes and demeanor of a female. On the one hand, our work has often described the crucial roles berdaches played for men in these patriarchal societies: in the military and religious spheres, in the communal sphere as sexual objects for leading men, and so forth. On the other, until the end of this work we shall meet with the notion that the berdaches, once having assumed the *nagua*, not only did women's work, but spent their time in women's space.[88] A vivid image can create this spaciality, one described by Hammond when in 1851 an old Laguna Pueblo chief took him to meet the village berdache:

> We therefore at once proceeded to the place where the public corn was being ground by the women detailed that day for the purpose. On entering the room . . ., we found about a dozen women on their knees before the *metates* . . . The chief spoke a few words, when immediately one, whom I would not have been able to distinguish on a cursory inspection from any of the others, rose and came towards us. '*Aqui esta el mujerado*' – 'Here is the *mujerado*,' said the old chief. 'You can do what you please with him.'[89]

In this women's space, the berdaches of an earlier period as well may indeed not only have swept or ground corn, but also spun and woven, 'domestic' activities, that is, that might produce objects not just for local consumption but also for trade. Unsurprisingly given the often superficial quality of our sources, I cannot confirm this notion in sixteenth- and seventeenth-century sources, although to this day the descendants of the American berdaches, alone among males, in some regions still do make such gender-specific objects.[90] My suspicion that the ancient berdaches did perform such tasks is heightened by the awareness of early observers that the berdache's advantage over other women consisted in his 'robustness' or strength. If husbands chose berdaches as wives on that score, there is every reason to believe that the berdache would have dominated women's space precisely because of that strength. Whitehead has noted that modern American berdaches were in fact sometimes placed in control of female production units.[91] Again, our much earlier sources cannot be expected to confirm such a detail, and they do not. Yet if the Latin sources prove unyielding on this question, the economic character of the berdache, quite convincingly demonstrated in other parts of the world, deserves further exploration.[92]

Women, Homosexual Behavior and the
Population Collapse

According to the European sources, American women hated the native berdaches; these sentiments will be examined in the next chapter. To conclude this chapter on quotidian behavioral realities, however, I shall here limit myself to describing and evaluating those behavioral interactions that link women to berdaches, or to male homosexual behavior.

Anal intercourse, of course, provides the foundation for such linkage, for men could physically practice it as readily with women as with other men. In the normal course of events, however, the earliest Iberian sources rarely refer to male anal intercourse with women, though they of course recognized that it, like similar concourse with males, prevented conception.[93] The only exceptions to this rule are the Iberians' descriptions of heterosexual marriage ceremonies among natives. At least two sources claim that, before the bride and groom retired on their wedding night, all the males of the groom's tribe had the right to take their pleasure with the bride. Thus in 1552 Gómara tells of Cuban brides going about naked on their wedding night, seducing any and all available men.[94] Then, referring to the Mantan tribes of today's Ecuador, Garcilaso de la Vega, perhaps describing anal intercourse, said they 'made it a condition of marriage that the bridegroom's relatives and friends enjoyed the bride before he did.'[95]

It was left to the Augustinian friar Calancha writing in the 1620s to exploit fully the anal linkage. He describes a sexual practice that had changed radically over time in the Pacasmayo valleys of northern Peru. Originally, he says, these natives had been much given to homosexual 'sodomy' – here using the word to refer to anal intercourse. Now things had changed:

> Today they are not free of this contagion, the wife being the accomplice. If as gentiles the accomplices were males, today [as Christians] they use matrimony to cover the treason done to nature, robbing from generation what they give sensuality.[96]

Clearly, Calancha believed that heterosexual anal intercourse had only recently spread, as the homosexual variety was suppressed. But this was not the only newfound evil. Somewhat earlier in his chronicle he had painted a picture of lesbian sexuality:

Today in the plains between Payta and Guarmey there is great damage; it has been some years since one began to use this iniquity. The accomplices are not man and man, but Indian woman and Indian woman.[97]

In the same text, he then reverts to the subject of heterosexual anal intercourse, and continues:

The dissolution [of sodomy] has become so public that as recognition that an Indian woman has committed this nefandous sin [with a man] for the first time, the man gives her a festive new dress, which they call a *capuz con listas*, so that everyone who knows of this evil custom knows about her abomination.

Calancha's detailed attention to the modalities of sodomy, and especially his sense that the heterosexual practice of anal intercourse was recent, was, as his reference to failing 'generation' intimates, brought on by the catastrophic decline in native population beginning in the last third of the sixteenth century. He asks:

What has caused the annihilation of the villages of the plains, so that their Indians no longer travel to the quicksilver, gold or silver mines? [Villagers] from the mountains grow in population in the mines, even as those [in the plains], more decimated, decline.

The answer was simple: God had consumed those guilty of sodomy and 'purified' their pueblos because they did not reform. What was needed was civil punishment to match the divinity's. After describing the alleged spread of marital sodomy, Calancha drew attention to, so as to praise the penalties he claimed the Incas had once levied against sodomy, then drew the obvious moral: 'Then when many were burned, there were thousands upon thousands of Indians. Today no one is killed and the pueblos are annihilated, without Indians. God castigates when judges don't judge.'[98] This typically terrifying man of God seems to have believed that, if the Spaniards started burning the natives, the population would rebound in the midst of illness and colonial repression.

For Iberians of this type, women had become part of the problem of male sexuality because they were evidently not bearing children. Thus Reginaldo de Lizárraga wrote about 1611 that God had punished the valley natives near the Pacific Ocean with low population because, once their mates were pregnant, husbands promptly practiced anal intercourse with someone else – as if, given the population emergency, he should have gone on to impregnate some other woman. Indeed, Lizárraga drove home that point by railing against men who married (post-menopausal) women because young girls *no saben servir*.[99] Much has been written about the pandemics of this period as causing the population collapse, and I would not gainsay the demographers' reading of the evidence. But many Iberians believed that, quite apart from diseases, the population was in decline because males and females, horrified at the future their children would surely face, avoided heterosexual intercourse. So bad was Mexican life, Zorita had already written in the mid-sixteenth century, that males conspired to avoid intercourse with all women.[100]

He meant, of course, heterosexual intercourse. For millions of American men, consigned by force to the mines of the Spanish realm, homosexual encounters, doubtless arranged with the same respect for age hierarchy as ever, obviously provided the only semblance of mutual carnal and emotional satisfaction available to two or more men.[101] The same must be surmised for the abandoned women who lived out their hopeless lives on the land, separated from their garrisoned mates. The awful arm of power laid heavy on the institution of the berdache. Only the Spanish *picada* forced all men, and not just the berdaches, to subjugate themselves to it.

7
Attitudes and Assessments

This filthy vice . . ., so vile and shameful, especially among the passives.[1]

See how just is God, to give them [syphilis] where [sodomy] is practiced.[2]

The dynamics evident in the organization of the previous chapters derive from three fundamental views about the means humans dispose of in creating knowledge. First, dealing with American sexual institutions, this work began by presenting a moral cartography of European sexuality, because we can only study American sexual institutions of this time through European sources. Second, I approached American sexuality from the field of battle, because I view warfare as the incubator of civil institutions, rather than believing, as do many scholars, that military institutions employed outside were created inside by 'civil,' read civilized, citizens. Third, to study the domestic practices of transvestism and homosexual comportment, I started on the mountain outside, before coming down into the village. I did so not because of a trickle-down elitist view of the nature of cultural contagion, but rather because the mountain, the religious field, is among the first organized and most enduring behavioral representations of the experiences gleaned from external warfare.

In all this, I have tried to avoid the presumption that actions are derived from ideas, with all that presumption's lazy if sometimes useful pitfalls. And that is why only toward the end of this work do I now turn to the ideas and attitudes that native Americans and Europeans had about homosexual relations, ideas which they, of course, erroneously believed explained homosexual actions and made them moral or immoral. Some readers will also decide that the ideational materials in this chapter do in fact explain what has gone before, rather than vice versa. In that case, the organization of the materials in the present chapter should facilitate their prejudice.

The materials are introduced as follows. I first present different histories of sodomy, as they emerge from Iberian sources. There appears to be no comparable native history of sodomy, though, as we shall see, at least one colonial historian wanted us to believe there was. Next comes the exposition of first native, and then Iberian, attitudes toward homosexual behavior, another difficult part of the work to articulate, given the constant filtering of such attitudes through European sources. The chapter concludes with comparisons of the native view with the peninsular one.

Histories of Sodomy

The Europeans who are our sources for American institutions did not want for long views on homosexual practices, but they had no similar generalizations to offer about male transvestism. This is probably because they came to the Americas armed with the one and not the other. While homosexual comportments were an ongoing reality in Europe, the durable male transvestism of the berdache type Europeans encountered in the Americas was rare in Europe. Inversely, transvestism had broad social applications in the games of European festivities, and even beyond the feastday governments sometimes encouraged prostitutes to transvest in order to seduce young men into 'decent' heterosexuality. Thus laws against transvestism were often not taken seriously, and so it was not the kind of topic that engaged social critics. That is, traditional Europeans in general were much readier to think of transvestism as a normal product of social interchange than they were to regard sexuality in the same way. All that having been said, however, the Europeans found transvestism to be an unsurprising accompaniment of homosexual 'infection,' because, while they might not be accustomed to European passives dressed permanently as women, they shared the American view that sexual passivity was womanly.

The active giants from the sea

From several areas of America, and especially from the region of Puerto Viejo (Ecuador), come reports of races of giants that once lived in these parts. They sometimes appear as a 'first race,' conquered or superseded by a historical people, such as the giant Central American race of the Quinomes, who according to tradition were overcome by the Olmecs. And sometimes they are said to have been 'sodomites,' that is, actives. In the case of the Quinomes, these men are said to have insisted on penetrating enemy males even though they had all the beautiful women they might desire at their beck and call.[3]

The giants of Ecuador and Peru were different, for in their more conventional story they turned to homosexual behavior because of the unavailability of women. It is a native legend that we witness the Spaniards transforming into one readable with European lenses. As told by those around Puerto Viejo, the story went that, sometime between the distant past and that of a century ago, giants appeared from the sea and settled in today's Ecuador. In some native accounts, they died out because they had no women with them and could not reproduce through local ones, whose vaginas were too small; in others, the giants raped the local women, who all promptly died of their wounds without reproducing. Some of these native accounts may have concluded by stating that the giants then turned to sodomy.[4]

Laid out in this fashion, the story explained to many Spaniards why, according to all reports, there were so many public homosexual acts in precisely this area of the Inca realm, the first Andean region conquered by the peninsulars. But what the latter did with this wisp of a legend was amazing. Combining the native tale with the public sexual practices they witnessed, many of the conquering historians easily recognized in these events a replay of the story of biblical Sodom. An artist who illustrated the demise of the giants at the hands of a wrathful fiery heaven for an early edition of Cieza de León's *Historia* (see figure 11) perhaps innocently added the figure of the archangel Michael carrying out the will of heaven. Perhaps on seeing this drawing, and certainly on hearing that a 'beautiful boy' had announced their impending demise to the giants, a Christian historian such as Calancha immediately knew that the visionary fine young man had been an angel, a fact Calancha said was hidden from the benighted natives because they 'did not know what an angel was.' Everything fit into place: the beautiful boy whom the Indians desired, to their ruin, was the seductive angel who appeared to Lot on the eve of the destruction of Sodom.[5] History had repeated itself. In the words of Zárate, writing in the mid-sixteenth century, 'since these [giants] were much given to unnatural vice, divine justice removed them from the earth, sending an angel for that purpose, *as at Sodom and other places.*'[6]

opiniones de el vulgo, y sus dichos varios, que siempre engrandece las cosas mas delo que fueron.

Cuentan los naturales por relacion que oyeron de sus padres, la qual ellos tuuieron y tenian de muy a-

Figure 11   St Michael destroys the Sodomitic Giant.

This is not the place to analyze the growth of this story: Cobo's determination that the giants came from Tierra del Fuego, 'since to this day men of more than ordinary stature live in this land,'[7] or Gutiérrez's suspicion that they instead came from the area of New Guinea[8] – the basic myth of Kon Tiki. Nor can the Spaniards' fascinating paleontological search for giants' bones throughout the Andes be detailed.[9] For our purposes, the important ideological element in this tale is its structural character. The giants of Puerto Viejo represented a particularly cataclysmic explanation for a basic principle of sexual lore in these times: the principle of sexual infection. And the important historical causality it yielded explained the outspokenly public character of homosexual interaction in these coastal equatorial societies: such behavior remained monstrous, even if the monsters had died off.

The principle of infection

There is no evidence in the Americas, or in medieval or early modern Europe, of the modern view that homosexual behavior was a normal and predictable part of social interchange. Cieza de León came close. In distinguishing levels of homosexual behavior in Peru, Cieza recognized that, of course, every populace harbored an occasional 'sinner' of this type. In fact, however, Cieza if pressed would have added that, just as surely, such behavior had become universal by spreading like a disease. This is the notion of all the sources: the unit under discussion is not the social facts surrounding the practitioners, but rather the act itself. Sodomy was essentially a pathology that spread from one area to another. In the language of the sources, it was 'contagious.'[10]

But what was the 'act itself,' or, more exactly, who became infected? Was it the passive's reception that was contagious for him, or the actor's penetration, or, indistinguishably, the 'unnatural' and yet contagious union of both individuals to both of them? The question is comparable with that raised earlier about what exactly was *contra naturam* in homosexual copulation. Let it be said now that, at least from the time of the medieval philosopher Albert the Great, the notions of pathology and contagion, in general, appear to have been associated mostly with the passive, who could not be turned away from such behavior once he had often enough received the penis.[11] It will not surprise the reader that the sources offer no explanation for the mechanism of such contagion.[12]

The contagions described by our sources were vertical and horizontal in nature. Vertical contagion proceeded in different ways, the first being from divinities to humans. Cieza de León, for instance, explains the existence of temple homosexual behavior in coastal Peru in a chapter entitled: 'How the demon gave the Indians of these parts to understand that it was a pleasing offering to their gods to keep Indians who would assist in the temples, so that the lords could know them, committing the most grave sin of sodomy.'[13] How was this done? In certain temples of the Americas the devil or demons spoke to their followers, Pachacamac being one of these. It was in these temples, according to Cieza, that the devil told those soliciting his responses that for lords to sodomize these boys was divinely pleasing.[14]

At about the same time, Las Casas described the same phenomenon for the Guatemalan area, which had, he claimed, previously been free of homosexual actions: the demon Cu (elsewhere Chan, Cavil, Maran) appeared in a vision and performed the act with another demon before his audience. Thus the natives came to believe that homosexual comportments were licit, and practiced them without constraint.[15] Torquemada elaborated on Las Casas's statement: the demon appeared in the form of a young man (*mancebo*) and proceeded to represent the act with another demon, who was a *niño*. After that, many of the natives came to believe that sodomy was not sinful. It was then that the fathers started giving their sons young berdaches for their pre-marital sexual pleasure.[16]

In addition to such divine pedagogy – a justification for homosexual behavior that was not unknown in Europe – another form of vertical pedagogy was on the minds of reporters: contagion downward from the top of the social ladder. The most striking case of this is Peter Martyr's report of the homosexual behavior Balboa encountered in the village of Quarequa on his trek across Panama to the Pacific Ocean in 1513. It was a practice of courtiers, concealed from the average people, Peter tells us.

> When the natives learned about it . . ., they spit upon those whom they suspected to be guilty of this vice. They begged [Balboa] to exterminate them, for the contagion was confined to the courtiers and had not yet spread to the people. Raising their eyes and their hands to heaven, they gave it to be understood that God held this sin in horror, punishing it by sending lightning and thunder, and frequent inundations which destroyed the crops. It was likewise the cause of famine and sickness.[17]

Imaginative this description certainly is; the whole segment on God's punishment is standard European fare, derived from the laws of

Justinian.[18] But the concern of the Europeans about the status of the practice was real. In another case, we find Oviedo bemoaning the fact that it had trickled down into the mass of the people, who imitate their rulers.[19]

Finally, one repeatedly encounters the claim that homosexual behavior passed horizontally, from one tribe to another. At the very outset of the conquests, Michele di Cuneo opined that the Caribbean Arawaks had 'caught' sodomy from the 'wilder' Caribs coming from the Tierra Firme of South America: they had perhaps seen the latter raping the former, and taken to it themselves.[20] And in the above referenced passage, Oviedo describes at length the 'spread' of homosexual behavior throughout Hispaniola and the Tierra Firme.

This was an old European saw, of course. We have seen the coastal Valencians and Catalonians fearing 'infection' by Italian merchants. Even the usually more subtle Gilberto Freyre insists that the Portuguese were lax in these matters because Italians came to do business in the port of Lisbon, and, despite the evidence, Brazilian indigenous peoples to this day believe that the 'contagion' arrived with the European whites.[21] Is there any doubt that such fantasies – alive and well in today's industrialized world in the fear gays will 'infect' children – all derive from the powerful if archaic notion that in its origins, before being corrupted by outsiders and their baleful influences, one's own heroic people had been free and innocent?

That notion of primordial innocence corrupted proved especially useful in accounting for the decline of great powers, such as the Inca or *orejones*, and here too the appropriate myth was not wanting. The mid-sixteenth-century Jesuit Joseph Acosta described the lecherous barbarians of the lowlands who surrounded the Andean Inca,[22] and in the early seventeenth century Fernando Montesinos named the Tierra Firme, lowland Brazilians, Tucumani, and Mantans as responsible for Incaic moral decline: they had ascended the mountains and, he gives us to understand, corrupted the hitherto innocent, if powerful, residents of Cuzco.[23] Thus the last mode of infection was from below, from the barbarians of the coastlines.

The coming of civilization

One of the unquestioned presumptions of the Iberian sources was that widespread homosexual behavior marked a tribe as barbaric. In Acosta's scheme, for example, there was a plateau on the road out of barbarism toward civilization where one had left cannibalism and human sacrifice behind but still practiced sodomy.[24] Many of the same sources desperately wanted to make a second presumption, whatever the evidence to the contrary, and that was that power and civilization proceeded upward in tandem. If not for a man such as Las Casas, then certainly for many other contemporaries, these two postulates in combination made for a third, often unspoken assumption that powerless nations were sodomitic, while the great empires of the American world, those of the Aztecs and Incas, were marvelously free and intolerant of such practice. This view was eminently useful, because the Iberians tried to rule by assuming the mantle of Aztec and Inca legitimacy that had extended over a good part of the American world.

While such notions of innocent power definitely extended to the Aztecs, the realm of the Incas was to prove the promised land for historians determined to elaborate such a past. The effort began unpretentiously enough in the pages of Cieza de León, who was not particularly an apologist for the Inca. It then realized its fruition in the *Royal Commentaries* of Garcilaso de la Vega, who, first among the major mestizo historians of Peru, projected a powerful vision of the Incas as a civilized people and their empire as the product of Incaic intellectual effort.

In many ways, Cieza de León adopted the position of his contemporary, Las Casas. With the exception of the area we call Ecuador, Cieza denied that homosexual behavior was public and common in the Andean world, and he resented statements to the contrary that had been made by earlier historians.[25] His claim that the Inca were free of the practice was, therefore, to a certain extent part of a more general argument against Oviedo and his descendants. Nevertheless, Cieza did not bypass the fact that the *orejones* had ruled over much of the Andes, and his comments in this regard did doubtless nourish the imagination of Garcilaso. In a chapter entitled 'How the Incas were Limpid of the Nefandous Sin and of Other Dirtinesses that are Found in other Princes of the World,' Cieza tells how the expanding Incas, as 'a people of great reason,' sought to suppress several practices, including cannibalism and sodomy, among 'those people who, before the Incas reigned, went about like savages.'[26] Not surprisingly, Cieza claimed that 'no one had ever said that any [of the Incas] had ever practiced that sin.' Indeed the whole tribe of the *orejones*, like many others, was free of the vice.[27] It was true that certain areas subordinate to the empire, especially that of Puerto Viejo (Ecuador), practiced homosexual acts, and that some places also featured temple sodomy. Cieza did his best to spare the lords:

perhaps the Incas did not know about this, or perhaps they decided to ignore it, as long as their subjects supported other Inca proscriptions and the cult to Inti, the sun.[28]

In all this, however, Cieza does not claim that homosexual behavior was outlawed. He does say that the Inca, with their 'santas y justas costunbres y leyes,' did outlaw and successfully suppress cannibalism among their subjects, but that is the size of it. Only in the Cuzco heartland are the Incas said by Cieza to have publicly shamed those found involved in the crime.

This modulated picture of moral relativism changed with Garcilaso de la Vega, writing a half-century later. Under his pen, a pan-imperial suppression of sodomitic behavior became part of a conscious Incaic process of civilization. Garcilaso was, in fact, determined to prove to the world that the Spaniards were not the first nor necessarily the greatest civilizing force to have swept across the Andes to the sea. Before the missionaries, the *orejones* had indeed come so far as to have essentially discovered the nature of the true, Christian, God![29]

The picture Garcilaso paints of his beloved nation is thoroughly Jewish and Old Testamental in character, a fact not sufficiently appreciated by many who have too easily swallowed the author's moral posture. The *orejones*, he said, exceedingly 'abominated' sodomy, ruler and people hating sodomy so much that they did not utter the word.[30] Thus, like Jews and Christians, the Incas too considered this the 'unmentionable sin.' Further, the *orejones* on conquering provinces for their empire punished homosexual behavior in a transparently Judeo-Christian fashion. On finding the vice hidden in some of the valleys along the northern sea coast, the Inca ordered that all accused 'sodomites' be burnt alive in the public square, their houses levelled, and the trees in their fields pulled up by the roots. Further, Garcilaso now has an 'inviolable law' prohibiting sodomy, which threatens to visit on all the penalty due any individual criminal.[31] All that was wanting to make this a completely recognizable European punishment was the sowing of salt on the land. The same cycle of punishments was also practiced on the Chinchas, including the laying waste of their fields, 'so that no memory should remain of anything the sodomites had planted with their hands,'[32] again, a commonplace European motivation for punishing homosexual comportment.

Much the same fate awaited other new subjects of the Incas, according to Garcilaso, and later authors have followed, largely uncritically. Thus the Augustinian Antonio de Calancha, writing not long afterwards, bemoaned the fact that the Spaniards were not punishing homosexual behavior as the Incas had done, and he blamed the decline of population on such judicial laxness, as we have seen.[33] More recently, Rowe has uncritically repeated not just Garcilaso but Calancha, the notion of Incan judicial rigorousness being so unquestioned that he does not bother actually to refer to those authors.[34] The Peruvian scholar Hector Cevallos Saavedra, in fact, went so far as to recommend that the 'just' legal strictures of the Incas against homosexual behavior be revived in contemporary Peru.[35]

The careful reader will grasp the way Garcilaso turned the ambivalent utterances of Cieza into the modern, powerful one-directional legend, and in any case we shall return to the question of whether the Incas or other peoples actually had laws against homosexual behavior. At this juncture, however, where we are examining the notion that the end of sodomy marks the achievement of civilization, there is a decisive point to be made about what underlying proposition Garcilaso was actually trying to drive home in these passages, what, that is, was at stake for this great mestizo scholar. It is an idea which, of course, other self-styled censors have difficulty appreciating.

That point is made by Garcilaso himself. It returns us to the gendered essence of conquest, emblematized in Cuzco and elsewhere by the great *picota* or *picana*, the penis-like 'prick' or gibbet for executions which in 1534, five years before Garcilaso's birth, Pizarro himself had had erected to found the Spanish city, taking a (subcutaneous?) slice out of it with his dagger as a mark of royal possession.[36] Conquest is in part about the gender of the competitors, and sixty years after the conquest *el Inga*, as Garcilaso was called, undertook to rescue the race of his mother from the imputation that the *orejones* were women. Another historian had written that Inca males spun cloth, and an outraged Garcilaso seized the occasion to retort. This was an understandable, but unacceptable, mistake of that historian, he said, for:

> Generally speaking there was no more manly people, or prouder of it, among all the pagans, than the Incas, nor any who so scorned feminine pursuits.[37]

This revelatory assertion, redolent of the submissiveness of the colonialized mentality, speaks volumes. Not only does it show how politicized was any Iberian description of the native division of labor. Further: who, in a nonpaternalistic society, would have thought to equate victory with maleness, and defeat with being a woman?

The rise of the Inca dynasty

While Garcilaso de la Vega does recognize that other peoples lived in Peru before the *orejones* arrived and erected Cuzco, in another sense they do appear *ex nihilo* in his account, for the author does not represent the Incas as having a moral history or development. Those coming before were savages. The Incas themselves came, and remained, civilized until they were overcome by the Spaniards. Yet even as *el Inga* was writing, the historiographic haze over pre-Incaic times had begun to lift. The now mostly lost works of Garcilaso's contemporary source, the mestizo Jesuit Blas Valera, for instance, provided a long list of pre-Inca 'kings,' which he claimed to have gotten from elder native scholars. Soon after, the priest-writer Fernando Montesinos seized upon this hot topic, and provided a dynamic, quasi-mythic history accounting for the rise of the *orejones*. In his *Memorias antiguas*, Montesinos told how invading barbarians from coasts, jungles, and the mountainous south had brought the highland kingdom of Peru from a flourishing imperial estate down into a spiral of decline from which there seemed no escape. The Incas had a moral history after all.

In Montesinos's account, the motor for this decline was homosexual behavior, which had reached alarming proportions in the kingdom. Salvation from this crash came from the insurgent dynasty of the Inca, which suppressed sodomy – bestiality, to use Montesinos's term – among the people of Cuzco. This decisive role of homoerotic behavior in the shaping of Andean historical epochs reminds one of the European notion that the biblical Flood was God's punishment for universal sodomy, which largely disappeared in the sequel, and of the story that all the world's sodomites died in the moment Jesus was born.[38] Despite its general familiarity, and despite the fact that, in the strict sense, Montesinos's tale is not fundamentally at odds with Garcilaso's notion of the Incas, the story is an important part of our analysis, for it shows credible moral and historical ambiguities emerging in the narration of Inca moral history.

Besides the environmental catastrophes which the people of Cuzco suffered in the latter days of the kings, Montesinos pointed to the rage of women against sodomy as a fundamental cause of the impending *coup d'état*:

Those who felt this calamity the most were the women, seeing that [the men] defrauded nature by not reproducing, and the women of their pleasures. In their meetings they dealt with nothing else but the miserable estate of little esteem at which they had arrived. They burned with resentment, seeing the men communicating among themselves the favors and gifts which were customarily theirs. They seized means to remedy the situation. They used herbs and [magical] arts, but nothing worked . . . [39]

We shall soon examine these alleged attitudes of women toward the 'unmentionable sin.'

Soon enough, the women found their leader in the person of Mama Ciuaco, a woman of royal blood, and her gifted sister, a witch who could talk to the demon. Allying herself with many men who disliked sodomy, Mama Ciuaco brought this exclusionary male bonding to an end through the instrumentality of her 20-year-old son Roca, who with her encouragement soon emerged as the first ruler (Inca) of the Inca dynasty, according to Montesinos. She convinced him that the Cuzceñans needed to return to the good old days of their ancestors, when everyone had obeyed natural law. Soon Inca Roca was addressing his fellows, trying to persuade them to follow him:

> Who doubts, my friends, the special love that my father the sun has for us . . . Vices and bestialities have been the fire that has consumed our greatness, which has been reduced to the point of disappearing. Everyone does what he wants . . . Instead of following the path of men, you walk that of animals. Valor has become so effeminized, that most of you have forgotten the sling and arrow.[40]

Having seized power and entertained his people with a week of festivities, Inca Roca got down to what, for today's historian, is the most fascinating part of this tale. On the command of his father the sun, and with the tender urging of his mother (and thus of her allied women), Inca Roca married 'so as to take care of the succession, and to replace those who had been lost in past pests and droughts.' Then on the next day, no fewer than 6,000 persons followed him into marriage. This was succeeded by a rigorous law that forever banned first any spilling of semen, and then any homosexual comportment, under the same penalties of cremation and destruction of property and trees which we have previously encountered.[41] Following these marriages, the men fell out to assume once again the military training of their ancestors, in short, to 'become men' again. Such was the beginning of the great dynasty of the Incas, according to Montesinos.

The decline of the Incas?

Doubtless, this author wanted to create the impression that, in a historic moment of ecological disaster and native population decline, the Incas had risen to power by adopting a strict moral stance favoring marriage and procreation and condemning sodomy. However, Montesinos would go beyond Garcilaso to reveal that, far from an unbroken series of virtuous Incas having reigned up till the Spanish conquest, the moral record was mixed. Indeed, the evidence for this other reading of Inca history was already piling up in Montesinos's historiographic predecessors.

Thus about 1613, some years before Montesinos, the native but, significantly, not Incaic historian Juan de Santa Cruz Pachacuti wrote that the second Inca, Sinchi Roca, 'always enjoyed pleasures, and, so that he could get used to fornication, they say he ordered them to search for men-women [that is, homosexual passives]. This is how they got so many [sexual] offerings, for the Indians brought them as presents. They say this unhappy Inca was barely able to have one son, Inca Lloque Yupanqui.'[42] Montesinos, then, merely filled in some of the blanks about the 'very sagacious' Inca Sinchi Roca. While not personally accused of homosexual behavior, Sinchi Roca presided over a period when 'the nefandous sin was very acceptable. The king did little to remedy this, so as not to alienate his vassals.'[43] Revealingly, Montesinos again picks up the theme of the alienation of women which, in his view, resulted from male sexual bonding:

> Those who were most affected by [such behavior] were the women. They got so out of sorts that they ordered the killing of many males by magic, maleficence that they practiced by means of *ariolos* and wizards; they also used love magic. This got to such a point that they killed many of the *principales*. The Inca Sinchi Roca called a meeting . . . [44]

The attribution of homosexual inclinations of one type or another continued. Santa Cruz Pachacuti alleged that Lloque Yupanqui, son of Sinchi Roca, though he punished sodomy in others, 'did not have relations with women until very old . . . He ordered all men to shave their beard to be like him, beardless . . ., and he raised many boys who were not to have relations with women. Later, these [boys] became passives for the soldiers at war.'[45] Buenaventura de Salinas upped the ante in 1630 by claiming that the same Inca 'had perfidious inclinations, being lascivious and given to idleness.'[46] In 1631 it was the turn of Mayta Capac Amaro, fourth in the classic line. Giovanni Anello Oliva says that this ruler 'had such a distaste for relations and intercourse with women, even the most beautiful. And despite being married to . . . the prettiest princess of that time, he never lived with her.'[47]

Let there be no mistake: these rulers, comprising the first four or five of the classic line imagined by the Spaniards, are not historically documented, but rather legendary sovereigns, whose names and reigns were dutifully passed on by elderly Inca intellectuals to their eager Spanish colleagues. I am, therefore, not making a case against any individual. The point is that it seems writers of the seventeenth century were proceeding through the canonized list of Incas and attributing sexual 'peculiarities' to one after the other. Nor did this practice limit itself to the earliest Incas. Certainly the most significant allegation among these early seventeenth-century Spanish writers was that the quite real imperial giant Pachacuti Inca (ca. 1438–71) was accused. Buenaventura de Salinas, copied by Calancha in 1638, wrote that this Inca 'was given to all sort of abominations, and during his time most people were sodomites, and this is why God locked the skies so that there was no rain for seven years.'[48]

Given that precedent, it is not surprising that Santa Cruz Pachacuti accused Huascar himself, the Inca whose power struggle with Ata- hualpa weakened the *orejones* at the moment of the Spanish invasion, of a terrible crime, one condemned at the time by the local rulers (*curacas*). He is said to have summoned all the local royal virgins (*acllas*) into the festive main square of Pomapampa, south of Cuzco, then ordering his minions to 'assault each one of the virgins, to use the [sin of] bestiality in public act, like the sheep of this land.' The text makes clear that Huascar meant this as his sacrifice to a sky divinity.[49] Whether this happened or not is less important than that an (indigenous!) historian thought such an act by an Inca credible. It decisively links *orejone* sexual practices to the temple practices with berdaches from which Cieza and Garcilaso had wanted to distance the Incas.

In reviewing the material above, it becomes evident that, despite Cieza's and Garcilaso's attempt to picture the imperial Inca as free of homosexual behaviors, there was just as powerful an inverse drive among slightly later authors. All allegedly deriving their information from elderly *orejones*, they might like Montesinos have the Incas rise to power as moral crusaders, but they picture the ruling line as, once having established its power, having its share of men who did not like women, but, alas, no women to rescue the 'effeminate' men from themselves, as had Mama Ciuaco long before.

Native Attitudes

We turn now away from early Spanish models of Andean moral history, and attempt to determine the attitudes that natives had toward transvestism and homosexual behavior. Such an attempt to unearth, much less generalize about these norms will, of course, be fraught with danger. Iberians and not natives, after all, were the almost exclusive recorders of such alleged norms. True, toward the end of the sixteenth century a group of impressive mestizo historians began to search out the 'true history' of America, and no one would deny the importance of what they have to say to our knowledge of the pre-Conquest past. In the last section, however, we have uncovered a second danger to our impending study of native attitudes, which derives in the first place from those mestizos. They were preoccupied with making their American ancestors appear, like their Iberian masters, *manly*. The historiographic gendering of the conquest and of colonial mutuality presents obstacles to our reaching back past these historians to earlier reality.

Any student of modern native Americans knows that, almost without exception, they will deny that there is or has ever been homosexuality or cross-dressing in their tribe.[50] Of course, such ignorance is especially common today, because in fact tribal customs like that of the berdache have often been lost.[51] But the significant question is through what process they were lost. The answer, at least in part, is that martial Europeans could not tolerate the notion of 'womanized' males as an institutionalized part of successful, even imperial societies. When the mestizo Garcilaso, in his telling phrase, sought to outdo even the Romans by claiming that 'there was no more manly people, or prouder of it, among all the pagans, than the Incas, nor any who so scorned feminine pursuits,' he revealed that, at the very beginning of the colonial period, male natives and mestizos recognized that they would have to deny their female side, so to speak, a central part of their human self-definition, if they were ever to be able to forget their conquest and claim their (illusory) equality with the oppressors.[52] It was the linkage of the natives' actual defeat to their own traditional rulership over their women, in part perhaps through men dressed as women, that was the essence of this denial.

This shame of many mestizo historians in their berdaches and in these peoples' homosexual behavior needs, therefore, to be watched for in the following pages, especially because many historians and anthropologists, on reading such denial, either share the sentiments of homophobia or discount them entirely as such. In fact, they are a product of history that, once understood, can be valuable evidence in itself. That is especially true in pursuing the question: did natives have laws against 'homosexuality'?

Law

Keep in mind from the start that this question is itself gender-specific in nature: only native men could have made such laws. With that in mind, we begin with the Incas, because they have generated the least evidence, though the most rhetoric, about laws against sodomy. Apparently the only evidence is contained in the so-called Anonymous Jesuit, usually attributed to Blas Valera, and dating to the end of the sixteenth century. This writer claimed the Incas did have a law, one that specifically prohibited homosexual activity. Citing a numbered law in a seemingly official fashion, this writer appears to paraphrase as follows:

> XX. Whoever commits the sin of sodomy is to be degraded and hung. Then he is to be burned with all his clothes. The same [happens] if he copulates with some animal.[53]

Yet neither the historians preceding nor those following the Anonymous do much to flesh out this notion of aboriginal legalism. Cieza, for instance, while claiming that the people of Cuzco themselves were above reproach, spent much time trying to explain why the Incas neither legislated against, nor punished, their other subjects for such comportment.[54] To be sure, Garcilaso, who fears his readers do not believe enough in the conquered Incas' manliness, does claim in the wake of the Anonymous that the Incas had prohibitions and penalties against practicing the 'sin,' but his report is so imprecise as not to distinguish between the active and passive partner to the act;[55] clearly, he sought to avoid the problem. And in the eighteenth century, in fact, the Dutch scholar De Pauw, who for his part was trying to prove the moral depravity of the indigenous American peoples, justly ridiculed Garcilaso on this score. As pointed out earlier, despite the desire of some modern Peruvians to 'return' to

Incaic law, there is substantial evidence that such laws did not, in fact, exist.[56]

Much the same can be said about the question of Inca punishment, as distinct from legislation. Usually, historians' statements that the Incas did punish were, and occasionally still are, transparent reveries for the 'good old days' with no substance. The one credible source on native sentiments might seem to be a group of aborigines who gave witness on whether sodomy had been punished and whether men had dressed as women in the south (Collasuyu) before the Spanish conquest. Their answers were transcribed by the Spanish authorities in 1571. As usual, most of these native men viewed cross-dressing as adopted *para usar*, as a step one took to play the passive; thus the reader of these responses cannot easily distinguish responses about punishments between the vestimentary and sexual questions. Still, the answers to these questions are unmistakably mixed. Of five groups responding, two said that the Incas punished 'it' when they encountered 'it,' but three were not ready to say so. Indeed, one witness stated positively that the passives involved (called *orua* in that region) were not punished but laughed at. The lesson is clear. Especially in light of the legends about giants, in which actives were punished by the heavens, it would be foolish to go further than to state that there is no credible evidence that the Incas punished by law homosexual behavior or transvestism. The fabled Incas were not, as Garcilaso would have it, haters of sodomy.

It will come as no surprise that, with the exception of one lapidary claim regarding Guatemala,[57] no region other than the Inca empire was said to have vice laws except Mexico, the other great empire of the American world. As always, the bigger and more powerful, the nearer were natives thought to be culturally similar to the Christians. Let us, however, say up front that around 1600, at the same time that Garcilaso was failing to convince some readers that, yes, the Incas had legislated against homosexual behavior, the same question as applied to the Aztecs was so open that the royal historiographer Antonio de Herrera came right out and said so:

Some say that in Mexico those who committed the nefandous sin were killed, others that one did not take [sodomy] seriously enough to legislate against it.[58]

Now we back up and follow the former group, mostly in the writings of early Franciscan friars.

As indicated earlier, the first detailed report on the general subject of Aztec sexual morality was filed in 1529 by the Franciscan lay brother Peter of Ghent, who claimed that homosexual behavior, and specifically passivity, was widespread among young and old.[59] That claim did not, however, fly. The interest of the Franciscans in Mexico was to represent the Aztecs to Spanish monarchs, who were moral because powerful, as naturally moral because powerful, so that those monarchs would entrust the Franciscans with the exclusive right to perfect these noble subjects.[60] Thus the story of Aztec legal actions against homosexual behavior emerges in the first full-scale work on that nation, written about 1538 by Toribio Motolinía:

> In the provinces of Mexico and Texcoco, and in those parts subject to these lords, the penalty of death was in place [for sodomy]. They not only do not permit it, but make incursions and search for such delinquents, as did the lord of Texcoco named Nezahualpilzintli. And his son Coauanacothzin, who later became lord of Texcoco, did the same as his father, making incursions and searching for those guilty of that bad evil crime, and publicly executing and hanging many of them. This [latter ruler] rose up to become a Christian and was baptized ... From this we can gather that they used natural law. They did not consider natural sexuality depraved or dark, but in this as in everything else they considered bad and outlawed everything that was against the Ten Commandments.[61]

From the beginning, therefore, the Franciscans searched for evidence that the Aztecs obeyed the Ten Commandments, in the form of natural law. The sagacious historian who knows Motolinía will, therefore, suspect that Coaunacothzin's alleged search for sodomites was connected in real life, as it is in Motolinía's text, to his baptism, the former hypothetically being a spoken or unspoken condition for the latter. It is but one last step to suspecting that the story that this prince's father, Nezahualpilzintli, made the laws against sodomy was retroactively invented to flatter the new convert. It was a standard enough move to entice young princes into the Christian camp.[62]

In 1543, shortly after Motolinía's work had been received in Spain, an otherwise unknown friar named Andrés de Alcobiz wrote that the series of laws he had just transcribed, which were observed in the Valley of Mexico, came from a work entitled *Historia de los Mexicanos por sus pinturas*. Among these 'laws' is one reading: 'They hung the passive [*puto*] and the active [*sométic*o] and the man they found dressed in women's clothes.' This more or less overlaps with Motolinía, which is not surprising because these so-called laws were found attached to the manuscript of Motolinía's *Memoriales*. Later writers, most importantly Las Casas, cited these 'laws.' Alas, for many reasons, their value is dubious.[63]

Motolinía's Franciscan follower, Geronimo Mendieta, was the first to expand his forerunner's relatively simple historical claims and ideology:

> Those who committed the nefandous sin, active and passive, were executed. And every now and then, judicial officials went to search them out, and inquired about them, so as to finish them off with death. For they were well aware that this so nefandous sin was against nature, because it is not found among the brute animals. Bestiality, however, was not found among the aboriginals. A male who went about dressed in women's clothes, and a woman who went about dressed in male clothes, both received death sentences.[64]

Thus in Mendieta, writing at the end of the sixteenth century, the Aztecs killed both the active and the passive partners; the berdache was outlawed, as were female transvestites. A fledgling principle of equality of punishment on multiple levels had been introduced, one which the contemporary monarchs of Spain had long since given up as unfair. Two forces were now in play. First, Mendieta was in effect pleading for a return to the good old Aztec days, when even passives and berdaches had been executed. Second, the mention of female berdaches may indicate that Mendieta was concerned by the catastrophic drop in population at that time.

The statement of Herrera at the turn of the century that there was no agreement on the matter of Mexican legalism regarding same-sex copulation did not immediately halt the flood of pro-Aztec statements in this area. Thus around 1606, Fernando de Alva Ixtlilxóchitl, a mestizo from Texcoco and related to the old ruling house, wrote that the great philosopher-king himself, Nezahualcoyotl – like some grave Jew or Roman – had punished traitors, revolutionaries and sodomites in that order. He had regularly hunted down the latter and had assigned quite distinct penalties to the passive and the active partner as follows:

> The nefandous sin [was punished] in two ways: through the lower parts, they removed the intestines from the one who served as a woman, who was tied to a post. And the boys of the city covered him with ashes, such that he came to be enclosed inside an artificial 'mountain.' And thereafter, they put a lot of kindling on top and set him on fire. And the one who served as a man they covered alive with ashes such that he came to be tied to a post until he died there.[65]

Authoritative as this statement might seem, on examination it appears largely to adhere to speech conventions used by the Franciscans friendly to the Aztecs, conventions that culminated in Juan de Torquemada's *Monarquia Indiana*, a work penned in the immediate wake of Ixtlilxóchitl's. Torquemada simply copied the latter's claims about Texcocan judicial traditions, and then paraphrased Mendieta's statements about the lords of Mexico, with two additions. He says that lesbian partners, who were both executed, were called *patlache*. And most curious – in the light of Peter of Ghent's outrage in 1529 about sodomitic practices among the temple priesthoods of Tenochtitlan – Torquemada claims that Mexican high priests caught in the nefandous sin were burned in some regions and hung in others.[66]

Thus the further one recedes from pre-conquest conditions and the more formally Christian the native leadership became, the more floridly assertive did the Franciscans and some mestizo nativists sound: before the conquest, these astute men basically claim, the lords of the Valley had been even more awful toward homosexual partners, including lesbians, than were their European counterparts, in that they heaped vengeance not only on actives, but upon passives as well. In its development, this historiographic tradition is a patent case of elaboration heaped on exaggeration to confirm a notion useful to its authors, and it says little for the common sense of many recent authors who still uncritically accept this sixteenth-century pap.[67]

Never mind contravening evidence, for example, the obviously anachronistic fact that toward the end of the century lesbianism is said to have been punished, whereas before that period of demographic collapse lesbianism went unmentioned. Or the absence from the Mapa de Quinatun, which illustrates Texcocan punishments, of Ixtlilxóchitl's disembowelment.[68] Or Herrera's statement in 1601 that many did not believe that homosexual behavior had been outlawed in Mexico. Or another mestizo historian's admission, contemporary to Ixtlilxóchitl, that in nearby Tlaxcala homosexual behavior, though unpopular, was not legally prohibited or punished.[69] Finally, never mind the historiographical record, which shows that two centuries ago the soundly ideological basis for the argument of Aztec judicial morality was clearly in place. In the 1770s, the Jesuit patriot Clavijero raged against the Dutchman De Pauw, who argued that the American races were degenerate. Even if it was true that sodomy was known in Mexico, wrote Clavijero, the Aztecs had strict laws against it.[70]

The present work is not, of course, arguing that the Aztecs did not harm certain persons practicing homosexuality, but only that there is precious little evidence of legal prohibitions. Indeed, what is revealing in the witness of Ixtlilxóchitl is this mestizo's recognition, by according their punishments differential attention, that actives and passives were not equal in cultural life. Indeed, in his account the stiffer punishment and the greater 'penalty of public shame' (*penas de vergüenza*) belonged to 'the one who served as a woman,' and s/he got most of the author's attention.[71] The customary, as distinct from legal, attitudes toward the berdaches will be dealt with in the following pages. For now, let it be said only that we have hit on an important aspect of native, but perhaps not just native, attitudes toward the partners to the homosexual act. A striking early text almost says it all. According to Oviedo, Nicaraguans were asked by the friars: 'What penalty is given to the sodomite (*puto*), whom you call *cuylon*, if he is the passive?'[72] Obviously, neither the locals, nor the friars, got very excited about the punishment of active practitioners.

Customary attitudes

Below the level of actual legislation lie worlds of customary proscriptions and tolerances among native peoples, at once the most fascinating and difficult to navigate and analyze. As with the study of so-called popular culture in Europe, so in grasping the native traditions of the ancient Americas, today's student must deal adequately with the fact that native traditions come down to us through so-called elite cultures, including in the Americas mestizo elites, that distort them to their own ends.[73]

These are male elite cultures, and our study has already shown how difficult it has been for this European or Hispanicized clerical culture to grasp the cultural forms – such as the alleged legal codes – projected by native males. The latter sometimes had a different, from the Iberian point of view more effeminate, division of labor than their European counterparts. Further, the former ruling men, though the talk was that they had become 'partners' in the colonial period, were in fact still conquered and thus still regarded as nationally effeminate or womanly. It was different with women's cultural forms, since both the Iberian and the native males considered them inferior. We start our examination of customary attitudes with native women's attitudes toward male homosexual comportment, as they are represented by the European writers.

First, a general observation. Beginning with the earliest sources, the Spaniards repeatedly assert that native American men maltreated native women:

> This is a people that thinks less of women than does any other nation on earth. For [the men] never communicate their business to them, even when they know that doing so would be in their interest.[74]

Gómara has the males of Rio de Palmas to the north maltreating their women, while, according to Zárate, south of the equator men did not like women any more.[75] And so it goes. There is interest here, to be sure. This oft-stated view helped make the Europeans, and especially the clergy, seem the defenders of women and, along with the flattery of children at the cost of their parents, this was a normal missionary strategy to neutralize the resistant older generation of (pagan) males.[76] Still, the allegation that, across the new Iberian realms, American women were treated badly does deserve our attention, especially because it comes from two of the most proudly misogynistic of contemporary European male cultures. Limiting ourselves purely to the obviously culturally determined notion that native women did much of the work for their men, it is clear that these reporters were impressed with what they saw.[77] Doubtless they did not see a great deal else, but their conviction on this score is, in any case, central to understanding what the Iberians said about native women's attitudes toward male homosexual behavior.

The general line came from Europe and was quickly applied across the American spectrum: women hated same-sex male sodomy. Early on, Oviedo assured his readers that this female hatred for homosexual sodomy was not, of course, 'due to their own principles, but more on account of their own interest.'[78] Uncustomarily, Las Casas chimed in with Oviedo, telling how an old Hispaniolan woman had told him in confession that, if sodomy had ever existed there, the women would have killed its practitioners or eaten them by the mouthful.[79] The essential in this male reading of the evidence is clear in Herrera. A professional caste of female prostitutes having been established in middle America precisely to prevent male homosexual behavior by selling sex, these public women stoned 'sodomites,' who were bad for business.[80]

But who exactly were the 'sodomites' the women are said to have hated? According to Oviedo, they were less the active partners, who were, after all, their own husbands – husbands were never accused of having been passives – than the passive ones. Describing the *mozos* whom the *señores y principales* kept around them, the author says that:

> These [passives] were extremely abominated by the women. But being very subject to their husbands, [the women] but infrequently dare speak to them about it, or to Christians.[81]

Thus the Iberians said that, in this paternalistic society, women hated the sweet-smelling berdaches who mimicked them, and not the men who were failing to copulate with them. Núñez de Pineda put it succinctly in describing the Araucanians: 'How can women not consider those men abominable and notorious who, doing what [the women] do, impudently rob them of their accustomed office?'[82]

There was, however, another side to this female hatred, according to the Spanish males, and that was male fear of female counter-attacks. The sources cited above as saying that males treated women badly usually explained this as resulting from males' homosexual preferences or preoccupations. So it was but a short step to Montesinos's notion that women might, after all, act against their husbands as well. Not only might they spitefully make themselves available to other men because their husbands were 'sodomites.'[83] If they 'saw their nature deceived and their pleasure unsatisfied,' they might take to killing men through types of amatory witchcraft.[84]

We certainly have no way of verifying this improbable scenario, dear as it has been to the fears of many paternalistic cultures. But on searching below the surface of such self-serving tales, a definite sense of genuine fear or concern may indeed be snatched. Often masked by slogans about women's lechery is a notion that, by developing sexual relations with men, the berdaches effectively isolated women from their husbands and thus made them vulnerable to desertion. If an active male chose not to fornicate with a particular woman, she could be excluded and exposed without protection. Through all the smoke that our ecclesiastical authors throw up, the Jesuit Montesinos hinted at an actual threat all women faced. We recall their resentment at the 'miserable state and low esteem they had reached,' and how they burned with jealousy of the berdaches. Was this sexual jealousy, or fear of abandonment?

In summary, for all the European sound of our sources' statements, there is certainly a modicum of truth in the assertion that women disliked berdaches. In a polygynous society of caciques and curacas, individual women must indeed have feared for their liveli-hoods, and been marginally more fearful of men playing women, to use the notion of the time, than of their husbands' other female spouses.

Passing now to the question of native male society's attitudes toward berdaches and homosexual acts, we face no want of problems, but they are of a more soluble character than the question of women's attitudes. Our conclusion may be stated at the beginning, quite apart from the question of whether berdaches were punished, and independent of the berdaches' undoubted importance for native societies. The governing attitude of male societies, one is tempted to say throughout the American world, was one of scorn for the men who dressed like, and assumed the tasks of, women.

Occasionally, our sources place these sentiments into the mouths of natives. Cieza de León, for example, says that the people of the Peruvian hills and valleys, on learning that one of theirs practiced the nefandous sin, 'shamed her [sic] greatly, called her a woman, and told her she should cease wearing the male clothing she bore.'[85] And the late sixteenth-century mestizo Muñoz Camargo, historian of Tlaxcala, criticizes first actives, then the berdaches: 'You bad and reckless men! Is there some lack of women in the world? And you berdaches, who assume the duties of women? Wouldn't it be better to be men?'[86] The Lampuna Indians around Guayaquil (Ecuador) ridiculed their neighbors the Chonos as 'dogs [and] queers' because they wore their hair short like women.[87] And further south, the slur *Asta Huayllas*, or 'May the men of Huayllas run after you,' refers to passives as well.[88]

While some of the above statements do echo Christian sentiments, they also reflect a certain truth about native mocking of such activity. Moving to a second and more common type of evidence on this score, one finds the Iberian sources, after describing native sodomy, simply stating that the indigenous peoples looked down upon certain of its practitioners. Thus the same Muñoz Camargo, obviously determined to rescue the 'honor' of his people in the eyes of the Spaniards, says that 'sodomites were looked down upon and thought less of and treated like women,' while the sin was 'considered a bad omen and an abuse.'[89] Torquemada said much the same. Though berdaches might take part in public festivals, this was truly a 'despised rabble, looked down upon and despised and not included in male society.'[90]

There is little to choose among perhaps a dozen such statements, and our time is better spent in an exact analysis of who exactly was being condemned. On this score, there can be no wavering. One does indeed encounter an occasional objection to the active party of the homosexual union; think of Soares's biting statement that the Brazilian natives considered mounting other men a sign of prowess, or of Cieza's curiosity at the fact that the sodomitic braves of the Manta area 'gloried' in their public penetrations.[91] Yet repeatedly, even when they do not specify sex role (which they commonly do), the equation our sources make between being of low status and being treated as a woman shows that, overwhelmingly, critics directed statements of this sort against berdaches, that is, against those presumed to be involved as passives in the homosexual act. Describing the Araucanians, Núñez de Pineda speaks in fact for many peoples. They:

> consider the nefandous sin vile and vituperous, with this difference: that he who practices the office of the male is not thereby shamed, as is he who subjects himself like a woman.[92]

The certain proof that the native males held this negative attitude emerges from the languages themselves. In their descriptions of native cultures, numerous Iberian writers recorded the words natives used to identify precisely the berdache, that is, the so-called passive partners in homosexual acts. These classificatory words were, in turn, often used as insults that one man directed against another, that is, also used against people who were not berdaches or did not engage in passive acts at all. Let us examine this linguistic evidence of ridicule.

The earliest information of this type comes from the royal historiographer Oviedo, who in describing a 1528 visit he made to Nicaragua says that, since 'there are *cuilones* (for they call the sodomite *cuilón*)' in that area, it was good to have female brothels.[93] The word is assumed to be Nahuatl, and was naturalized by Aztec garrisons in this outlier of the empire. We recall that this was the same word that the Aztecs hurled against the fleeing Spaniards on the Noche Triste; it thus assuredly refers to passive partners in homosexual behavior. Early in the seventeenth century, Herrera, in turn, confirms that it was a formal insult term: 'it was a despicable thing to be called *cuy lumpult*, which means consenting sodomite, and because of it they had fights with swords and shields and the challenge was allowed . . .'[94] Because of the Aztec Empire's extension, the word was probably the most widely used of any term of the type.[95]

Oviedo introduced a second such term into the European ken, the Chibcha word *camayoa*, used in the Panamanian province of Cueva. He carefully limited its use to 'those who are passives,' and noted it was an insult term: 'Thus among them, when an Indian wanted to insult another or vituperate someone who is effeminate and of little worth, they called her [sic] *camayoa*.'[96] The historiographic habit continued. From a native judicial witness in 1571 we learn that 'those who acted like women' in Collasuyu by dressing and rougeing themselves so were called *oruas*; they were not punished, just laughed at.[97] Though berdaches of the Guaicuru (Brazil) thought of themselves as women, tribesmen called them *cudiñas* (*castrati*); Mohave berdaches were named *alyhas*; Angolans in Brazil named their own passives *quimbandas*, who wore special dress, and so forth.[98]

Certainly the most precise source in this regard is Núñez de Pineda, writing about the Araucanians in 1673. This writer distinguished two types of shamans or *machis*. One type did not transvest, the other was composed of passive homosexuals (*hueyes* or *weye*), who did wear women's clothes, and who alone, to the exclusion of the active party, were considered vile and disgusting.

> These they call *hueies*, which in our [Castilian] language means nefandous or, still better, *putos*, which is the true meaning of the name *hueies*.[99]

The list of primary sources linking the names of passives to their derogatory usage against enemies could easily be extended by exploiting existing vocabularies.[100] But what is it that such statements say and do not say? To some, the existence of such a term indicated actual practice. Thus the sixteenth-century Huguenot missionary Jean de Lery notes that the Tupis of Brazil insulted each other with the term *tyvire*, meaning 'man with a broken behind' or passive partner, then concludes from this 'that the abominable sin is [possibly] committed amongst them.'[101] Oviedo had come to the same conclusion on seeing sculptures of one male mounted on another.[102] This is circumstantial evidence at best, and can say nothing about how widespread the practice was. The point being made here is rather about attitudes. In modern compilations, one occasionally encounters a native word for a homosexually involved active male,[103] but rarely is such a word encountered in the early colonial sources I have consulted.[104]

An exception helps make the point. In Nahuatl, the words 'ni-te-cuilontia,' as well as 'tecuilónti,' do refer to actives, but through highlighting passivity: they mean in fact 'I make someone into a passive,' as if to say that the passive is the substantive party, the one being identified through the ridicule of penetration.[105] The native attitude is unmistakable. For male culture at least, berdaches and passive homosexual partners, not actives at all, were the exclusive object of public scorn and ridicule. The reason for this hardly needs repeating. An active male in the homosexual act was doing the 'natural' thing: penetrating.

Let us conclude this section on native attitudes by observing that, in all this native disdain for the berdaches and their homosexual behavior, there is no native expectation that such behavior was expected from people of low (or high!) social origins. We have occasionally heard both that berdaches were the sons of caciques, and inversely that they came from those subject to lords. The one absolutely uniform assumption of all the sources is, rather, that the passives, usually of young age in any case, incurred low status from their behavior.

Iberian Attitudes

In Chapter 2 of this book, we examined Iberian attitudes toward their own and North African transvestism and homosexual practices. Now it is a matter of inquiring into their reactions toward the same phenomena on the American side of the Atlantic. Recall, however, that the eyes trained on native American practices in this period were only those of conquerors. The resulting authoritarian tenor of European reports about American sexuality must affect our perception of them. Even from the mouths of historians as sympathetic to the Amerindians as Cieza or Las Casas, an unquestioned linkage between such allegedly 'unnatural' behaviors and the natives' presumed inferior level of 'civilization' could not help but make itself felt. The fact is that not a single source even hinted that homosexual comportment might be other than evil. Fundamentally, all 'sodomy' was viewed as a sin, and most sodomy as evidence of barbarism.

And yet, beneath such verbal proclamations, the Iberian discourse on the character of conquest was itself unmistakably gendered, indeed phallic, in character. That was apparent in the Spanish ritual that erected a *picota* or penis-shaped garrot outside the gate of every new American city, and then carved out pieces from it. It was an 'obscene' language that must have been grasped, at least subliminally, especially since some of the surviving *picotas* unmistakably imitate penises.[106] Sodomy is barbarous, that *picota* (later *picana* in America) proclaimed, and we will punish it, along with other serious crimes, with sodomy.[107] The New World *picota* was indeed a descendant of ancient Priapus, the god who threatened intruders with rape, and even of the male apes, who still can be seen standing guard on hills, penises erect.[108] Thus though we are forced to rely on words to document Iberian attitudes, there is another world of Spanish sexual violence against not just native women, but native males, that the sources seldom mention.

The Iberians always condemned the homosexual sodomitic act, 'sodomía.' Our sources rarely mention male anal penetration of women, as we have seen, and then only to explain population stagnation, while female homosexuality was hardly ever reported, and still less commonly termed 'sodomy.'[109] *Sodomía* was, therefore, bad, the more easily so because focusing on the act obscured the partners' individual culpability.

The matter becomes interesting and more ambiguous when the transitive verbs for this behavior are examined, precisely because the question of those responsible for the verbal action is raised. They are limited. In Italian, 'to sodomize' (*sodomitare*) is common enough at the time, but in the contemporary Castilian and Portuguese languages the verb *cometer* is usually combined with a noun, as in *cometer el pecado de sodomía*.[110] On reflection, the question as to who commits the crime is evidently significant. Since in anal intercourse the penetrator was always considered the (kinetically) active partner, while the recipient was said to be passive, it might seem that, in the sources, only the penetrator would be said to *commit* the sin or to 'sodomize.' This way of stating the matter does, in fact, overlap with both reality and law. In American reality, but in Iberia as well, the berdache's passivity often did originate in constraint or absence of free will. And indeed, the laws of the homeland, now applicable in the Indies as well, did generally excuse the passive from prosecution when constraint was evident.[111]

On the other hand, everywhere there was a strong tendency to blame the passive, intimating that s/he had seduced the active male. This self-serving notion, a second nature in Europe, made the passive active enough, so to speak, as to be thought guilty at times of having 'committed' the sin along with the active partner. To the point: a survey of the source use of the word *cometer* reveals first of all that it is usually the active who is said to have 'committed' sodomy. This is owed in large part to the penetrator being the one in control, that is, it is related to notions of authority. Thus in Torquemada's explanation for the origins of sodomy in Central America, it is an active *mancebo*-god Chin or Chan who in a vision mounts a *niño*-demon to persuade his American subordinates that homosexual behavior was permissible.[112] However, in cases where the passive appears as seductive, the opposite is true and s/he is said to 'commit' the sin. A good example is furnished by the berdaches of Collasuyu, who had a reputation for aggressive hawking of their wares. They were said to commit sodomy. Just as convincing in this regard is Calancha's description of an *India* who won a prize when she was anally penetrated for the first time by her husband. She too is said to have 'committed' the nefandous sin.[113]

The same general rule, that active terms tend to be applied to the active party in homosexual behavior, can be observed in the nouns employed to describe the partners. The usual Iberian term for the passive party is *puto*, and *sodomita* or one of its cognates refers to the active party in most cases in our sources.[114] Still, there are important exceptions. Gómara, for example, states that many Venezuelan 'sodomites' appear thoroughly womanish, except for their small breasts and the fact they cannot give birth.[115] Sahagún refers to the (effeminate) 'sodomites' who eat chicle, and at another point speaks of the *somético paciente*, clearly indicating that, for him, the term 'sodomite,' unless further delimited, refers to either party to the act.[116] Last but not least is the passage in Muñoz Camargo, which, after referring in general to 'sodomites,' proceeds to condemn first active, and then passive, partners, both, that is, being subsumed under the term 'sodomites.'[117]

To add to the uncertainty, Muñoz says that these Tlaxcalan 'sodomites' were ridiculed by being treated as women, allowing the reading that, just as today, the penetrating party, also being considered by straight society as 'effeminized,' was punished in this way as well. But this is too modern a reading, by those who would ignore the dominance of age and power in this past age, the specifically pedophilic character of the era we are describing. In fact, this is the only source I have found that allows such a modern reading; almost universally, the passive is the party who is said to be effeminized by and for his/her behavior, and no one describes the active male in the homosexual act as womanish.

The berdache is always described as a passive, *not* an active, and never as a heterosexual in drag, as is so common in today's society. Indeed, it can be demonstrated that, far from considering all participants in homosexual acts as indifferently condemnable, the Spaniards, like the peoples they had conquered, believed passives to be the reprehensible partner in that act. This Iberian attitude emerges not from description of European behaviors, of the type we found early in this book, but rather from Iberian descriptions of native behaviors. The peninsulars merely intimate that the preference for the active over the passive life was as natural for them as it was for their subjects.

The specific Spanish detestation of passivity can be seen in some emotional reports that come close to identifying less sodomy than the assumption of the woman's sexual and work roles as the 'abominable sin.' Take the sequence of words used by Pedro Pizarro, who says that the natives around Lake Titicaca were 'a dirty folk, indulging in many abominable sins, and many men go about in the clothes of women, doing evil.'[118] Sin was dirty, but what was notably abominable was wearing women's clothes, which pointed to passivity in the sexual act.

Second, consider the heated commentary of the Franciscan Bernardino de Sahagún, which, while putatively reporting on Aztec attitudes, revealingly mirrors the author's own, Spanish, values:

> The passive sodomite is abominable, nefandous and detestable; he deserves to be mocked and laughed at by people. And one cannot tolerate the stench and foulness of his nefandous sin, because of the nausea he brings upon men. He shows himself womanly and effeminate in everything, in walking or in talking. For all this he deserves to be burned.[119]

There is no remotely comparable attitude toward actives. Effectively, it is the passive who is the 'abominable, nefandous and detestable' party according to both the Mexicans and to Spaniards such as Sahagún. Interestingly, the passive deserved to be ridiculed because his sin made *males* sick, that is, presumably including actives involved homosexually as well as heterosexually. And the sin that merited the stake was the passive demonstration of self as totally womanish and effeminate – a crime of representation more than a sexual crime.[120]

Sahagún was certainly not alone among Spaniards in sharing the attitudes of the native males on this question. Rather, one supposes his was the customary view of the peninsular male. Almost a century later, the Jesuit missionary Pérez de Ribas reported a Sinaloan attitude toward homosexual comportment that he obviously fully shared:

> This filthy vice, which is unmentionable because of its indecency, is found among these peoples in some areas. But since it is worse than brutish, because it is not found among the brute animals, [even] these nations so blind and foreign to the light of reason consider it so vile and shameful, *especially among the passives*, that [these passives] were known and looked down upon by all. And they [used] a shameful word and phrase to

name them in their language. And such [passives] did not use the bow or arrow. Rather, some of them dressed themselves as women.[121]

Thus Pérez slips rapidly from a passionless reference to sodomy in general to a ringing putdown of passivity in particular. His formulation makes our point winningly, so forcefully does it illuminate the Spanish and Sinaloan double standard as it applied to those involved in homosexual acts, for then and now it takes two to have intercourse. Less sodomy *per se* than the assumption of the 'female' role by the young and by prisoners, with all its submissive associations to force and conquest, was that which repelled natives and Spaniards. The abomination, and yet the precondition of power, was submission.

In all this, there was no comparable social action against actives, and no tradition of ridicule at all, either in the native or in the Iberian sources. To be sure, Soares did make fun of the Brazilian actives who thought their mounting of passives was a sign of prowess.[122] But we have seen too much in the European past to blind us to the reality. Indeed, the weight of the evidence now allows us to understand with some cultural depth the European maxim that male homosexual behavior might bestow a 'just title' for conquest. According to Hanke, both Oviedo and Las Casas in their incessant dispute knew that the question of the natural slavery of the Indians was at stake.[123] We may read: the natural slavery of the passive subordinate to another male, and catch the drift.

Nor does Europe's and Latin America's present, any more than its past, allow us to hold to the curious notion that we have outlived the ancient link between sexual force and political power. At the verbal level, a substantial body of work now exists showing that, specifically in Andalusia, and more generally in the Mediterranean world, accusations of homosexually passive, and not active, behavior remain to this day the standard fare for insulting one's enemies or competitors. In the social play of gaining dominance and avoiding submission, modern Andalusian villagers, like their Iberian neighbors of the thirteenth century, retain a strong fear of being forced into a passive role, of having something 'stuck up one's ass' (*tomarlo por culo*).[124] Nor is this fear unfounded, as one source for this information has also demonstrated.[125]

At an earlier point in this work, I showed how powerful, in certain contexts of social interchange, the male tendency to rape other males remains in today's European and North American practice. It is not surprising, therefore, that the same tendency remains close to the surface in the Latin American world as well. We need mention only two countries where sexual torture of this type has been widely reported in recent years. During the latter days of Manuel Noriega's rule in Panama, repeated reports of threatened prisoner sodomization surfaced in major North American newspapers. Sexual humiliation was central to the judicial practices of the regime, political prisoners, for example, being dressed up in prostitutes' clothing, or threatened with rape by AIDS-infected prisoners.[126] Threats of this type are also implemented at times, as is clear from reading the harrowing descriptions of quotidian sexual torture, including homosexual rape by both humans and *picanas*, furnished by Graziano in his work on the Argentine 'Dirty War' of 1976–81.[127]

Nor does this recent history suggest that the active homosexual male is culturally confused or disordered. The torturers were doing what came naturally, if not theologically. The active partner was powerful, and the presence of power showed the world was in order. To this day, the word 'homosexual' in this region refers not to actives, but only to passives.[128]

The surprising conclusion to this chapter is that Amerindian and European straight attitudes toward male homosexual behaviors bore significant similarities to each other. Let us not ignore the differences: a European tendency to equate automatically transvestism with homosexual comportment, an Amerindian rule that, outside the festive world, at least, once dressed as a woman, always dressed as one, the seeming absence of a traditional native antagonism of officialdom to active homosexual behavior, as one finds in Europe, and the at least allegedly more misogynistic attitude of Amerindian males toward their females. However, the presence in both cultures of a declamatory ridicule against passives more than actives, and, most fundamentally, the underlying despisal in both these cultural universes of a state of dependency that informed the hate of passives, are quite striking, and provided the possibility of a working together of the males of both the victors' and the losers' cultures in colonial times. Obviously, the imputed beneficence of Spanish men toward their women must be taken with a grain of salt.

8
Yesterday and Today

I saw with my own eyes the Indians committing these crimes of sodomy and other crimes against nature.[1]

If they win . . . all the pretty girls of America will be ravaged time without number, as well as many ugly ones, and some men.[2]

The headline reads: 'Philippine Town's Parents Battle Effort to Stop Their Children's Sex Trade.'[3] The scene is present-day Pagsanjan in that nation of islands. The parents, along with the town mayor, describe the benefits of the local trade in boys and the generosity of the boys' foreign patrons. 'The moral attitude of the town is pro-prostitution,' says the writer. 'The attitude is, everyone's doing it, you're not going to get pregnant, and you get the money.'

There can be no doubt about it. Still today, the sexual experiences of boys must be seen from within the social and political contexts the elders create and command, and from within the economic structures that victimize these parents as well. When then we read that in 1975 American children were paying off local bullies not with lunch money but with their bodies, and that the sexual domination of other males had become a fashionable street means to show off one's machismo, we know well enough to look for the causes of such behavior in the world into which these youngsters were born.[4]

Such cultures of deprivation remember what went before as so many machismos past. The scene now is a contemporary brothel in Cuzco. Male clients relax in the drawing room and describe to each other the various postures that their lovers had been willing to assume for them. It is an effect a theatre of braggadocio, a setting in which one client tries to prove to another that his woman, and she alone, had gone to the most 'unnatural' extremes of coupling in order to fulfill his demands. In conservative upland Peru, two of these extreme positions are said to be the *caballo*, with the woman on top, and the *perrito*, in which the man mounts and comes from behind, 'like a dog.'[5] In this enclosed 'plaza' of an Hispanic-American consumer society, even the simplest men ask us to imagine such poses to prove that, after all, for a price they had totally dominated somebody outside their family, but within their society. Memories of glories past, heralds of futures whose illusory sexuality poorly conceals a very real poverty of force in their relations with other men.

True, this Felliniesque parlor scene is vastly different from the world studied in the pages of this book. Quite apart from difficult comparisons, the time when peninsulars could simply take any native American woman they wanted is more or less past.[6] And yet, social power is still constructed by the repression of the defenseless, whether they be boys or men, girls or women, and this fact allows, even requires, us to follow a summary of our findings regarding the early modern past with some reflections on forced sexuality in today's world.

This book concerned itself largely with the organization of society and political culture by means of the constraints that adult males placed on young boys to foster the former's status. At the outset I showed that the explorers and conquerors were familiar from Europe with many of the practices and sexual notions they found at work in the Americas: of course quotidian sodomy, but also the homosexual rape exercised against conquered soldiers. The Iberians and native Americans understood, I think, that social forms begin in the violence of the field, only later to serve as a foundation for civil institutions. Further, common to both cultures was a deeply ingrained tradition of insult that, beginning with verbal sexual insults, ranged up to castration, perhaps to circumcision, even to a fear of cannibalism. The Spaniards knew that a taste for young men was common among their Moorish neighbors, and so was automatically a part of late fifteenth-century Iberian Christian culture as well. Knowledgeable at least about males who dressed constantly as women, the peninsulars were also familiar with the *bardasse* of the Mediterranean, that is, of the boyish sex slaves who took the passive sexual role in homosexual liaisons.

Yet they probably did not recognize the berdaches they encountered in the Americas, that is, men of all ages who for life played women in all conceivable manners; they certainly had not encountered such figures in Europe to the extent they met with them in the Americas. That having been said, however, the Spaniards proved themselves capable of a quick understanding of these berdaches and of their role in military and civil society, varied as this was among the many American nations. On the basis of evidence from the Tierra Firme, the

Caribbean Islands, and from the east coast of Mexico, I could show that lords made and used such berdaches to help build their polities.

Rulers created retinues of passives for their own and their clients' pleasure and profit. Shown off on feast days by the same active lords, those retinues proved their submission and the lords' power. Did the berdaches continue to provide sex once they had passed youth? The question cannot be fully answered, given the austerity of the Iberian sources. Still, older berdaches, as their masters' wives, and as teachers or leaders of women's work contingents, did continue to reflect their masters' and the tribal authority, and the same broad use of these berdaches was then found among the Andean nations and within the southwestern part of the present-day United States of America. In general, these homosexual unions were eminently directed toward the good of the parents and of the larger society.

In this we follow the Spanish sources, who understood well enough that state or community building was talked of in male–female terms. Seen from this angle, it is not surprising that peninsulars and Americans so often labelled Aztecs and Incas as homophobic 'manly people,' who ruled over 'effeminate and subjected' persons. Nor is it unexpected that, in turn, the Iberian conquerors would view even such ruling or 'manly people' as feminine in relation to them, just as *The Book of Chilam Balam* characterized this relation. Europeans had long imagined conquest in gender terms.[7]

And the same conquerors knew from the old country that it was in religious ritual that the gendered representation of conquest was at its most stable. Now, across the Americas they found berdaches within a context of religious sacrifice that we are still far from fully understanding apparently providing sexual servicing to leading tribal males. What proved particularly intriguing was the 'backwards gesture' of approaching the gods at least at Peruvian Pachacamac, the use of a sexual gesture to express reverence that was probably not limited to the Americas at all.[8]

The record the Iberians made of what they saw or heard in the New World has turned out to offer a good basis for studying homosexual behavior and transvestism in the Americas, despite the notorious shortcomings of that evidence pointed out along the way. Perhaps the Iberians' most stunning error was their ability to imagine an anti-sodomitic legal structure in the high cultural centers of Tenochtitlan and Cuzco where there was none. Their most important success, on the contrary, was their ability to convince us that they indeed shared with native Americans a very similar distaste for the passive partners to the sodomitic act, which, in the American case at least, was but an agreement to hate those they themselves had reduced to dependence for life.

At the cultural level, we found in these Iberian sources a lively if unfounded fear that homosexual behavior would spread from one people to another. Indeed, what is missing is any more than a hint that the berdaches ever formed a unit that extended between tribes. Though today many are amused by the notion that sodomy is a mark of a lower stage of evolution, the Spaniards believed just that. They then transferred that conviction so successfully to the native Americans that their outstanding mestizo historians, while praising much of the life of their ancestral cultures, condemned the berdaches of their own past to silence or to the most heartfelt condemnation.

This book has established that cultures have existed in which transvested homosexual passives were creations of their human environment rather than of biology. What we have not found is that all those participating as passives in homosexual acts were berdaches. Indeed, it would be as folly to think that as to imagine with the Spaniards that, inversely, all (transvested) berdaches were homosexually involved. To the contrary, the berdaches who assumed their costume at an advanced age gave us fairly strong evidence that many were not so sexually involved, at least not as anal receptors. Finally, despite our effort, we have been unable to do more than hazard guesses about the life cycle of the sexually active berdache. In Europe, age was a dominant factor in determining homosexual role. But the Iberian sources simply never attach an age to the sexual activities of the American berdaches. Thus comparisons with homosexual behavior in Antiquity and medieval Europe dealing with the life cycle of sexual involvement have proven hard to make.

All this means that there could yet be hidden in the American past some evidence, left unreported by the Iberians, which would allow us to maintain that homosexual behavior was biologically determined. But operating with what we do know, the American berdaches do strongly confirm the environmental base of *some* homosexual behavior. Not of 'homosexuality,' which is not documented in this period. Avoiding that term and the word 'homosexuals' has, in fact, allowed us to understand that, as the saying goes, there were only tops and bottoms. The general public considered the former normal because they penetrated, as was natural; the latter, beyond a certain age, were scorned even as they were treasured.

Thus the association between forced sexuality and the construction of social and political identities is evident in the distant past despite denial among historians. That linkage is all the more forcefully denied by students of the recent past and of the present. Thus Magnus Hirschfeld, one of the first serious students of homosexual customs, after describing some of the unpleasant facts we have also recorded, voiced his conviction that 'primitive acts of cruelty have been overcome, and [such] happenings [today] are reversions.' Indeed, Hirschfeld was even unwilling to admit that rape occurred in modern military operations.[9] Thorkil Vanggaard, one of the most innovative contemporary thinkers on the subject and among the first to compare animal and human sexual gestures, in his *Phallós* of 1972, repeatedly insisted that the old notions and practices of domination no longer existed.[10] And even Sigmund Freud, not particularly known for benign interpretations, was convinced that anal eroticism had largely disappeared through evolution.[11]

That a terrible illusion lay behind such notions must be clear to all readers of the outgoing twentieth century, certainly one of the most violent in world history.[12] Because of the racism of the European imperial past, we may choose to play down the several reports I chronicled from the Near East and Africa that document sexual punishments at the beginning of the century, but there is no ignoring the terrifying mutilations of a quarter to a half million Rwandans in 1994. Nor have such brutalities occurred only outside Europe, as the example of 'punishment rape' or *Strafvergewaltigung* in Southeast Europe manifestly shows.

The report of the Carnegie Peace commissioners from the Balkans during the so-called Second War of 1913 contains seemingly endless accounts of the rape of women in hundreds of Balkan villages, of the physical butchery of many men, and, yes, even of the 'shameful' cases of the violation of young males as well, as hard as it was for the male writers to bring themselves to comment on such acts.[13] Certainly, the deeds of some units involved in the First and Second World Wars in Europe must have been comparable with those perpetrated in the Balkans, or with those carried out by the Japanese in Asia during the same period.

Any doubt about such continuity is set aside by the facts of the new Balkan wars. In 1994, in the midst of this new horror, we may compare its journalistic record with that of the original Carnegie Endowment report, and find out that little has changed in this regard: rape, butchery, excision of eyes, ears, noses, genitalia, and the occasional references to the sexual abuse of males do not disappear.[14]

Nor is such behavior among 'developed nations' limited to the Balkans. If Western countries appear less involved in such actions, it is because they are relatively wealthy and have sustained civil order.

Inside, that order has meant concentration camps in Germany,[15] and homosexual force in the prisons of other countries – in Noriega's Panama, where the political authorities threatened prison detainees with homosexual rape by AIDS-infected prisoners, and in the United States as well, where a Commissioner of Corrections at Attica Prison frightened the public with the story that prisoners had killed and castrated hostages, then stuffed their testicles and penises in their mouths.[16] And outside, that regime has meant that in Vietnam, for example, the old order of the battlefield persists. American soldiers cut off ears and the like, and raped with the 'best' Serbia has to offer – or so it seems in the absence of serious study of this subject matter.[17] Yet in his introduction to the republication of the Carnegie report, George Kennan says that Balkan brutality is due to the fact that some of its inhabitants preserve customs from outside Europe![18]

Thus both the past and the present made politics by sexual force, showing the power of the sexual posture as a political gesture. What then could bring a scholar such as George Kennan, and indeed most Westerners in his train, to claim that brutality of the Bosnian type is foreign to European culture, or 'to a civilized country,' as is said? It is the repression and denial of the reality of sexual abuse, especially of children, in their own societies. Child abuse is a major social reality in advanced Western countries as well as in the developing world, and it is not limited to female victims. What has surprised many observers is the large and growing number of young boys who appear in these statistics, ranging between one-quarter and one-half of all reported cases of child sexual abuse.[19] In 1989, some 16 per cent of American males said they were sexually abused as children.[20] To this figure belong, of course, those many young adolescent males victimized by Roman Catholic priests in the recent past.[21] Such crimes were long enormously underreported and understudied, one scholar has written, in part because such abuse was so terribly shameful for a male in a macho society.[22] How unwilling has the social order been to face this reality? What has been found in the case of the Catholic scandals may be applied more generally: time after time, the financial resources of the dioceses were expended not to assist the victims or even the perpetrators, but to conceal the whole matter from the public ken. Often enough, civil authorities have conspired in this policy of seeing, hearing and speaking no evil.

Purely on the evidence from the United States, it is clear that a broad-based behavior exists that abuses children in their early years, but then as adults as well, either through memories or in other prisons. The world of sexual abuse did not go away; it is clearly still with us. It is important that we understand why. And in this search, Sigmund Freud, for all his denial that modern child abuse was real, provides important guidance.[23]

The male child lives in a world where people threaten him with castration, just as girls are threatened by their own horror. That Freudian notion, broadened to include other types of sexual violence as well, has been the import of our historical evidence as well. The statement comes in the midst of Freud's explanation of how the Oedipal complex works in young boys: boys three to five years of age, drawn to their mothers, become afraid that their jealous fathers will castrate them. The fear may be fantasy, it may be exemplified in the circumcisions or substitute castrations the boy sees happening around him, or he may actually be threatened with castration (Freud does *not* mention the anal intercourse which we know now is common enough among adult child molesters). Out of this fear of the father, male children detach themselves from their mother and identify with their fathers and the latters' super-egos.[24]

The import of our evidence takes us further, however. Once males transcend the fear of fatherly castration, they still have social reality to fear, and the collectivity, for example, one's high school class, does not let them forget it. A particular punishment recommended in late medieval Florence may stand for all the evidence of this that we have presented. The sodomite should have one testicle removed, said the writer. This would be a serious punishment, and yet would allow the guilty party to reproduce. Only after a third conviction would the second testicle be severed.[25]

Freud's Oedipal explanation of boyish fears was not, however, his only foray into the relations between fathers and sons. In his *Totem and Tabu*, the author does little short of explaining the origins of civilization through the myth of a climactic act of violence of sons against fathers. Elsewhere citing approvingly Diderot's statement to the effect that, without civilization, a young man would 'twist his father's neck and sleep with his mother,'[26] Freud in the *Totem* began history with a father who, lord of the harem and of the horde, monopolized women until his desperate sons conspired together and killed and ate him. Then, to prevent such acts of mayhem happening in the future, the brothers ordained a series of legal constraints, called civilization. No longer would fathers corner social resources as they once had, because the alternative was murder and social disorder.[27]

Thus again, the conditions that Freud describes resonate out of the material we have presented in this book, for to what end did fathers (and mothers) make their sons berdaches if not as part of a family and political strategy? Whether in Antiquity or traditional North Africa or in Europe or in early America, fathers had reason to fear that their sons wanted them dead at almost all costs.[28] Perhaps Gerald Creed put it best, though he was studying not berdaches but Melanesian initiations through the fellation of superiors. What was at stake was the father's control of his wives and sons, and this ritual homosexuality was a mechanism to maintain the female quality of youth as a way of perpetuating their inferiority.[29] Nor does Creed limit himself to father–son relations. He notes that slightly older boys at times have intercourse with younger ones, and to much the same end: to control a 'wife' even while they remain under the control of their father.

In the West, the boy became a man and has too often visited on his children what had been visited on him. Not in ancient America, where a boy, made a berdache, remained forever 'like a woman.' For better or worse, these berdaches had no history, because, generally speaking, they had no children. No descendants to witness the great anti-homosexual rampages of 1658 in Mexico City, or to see the famous eunuchs Ardian and Bucendo riding through the festive streets of that same city mounted on ostriches.[30] In any case, these tales belong to an age of full-fledged colonialism, and not to the period of contact we have studied in these pages.

In those centuries, we found cultures in a small way making boys into girls, as the saying goes – one more paragraph for an unwritten history of child rearing and abuse, and of state formation, a tale that of course now will include the abuses of the white conquerors as well. Clearly, the moral of our tale of the past is that brutality to one's own body and to those of others was widespread.[31] Now, it remains to recognize the brutality among today's 'civilized countries.' Only then can we freely revel in the distinctive genius of each human culture.

Notes

INTRODUCTION

1 '... por tener mejor declarada la culpa por donde Dios castiga estos indios'; G. Fernández de Oviedo, *Historia general y natural de las Indias*, 5 vols (Madrid, 1959 [BAE], 117–21), 118: 144 (bk 17, chap. 17).
2 A. Karlen, *Sexuality and Homosexuality: a New View* (New York, 1971), 554, describing prisons.
3 H. Cortés, *Cartas y documentos* (Mexico City, 1963), 25 (10 July).
4 P. Sarmiento de Gamboa argued that, because natives sinned against nature, the Spanish had this right even if the Incas were natural lords; *Historia Indica* (Madrid, 1960), BAE, 135: 199; see further P. Duviols, *La lutte contre les religions autochtones dans le Perou colonial: 'l'extirpation de l'idolâtrie' entre 1532 et 1660* (Lima, 1971), 44. J. Acosta maintained 'el pecado nefando con varones,' and apparently not anal intercourse with women, was said to give this right; *De procuranda indorum salute*, in his *Obras* (Madrid, 1954), BAE, 73: 432f. Unless otherwise indicated – e.g., by referral to male anal intercourse with a female – this is the meaning I too assign to 'sodomy.' On the concept, see J. Chiffoleau, 'Dire l'indicible: remarques sur la catégorie du *nefandum* du XIIe au XVe siècle,' *Annales E.S.C.*, 45 (1990), 289–324.
5 The *Sumario de la natural historia de las Indias* was out in 1526; in *Historiadores primitivos de Indias* (Madrid, 1946), BAE, 22. The *Historia* proper appeared from 1535 on.
6 'Solo su interés temporal'; 'Entre los remedios,' *Obras Escogidas*, vol. 5 (Madrid, 1958), BAE, 110: 81. Las Casas cautioned that, 'whether it be idolatry or sodomy,' the Spaniards had to preach against the crime before

182

NOTES TO PAGES 2-4

attacking practitioners; L. Hanke, *All Mankind is One: a Study of the Disputation between Bartolomé de Las Casas and Juan Ginés de Sepúlveda in 1550 on the Intellectual and Religious Capacity of the American Indians* (DeKalb, 1974), 88.

7 Junipero Serra's *entrada* in California dates from the 1750s; otherwise, most of my subject matter comes from the sixteenth and seventeenth centuries.

8 E.g., P. de Cieza de León notes that the Cañari women of Ecuador were those who worked the land, while their men stayed at home weaving and making up their faces and 'otros oficios afeminados.' Yet they did not practice homosexuality; *Crónica del Perú*, 3 vols (Lima, 1984–6), 1: 146f (chap. 44).

9 Foucault seems in fact to be describing *male* sexuality; M. Foucault, *The History of Sexuality*, 3 vols (New York, 1980–8), 1: 103. Beneath this conception is the more fundamental understanding of a relationship between sexuality and violence, especially as expressed in the solemn, or religion; R. Girard, *Violence and the Sacred* (Baltimore, 1972), 34f.

10 On this matter, see J. Boswell, *Christianity, Social Tolerance, and Homosexuality: Gay People in Western Europe from the Beginning of the Christian Era to the Fourteenth Century* (Chicago, 1980). Further on monastic discipline to avoid such friendships, see P. Quinn, *Better than the Sons of Kings* (New York, 1989). On the pressure on Mexican boys in friaries in the sixteenth century, see R. Trexler, 'From the Mouths of Babes: Christianization by Children in Sixteenth-Century New Spain,' in his *Church and Community, 1200–1600: Studies in the History of Florence and New Spain* (Rome, 1987), 549–73.

11 'Primariorum filios nutriebant,' and, citing Tomas Ortiz O. P. on this 'betrayal': 'Son sodométicos más que generación alguna'; P. Martyr d'Anghiera, *De orbe novo decades octo*, in his *Opera* (Graz, 1966), 221, 223 (dec. 7, chap. 4). My English translation, after verification, usually comes from F. MacNutt's edition of *De orbe novo*, 2 vols (New York: Burt Franklin, 1970).

12 Many of Las Casas's pronouncements are together in English in F. Guerra, *The Pre-Columbian Mind* (New York, 1971), 67–76; a number are given in Spanish in the following pages. Las Casas compared the Americans favorably with Pre-Christian Europeans (the French, Scots, Greeks, and Romans by name) as regarded homosexuality, but, as was his wont, he avoided comparisons with contemporary Europeans; *Apologética historia Sumaria*, 2 vols (Mexico City, 1967), 2: 314, 364, 625. Pedro de Cieza de León refers to the 'pública y descubiertamente' practice of sodomy in his *Crónica*, 1: 160 (chap. 49); further 1: 166ff (chap. 52). After verification, I use Harriet de Onis's translation in *The Incas of Pedro de Cieza de León*, ed. V. von Hagen (Norman: University of Oklahoma Press, 1959). For the coastal island of Puna, see further 1: 174f (chap. 55). But 'dexando aparte lo de Puerto Viejo,' the sodomite was an individual and isolated sinner, 'como es en cada cabo y en todo lugar uno o seys o ocho o dies'; 2: 74

(pt 2, chap. 25), and no more 'que es en todo el mundo, que avia algun malo'; 1: 195 (chap. 62).

13 'Pecado político'; F. Montesinos, *Memorias antiguas historiales y políticas del Perú* (Madrid, 1882), 90 (chap. 15); and in F. Guerra, *'The Pre-Columbian Mind*, 195. I use Guerra's translations only after verification. 'Quasi permitida'; Toribio Motolinía, *Memoriales e historia de los Indios de la Nueva España* (Madrid, 1970), BAE, 240: 142. See also J. Imbelloni, 'La "Essaltatione delle Rose" del Codice Vatican Mexicano 3738, el "Nictekatun" de las Fuentes Maya y el "Pecado Nefando" de la Tradición Peruana mas Remota,' *Anales de arqueología y etnología*, 4 (1943), 189.

14 *Obras de Francisco de Vitoria: relacciones teológicas* (Madrid, 1960), 1050; also Guerra, *The Pre-Columbian Mind*, 62.

15 What research there is begins with the surfacing of Spanish and Portuguese Inquisition records in the late sixteenth century; see the admirable survey in E. W. Monter, *Frontiers of Heresy: the Spanish Inquisition from the Basque Lands to Sicily* (Cambridge, 1990).

16 Guerra, *The Pre-Columbian Mind*, 222f, 229. The evidence, of course, belies Guerra's easy confidence. The case of the Spanish sodomites whose activity ruined the departure of Nicholaus Federman from Cádiz in 1533 is extensively described in P. Simon, *Noticias historiales de las conquistas de tierra firme en las Indias Occidentales*, 2 vols (Bogotá, 1882), 1: 93 (pt I, 3rd Noticia Historial, chap. 1). A. Requeña also takes seriously the inner-American contagion theory found in the sources; 'Noticias y consideraciones sobre las anormalidades de los Aborígenes Americanos: sodomía,' *Acta Venezolana*, 1 (1945), 44–73; on this subject, see Boswell, *Christianity*, 316.

17 By the eighteenth century, Mexican nationalists conceded that there had been a contagion; however, it stemmed not from America or Spain, but from Africa and its 'Nègres, qu'on a faussement accusés d'avoir transporté cette corruption d'un monde à l'autre'; C. De Pauw, *Recherches philosophiques sur les Americains*, 3 vols (London, 1770), 1: 63.

18 Thus Boswell accuses Philo of 'conflat[ing] the concepts of pederasty and homosexual relations,' and elsewhere condemns the 'association of homosexuality with child molesting'; allowing for a few exceptions, he denies that 'the apparent prevalence of erotic relationships between adults and boys in the past corresponded to reality'; Boswell, *Christianity*, 28, 143, also 243. In this book, by pederasty I mean a sexual relation between a man and a boy or adolescent, whether or not the boy is transvested; I do not use derivatives of the word ephebe or late adolescent, for the simple reason that the age of passives has proved to be difficult to determine. See, however, G. Bleibtreu-Ehrenberg's unfortunately titled 'Pederasty among Primitives,' *Journal of Homosexuality*, 20 (1990) (a special issue on *Male Intergenerational Intimacy*), 28. She argues that, since a berdache is socially a female, one cannot describe a relationship with him as pederasty. This might be true if we knew that berdaches *wanted* to be women; we do not. As we shall see, the world I will describe is not the modern one of M. Garber's, where

free choice in these matters may apparently be assumed; see her *Vested Interests: Cross-Dressing & Cultural Anxiety* (New York, 1992).

19 The title of David Halperin's book *One Hundred Years of Homosexuality and Other Essays on Greek Love* (New York, 1990) makes the point well: in traditional Europe, the notion of a 'gay' life style shared by everyone participating in homosexual behavior, both the active and the passive practitioners, was unknown, and such language is not found in the sources. See in general on European terminology, Boswell, *Christianity*, M. Goodich, *The Unmentionable Vice: Homosexuality in the Later Medieval Period* (Santa Barbara, 1979). Important developments are, however, traceable to the years around 1700; see R. Trumbull, 'Gender and the Homosexual Role in Modern Western Culture: the 18th and 19th Centuries Compared,' in *Homosexuality, Which Homosexuality?*, ed. D. Altman et al. (Amsterdam, 1989), 149–69.

20 W. Williams, *The Spirit and the Flesh: Sexual Diversity in American Indian Culture* (Boston, 1986), concentrates on natives in the United States; the strongest pro-subculture statement by an early colonial specialist is L. Mott, 'Pagode português: a subcultura *gay* em Portugal nos tempos inquisitoriais,' *Ciencia e cultura*, 40 (1988), 120–39. Without ideological significance, the contemporary term 'passive' (Latin: *patiens*) is preserved in this work precisely because physical passivity – in anal intercourse – was its defining characteristic.

21 E. Westermarck titled his chapter on our subject 'Homosexual Love,' though neither the word nor the idea occurs in it; *The Origin and Development of Moral Ideas*, 2 vols (London, 1917), 2: 456 (chap. 43).

22 G. Herdt, *Guardians of the Flutes: Idioms of Masculinity* (New York, 1981); M. Godelier, *La production des grands hommes* (Paris, 1982); and the impressive article by G. Creed, 'Sexual Subordination: Institutionalized Homosexuality and Social Control in Melanesia,' *Ethnology*, 23 (1984), 157–76.

23 M. Rocke is the first Europeanist who has been able to ground his understanding of homosexual practices in the actual ages of practitioners; *Male Homosexuality and its Regulation in Late Medieval Florence* (diss.: SUNY, Binghamton, 1989).

24 *The Creation of Patriarchy* (New York, 1986); Silverblatt, *Moon, Sun, and Devil: Inca and Colonial Transformations of Andean Gender Relations* (Princeton, 1987). A rare work on so-called female berdaches is E. Blackwood, 'Sexuality and Gender in Certain Native American Tribes: the Case of Cross-Gender Females,' *Signs*, 10 (1984), 27–42. The best collection of modern evidence on them is in the dissertation of S. Lang, *Männer als Frauen–Frauen als Männer: Geschlechtsrollenwechsel bei den Indianern Nordamerikas* (Hamburg, 1990), 310–63. Barbara Tedlock says she has a great deal of information on modern Zuni female cross-dressers, and has promised to make it available to the scientific world; she would do everyone a service by such an action.

25 Nor, in particular, was the distance that great before the conquests; on the

application of warpaint in Europe, see R. Trexler, 'Follow the Flag: the Ciompi Revolt Seen from the Streets,' *Bibliothèque d'humanisme et Renaissance*, 46 (1984), 364.

CHAPTER I BACKGROUNDS

1   A. Kirk Grayson and D. Redford (eds), *Papyrus and Tablet* (Englewood Cliffs, NJ, 1973), 149; cited in D. Greenberg, *The Construction of Homosexuality* (Chicago, 1988), 126.
2   Herodotus, *The Persian Wars*, ed. G. Rawlinson (New York, 1942), 164 (bk 2, chap. 102).
3   Cited in R. Burton, *The Erotic Traveler*, ed. E. Leigh (New York, 1967), 28.
4   A. Edwardes, *Erotica Judaica: a Sexual History of the Jews* (New York, 1967), 87.
5   According to J. Boswell, *Christianity, Social Tolerance, and Homosexuality* (Chicago, 1980); Foucault, *The History of Sexuality* (New York, 1980-8), esp. vol. 2. See in general V. Bullough, *Sexual Variance in Society and History* (Chicago, 1976), and Greenberg, *Construction*. Recently on the Chinese tradition, B. Hinsch, *Passions of the Cut Sleeve* (Berkeley, 1990); and J. Spence, *The Memory Palace of Matteo Ricci* (New York, 1985), 220-9, on Chinese boys constrained to dress, sing and dance. For Japan, see P. Gordon Schalow's superb introduction to Ihara Saikaku, *The Great Mirror of Male Love* (Stanford, 1990).
6   G. Lerner, *The Creation of Patriarchy* (New York, 1986), 76-100.
7   P. Meulengracht Sørensen, *The Unmanly Man: Concepts of Sexual Defamation in Early Northern Society* (Odense, 1983), 82. The author lists the sexual humiliations mentioned in the sagas that were visited on the defeated; anal rape of males is often accompanied by the notion that the victim thereafter bore children.
8   K. Dover, *Greek Homosexuality* (Cambridge, MA, 1978), 105; D. Fehling, *Ethologische Überlegungen auf dem Gebiet der Altertumskunde: phallische Demonstration-Fernsicht-Steinigung* (Munich, 1974), 103. The victory of the Greeks over the 'womanly' Persians at Eurymedon took place ca. 466 BC. Some daring associations of the representation of the rape of women (Lucretia, etc.) to claims of absolute political domination are in M. Carroll, 'The Erotics of Absolutism: Rubens and the Mystification of Sexual Violence,' *Representations*, no. 25 (1989), 3-30.
9   The ancient practice of taking sons hostage obviously carried a clear sexual threat with it since, if a treaty were broken, hostages could be treated as slaves. Note the distinction between children and men taken as hostages in the Peloponnesian War in A. Panagopoulos, *Captives and Hostages in the Peloponnesian War* (Athens, 1978), 112-13, 189-91. Note also the action of the tyrant Periander of Corinth (625-585 BC), who in revenge is said to have sent 300 sons of the Corcyraean elite to Sardis

to be castrated; Herodotus, *Persian Wars*, 234–5 (bk 3, chap. 48). See also the Notarus case in Constantinople in 1453 cited below. Much later, Russian settlers seized and kept boy hostages to insure peaceful relations with the Aleuts; L. Black, 'Russia's American Adventure,' *Natural History* (Dec. 1989), 50.

10 'Productis omnibus elegisse impubes dicitur: quod et virginitate decorum et consensu obsidim ipsorum probabile erat eam aetatem potissimum liberari ab hoste quae maxime opportuna iniuriae esset'; T. Livy, *History*, trans. B. O. Foster, vol. 1 (London, 1988), 262 (bk 2, chap. 13). Carlin Barton kindly passed this to me.

11 On punishing humans like animals by quartering them, see P. Browe, *Zur Geschichte der Entmannung* (Breslau, 1936), 80–1. 'Sparato come porco e sbarrato,' is in *Croniche di Giovanni, Matteo e Filippo Villani*, 2 vols (Trieste, 1857), 1: 454 (Giovanni Villani, bk 12, chap. 17); R. Van Dülmen, *Theater des Schreckens* (Munich, 1985), 127ff, describing the ritual of quartering as a *Schlachtfest*. See also E. Muir, *Mad Blood Stirring: Vendetta and Factions in Friuli During the Renaissance* (Baltimore, 1993). For dismemberment followed by burning as a punishment for homosexual acts in eighteenth-century Switzerland, see Greenberg, *Construction*, 303. In Moroccan (Meknès) slang, the house where an assignation occurs is called a slaughterhouse, the penis a knife, the woman a victim, intercourse a sacrifice, etc.; V. Crapanzano, *Tuhami: Portrait of a Moroccan* (Chicago, 1980), 102. Cf. the Spanish words *cingar* and *la cingada*, the latter being 'ripped open' in the sexual act; O. Paz, *Labyrinth of Solitude* (New York, 1961), 77, and T. Almaguer, 'Chicano Men: a Cartography of Homosexual Identity and Behavior,' *Differences*, 3 (1991), 80. See further M. Combs-Schilling, *Sacred Performances: Islam, Sexuality, and Sacrifice* (New York, 1989).

12 Such as banging and stabbing, thrusting and piercing; *Homo Necans* (Berkeley, 1983), 59. My italics.

13 Cited by D. Henwood in *The Nation*, 5 Oct. 1992, 1.

14 Although B. Bennassar noted that, in early modern Spanish Inquisitorial prosecution of male bestiality, the beasts in question were usually females; *L'inquisition espagnole, XVe–XIXe siècle* (Paris, 1979), 349. Thus eventual criticisms of such 'bestiality' were directed against homosexual actives, not passives. See below, Chapter 2.

15 The use of altars has been common. Thus a Midrash claims that, on conquering Jerusalem, Titus spread out a scroll of the law on the Temple altar, put two Jewish harlots over it, and mounted each of them, spilling seed on the scroll; Edwardes, *Erotica Judaica*, 161; and in 1512 French troops are said to have butchered a priest on the altar along with a series of other sexual depradations; Giangiacomo Martinengo, cited in E. Cochrane, *Historians and Historiography in the Italian Renaissance* (Chicago, 1980), 184. For postures, see J. Brundage, 'Let Me Count the Ways: Canonists and Theologians Contemplate Coital Positions,' *Journal of Medieval History*, 10 (1984), 82f.

16 Remember that, at least in early centuries, the passive's, and not the active's, posture tended to be labelled *contra naturam*; see Cassian, cited in Boswell, *Christianity*, 157. This was a continuation of the classical meaning: *contra naturam* meant something that did not conform to social conventions; P. Veyne, 'L'homosexualité à Rome,' *Communications*, 35 (1982), 26; J. Winkler, *Constraints of Desire; the Anthropology of Sex and Gender in Ancient Greece* (New York, 1989), 17–45. Still, what could be more *contra naturam* than an active treating another man like a woman? See Foucault glossing Pseudo-Lucian, in his *History of Sexuality*, 3: 215. There he also points out the 'political relation' inherent in male homosexuality: 'What enables one to do violence and to deceive – tyrannical power and the art of persuasion – [is] brought into relations between men.' On the dog language for this posture, see Edwardes, *Erotica Judaica*, 86. Note as well the English word 'underdog'; T. Vanggaard, *Phallós* (New York, 1972), 77.

17 'Homo peccando ab ordine rationis recedit; et ideo decidit a dignitate humana ... et incidet quodammodo in servitutem bestiarum ... Et ideo ... hominem peccatorem occidere potest esse bonum, sicut occidere bestiam; peiior enim est malus homo bestia et plus nocet, ut Philosophus dicit in I Polit. [c. 1, no. 12] et in VII Ethic. [c. 6, no. 7]'; T. Aquinas, cited in Browe, *Zur Geschichte der Entmannung*, 81.

18 Meulengracht Sørensen, *The Unmanly Man*, 82; for China, Greenberg, *Construction*, 162; Herodotus, *Persian Wars*, 434, 443, 636–7 (bk 6, chaps 9, 32; 8: 104–6). Thomas Africa kindly passed on the Herodotus references. I finished this book before the appearance of H. P. Duerr's *Obszönität und Gewalt* (*Der Mythos vom Zivilizationsprozess*, vol. 3) (Frankfurt am Main, 1993). Different from my own work, this excellent collection deals mostly with the male abuse of women and women's symbolic defenses. See, however, chap. 16 on the rape of rivals, chap. 18 on the castration of males, and chap. 32 on rape as humiliation with important references also to male victims.

19 W. Burkert, *Homo Necans*, 68. Surprisingly, this seminal work does not mention homosexuality.

20 Greenberg, *Construction*, 121. Reference to the Rameses II frieze with castration underway is in Edwardes, *Erotica Judaica*, 77. Further on castration of prisoners in E. Bethe, 'Die Dorische Knabenliebe: ihre Ethik und ihre Idee,' *Rheinisches Museum für Philologie*, neue Folge 62 (1907), 464–5.

21 Edwardes's reading from a passage in Deuteronomy; *Erotica Judaica*, 56f.

22 1 Samuel 18–27, noted in Bethe, 'Dorische Knabenliebe,' 464f. Bethe suggests, however, that in this case the call for foreskins may be understood to refer to the removal of the whole penis; see further, Edwardes, *Erotica Judaica*, 71–3, with a host of biblical stories on such battle trophies.

23 'To be symbolically a man,' a recent student of Morocco says, 'one must be rendered as really as possible a woman'; Crapanzano, *Tuhami*, 51. Cf.

an interesting approach to homosexual rites of passage to manhood in Melanesia: 'Ritualized [male] homosexuality may actually be a mechanism to maintain the feminine quality of youth as a way of perpetuating their inferiority.' Thus rites of passage to make boys into men can also be seen to keep them women!; G. Creed, 'Sexual Subordination,' *Ethnology*, 23 (1984), 167. Adam's and Trumbach's attempt at an age typology featuring masculinization, placed over and against a gender typology emphasizing the feminization of boys, has no experiential base: there is no evidence of a contradiction between being despised as effeminate and yet being masculinized; see in S. Murray (ed.), *Social Theory, Homosexual Realities* (New York, 1984), 46.

24   For Ethiopia, see J. Bruce, *Travels to Discover the Source of the Nile in the Years 1768 . . . 1773*, vol. 6 (Edinburgh, 1813), 116–18; for female circumcisions, see a recent edition of F. Hosken, *The Hosken Report: Genital and Sexual Mutilation of Females* (Lexington, MA, 1982).

25   On military castrations practiced by the East African Galla, in part to win brides, see the reports of P. Paulitschke, *Beiträge zur Ethnographie und Anthropologie der Somali, Galla, und Harari* (Leipzig, 1888), 59; F. Caillaud, *Voyage à Méroé, au fleuve blanc, au delà de Fazoqul . . . 1819 . . . 1822* (Paris, 1824), 32–3. In both these reports, victors then hung the testicles about the neck; see below the Spanish and American practices of hanging testicles as ornaments. On the Umayad mother-figure Hinda, who hung the penis and testicles of her father's murderer about her neck, Edwardes, *Erotica Judaica*, 77, citing Burton. J. Krapf reported that, when the Galla did not have enough castrated penises for their social needs, they purchased 'Swahili' slaves to obtain their penises; *Reisen in Ostafrika Ausgeführt in den Jahren 1837–1855*, vol. 1 (Stuttgart, 1964), 274. Spanish castration of Caribbean islanders is documented in R. Laudonnière, cited in Chapter 3.

26   On the formulation that total castration made Sporus 'into a woman,' see Suetonius, cited in G. Devereux, 'Greek Pseudo-Homosexuality and the "Greek Miracle",' *Symbolae Osloenses*, 42 (1968), 85. Further E. Cantarella, *Bisexuality in the Ancient World* (New Haven, 1992), 160f, where 'women' like Sporus promptly married men.

27   'Et percussit inimicos suos in posteriora, / Opprobrium sempiternum dedit illis'; Psalm 77.66; Latin biblical texts are of course taken from the Vulgate. See also K. Wentersdorf, 'The Symbolic Significance of *Figurae Scatologicae* in Gothic Manuscripts,' in C. Davidson (ed.), *Word, Picture, and Spectacle* (Kalamazoo, MI, 1984), 5.

28   The punishment might be linked to the monarch's own alleged homosexual behavior; Boswell, *Christianity*, 300; A. Karlen, *Sexuality and Homosexuality* (New York, 1971), 86.

29   D. Fehling, *Ethologische Überlegungen auf dem Gebiet der Altertumskunde* (Munich, 1974), 223. Castration was also used to punish adulterers; E. Evans-Pritchard, 'Sexual Inversion among the Azande,' *American Anthropologist*, 72 (1970), 1431.

30 'In past times, the defilers of virginity and chastity suffered capital punishment . . . But in modern times the practice is otherwise and for the defilement of a virgin they lose their members'; cited in G. Constable, 'Aelred of Rievaulx and the Nun of Watton: an Episode in the Early History of the Gilbertine Order,' in *Medieval Women*, ed. D. Baker (Oxford, 1978), 215.

31 The reference is to the Julian law against adultery; L. Apuleius, *Opera Omnia*, ed. G. F. Hildebrand (Hildesheim, 1968), 822–4 (bk 9, chaps 27–8).

32 Mortality depended on the type of castration and circumcision, reaching up to 90 per cent when members were excised; *The Hosken Report*, 63. A. Richlin, *The Garden of Priapus: Sexuality and Aggression in Roman Humor* (New Haven, 1983), 215, has a list of punishments satirists had husbands inflict upon adulterers. See also ibid., 140f, for rape as punishment for property crimes.

33 Isaiah 20.4; Edwardes, *Erotica Judaica*, 75.

34 For the punishment, Aristophanes, 'Clouds,' 1083f, cited in K. Dover, *Greek Homosexuality*, 105–6, further 144. Boys shaved because the 'hairy pelt' of a grown boy, for example on his buttocks, dissuaded lovers; ibid., 99. For medieval humiliation, H. P. Duerr, *Nacktheit und Scham* (Frankfurt am Main, 1988), 262–3, and his *Obszönität und Gewalt*, respectively vols 1 and 3 of his *Der Mythos vom Zivilizationsprozess*.

35 Edwardes, *Erotica Judaica*, 69, 75–6, 161.

36 However, 'when that wicked man [Nebuchadnezzar] attempted to submit the righteous Zedekiah to sexual abuse, his phallus was outstretched three hundred cubits and wagged in front of all the captives'; Edwardes, *Erotica Judaica*, 98, reference being to Rabbah b.R. Huna, *Mo'ed: Shabbath*; Greenberg, *Construction*, 200.

37 Edwardes, *Erotica Judaica*, 96f; M. Goodich, *The Unmentionable Vice* (Santa Barbara, 1979), with reference to the Torah Sanhedrin.

38 In Aristophanes, the horseradish insertion (*raphanidosis*) followed right after the depilation so that the boy became a pathic or *europroklos*; Aristophanes, 'Clouds,' 1083f, cited in Dover, *Greek Homosexuality*, 106, with other references; the same act in Rome, in Richlin, *The Garden of Priapus*, 215, 256. D. Cohen doubts there was such a punishment; 'A Note on Aristophanes and the Punishment of Adultery in Athenian Law,' *Zeitschrift der Savigny-Stiftung für Rechtsgeschichte, Romanistische Abteilung*, 102 (1985), 385–7. Dover has discovered yet another gender punishment or, rather, insult: painting enemies with the more whitish color reserved for women in Greek art; the vase tells the story of a youth who had cuckolded a husband; Dover, *Greek Homosexuality*, 106.

Many other cases of ancient anal rape are documented in what follows. Random cases of symbolic rape in today's American life, both real and feared, have involved pipes: *The Weekly Guardian*, 4 January 1987, 6 (white Toledo racists vs. a black); nails: L. Tiger, *Men in Groups* (New

York, 1969), 187–8 (Cornell University fraternity initiation); screwdrivers: J. Bremmer, 'An Enigmatic Indo-European Rite: Paederasty,' *Arethusa*, 13 (1980), 291 (guard vs. prisoner, Attica Prison, 1972).

39 Dover, *Greek Homosexuality*, 106.

40 Fehling, *Ethologische Überlegungen*, 10, 19. For anal rape as a punishment for thievery in Nordic areas, see K. Gade, 'Homosexuality and Rape of Males in Old Norse Law and Literature,' *Scandinavian Studies*, 58 (1986), 136. The exact opposite of this Priapian threat was the practice of infibulation, in which, as exercised on males, the foreskins of Roman slaves were sewn together to obviate sexual behavior; E. Dingwall, *Male Infibulation* (London, 1925).

41 Browe, *Zur Geschichte der Entmannung*, 64.

42 Fehling, *Ethologische Überlegungen*, 104f; further Veyne, 'L'homosexualité,' 28.

43 See the Apuleian case above, at note 31. A comparable story is told in Gautier le Leu's 'Prestre taint', C. Livingston (ed.), *Le Jongleur Gautier le Leu* (Cambridge, MA, 1951), 264–9, including a variant in which the boy was castrated. Featuring a husband who is a confirmed sodomite, the story then appears in Boccaccio's *Decameron; Opere* (Milan, 1966), 386–7 (day 5, tale 10).

44 Fehling found such records, *inter alia*, in Horace and in Valerius Maximus; *Ethologische Überlegungen*, 21–2. For another list of *Strafvergewaltigungen*, see Cantarella, *Bisexuality*, 103f, 143.

45 Greenberg, *Construction*, 126; see further Winkler, *Constraints of Desire*, 48, who makes the case for a 'Solonic' prohibition against touching free boys. It takes little imagination to guess that the only person who would have demanded such punishment would have been the owner of such a male victim.

46 See the Roman *lex Scantinia*, to the same end, discussed below at note 110.

47 In Old Norwegian law, it was forbidden to have carnal intercourse with a man's male as well as his female slaves; K. Gade, 'Homosexuality and Rape of Males,' 136. Further rights to violate because of the violation of *male property*: D. Halperin, *One Hundred Years of Homosexuality* (New York, 1990), 92; Dover, *Greek Homosexuality*, 106. See also the case of Pausanias, a lover of Philip of Macedon, given over by Attalos to mule drivers to be sexually abused because of what Pausanias had done to Attalos's boy; in *Diodorus of Sicily*, trans. C. Welles (Cambridge, MA, 1963), vol. 8: 95–103 (bk 16, chaps 93–5), and referenced by N. Machiavelli (*Discourses* [bk 2, chap. 28]); A. Saxonhouse, *Women in the History of Political Thought: Ancient Greece to Machiavelli* (New York, 1985), 162.

48 Fehling, *Ethologische Überlegungen*, 22.

49 See Duerr, *Obszönität*, 280–3. Of course, attention to the punishment of the female partner to adultery is objectively just as important; see, for example, Trexler, '"*Correre la Terra*"': Collective Insults in the late

Middle Ages,' in my *Dependence in Context in Renaissance Florence* (Binghamton, 1994), 113–70.

50 See, e.g., M. Chebel, *L'esprit de sérail; perversions et marginalités sexuelles au Maghreb* (Paris, 1988).

51 Curiously, E. Goffman in his classic *Asylums* (New York, 1961) did not broach the subject. But modern penology presumes this relation, and the movement toward giving prisoners conjugal rights stems in part from this insight; see, e.g., A. Scacco (ed.), *Male Rape: a Casebook of Sexual Aggression* (New York, 1982). I am not suggesting, of course, that there would be no homosexual behavior but for such separate sex institutions. I am stating that coercive homosexual behavior can be brought on by such exclusivism.

52 A Persian case of 1885 is that of Burton, cited in Fehling, *Ethologische Überlegungen*, 22.

53 Greenberg, *Construction*, 135–6; Edwardes, *Erotica Judaica*, 46–7; Vanggaard, *Phallós*, 110–12.

54 This approach does not conflict with Sigmund Freud's myth of sons conspiring to build 'civilization' by killing the primal father; *The Basic Writings of Sigmund Freud* (New York, 1977), 914–30 (*Totem and Taboo*, chap. 5). Alas, that 'father's' actual abuse, one focus of the present work, remained more active than Freud wanted to believe; notoriously, in his analyses he dismissed as fantasy fathers' actual violence against their children; J. Herman with L. Hirschman, *Father–Daughter Incest* (Cambridge, MA, 1981), 7–11; J. Masson, *The Assault on Truth: Freud's Suppression of the Seduction Theory* (New York, 1984). Despite the promising title, E. Pellizer and N. Zorzetti (eds), *La paura dei padri nella società antica e medievale* (Rome, 1983), is not very helpful. On the regular application of the word 'sodomite' only to the active, see M. Rocke, *Male Homosexuality and its Regulation in Late Medieval Florence* (diss.: SUNY, Binghamton, 1989).

55 Greenberg, *Construction*, 115–16; on how female slaves were castrated, see Devereux, 'Greek Pseudo-Homosexuality,' 84f. Dover notes that on vases it was pre-military boys whom the Greeks called 'beautiful'; 'youth' on the other hand were never so called; *Greek Homosexuality*, 86; P. Cartledge, 'The Politics of Spartan Pederasty,' *Proceedings of the Cambridge Philological Society*, 207 (1981), 22. With minimal documentation, Devereux distinguished between those Greek boys who began homosexual behavior at a very young age – to then remain lifelong passives – and those (pre-military) boys who began to engage in 'pseudo-homosexuality' in early adolescence, but ceased that behavior when they later married heterosexually; 'Greek Pseudo-Homosexuality,' 73. The most extensive discussion of age, at least in Greece, is in Cantarella, *Bisexuality*, 36–44. She says it was considered awful to relate sexually to a boy below 12 years of age.

56 Dover, *Greek Homosexuality*, 84f. Ihara Saikaku's *The Great Mirror* provides an important introduction to this understudied Japanese phenomenon.

57 In the West, not only 'boy,' but also *garçon*, *Knecht* and *ragazzo* are notorious in this respect; for the Greek word *douloi*, see Bremmer, 'Enigmatic Indo-European Rite,' 288f, and for the Arabic word *ghulam*, see B. Lewis, *The Political Language of Islam* (Chicago, 1988), 16. On vestigial European 'initiation homosexuality,' strictly speaking, see B. Sergent, *L'homosexualité initiatique dans l'Europe ancienne* (Paris, 1986); also G. Bleibtreu-Ehrenberg, *Homosexualität: die Geschichte eines Vorurteils* (Frankfurt am Main, 1981), 43f.

58 Cantarella, *Bisexuality*, 51.

59 Bremmer, 'Enigmatic Indo-European Rite,' 282. The authoritarian character of the *paideia* ideal is noted by Cartledge, 'Politics,' 19.

60 Dover, *Greek Homosexuality*, 192. Cf. the paradigm older–younger brother discussed at the end of Chapter 3.

61 Greek boys were no different in this respect than others; Dover, *Greek Homosexuality*, 84f, 106f, 140, 145. On 'Greek hypocrisy' of this type, see further Foucault, *The History of Sexuality*, 3: 201, 219, for the Pseudo-Lucian, who says: 'You pretend to be disciples of Socrates who are not enamored of bodies but of souls. How is it then that you do not pursue old men full of wisdom, but rather children, who are unable to reason?'

62 L. Coser, 'The Political Functions of Eunuchism,' *American Sociological Review*, 29 (1964), 880–5; also G. Kadish, who answers 'no' to 'Eunuchs in Ancient Egypt?,' in *Studies in Honor of John A. Wilson* (Chicago, 1969), 55–62.

63 The castration business of Panionius of Chios was mentioned earlier; see also Muhammad ibn Ahmad Al-Muqaddasî [ca. 950 AD], *Description de l'Occident Musulman au IVe–Xe siècle*, ed. C. Pellat (Algiers, 1950), 57.

64 'For the barbarians value eunuchs more than others, since they regard them as more trustworthy', Herodotus, *Persian Wars*, 637 (bk 8, chap. 105). N. Penzer, *The Harem* (London, 1965), 149, says that the Turks got from the Byzantines the practice of using eunuchs to guard harems.

65 Greenberg, *Construction*, 115.

66 See Bethe's brilliant argument contrasting the semen of the kiss and of anal intercourse; 'Dorische Knabenliebe,' 459–62; also Cartledge, 'Politics,' 23; Halperin, *One Hundred Years*, 56. Further Dover, *Greek Homosexuality*, 202–3. See Chapter 2, at note 57, for the medieval continuation of this idea.

67 See G. Herdt, *Guardians of the Flutes* (New York, 1981); M. Godelier, *La Production des grands hommes* (Paris, 1982), and Creed, 'Sexual Subordination,' the last noting (166) that, despite the subordination of boys that is central to the rites, participants view that subordination as a statement of male superiority over females. Dover disagrees with those scholars who have found initiation in Greek society; K. Dover, 'Greek Homosexuality and Initiation,' in his *The Greeks and their Legacy* (Oxford, 1988), 115–34.

68 Evidence of shaving and depilation is in Halperin, *One Hundred Years*,

88, and in Dover, *Greek Homosexuality*, 144; an informative article on types of female depilation is M. Kilmer, 'Genital Phobia and Depilation,' *Journal of Hellenic Studies*, 102 (1982), 104–22; see also D. Bain's gloss on 'Aristophanes, *Ekklesiazousai*, 724,' *Liverpool Classical Monthly*, 7 (1982), 7–10. Eunuchs, of course, often did not assume expected male characteristics such as beards; see E. and R. Peschel, 'Medical Insights into the Castrati in Opera,' *American Scientist*, 75 (1987), 578–83. Isaiah (20.4) prophesied depilation as a humiliating punishment of the Jews; Edwardes, *Erotica Judaica*, 75.

69   A. Richlin is aware of the relation between property and rape; *The Garden of Priapus*, 140–1.

70   Comparative information on warriors' and merchants' retinues of (also sexual) servants is in Greenberg, *Construction*, 115 (the Azande), 180 (Afghan merchants), 188 (Darius's army), 110.

71   Obviously the obscene image of grown men forming a queue behind an 'estrous' young male provides false consciousness which is useful in dominating these boys: these lords are indeed in, and appear not to be out in front of, a queue.

72   For the text, see M. Lichtheim, *Ancient Egyptian Literature*, vol. 2 (Los Angeles, 1976), 214–23, and for interpretation, J. Gwyn Griffiths, *The Conflict of Horus and Seth* (Liverpool, 1960), 41–6, esp. 44, where the author allies himself with C. S. Seligman in maintaining that there is no evidence of such actual behavior in Egypt; he then turns about and cites a case from 1936–7. On the Seth–Horus conflict, see also V. Bullough, 'Homosexuality as Submissive Behavior: Example from Mythology,' *Journal of Sex Research*, 9 (1973), 283–8. My thanks to Gerald E. Kadish for discussing this and much other ancient Near Eastern material with me.

73   Cartledge, 'Politics,' 29, 36, no. 78; Dover, *Greek Homosexuality*, 189ff. The Ephorus fragment is analyzed in J. Bremmer, 'An Enigmatic Indo-European Rite,' 283; Strabo preserved it; *The Geography of Strabo*, ed. H. Jones, vol. 5 (Cambridge, MA, 1944), 155–9.

74   See the solid dissertation of G. Koch-Harnack, *Knabenliebe und Tiergeschenke: ihre Bedeutung im päderastischen Erziehungssytem Athens* (Berlin, 1983). These vases also reveal a whole world of male aggression against Athenian women; E. Keuls, *The Reign of the Phallus: Sexual Politics in Ancient Athens* (Berkeley, 1985).

75   Koch-Harnack, *Knabenliebe*, 46, 200, 206.

76   Ibid., 240, 131.

77   Interestingly, she concludes that, while such aggression may have helped Athens survive, 'from the point of view of culture it has rather had a negative effect on western thought'; ibid., 244.

78   See Cantarella, *Bisexuality, passim*, and Dover, *Greek Homosexuality*.

79   Dover, *Greek Homosexuality*, 190.

80   Cf. J. Le Goff and J.-C. Schmitt (eds), *Le Charivari* (Paris, 1981), 165–76. The charivari, E. P. Thompson observes, 'nous amène à la plus complexe

et fondamentale des questions: les définitions idéales, dans des communautés différentes, de la féminité des femmes et de la virilité des hommes'; '"Rough Music": le charivari anglais,' *Annales*, 27 (1972), 303.

81   In a personal communication (29 May 1989), Y. Roumajon confirms that, in the early 1960s he reported to a Heidelberg conference (not Parisian, as in Wickler below) on his study of three youth groups in the suburbs of Paris: as a sign of their authority, the male leaders of these voluntary associations imposed anal intercourse on their male and female followers; Roumajon's report was never published; cf. W. Wickler, *The Sexual Code* (Garden City, 1973), 228f. On Parisian *écoles* initiations (*le bizutage*) today, see M.-O. Dupé (ed.), *Bizutages* (Paris, 1992). The modern fraternity's fear of being thought homosexual in orientation is analyzed by P. Reeves Sanday, *Fraternity Gang Rape: Sex, Brotherhood, and Privilege on Campus* (New York, 1990), 123.

82   Scacco, *Male Rape*, vii.

83   In seventeenth-century Japanese culture, there was a ceremony when a hitherto passive boy reached 19 years of age: after it, he took only the active role with boys; Saikaku, *The Great Mirror*, 1. I have yet to find a coming-of-age ceremony in the ancient Mediterranean that resulted in a clear change in mode of homosexual activity.

84   Devereux, 'Greek Pseudo-Homosexuality,' 84f. Late medieval Florentine female prostitutes undertook similar cross-dressing to the same end (though another reason may have been to announce to males: 'you may sodomize me'); Trexler, *Dependence in Context in Renaissance Florence* (Binghamton, 1994), 394f. In Palma de Mallorca, cross-dressing was done 'per provocar los homes a pecat'; R. Rossello, *L'Homosexualitat a Mallorca a l'Edat Mitjana* (Barcelona, 1978), 19. 'The hope of inducing [males] to adopt more conventional morals,' that is, to slide them toward heterosexuality, was also at the roots of the Islamic *ghulamiyyat*, girls dressed like boys; *Encyclopedia of Islam*, new edn, vol. 5 (Leiden, 1986), 777.

85   Dover, *Greek Homosexuality*, 189f. Bethe, 'Dorische Knabenliebe,' 456f.

86   On these 'buddy' institutions, see V. Bullough, *Sexual Variance in Society and History* (Chicago, 1976), 106; Dover, *Greek Homosexuality*, 192.

87   On Greco-Roman hierodulia, see D. Hogarth in *The Encyclopedia of Religion and Ethics*, vol. 5 (New York, 1981), 671f; and for comparable Semitic and Egyptian practice, G. Barton, ibid., 672–6. On Mesopotamia, see F. Apffel-Marglin, 'Hierodouleia,' in *The Encyclopedia of Religion*, vol. 6 (New York, 1987), 309–13, and G. Bleibtreu-Ehrenberg, *Der Weibmann* (Frankfurt am Main, 1984), 162f.

88   Dover, *Greek Homosexuality*, 84f.

89   Note that, in parts of today's Latin America, the word homosexual refers not to the active but only to the passive partner; J. Carrier, 'Cultural Factors Affecting Urban Mexican Male Homosexual Behavior,' *Archives of Sexual Behavior*, 5 (1976), 116.

90 Preference for macho athletic types in antiquity is documented in Dover, *Greek Homosexuality*, 69–72; however, the author does think that actives may have increasingly preferred effeminates to macho types in the Hellenistic period. Eloquent modern witness of some actives' desire to demonstrate dominance is in D. Rabinowitz, 'Arms and the Man: a Sex Scandal Rocks Princeton,' *New York* (17 July 1989), 36; see also the novel by M. J. Engh, *Arslan* (New York, 1976), where the anti-hero tells the mother of a just-raped boy: 'You should be proud of your son, madam. He fights well – well' (24; brought to my attention by Warren Wagar). Exceptions to this general rule regarding macho passives in antiquity were, of course, many. For example, the so-called *cinaedi* of Rome were effeminate males who, among other activities, danced at dinner parties in part to seduce males; A. Richlin, 'Not Before Homosexuality: the Materiality of the *Cinaedus* and the Roman Law against Love between Men,' *Journal of the History of Sexuality*, 3 (1993); 523–73, esp. 546; see also Winkler, *Constraints*, 45–54. My thanks to Carlin Barton for discussing the *cinaedi* with me.

91 On this subject, much caution can be learned from M. Garber, *Vested Interests* (New York, 1992), 128–46.

92 The best summary of behavioral 'effeminacy' in ancient times is in E. Rowson, 'The Categorization of Gender and Sexual Irregularity in Medieval Arabic Vice Lists,' in J. Epstein and K. Straub (eds), *Body Guards: the Cultural Politics of Gender Ambiguity* (New York, 1991), 69–72; and Rowson, 'The Effeminates of Early Medina,' *Journal of the American Oriental Society*, 111 (1991), 671–93. On the Romans, see Richlin, 'Not Before Homosexuality,' 544–8.

93 Rowson, 'Effeminates,' 671f; for American practice, see the study by H. Whitehead, 'The Bow and the Burden Strap: a New Look at Institutionalized Homosexuality in Native North America,' in S. Ortner and H. Whitehead (eds), *Sexual Meanings* (Cambridge, 1981), 80–115.

94 On such irrational 'effeminacy,' P. Veyne (ed.), *A History of Private Life*, vol. 1 (Cambridge, MA, 1987), 204f. Richlin, *The Garden of Priapus*, 221, notes that bisexuality itself could be branded effeminate, 'promiscuity' with both sexes being deemed 'excessive.' Links of military cowardice and 'effeminacy' in European antiquity are found in the polarity hoplite–*cinaidos* in Winkler, *Constraints*, 45–51. In old Nordic languages, the word for cowardice and effeminacy was the same; Meulengracht Sørensen, *The Unmanly Man*, 24; Gade, 'Homosexuality and the Rape of Males,' 134; Vanggaard, *Phallós*, chap. 5. See Greenberg, *Construction*, 43, for the dressing of losers or adult noncombatants as women.

95 See the wise statement of Crapanzano regarding modern Morocco cited above, note 23.

96 Halperin, *One Hundred Years*, 98f. For the same notion in the ancient North, see C. Clover, 'Regardless of Sex: Men, Women, and Power in Early Northern Europe,' *Speculum*, 68 (1993), 377, and 384f, as it applies to ageing: 'Everyone becomes *argr* [a passive] as he becomes older.'

97   Halperin, *One Hundred Years*, 98f.

98   On which rite, accomplished at about age 17, see Richlin, 'Not Before Homosexuality,' 546ff, who also mentions a rite of *depositio barbae*, near age 20. Note that the Latin word for what I call young men (ages 20 to 40) was *iuvenes* (youth). On continuities of 'effeminate' behavior in modern times, cf. J. Brody, 'Boyhood Effeminacy and Later Homosexuality,' *New York Times* (16 Dec. 1986), C1.

99   No beard would grow on Cleisthenes' face; Dover, *Greek Homosexuality*, 144. As noted earlier, other youths shaved so they would continue to look young. On Demosthenes, suspected of 'shameful practices' because of his boyish lisp, see Dover, *Greek Homosexuality*, 75. P. Farb, *Word Play* (New York, 1973), 52-6, provides an excellent sketch of genderized assumptions about speech patterns.

100 P. Veyne, 'L'homosexualité,' 26, and above, note 16, where the Christian notion of *contra naturam* also referred originally only to passives, and not to actives. See also Veyne's summations of Roman sexuality in his *A History of Private Life*, 1: 79, 202-5, 242f.

101 *Valerii Maximus factorum et dictorum memorabilium libri novem*, ed. K. Kempf (Leipzig, 1988), 273f (bk 6, chap. 1), cited in Richlin, *The Garden of Priapus*, 225.

102 Respectively Greenberg, *Construction*, 187, and Boswell, *Christianity*, 229. Note that William and Henry were themselves suspected of homosexual behavior.

103 The linkage of treason and homosexual behavior would have a long history. The early sources blame (effeminate) passives for such *lèse-majesté*; see Halperin, *One Hundred Years*, 186.

104 Richlin cites Suetonius' *Life of Domitian* (10.5) that, in the wake of an uprising against the emperor, two junior officers escaped the accusation of complicity in the conspiracy by proving that they were passives (*impudici*) and thus 'could have been of no account either with the commander or the soldiers'; 'Not Before Homosexuality,' 540. 'Contennendo lo fa essere tenuto vario, leggieri, effeminato, pusillanime, irresoluto: da che uno principe si debbe guardare come da uno scoglio'; N. Machiavelli, *Il Principe e Discorsi sopra la prima deca di Tito Livio*, ed. S. Bertelli (Milan, 1960), 75 (chap. 19 of *The Prince*).

105 Richlin, 'Not Before Homosexuality,' 531f. C. Barton, 'All Things Beseem the Victor: Paradoxes of Masculinity in Early Imperial Rome,' in R. Trexler (ed.), *Gender Rhetorics: Postures of Dominance and Submission in History* (Binghamton, 1994), 88-92. An inconclusive, but helpful, review of the evidence of passivity among the powerful is in Cantarella, *Bisexuality*, 156-64.

106 'Sed illae puellae chorus erat cinaedorum, quae statim exultantes in gaudium, fracta et rauca et effeminata voce clamores absonos intollunt . . .'; Apuleius, *The Golden Ass* (Cambridge, MA, 1977), 386-8, (bk 8, chap. 26). Richlin omits any mention of Apuleius' account of *cinaedi* in her extensive article on the subject ('Not Before Homosexuality').

107 Richlin fails to see that this is one reason Roman *cinaedi* also commonly
     had intercourse with women; 'Not Before Homosexuality,' 532f, 549; *The
     Garden of Priapus*, 139. On their 'effeminate' dancing, see *The Garden of
     Priapus*, 92, 98, 101, 222; cf. Bleibtreu-Ehrenberg, *Der Weibmann*, 111,
     where they are linked to shamanism. Apuleius' tale is more revealing than
     others these authors cite. On the singing Medinans who earned money as
     homosexual passives to spend heterosexually, see Rowson, 'Categoriz-
     ation,' 57, 66. They presumably danced as well, since their delicate
     movements were part of their social identity.

108 Dover, *Greek Homosexuality*, 140. This disdain lies behind the 'hail fellow
     well met' attitude toward the pathic, or the image of the actives lapping
     behind a boy as if he were in heat, that is encountered in some literature,
     such as Petronius' *Satyricon; Petronius*, trans. M. Heseltine (London,
     1987).

109 An alternative derivation is from an Old English word for a man impressed
     into slavery; *The Compact Edition of the Oxford English Dictionary*
     (Oxford, 1971), 'bad'; Greenberg, *Construction*, 249. (Cf. the similar
     original meaning of (sexual) enslavement of the ancient word *berdache*.)

110 It was assumed, of course, that the average youngster did not enjoy being
     anally penetrated, but only 'suffered' it; Dover, *Greek Homosexuality*, 36,
     52. Richlin, 'Not Before Homosexuality,' 569ff, misunderstands the *lex
     Scantinia* and the later *lex Julia* to apply only to passives; also Cantarella,
     Bisexuality, 106–14. See better Bleibtreu-Ehrenberg, *Homosexualität*,
     187f. Comparable laws of Domitian and Hadrian forbade castration, so
     that according to Justin Martyr, a Christian wishing to be castrated had
     to appeal to the authorities; H. Hitzig, 'Castratio als Verbrechen,' in
     *Paulys Realencyclopädie der classischen Altertumswissenschaften, neue
     Bearbeitung*, vol. 3, pt 2 (Stuttgart, 1899), 1772f. On the Athenian
     penetration law, see Winkler, *Constraints*, 45–70, esp. 48.

111 Vanggaard, *Phallós*, 77. I am forced largely to neglect this Scandinavian
     complex in the present work because of its seeming marginal contacts with
     the Iberian world, the focus of our interest. The literature is, however,
     significant for our topic. See also Meulengracht Sørensen, *The Unmanly
     Man*; Gade, 'Homosexuality and the Rape of Males'; Clover, 'Regardless
     of Sex,' 363–87.

112 For anal rape or castration as part of political leadership in antiquity, see
     the cases of Periander of Corinth and Nebuchadnezzar, cited above. Anal
     rape's use in contemporary French gangs is noted above, at note 112. Of
     course, male rape in prisons is a microcosm of this form of political
     ascendancy. The representation of power and submission through mount-
     ing is a standard part of animal representation, though the complexities in
     reading it, at least among the higher apes, are not to be underestimated;
     see F. De Waal, 'The Relation between Power and Sex in the Simians:
     Socio-Sexual Appeasement Gestures,' in Trexler, *Gender Rhetorics*,
     15–32. See Chapter 5 for the politics of public mounting among humans,
     and the latter's conversion into a prayer form. On the alleged dress of the

followers of the conspirator Cataline, see Richlin, 'Not Before Homosexuality,' 541f.

113 Meulengracht Sørensen presents no evidence for his assertion that pre-Christians in far Northern Europe punished only passives, whereas the evangelizing Christians, according to him, equally denounced passivity and activity; *The Unmanly Man*, 26. I will address this question in what follows. For ancient hints, see the warnings of the pedagogue Quintilian in Richlin, *The Garden of Priapus*, 223f.

114 Dover, *Greek Homosexuality*, 144f. Machiavelli was drawing on his reading in Roman texts when he observed much the same, as cited just above, note 104. The standard polarity hoplite–*cinaedus* was mentioned above, note 94. See the same sentiments in the forgery of Benedictus Levitus, described in Chapter 2.

115 Note the plural husbands; 'Mollem episcopum, effeminatum Palladius vocitaret: 'Ubi sunt mariti tui, cum quibus stuprose ac turpiter vivis?'''; *Histoire ecclésiastique des Francs*, vol. 2 (Paris, 1837), 114ff (bk 4, chap. 40); Greenberg, *Construction*, 250.

116 See the discussion of Byzantine *castrati* below, Chapter 2.

CHAPTER 2 IBERIAN EXPERIENCES

1 Martial (10.65), cited in A. Richlin, *The Garden of Priapus* (New Haven, 1983), 137.

2 'Neque molles neque masculorum concubitores . . . regnum dei possidebunt'; 1 Corinthians 6.9; see W. Johansson, 'Ex Parte Themis: the Historical Guilt of the Christian Church,' in *Homosexuality, Intolerance, and Christianity: a Critical Examination of John Boswell's Work* (New York, 1981), 1–4.

3 Cf. H. P. Duerr, *Der Mythos vom Zivilizationsprozess* (Frankfurt am Main, 1988), vol. 1, attacking Elias for this assumption. As mentioned earlier, Elias's 'civilizing process' studiously ignores sexuality. Further reflection on this common error of 'progress' away from sexual violence is in Chapter 8.

4 'Obtuli mancipia quatuor Carsamatia Imperatori nominatis omnibus gratiosora. Carsamatium autem Graeci vocant amputatis virilibus et virga eunuchum, quos Verdunenses mercatores ob immensum lucrum facere solent, et in Hispaniam ducere'; Liutprand of Cremona, bk 6, chap. 3, of his *Relatio de legacione Constantinopolitana*, cited in C. Du Cange, *Glossarium.mediae et infimae latinitatis* (Paris, 1937), 2: 192 ('carsamatium'); see also N. Daniel, *The Arabs and Medieval Europe* (London, 1979), 74. I could not verify the common statement that *the Jews* of Verdun were famous for these castrations, as in A. Mez, *The Renaissance of Islam* (Patna, 1937), 354.

5 Al-Muqaddasî, *Description de l'Occident Musulman au IVe–Xe siècle* (Algiers, 1950), 57 (facing French and Arabic texts). The immediately

NOTES TO PAGES 39–40

preceding text assures the reader that this Jewish town was in Spain; nonetheless, authors have suggested that the town 'beyond' Pechina was Verdun! See, e.g., A. Arjona Castro, 'Los eunucos y la cirugia de la castración en la España musulmana,' *Axerquia*, 3 (1981), 279–82.

6 Browe cites the Benedictine Christian von Stablo in his *Expositio in Mattaeum* to this effect: 'Ex antiquo usu gentilium adhuc permanet in multis gentibus atterere testiculos infantium in tenera aetate sive macerare vel etiam penitus auferre pro multis causis, sive ut assidui sint in servitio dominorum seu ut creditam sibi substantiam non dispergant in mulieribus. Nam ante christianitatem ad turpe ministerium a quibusdam fiebant. Nunc vero in Benevento quoscunque clericos facere disponunt, pater et mater in infantia atterunt testiculos et videntur semper iuvenes esse, usquequo canescere incipiunt. Nam in perfecta aetate si factum fuerit, debilitantur statim et vires amittunt'; P. Browe, *Zur Geschichte der Entmannung* (Breslau, 1936), 86f. Needless to say, Al-Muqaddasî has the Mohamme-dans who overran such institutions releasing the innocent children; *Description*, 57. Also M. Chebel, *L'esprit de sérail* (Paris, 1988), 37. Note that several *typica* tried to protect monks from temptation by denying eunuchs or those who suppressed beards access to monasteries; *Oxford Dictionary of Byzantium*, 3 vols (Oxford, 1991), 2: 946. On a Byzantine monastery reserved for eunuchs, however, see ibid., 747. For future reference, note the alleged Templar claim that homosexual unions were permitted to avoid the scandal of heterosexual liaisons; P. Mantegazza, *The Sexual Relations of Mankind* (New York, 1935), 91.

7 Mez, *Renaissance*, 354. There is reason to believe that some Muslims copied their use of eunuchs from the Byzantines.

8 Chebel, *L'esprit de sérail*, 37–8.

9 N. Penzer, *The Harem* (London, 1965), 149. It is not clear whether Coptic monks already specialized in castrating Sudanese for the markets of the eastern Mediterranean, as they still did in the nineteenth century; D. B. Davis, in *The New York Review of Books* (11 Oct. 1990), 36; and for the monks' fairly recent operations on Mount Ghebel-Eter, to supply the harems of the Near East, see F. Hosken, *The Hosken Report* (Lexington, 1982), 63.

10 Daniel, *Arabs and Medieval Europe*, 224f. On the *bardadj*, see Chebel, *L'esprit de sérail*, 61.

11 On the prevalence of sexy young passives at Seville in the high Middle Ages, see below, at note 50. For sale at the modern markets were boys stolen from or sold by their families; one such market closed only during the Spanish occupation; C. Coon, *Tribes of the Rif* (Cambridge, MA, 1931), 110–11, who notes the very low standing of women in the whole Jebala area. The age of such passives is always difficult to determine, so Coon's statement is important that, when the boys reached an age at which they were no longer sexually attractive to the buyers, the latter released them. This presumably indicates an age of about 18 years.

12 Text cited in J. Boswell, *Christianity, Social Tolerance, and Homosexuality* (Chicago, 1980), 282.

13 Boswell, *Christianity*, 281, citing Odericus Vitalis with the grand old (already in Herodotus) stereotype that Europe was ruined by the importation of Eastern 'softness.'

14 Cited in Boswell, *Christianity*, 282.

15 A 1616 English usage of the word berdache applied to Malta, however, referred to them as boys: the night after a Spanish soldier and a Maltese boy were burned for sodomy, 'there were above a hundred Bardassoes, whoorish boyes that fled away to Sicilie in a Galleyot for feare of fire'; W. Lithgow, *The Totall Discourse of the Rare Adventures and Painful Peregrinations of Long Nineteene Years Travayles* (Glasgow, 1906), 335–6. For the ambiguous evidence regarding attitudes toward transvestism in Antiquity, where there is little evidence of the continual wearing of the clothes of the opposite sex, see E. Cantarella, *Bisexuality in the Ancient World* (New Haven, 1992), 178.

16 A. Heriot, *The Castrati in Opera* (London, 1956), 10–12. In Antiquity, *causa vocis* was the usual reason given for infibulating men; see C. Widstrand, 'Female Infibulation,' *Studia ethnographica Upsaliensia*, 20 (1964), 95f, and E. Dingwall, *Male Infibulation* (London, 1925), chaps 2, 3. Besides noting that *castrati* sang in the Byzantine church for centuries, J. Rosselli, 'The Castrati as a Professional Group and a Social Phenomenon, 1550–1850,' *Acta Musicologica*, 60 (1988), 146, brings together evidence that Spain furnished the first *castrati* singers for Ferrara and Rome. Despite the assertion that in the seventeenth century almost all European castrations for vocalists were done in southern Italy, the 'capons' singing in the cathedral of Seville at the time were all from Spain; S. De la Rosa y López, *Los seises de la catedral de Sevilla* (Seville, 1904), 137–8. Recall that the eighth-century *mukhannathün* (effeminates) of Medina were precisely famous for singing; on the possibility that they were falsettists, see E. Rowson, 'The Effeminates of Early Medina,' *Journal of the American Oriental Society*, 111 (1991), 683, note 83. And note that a fundamental usage of falsetto is by priests who copy or utter the words of a female deity; in the Andes, cf. I. Silverblatt, *Moon, Sun, and Devil* (Princeton, 1987), 99.

17 In 1462, a group of five led by Bartolomé del Marmol 'arrancáronles las lenguas, cortáronles las orejas y partes vergonzosas, y se presentaron a recibir el premio infame que suelen dar los moros por semejantes hazañas'; Alonso de Palencia, *Crónica de Enrique IV* (Madrid, 1973), BAE, 257: 189–90 (bk 8, chap. 7); cf. the chronicle of Galíndez: 'cortándoles las lenguas y orejas y llevándolos a Granada por aver el prezio como con cabeza de lobo que los moros acostumbran dar a los que aquella abominable ganancia quieren aver'; Juan Torres Fontes, *Estudio sobre la 'Crónica de Enrique IV' del Dr Galíndez de Carvajal* (Murcia, 1946), 262. On his selling Christian foreskins to same, see T. Miller, *Henry IV of Castile, 1425–1474* (Philadelphia, 1972), 90.

18 R. Menéndez Pidal's emphasis on the 'moorophile' character of fifteenth-century Christian life is elaborated in dress style by C. Bernis, 'Modas moriscas en la sociedad cristiana española del siglo XV y principios del XVI,' *Boletín de la Real Academia de la Historia*, 144 (1959), 199–228. Generally on the problem A. Hess, *The Forgotten Frontier: a History of the Sixteenth-Century Ibero-African Frontier* (Chicago, 1978).

19 The Spanish word for a boy at this stage is *mancebo*; N. Roth, '"Deal Gently with the Young Man": Love of Boys in Medieval Hebrew Poetry in Spain,' *Speculum*, 57 (1982), 39; J. Schirmann, 'The Ephebe in Medieval Hebrew Poetry,' *Sefarad*, 15 (1955), 55–68.

20 That is, the curved rising moon is linked to the prostrate Muslim at prayer; written ca. 1124 by Muhammad Ibn Malike, secretary to the king of Murcia; Roth, 'Deal Gently,' 28.

21 S. Goitein, 'The Sexual Mores of the Common People,' in A. Lutfi al-Sayyid-Marsot (ed.), *Society and the Sexes in Medieval Islam* (Malibu, 1979), 59.

22 Mez, *Renaissance*, 359–60.

23 Boswell, *Christianity*, 200, 233–4.

24 See the examination of Lourie's argument in Boswell, *Christianity*, 233–4.

25 Thus the author notes that Pelayo's persecutor was criticized less for his homosexual desires than miscegenation; Boswell, *Christianity*, 198–200.

26 In 854, the Christian Paul Alvarez of Córdoba denounced these Andalusian Muslim refinements that in his view did indeed successfully seduce Christianity's young men; cited in W. Montgomery Watt, *A History of Islamic Spain* (Edinburgh, 1965), 56; see Patricia Smith's unpublished paper, 'The Cult of St Pelagius in 10th Century Spain,' read at the CEMERS conference in Binghamton, NY, 1991, note 8; also Boswell, *Christianity*, 198. The cult of Pelayo was fast off the mark. Both a local and a German *passio*, respectively by one Raguel and Hrotsvit of Gandersheim, date to the mid-tenth century; *Acta Sanctorum*, June V (Brussels, 1867–8), c. 267.

27 Boswell, *Christianity*, 176.

28 'Stupratoribus puerorum, nec in fine dandam esse communionem'; cited in Boswell, *Christianity*, 179 (ca. 305). According to the author of this decree, males were thought able to resist coercion at age 14. For an overview of Roman legislation in the period from Theodosius through Justinian which is sensitive to the distinction passive–active, see Cantarella, *Bisexuality*, 182–4.

29 See the text in 'De masculorum stupris' (On the Rape of Males); *Monumenta Germaniae Historica: Leges Visigothorum* (Hannover, 1902), 163. Those *inferens quisque vel patiens non voluntarius* who revealed the crime to the authorities and claimed that they had been forced to participate might be rendered exempt from punishment. This became a standard way to get passives to denounce actives. Tolerable translations of this and the following are in D. Bailey, *Homosexuality and the Western Christian Tradition* (London, 1955), 92–4, but the reconstruction of Visigothic

legislation that follows is my own; previous scholars have failed to distinguish the active and passive parties referred to in the laws.

30   'Inter cetera tamen obscenum crimen illud de concubitoribus masculorum extirpandum decernite, quorum horrenda actio et honestae vitae gratiam maculat et iram caelitus superni vindicis provocat'; ibid, 483. Keep in mind that, from one vantage point, a royal court by definition is one 'that keeps males.' Keep also in mind that losing 'the grace of a decent life' may have meant that such boys, having been penetrated, were undesirables as spouses.

31   'Quicumque hujus nefariae actionis patratores extiterint, quique in his turpitudinibus sese implicari permiserint, & contra naturam masculi in masculos hanc turpitudinem operaverint. Siquidem episcopus, presbyter, aut diaconus fuerit, de proprii honoris gradu dejectus, perpetui exilii manebit damnatione proculsus'; J.-D. Mansi, Sacrorum Conciliorum ... Collectio (Florence, 1766), 12: 71; see also Boswell, Christianity, 349; V. Bullough, Sexual Variance in Society and History (Chicago, 1976), 352.

32   'Illius sane facinus detestande libidinis abrogare contendimus, quibus masculi masculos inlicita stupri actione inmundis sordibus maculare'; Lex Visigothorum, in Monumenta Germaniae Historica, Leges, sec. 1 (Hannover, 1902), 165.

33   Urban brothels are difficult to imagine at this time, but there was pre-existent Roman imperial law to burn their (passive) inhabitants, that is, the property of the actives; Boswell, Christianity, 124 (who erroneously has Valentinian's letter as directed against those who put boys in them); J. Lauritsen, ' "Culpa Ecclesiae": Boswell's Dilemma,' in Homosexuality, Intolerance, and Christianity (New York, 1981), 18f, 21f. Boswell's reading of Justinian's Institute (4.18.4) in the Code is also erroneous: the law begins by referring to property rights over women; thus what follows is not directed 'against all homosexual relations,' but, as our reading of these laws indicates, against those who violate other men's passive males, that is, actives; Boswell, Christianity, 171.

34   J. Noonan, Contraception (Cambridge, MA, 1966), 236. On the seed, see the quote of Peter Chanter, ibid.

35   Cited in Boswell, Christianity, 377.

36   See Chapter 1, note 14.

37   'Et novissime nec in bello seculari fortem nec in fide stabilem et nec honorabilem hominibus nec deo amabilem esse venturam: sicut aliis gentibus Hispaniae, Provinciae et burgundionum populis contigit.' Because of such sodomíticas luxurias with human males and with animals, 'iudex omnipotens talium criminum ultrices poenas per ignorantiam legis dei et per sarracenos venire et servire permisit'; forged capitulary of ca. 850 by Benedictus Levitus of Westphalia, in Monumenta Germaniae Historia, Legum, vol. 2, ed. G. Pertz (Hannover, 1837), 156 (separate pagination in rear of pars altera: Spuria) (Additio IV, number 160); also 111 (bk 3, chap. 143), 136 (Additio II, number 21). See also G. Bleibtreu-Ehrenberg, Homosexualität (Frankfurt am Main, 1981), 218-27, 392f. Perhaps not

until Voltaire did Europeans discover that 'courage is not incompatible with effeminacy'; N. Nichols Barker, *Brother to the Sun King: Philippe, Duke of Orléans* (Baltimore, 1989), 236.

38   For uncertain reasons, J. Brundage assumes that homosexual behavior was widespread in subsequent centuries: *Law, Sex, and Christian Society in Medieval Europe* (Chicago, 1987), 149.

39   'Amos á dos sean castrados ente todo el pueblo, e despues a tercer dia, sean colgados por las piernas fasta que mueran, e nunca dende sean tollidos'; cited in Boswell, *Christianity*, 288. Also R. Carrasco, *Inquisición y represión sexual en Valencia: historia de los sodomitas (1563–1785)* (Barcelona, 1985), 41. These provisions were in place in Portugal as well; A. De Oliveira Marques, *Daily Life in Portugal in the Late Middle Ages* (Madison, 1971), 180. In Italy, Siena also prescribed hanging, but 'by the virile members'; Brundage, *Law, Sex, and Christian Society*, 473.

40   A less lethal instance of popular, or at least rural, justice is provided in a Gloucestershire event of 1716 in which, to mock and punish an active, the passive was made to dress up as a woman and be shown giving birth to a boy in a mock groaning, elsewhere called *couvade*; D. Rollison, 'Property, Ideology and Popular Culture in a Gloucestershire Village, 1660–1740,' *Past and Present*, no. 93 (1981), 72f.

41   Boswell, *Christianity*, 289; B. Bennassar, *L'Inquisition espagnole, XVe–XIXe siècle* (Paris, 1979), 333; D. Greenberg, *The Construction of Homosexuality* (Chicago, 1988), 272; this is the first known specification of age in the Christian law of Spain regarding homosexual behavior. Byzantine exempted adolescents under 15 from execution for sodomy; *The Oxford Dictionary of Byzantium*, 2: 945. The question of age invites comparison with Jewish practice in Andalucía a half century earlier. Writing in his *Mishneh Torah* about 1200, Maimonides of Córdoba said he would follow Talmudic authority on the subject: neither partner would be prosecuted if the boy was under nine years of age. If the latter was between nine and 13, not he, but the active would be punished. Presumably passive boys 14 and up were punished along with actives; Roth, 'Deal Gently,' 23; on anti-Semitic use of this passage, see J. Schoeps, 'Antisemitische Stereotypen,' *Die Zeit* (2 Feb. 1990). Mary performed a miracle in Avignon in 1310, saving an innocent 14-year-old boy from an unjust death sentence for sodomy; see Bibliothèque nationale, Paris, ms. latin 5931, ff. 95v–102v (kindly brought to my attention by M. Rocke). Finally, a fascinating light regarding dependence is thrown on lesbian behavior by an opinion of the late sixteenth-century Italian jurist Farinacci, who warned that, if a woman behaved like a man with another woman, she would be in danger of the penalty of death used against male homosexual actives; cited in J. Brown, *Immodest Acts: The Life of a Lesbian Nun in Renaissance Italy* (New York, 1986), 14

42   'Por este pecado foi destruida a Ordem dos Templários por toda a Cristandade en um dia'; cited in L. Mott, 'Pagode português, Ciencia e

cultura, 40 (1988), 121. The suppression of the Templars had taken place scarcely a century and a half earlier; De Oliveira Marques, *Daily Life*, 180. According to the Portuguese historian Fernão Lopes, an earlier king, Pedro I (1357–67) was also suspect of homosexual interests – in his squire Afonso Madeira; ibid., 181. On Henry IV of Castile and his minions, see A. Edwardes, *Erotica Judaica* (New York, 1967), 203; Miller, *Henry IV*. An analysis of the king's alleged homosexuality is in W. Phillips, Jr., *Enrique IV and the Crisis of Fifteenth-Century Castile* (Cambridge, MA, 1978), 90–5.

43   J. Trevisan, *Perverts in Paradise* (London, 1986), 66.

44   Bennassar, *L'Inquisition*, 333–4; Carrasco, *Inquisición*, 40–1. Portuguese law by 1540 linked heresy, treason, sodomy and counterfeiting; Trevisan, *Perverts*, 40.

45   Trevisan, *Perverts*, 66.

46   'Las penas ántes de agora establecidas no son suficientes para estirpar, y del todo castigar tan abominable delito'; cited in Carrasco, *Inquisición*, 41.

47   Carrasco, *Inquisición*, 18. Recall that the active role was not generally thought pathologic. For Albert the Great and Aquinas on the infection among passives, see Boswell, *Christianity*, 52, 235, 316.

48   Carrasco's interpretation of this bull is convincing; *Inquisición*, 11–12, 58. The talk about infection in this bull is a cover to justify the Inquisition's unusual step of assuming authority over non-Christians and, in fact, the prelates went all the way in 1525, forcing all Moors in Spain to convert.

49   Chebel, *L'esprit de sérail*, 1–71, provides a helpful introduction.

50   Meant are effeminate passives selling their services; see the Arabic passage and gloss in E. Lévi-Provençal, 'Un document sur la vie urbaine et les corps de métiers à Séville au début du XIIe siècle. Le traité d'Ibn Abdun,' *Journal Asiatique* (April–June 1934), 241, 255f (section 170 of the treatise), and esp. 265. Norman Stillman kindly helped me with this passage.

51   Cited in Boswell, *Christianity*, 233, 198.

52   Alexander of Diospolis in Thrace; *Oxford Dictionary of Byzantium* 2: 945; it is not known if this bishop was married or not. For Gregory of Tours, see Chapter 1, note 115. For a list of clerks castrated for sexual offenses, see G. Constable, 'Aelred of Rievaulx and the Nun of Watton: an Episode in the Early History of the Gilbertine Order,' in D. Baker (ed.), *Medieval Women* (Oxford, 1978), 215. Like an ancient Egyptian, Geoffrey of Anjou is reputed to have had a bishop and some of his clerks castrated, and the testicles of these eunuchs brought to him in a basket; ibid., 216. For Hugh le Despenser's testicles being burned, see Boswell, *Christianity*, 300.

53   P. Meulengracht Sørensen, *The Unmanly Man* (Odense, 1983), 54–5. In a notorious mid-sixteenth-century case, Pier Luigi Farnese, brother of the pope, raped the bishop of Fano; B. Varchi, *Storia fiorentina* (Florence, 1963), 2: 651–5 (bk 16, chap. 16).

NOTES TO PAGES 48-49

54 See, e.g., M. Perry, *Crime and Society in Early Modern Seville* (Hanover, 1980), 132; B. Bennassar, *The Spanish Character* (Berkeley, 1979), 207–11; V. Pandolfi and E. Artese (eds), *Teatro goliardico dell'Umanesimo* (Milan, 1965), introduction (on *Janos sacerdos*). It is not clear what relation if any the hundreds of cases of clerical sexual abuse in the contemporary United States of America have to this past; see J. Berry, *Lead Us Not into Temptation: Catholic Priests and the Sexual Abuse of Children* (New York, 1992).

55 'Aliquis ex monachis sodomitas esse auditum . . . Certe si amplius quot tales ad aures nostras pervenerit, non solum in eos, sed etiam et in ceteris, cum talia consentiant, talem ultionem facimus, ut . . .'; *Monumenta Germaniae Historica, Legum* I (Hannover, 1835), 93. That is, he would act not only against actives, but against consenting passives as well.

56 Boswell, *Christianity*.

57 In Islam, E. Westermarck, *Ritual and Belief in Morocco*, 2 vols (London, 1926), 1: 198. Cf. Aquinas's notion that the *virtus activa quae est in semine maris intendit producere sibi simile, perfectum secundum masculinum sexu*, in Boswell, *Christianity*, 326. The associated Christian notion of kissing as passing moral qualities in saliva or breath is in N. Perella, *The Kiss Sacred and Profane* (Berkeley, 1969), passim, esp. 159, 299; and, in general, K. Schreiner, '"Er küsse mich mit dem Kuß seines Mundes," in *Höfische Repräsentation: das Zeremoniell und die Zeichen*, ed. H. Ragotzky and H. Wenzel (Tübingen, 1990), 89–132. The notion is later encountered among the healers (*paje*) of Brazil; Trevisan, *Perverts*, 22.

58 The literature on monastic recruitment is in J. Lynch, *Simoniacal Entry into Religious Life from 1000 to 1260* (Columbus, 1976); classic is U. Berlière. 'Le recrutement dans les monastères bénédictins aux XIIIe et XIVe siècles,' *Académie royale de Belgique, Mémoires de la Classe des lettres et des sciences morales et politiques*, 18 (1924), fasc. 6.

59 Cited in Chebel, *L'esprit de sérail*, 37. Perhaps among these souls were the warehoused children referred to by Al-Muqaddasî: having been castrated outside the monastery by their parents, they were then 'interned in monasteries so they won't get involved with girls and so as to spare them the tortures of carnal desire . . .'; see above, at note 6.

60 Boswell, *Christianity*, 143.

61 On oblation, J. Boswell, *The Kindness of Strangers* (New York, 1988), 238ff; on abuse, 241f; on child trading, 407f. See also P. Quinn, *Better than the Sons of Kings* (New York, 1989). In later urban Europe, schools were often thought of as instruments for suppressing male homoeroticism; B. Krekic, '*Abominandum crimen*: Punishment of Homosexuals in Renaissance Dubrovnik,' *Viator*, 18 (1987), 337–45, and R. Trexler, 'Ritual in Florence: Adolescence and Salvation in the Renaissance,' in my *Dependence in Context*, 259–325. To my knowledge, the Freudian notion of castration fear stemming from the Oedipal complex, so familiar a feature of analyses of natural father–son relations, has not been applied to *spiritual*

father–son relations, thorough as was the monastic assumption of the role of 'father' to these 'sons.'

62   I. Forsyth, 'The Ganymede Capital at Vézelay,' *Gesta: International Center of Medieval Art*, 15 (1976), 241–6; Boswell, *Christianity*, 251. Goodich also saw Ganymede's terrorized face as evidence of a fear of homosexual rape only within monasteries; *The Unmentionable Vice* (Santa Barbara, 1979), 18.

63   I obviously differ from B. Sergent, *Homosexualité initiatique dans l'Europe ancienne* (Paris, 1986), 288f, who theorizes that clerks were against, warriors for, homosexual behavior. Emblematic of the cultural despisal of passives is a constitution of the Council of Nablus in 1120: a man who was raped was not executed, but he nonetheless had to submit to canonical penance, presumably, says Brundage, because of the ritual pollution that he had suffered; *Law, Sex, and Christian Society*, 213.

64   C. Walker Bynum, *Jesus as Mother* (Berkeley, 1982), 157f; see further 128 for monks as women and bishops as men, and 161 for monks casting themselves as females to pray to the male god. The same strategy was followed by lay confraters in late medieval Florence; J. Rondeau, 'Prayer and Gender in the *Laude* of Early Italian Confraternities,' in Trexler, *Gender Rhetorics*, 228f. As indicated, Sergent, *Homosexualité initiatique*, 228f, puts forward an alternate theory of antagonism between (ancient) clerks and warriors.

65   Text in Boswell, *Christianity*, 367f. By the early ninth century, the Arabian historian Tabari had determined that Islamic men could penetrate their wives from behind, but only into the vagina; F. Mernissi, *Le harem politique: le prophète et les femmes* (Paris, 1987), 184–8. But by the high Middle Ages, Christians considered the *mos animalium* or coital mounting to be *contra naturam*, even worse than the woman on top; Albertus Magnus, cited in T. Tentler, *Sin and Confession on the Eve of the Reformation* (Princeton, 1977), 189.

66   See the case in Florence further below. G. Ruggiero has shown that the prejudice extended to legal penalties; *The Boundaries of Eros: Sex Crime and Sexuality in Renaissance Venice* (New York, 1985), 125. For Bernardino of Siena's succinct view to the effect that it is also morally more reprehensible, see M. Rocke, 'Sodomites in Fifteenth-Century Tuscany: the Views of Bernardino of Siena,' in K. Gerard and G. Hekma (eds.), *The Pursuit of Sodomy: Male Homosexuality in Renaissance and Enlightenment Europe* (New York, 1989), 12.

67   On the link between clerical homosexual behavior and the origins of modern Italian theatre, see Pandolfi's introduction to the 1427 play *Janus sacerdos*, in *Teatro goliardico*.

68   C. Marchello-Nizia, 'Amour courtois, société masculine et figures du pouvoir,' *Annales E.S.C.*, 36 (1981), 980.

69   P. Linehan, *History and the Historians of Medieval Spain* (Oxford, 1993), 609.

70   M. Rocke, *Male Homosexuality and its Regulation in Late Medieval Florence* (diss.: SUNY, Binghamton, 1989), 62. On the harem complex,

see N. Penzer, *The Harem*, and for the father horde archetype, S. Freud, *Totem and Taboo*, in *The Basic Writings of Sigmund Freud* (New York, 1977), 914 seq.

71   Daniel, *Islam and the West* (Edinburgh, 1962), 143. William's claim is that husbands in Islam had a sexual preference for boys, or at least bisexual proclivities; he does not mention single men. Muslim law allowed a man who could not afford to marry the four permitted wives to take 'a slave' to fill out the number (Sura iv.29). I have not, however, been able to confirm Numa Praetorius's sensational report that an oral tradition existed early in this century that meant that a male (*Junge*) might be taken on as such a substitute; N. Praetorius, 'Ueber gleichgeschlechtlichen Verkehr in Algerien und Tunis,' *Anthropophyteia*, 7 (1910), 186.

72   Trexler, 'Florentine Prostitution in the Fifteenth Century,' in my *Dependence in Context*, 373. Nowhere do the Florentine authorities refer to the danger of women being raped. But in France, J. Rossiaud found youth's widespread, even public rape of women reason enough for the establishment of public brothels; ibid., note 4; see J.-L. Flandrin, *Le sexe et l'Occident* (Paris, 1981), 283ff.

73   G. Shepherd, 'Rank, Gender and Homosexuality: Mombasa as a Key to Understanding Sexual Options,' in P. Caplan (ed.), *The Cultural Construction of Sexuality* (London, 1987), 261.

74   Chebel, *L'esprit de sérail*, 20.

75   Mez, *Renaissance*, 358.

76   It is significant that the French word *barda* derives from the Arabic word *bardah*, meaning luggage, or a soldier's kit. The berdache may ultimately be traceable to a military servant or slave.

77   According to one source, they were militarily organized with their own flags. This unstudied subject can be approached through W. Haberling, *Das Dirnenwesen in den Heeren und seine Bekämpfung: eine geschichtliche Studie* (Leipzig, 1914), 21–4.

78   'Pues habia soldado que traia Cien y cincuenta piezas de servicio Entre machos y hembras amorosas, Las quales regalaban á sus amos En cama y en los otros ministerios'; source cited in G. Friederici, 'Über die Behandlung der Kriegsgefangenen durch die Indianer Amerikas,' in *Festschrift Eduard Seler*, ed. W. Lehmann (Stuttgart, 1922), 73. Despite the women, the danger was always present. In the later sixteenth century in Seville, the accused often said that they began committing sodomy after entering the military; M. Perry, *Gender and Disorder in Early Modern Seville* (Princeton, 1990), 125. Otherwise, recent literature on Spanish women contributes little on this score; see, e.g., H. Dillard, *Daughters of the Reconquest: Women in Castilian Town Society, 1100–1300* (Cambridge, 1984); J. Powers, 'Townsmen and Soldiers: the Interaction of Urban and Military Organizations in the Militias,' *Speculum*, 46 (1971), 655–71.

79   'Quinque milia scortorum quae eius comitatum [sic] sequebantur; Alvarus Pelagius, *Speculum regum*, ed. M. Pinto de Meneses, vol. 1 (Lisbon, 1955), 368. Praising continence ca. 1341–45 to Alfonso XI of Castile, Alvarus

implicitly urged the monarch to again empty the royal camp of prostitutes. To make his point, he paraphrases the *Historia hispanorum*'s account of how the Muslims learned to dangle 'virgins' before the knightly orders of Calatrava and Santiago to insure victory in battle. See below for avoiding worse. My warm thanks to Peter Linehan for making these passages available to me.

80 On the other hand, Bianchi bemoaned the fact that local women were copying the comportments of these prostitutes: 'le done vano vestite e cavalchano come fano li homini ... perchè hano imparato queste fogie dalle ... [sic!] Spagnole'; Tommasino de' Bianchi, called de' Lanzalotti, *Cronaca Modenese*, vol. 1 (Parma, 1866), 141. On rape in military actions at this time, see L. Carroll, 'Machiavelli's Veronese Prostitute: *Venetia Figurata?*,' in my *Gender Rhetorics*, 105.

81 Bianchi, *Cronaca Modenese*, 1: 141.

82 Jacopo Modesti, 'Narrazione del Sacco dato alla terra di Prato dagli Spagnoli,' *Archivio Storico Italiano*, 1 (1842), 242; for Florence, see R. Trexler, *Public Life in Renaissance Florence* (Ithaca, 1991), 541f.

83 'Nec dicant, maxime hispani, qui inter caeteros immundos christianos magis libidini et fornicationibus vacant, quod ideo meretrices ducunt secum ne peius incurrant, scilicet flagitium sodomiticum'; Alvarus Pelagius, *Speculum Regum*, 1: 270, 272.

84 Comparative attitudes and numbers are discussed by J. Hale, *War and Society in Renaissance Europe* (Baltimore, 1986), 161f; G. Parker, *The Army of Flanders and the Spanish Road, 1567-1659* (Cambridge, 1972), 175f. The term 'wife' may conceal a different reality. The 'travelling wives' (*zun-e-suffuree*) who in camel caravans crossed the Khyber Pass into the Punjab, at least in recent times, were in fact five- to twenty-year-old berdaches, indistinguishable from women; A. Edwardes, *The Jewel in the Lotus: a Historical Survey of the Sexual Culture of the East* (New York, 1959), 249.

85 For this and the following, see G. Ramusio (ed.), *Navigationi e viaggi*, 6 vols (Turin, 1978-85), 1: 168f. The oldest text is Italian. The term *cheua* was commonly used in Spain as well; see the article *liwat* (homosexual activity) in *Encyclopedia of Islam*, new edn, 5: 778. It should also be mentioned that, according to Leo, the witches of Fez 'have a damnable custom to commit unlawful venerie among themselves'; cited in E. Westermarck, *The Origin and Development of Moral Ideas* (London, 1917), 2: 484.

86 'Uomini ribaldi e di sangue vile'; Ramusio, *Navigationi e viaggi*, 1: 169. Note that Leo saw the prostitutes as crucial because they alone in the army could cook! William Lithgow furnished a traveller's report on the brothels of Fez, full of 'sodomiticall boyes,' in 1615: *Totall Discourse*, 322f.

87 Unfortunately, Leo does not mention the many young male Jews who, driven destitute from Portugal and Spain beginning in 1492, became prostitutes in North Africa, perhaps in these very brothels, sometimes to service only other Jews; Edwardes, *Erotica Judaica*, 208f. Their history

might provide some insight into comparative Moroccan-Iberian sexual institutions at this moment.

88 Miller, *Henry IV*, 90.

89 In Trexler, '*Correre la Terra*: Collective Insults in the Late Middle Ages,' in *Dependence in Context*, 123, 150.

90 F. Guerra (ed.), *The Pre-Columbian Mind* (New York, 1971), 222f, 229.

91 Indeed this feminine presence at war may, perversely, help our comprehension of the central, yet poorly understood cultural – and not just thespian – phenomenon of the Golden Age 'manly woman' (*mujer varonil*), the 'woman dressed as a man' (*mujer vestida de hombre*). Such transvestisms, and the psychology of male weakness implicit in them, offer an excellent base from which a social historian could push further back into Iberian culture. On transvested women in the theatre (the roles were played by women), see M. McKendrick, *Women and Society in the Spanish Drama of the Golden Age: a Study of the Mujer Varonil* (Cambridge, 1974); the *hombre mujeril* is broached in G. Bradbury, 'Irregular Sexuality in the Spanish "Comedia",' *Modern Language Review*, 76 (1981), 566–80. According to Bradbury (567), the literary tradition was imported from Bandello's Italy, but with rare exceptions avoided the homosexual allusions common to the established Italian trope. See also T. O'Connor, 'Sexual Aberration and Comedy in Monroy y Silva's *El Caballero Dama*,' *Hispanófila*, 80 (1984), 17–39.

92 Already the Roman 'page' (*paedagogium*) was a type of sexual plaything; P. Veyne, *A History of Private Life* (Cambridge, MA, 1987), 1:79. A categorical approach to preparing for the neglected study of such males in armies would be to survey young boys' behavior in trains of merchants and their positions within societies of vagabonds; on the latter, see the small classic by 'J. Flynt,' 'Homosexuality Among Tramps,' in H. Ellis and J. A. Symonds (eds), *Sexual Inversion* (New York, 1975), 252–7.

93 See now E. W. Monter, *Frontiers of Heresy* (Cambridge, 1990), chap. 13, with an excellent bibliography of the many works on these records.

94 See, for instance, Mott, 'Pagode.'

95 Boswell, *Christianity*, 293.

96 Unsurprisingly, Yom Tov Assis documents from the same Aragonese records that for a payment the crown waived charges of sodomy and other sexual crimes; 'Sexual Behaviour in Mediaeval Hispano-Jewish Society,' in *Jewish History: Essays in Honour of Chimen Abramsky*, ed. A. Rapoport, A. and S. J. Zipperstein (London, 1988), 50f.

97 R. Rossello Vaquer, *L'Homosexualitat a Mallorca a l'Edat Mitjana* (Barcelona, 1978).

98 Ibid., 12f.

99 Ibid., 16f.

100 Ibid., 19.

101 Benassar, *L'Inquisition*, 346.

102 Chebel, *L'esprit de sœrail*, 40.

103 'Eodem die peracto prandio Almariam exeuntes extra portam vidimus

columpnam unam altam muratam, in qua in pedibus pendebant 6 Christiani italici, qui sodomia erant convicti. Suspendunt autem eos primo ad collum, ut apud nos, et post invertunt eos ad pedes. Et ante judicium abscindunt testes et appendent eis ad collum. Nam Hispani odio habent hoc vicium et in ipsum maxime animadvertunt, et merito, quia contra naturam est et bestiale quid'; H. Münzer, 'Itinerarium Hispanicum Hieronymi Monetarii, 1494–1495,' ed. L. Pfandl, *Revue Hispanique*, 48 (1920), 41f; leaving Madrid '25 Januarii [1495] exeuntes extra portam vidimus duos homines in pedibus pendentes cum suis testiculis ad collum libatis, qui convicti erant ex sodomia'; ibid., 133. In East Africa, women wore testicles, given them by their paramours, around their necks; F. Caillaud, *Voyage à Méroé* (Paris, 1824), 32f. Cf. the story of Hinda, mother of Mu'āwiya, founder of the Umayad Caliphate, who encouraged her followers to use their scimitars to slash foreskins and the total genitals from their foes. She avenged the loss of her own father by having his killer brought before her, whereupon she hacked off his penis and testicles, and strung them around her neck. The victim's ears, nose, fingers and toes followed; Edwardes, *Erotica Judaica*, 77, citing R. Burton, *Personal Narrative of a Pilgrimage to Al-Madinah and Meccah.*

104 'De hac urbe aliud, quod scribam, non habeo, nisi eam ab hominibus incoli, ipsis ethnicis [i.e., Moors] deterioribus. Nam sacrifico corpus Domini cum in missa elevante nemo in genua procumbit, sed stantes permanent tanquam bruta animalia.[!] Vitam vero tam impuram et Sodomiticam agunt, ut me eorum scelera enarrare pigeat pudeatque'; Leo de Rozmital, *Commentarius brevis et iucundus itineris atque peregrinationis, pietatis et religionis causa susceptae ab Illustri et Magnifico Domino, Domino Leone, libero barone de Rosmital et Blatna*, ed. K. Hrdina (Prague, 1951), 62.

105 The valuable texts are in *Les cròniques valencianes sobre les Germanies de Guillem Ramon Català i de Miquel Garcia (Segle XVI)*, ed. Eulalia Duran (Valencia, 1984), 1263–75, kindly made known to me by W. Monter; see also Carrasco, *Inquisición*, 18. Note the prejudice against clerks as suspect of sodomy.

106 *Les cròniques valencianes*, 104f; see in general Monter, *Frontiers*, 280.

107 'Este dia sacaron a quemar tres onbres e un mochacho, que disen que eran de fuera, por el pecado contra natura. Dios los perdone sus ánimas, amén'; K. Wagner, 'La Inquisición en Sevilla (1481–1524),' in *Homenaje al profesor Carriazo*, vol. 3 (Seville, 1973), 449.

108 M. Perry, 'The "Nefarious Sin" in Early Modern Seville,' in Gerard and Hekma, *Pursuit of Sodomy*, 82. See also the significant case in 1585 of a black man, a procurer of young boys, who was executed for sodomy. He was dressed up like a woman for the procession to his death; Perry, *Crime and Society*, 142. It would seem at first glance that he was an active sodomite, which would make his forced transvestism of special interest. But the matter is not certain. More typical of forced judicial transvestism is the case of the groaning cited above, at note 40.

109 Carrasco, *Inquisición*, 217.

110 'Testiculi sui abscissi fuerunt et appensi ex utraque parte nasi sui'; see this and other texts in C. Bemont, *Simon de Montfort, Earl of Leichester (1208–1265)* (Oxford, 1930), 243. On the castration of Edward II of England while he was alive, see Boswell, *Christianity*, 300.

111 The hangman 'luy fandit sa chemise; et mist ung cuviaulx devant luy entre ces jambe. Puis samblait à plusieurs qu'il lui eust couppés le mambre viril avec les gènitoire, et lez gectait on cuviaulx . . .' Jean de Landremont's execution is described in detail in *La Chronique de Philippe de Vigneulles*, ed. C. Bruneau, vol. 3 (Metz, 1932), 264 (bk 4). Jacques Rossiaud kindly passed me this reference. Earlier cases of judicial castration: in 1078 the Count of Breisgau castrated a group of rebellious farmers; Browe, *Zur Geschichte der Entmannung*, 64; a Perugian's testicles were removed in the second half of the thirteenth century as a punishment for adultery; kindly passed to me by A. Zorzi. A thief had his testicles removed on order of a Florentine judge; *Archivio di Stato, Firenze, Provvisioni*, 61, f. 202v (23 Dec. 1373), passed to me by Christiane Klapisch-Zuber; a list of sexual humiliations in the Norse sagas, castration being the most common, is in Meulengracht Sørensen, *The Unmanly Man*, 82.

112 'Decianme en Roma que ya era imposible en Italia remediarse ni castigarse el pecado nefando. Yo les respondí que no me parecía asì a mi, sino que se atajaba si se ordenase y ejecutase que el muchacho corrompido que no le denunciase dentro de algún día después de violentado lo quemasen por ello, y desde niños lo supiesen y cobrasen aquel miedo (que ahora pasan ligeramente por ello) y no perdona lo pasado'; Carrasco, *Inquisición*, 19.

113 See Rossello, *L'homosexualitat*. Rape as common on the mainland in Bennassar, *L'inquisition*, 346.

114 J. Deleito y Piñuela, *La Mala Vida en la España de Felipe IV* (Madrid, 1987).

115 Deleito y Piñuela, *Mala Vida*, 75.

116 'De hombres convertidos en mujeres, de soldados en afeminados, llenos de tufos, melenas y copetes, y no sé si de mudas y badulaques de las que las mujeres usan'; cited in C. Viñas y Mey, *El problema de la tierra en la España de los siglos XVI–XVII* (Madrid, 1941), 47.

117 A. de Sandoval, *Un tratado sobre la esclavitud* (Madrid, 1987), 157. On the Delaware 'women' and Iroquois 'men,' see Chapter 3.

118 'Maior preterea Hispaniorum pars annullatos aut gemmatos derident & probra ascribunt gennarum gestamina, populares precipue. Nobiles autem si quando nuptiales vel alias regiae parentur pompae celebres, tot quibus aureis gemmis consutis gaudent & vestibus margaritas gemmis admixtas intertexunt. Alias minime, effoeminatorum esse huiuscemodi ornatus atque Arabicorum odorum spiritus & suffumigationes continuas diiudicant. Obscoena Venere obvolutum putant si cui castoreum vel muscum olenti occurrant'; *Opera* (Graz, 1966), 121 (decade 3, chap. 4). NB, the title 'De suffumigiis, & odoribus harum terrarum, dulcia, molliaque verba dici quirent, quae pretermittimus, quia magis ad effoeminandos animos, quam ad bonos mores faciunt'; ibid., 150 (decade 4, chap. 4). Some excellent

thinking on this problem of power seductions is in Marchello-Nizia, 'Amour courtois,' especially 980.

119 As an example of the codpiece, see Bronzino's contemporary portrait of the Duke of Urbino, reproduced opposite the title page of T. Vanggaard, *Phallós* (New York, 1972). See also P. Simons, 'Alert and Erect: Masculinity in some Italian Renaissance Portraits of Fathers and Sons,' in my *Gender Rhetorics*, 163–86.

120 See the slim pickings in V. and B. Bullough, *Cross Dressing, Sex, and Gender* (Philadelphia, 1993). Note also the absence of clothing terms in Richard of Devizes' 1192 account of London's netherworld; W. Dines and W. Johansson, 'London's Medieval Sodomites,' *The Cabirion and Gay Books Bulletin*, 10, nos 6 and 7 (1984), 5ff. A suggestive case that needs separate study is that of the knight Ulrich von Liechtenstein, who in his *Frauendienst* (ca. 1226) tells of searching for jousting challenges dressed as 'Lady Venus' both on the field and off; R. Barber and J. Barker, *Tournaments: Joust, Chivalry and Pageants in the Middle Ages* (Woodbridge, Suffolk, 1989), 49–52. Beatrix Bastl kindly passed this on to me.

121 See F. Rogers, *The Quest for Eastern Christians* (Minneapolis, 1962); *The Travels of the Infante Dom Pedro of Portugal* (Cambridge, MA, 1961), *passim*.

122 The *donne publiche* 'con molte lusinghe e parole accarezzano mirabilmente gli uomini, ciascuno secondo l'età loro, e sono molto accorte e gran maestre a provocar gli uomini ai lor diletti: e di qui nasce che tra gl'Indiani non si sa ciò che sia quel vizio abominevole.' Ramusio, *Navigazioni e viaggi*, 2: 809. See also Cesare Federici's mid-sixteenth-century description of Burmese women's seductions, to the same end and with the same success, in J. Spence, *The Memory Palace of Matteo Ricci* (New York, 1985), 225; J. Boon, *Other Tribes, Other Scribes* (Cambridge, 1982), 165. And for the notion that homosexual behavior was completely foreign to the consciousness of some peoples, see further Alberto Campense's description (1523–5) of the Muscovites: 'li vizi contra natura sono a essi del tutto incogniti'; Ramusio, *Navigazioni e viaggi*, 3: 655.

123 Trexler, *Dependence in Context in Renaissance Florence* (Binghamton, 1994), 374.

124 'I quali sono senza barba e vestono da donna di continuo: e li Persiani si fanno beffe di noi, che riputiamo questa cosa per brutta'; Ramusio, *Navigazioni e viaggi*, 2: 727. A study of modern practice in the nearby region of Sohar is U. Wikan, *Behind the Veil in Arabia: Women in Oman* (Baltimore, 1982), 168–86 ('The *Xanith*: a Third Gender Role?'). This article is especially valuable on the difficult question of the life of *older* passives; see at Chapter 4, note 65.

125 Ones in Florence are referred to by Rocke, *Male Homosexuality*, 366f; one at Valencia, established by the Neopolitan Nicolas Mont, is described by Bennassar, *Spanish Character*, 208f; also Hale, *War and Society*, 189. Twelfth-century male brothels in France are listed by Boswell, *Christianity*, 254.

126 Cf. the situation in Florence in 1551, when 13 per cent of the female population was in nunneries; Trexler, 'Celibacy in the Renaissance: the Nuns of Florence,' in *Dependence*, 355. Individual adolescents, if not organized houses of male prostitutes, were, in such circumstances, tolerable substitutes for the absence of women.

127 'Sono malvoluti dalle donne, perchè il più delle volte menano seco schiavi gioveni eunuchi con li quali dormono'; Ramusio, *Navigazioni e viaggi*, 2: 572. The Spaniards in the Americas will also comment on women's attitudes toward effeminates. For the topos in Europe, see, e.g., the preacher Bernardino of Siena in Rocke, 'Sodomites,' 20.

128 Note that, after the decrees of the Council of Trent were put in place in Aragon in the 1570s, almost all those prosecuted for homosexual behavior by the Inquisition were Old Christians; Bennassar, *L'inquisition*, 342.

129 When Notaras refused, so the story goes, Mehmet had both of them killed; S. Runciman, *The Fall of Constantinople 1453* (Cambridge, 1965), 151. So political loyalty was a gendered quantum. Note that the famous Dracula, or Vlad the Impaler (d. 1477), whose favorite punishment was employed against suspected traitors, was also well known across Europe; J. Striedter, 'Erzählformen als Antwort auf den Schrecken in der Geschichte, oder: Wie Drakula überlebte,' in H. Eggert et al. (eds), *Geschichte als Literatur: Formen und Grenzen der Repräsentation von Vergangenheit* (Stuttgart, 1990), 104–27.

CHAPTER 3 THE MILITARY AND DIPLOMATIC BERDACHE

1 'E se ne serviriano come di femine,' Girolamo Benzoni, *La historia del Mondo Nuovo* (Graz, 1969), fol. 73r.

2 'Qu'il craignoit estre tombé en la main des Espagnols, desquels autrefois il avoit este pris, et lesquels, comme il montra, luy avoient coupé les genitoires'; R. Laudonnière, *L'histoire notable de la Floride* (Paris, 1853), 64.

3 See Castellanos's full verse in Chapter 2, note 78; and G. Friederici, 'Über die Behandlung der Kriegsgefangenen durch die Indianer Amerikas,' in *Festschrift Eduard Seler* (Stuttgart, 1922), 73. Did the curse 'dogs' derive from the posture of the passive on all fours? That was the assumption in a sixteenth-century English dispute about transvestism in theatre, where 'men are transformed into dogges'; J. Binns, 'Women or Transvestites on the Elizabethan Stage?: an Oxford Controversy,' *Sixteenth-Century Journal*, 5 (1974), 103.

4 The term 'berdache,' which in medieval Europe was used to refer to a male prostitute or slave, appeared in the Americas in the late sixteenth century. *Bardaje* can be found in D. Muñoz Camargo, *Historia de Tlaxcala* (Mexico City, 1978), 138, and in J. de Torquemada, *Monarquia Indiana*, 3 vols (Mexico City, 1969), 2: 393 (bk 12, chap. 11), where it refers to the

emperor Hadrian's 'mancebo, que le servia de bardaje.' The institution was widely spread in East Asia, presumably before it spread almost universally to the tribes of the American continent. See recently E. Blackwood (ed.), *The Many Faces of Homosexuality* (New York, 1986), 137 and seq.; also H. Whitehead, 'The Bow and the Burden Strap,' in S. Ortner and H. Whitehead, *Sexual Meanings* (Cambridge, 1981). The classic work on the Asian berdache is M. Eliade, *Shamanism* (Princeton, 1972). In 77 pages on 'Les Indiens sodomites,' Ragon makes only one reference to the berdache. He does not mention transvestism, the berdache's most common characteristic. Instead, he defines the berdache as an 'institution ... [qu'] admettent l'homosexualité comme un comportement licite, socialement reconnu ...' Yet even given this novel definition, more attention to the sources would have saved him from saying 'qu'aucune source incontestable n'atteste son existence au Mexique central, ni à l'époque de la conquête, ni ultérieurement'; P. Ragon, *Les amours indiennes, ou l'imaginaire du Conquistador* (Paris, 1992), 37f.

5 'Los mochachos que cativan cortanlos el miembro, e sirvense de ellos hasta que son hombres, y despues cuando quieren facer fiesta matanlos e comenselos ... Destos mochachos se vinieron para nosotros huyendo tres, todos tres cortados sus miembros'; *Colección de los viajes y descubrimientos que hicieron por mar los españoles*, ed. M. Fernández de Navarrete, 5 vols (Buenos Aires, 1945–6), 1: 333 (letter of the end of January, 1494); cf. also the letter of December 5, 1494, of the Italian Peter Martyr d'Anghiera to the humanist Pomponio Leto regarding the same Caribs: 'Pagos incolarum adoriuntur, quos capiunt homines, comedunt recentes. Pueros castrant, uti nos pullos. Grandiores pingioresque effectos iugulant, comeduntque ...'; *Opera* (Graz, 1966), 367 (*Opus Epistolarum*, bk 7, letter 147); also F. Guerra (ed.), *The Pre-Columbian Mind* (New York, 1971), 45. Some Brazilian tongues link homo- and heterosexual intercourse with eating; C. Lévi-Strauss, *The Raw and the Cooked* (New York, 1975), 269f; P. Fry, 'Male Homosexuality and Spirit Possession in Brazil,' in Blackwood, *Many Faces*, 141. Notoriously, the English term 'eat me' has a sexual meaning. A. Métraux downplays sexual behavior as a theme in triumph; 'Warfare, Cannibalism, and Human Trophies,' *Handbook of South American Indians*, vol. 5 (New York, 1963), 383–409, and esp. 404. G. Friederici accords it a somewhat more prominent place: *Skalpieren und ähliche Kriegsgebräuche in Amerika* (Braunschweig, 1906), 74f; 'Über die Behandlung,' 117f.

6 'Per quello habiamo visto in tute le isole dove siamo stati, cossì li Indiani como li Camballi sono forte sodomiti, non sapendo, como io credo, se fanno male o bene. Habiamo iudicato che questo maledetto vicio sii proceduto in dicti Indiani da dicti Camballi, perciò che, como vi ho dicto di sopra, sono homini più feroci, et che subiugando li dicti Indiani et mangiandoli, per vilipendio etiam li habiano facto quello excesso, il quale poi procedendo sia cresiuto de l'uno in l'altro.' Michele says twice that the Caribs 'haveano tagliato il membro genitale in fino al ventre'; letter of

October 28, 1495, in *Raccolta di documenti e studi pubblicati dalla r. commissione colombiana pel quarto centenario della scoperta dell'America*, ed. C. de Lollis, pt 3, vol. 2 (Rome, 1893), 102f, 97; trans. in S. Morison (ed.), *Journals and Other Documents on the Life and Voyages of Christopher Columbus* (New York, 1963), 220. Hinting at homosexual rape among the Caribs, López de Gómara describes these 'sodomitas idolatras' as so 'inhumanos [y] crueles' that Christians could sell them as slaves; *Historia de las Indias* (Madrid, 1946), BAE, 22: 189. A. Requeña suspects that natives used homosexual rape in war, but he misses the information to that effect in Michele's letter; 'Noticias y consideraciones sobre las anormalidades de los aborígenes Americanos: sodomía,' *Acta Venezolana*, 1 (1945), 59–60.

7 Trexler, *Public Life in Renaissance Florence* (New York, 1980), 540f; and see Chapters 1 and 2.

8 'En el tiempo que así estaba, entre estos vi una diablura, y es, que vi un hombre casado con otro, y estos son unos hombres amarionados impotentes, y andan tapados como mujeres y hacen oficio de mujeres, y tiran arco y llevan muy gran carga, y entre estos vimos muchos de ellos asi amarionados como digo, y son más membrudos que los otros hombres, y mas altos; sufren muy grandes cargas'; Núñez Cabeza de Vaca, *Naufragios* (Madrid, 1946), BAE, 22: 538 (chap. 26). The Amazon myth may have framed such descriptions. Rolena Adorno, who is working on a critical edition of Núñez Cabeza, was kind enough to point out to me that the BAE text follows a 1555 edition; the original 1542 print, however, says these people '*no* tiran arco.'

9 The 'señores' 'tienen mancebias publicas de mujeres, y aun de hombres en muchos cabos, que visten y sirven como hembras sin les ser afrenta, antes se excusan por ello, queriendo, de ir a la guerra'; López de Gómara, *Historia*, 22: 199 (pt 1). The significance of grown men (*hombres*) assuming women's clothing will be returned to at a later point.

10 'No se ocupan en el uso de las armas, ni hacen cosa que los hombres ejerciten'; Oviedo, *Sumario de la natural historia de las Indias*, in *Historiadores primitivos de Indias* (Madrid, 1946), BAE, 22: 508 (chap. 1).

11 'No usan de arco ni flecha, antes algunos se vestían como mujeres'; A. Pérez de Ribas, *Páginas para la historia de Sinaloa y Sonora; triunfos de nuestra santa fe entre gentes las mas barbaras y fieras del Nuevo Orbe*, 3 vols (Mexico City, 1944), 1: 132.

12 'Ils vont pourtant en guerre, mais ils ne peuvent se servir que de la massue, et non pas de l'arc n'y de la flèche qui sont les armes propres des hommes'; Marquette's berdaches are cited in A. Karlen, *Sexuality and Homosexuality* (New York, 1971), 463f. Since different tribes used different types of arms, evidently their representation was, as here, a matter of gender.

13 How such *castrati* become outsized is described in E. and R. Peschel, 'Medical Insights into the Castrati in Opera,' *American Scientist*, 75 (1987), 578–83. López de Gómara's text: 'Cásanse unos hombres con otros, que son impotentes o capados, y que andan como mujeres, y sirven

y suplen por tales, y no pueden traer ni tirar arco'; *Historia*, 22: 182. B. de Las Casas in turn repeated Gómara's account, adding: 'No se sabe si aquella impotencia se causan ellos por cerimonia y religión, como los gallos dedicados a la [Roman] diosa Bericintia . . . o porque la naturaleza, errando, haya causado aquella monstruosidad'; *Apologética historia Sumaria*, 2: 359 (chap. 206). Note also that, quite recently, berdaches among the Lango of Uganda were believed to be impotent; C. Ford and F. Beach, *Patterns of Sexual Behavior* (New York, 1951), 131.

14   See, for example, the plate 'Functions of the Hermaphrodites' (*Hermaphroditorum officia*), in M. Alexander, *Discovering the New World* (New York, 1976), 34.

15   'Frequentes istic sunt Hermaphroditi utriusque naturae participes, ipsis etiam Indis exosi; eorum tamen opera, quod robusti & validi sint, ad onera ferenda utuntur jumentorum loco. Proficiscentibus ergo ad bella Regibus, hermaphroditi annonam ferunt: & vulnere vel morbo Indis, illi ipsi binis longuriis satis firmis . . . atque sic defunctos gestant ad sepulturae locum'; *Brevis narratio eorum quae in Florida Americae provincia Gallis acciderunt, secunda . . . Laudoniere . . . anno MDLXIII, quae est secunda pars Americae, additae figurae . . . auctore Iacobo de Moyne, cui cognomen de Morgues . . .*, ed. T. de Bry (Frankfurt am Main, 1591), c. xvii-r. In the eighteenth century, it was determined that earlier Frenchmen had erroneously applied the term 'hermaphrodites' to what were in fact occasionally eunuchs and usually transvested passives, or berdaches; C. De Pauw, *Recherches philosophiques sur les Americains* (London, 1770), 2: 98. See, however, the occasional hermaphrodites of central Sulawesi (Celibes), who transvest, just like those who want to avoid battle; J. Van der Kroef, 'Transvestism and the Religious Hermaphrodite in Indonesia,' *Journal of East Asiatic Studies*, 3 (1959), 259.

16   Alexander, *Discovering*, 205. Laudonnière adds that these painted 'hermaphrodites' 'ont tout le plus grand travail, mesmes ils portent leurs vivres quand il vont à la guere.' The Tumucua priests did enjoy females, he says, 'toutefois quelques uns sont sodomites'; Laudonnière, *L'histoire notable*, 8f. On the association of priests with passive boys in Tenochtitlan, see further below.

17   'Unum sum miratus . . . numquam eos pugnae loco exceder, quin cadaveribus hostium sic mutilatis, sagittam per anum ad summum usque traijciant; quod sané non sine magno periculo interdum fieret, nisi qui ad hoc munus sunt delegati, perpetuò turmam militum auxiliarem haberent'; *Brevis narratio*, c. xv-r. The illustration, 'How Outina's soldiers treated their slain enemies' (*Outinae milites ut caesis hostibus utantur*), in Alexander, *Discovering*, 31. In general on the treatment of corpses, see Friederici, 'Über die Behandlung,' and his *Skalpieren*. On symbolic sodomization among the Zulu, see D. Fehling, *Ethologische Überlegungen auf dem Gebiet der Altertumskunde* (Munich, 1974), 23.

18   On this and other alleged laws, see Chapter 7. For stomach evisceration, see C. Klein, 'Snares and Entrails: Mesoamerican Symbols of Sin and

Punishment,' *Res*, 19/20 (1990–1), 81–104; and the graphic sculptural vestiges in L. Schele and M. Miller, *The Blood of Kings: Dynasty and Ritual in Maya Art* (New York, 1986), 228, 240. Klein does not note the fact that such punishment was also dispensed anally, as, e.g., in her figure 14.

19 See the relevant text in *The Chronicles of Michoacan*, ed. E. Craine and R. Reindorp (Norman, 1970), 30, the image being pl. 9.

20 'Metieron una lanza de palma por el sieso, atravesándole con ella el cuerpo todo hasta la cabeza'; Martin de Murúa, *Historia general del Perú* (Madrid, 1986), 277; see also F. Graziano, *Divine Violence: Spectacle, Psychosexuality, & Radical Christianity in the Argentine 'Dirty War'* (Boulder, 1992), 284.

21 In a letter of 8 July, Guzmán narrated how bravely the men of Cuizco (west of Tenochtitlan) had resisted the conquest of their area, 'como si fueran españoles': 'Entre esta gente que en esta isleta se defendió, peleó un hombre en abito de muger, tan bien y tan animosamente, que fue el postrero que se tomo, de que todos estaban admirados ver tanto corazón y esfuerzo en una muger, porque se pensaba que así lo era por el ábito que traía, y después de tomado, biose ser hombre, y queriendo saber la cabsa por que traie ábito de muger, confesó que desde chequito lo havia acostumbrado y ganava su bida con los hombres al oficio, por donde mande que fuese quemado y así lo fue'; in *Colección de documentos ineditos relativos al descubrimiento, conquista y organización de las antiguas posesiones españolas en America y Oceania*, vol. 13 (Madrid, 1870), 367f.

22 Indications that such prisoners thereafter became berdaches for the victors remain rare: 'statements that male war captives were forced to become berdaches seem mostly an anthropological myth,' according to C. Callender and L. Kochems, 'The North American Berdache,' *Current Anthropology*, 24 (1983), 451, with reference to the Winnebago. Helms, however, claims that, in ancient Panama, *pacos* – war prisoners who served the elite Cuma as slaves – were at times used as homosexual partners or *camayoa*; M. Helms, *Ancient Panama* (Austin, 1979), 14. Modern Osage evidence is especially interesting. According to the traveller Tixier, hermaphroditic wild beasts, called *bredaches* by the Creoles, were prized for their meat in the hunt. This unique link of the berdache to hunted animals appears to cast the berdache as a war victim; V. Tixier, *Travels on the Osage Prairies* (Norman, 1940), 197, 182.

23 B. Isaac gives no hint of such practices in his 'Aztec Warfare: Goals and Battlefield Comportment,' *Ethnology*, 22 (1983), 121–31. I also came up blank in Schele and Miller, *Blood*, despite the authors' emphasis in chap. 5 upon Maya 'Warfare and Captive Sacrifice.' While a mine of information, Friederici, 'Über die Behandlung,' is wanting in frankness in matters regarding sexuality.

24 See her important 'Fighting with Femininity: Gender and War in Aztec Mexico,' in Trexler, *Gender Rhetorics*, 107–46.

25 C. Klein, 'Rethinking Cihuacoatl: Aztec Political Imagery of the Conquered Woman,' in *Smoke and Mist: Mesoamerican Studies in Memory of Thelma D. Sullivan*, ed. J. K. Josserand and K. Dakin, 2 vols (Oxford, 1988), 1: 237–77.

26 As told to F. Karsch-Haack, *Das gleichgeschlechtliche Leben der Naturvölker* (New York, 1975), 380.

27 Klein, 'Fighting with Femininity,' 113. The insult *cuilone!*: '*Oh cuilones, y aun vivos quedáis*'; B. Díaz del Castillo, *Historia verdadera de la Conquista de la Nueva España*, 2 vols (Mexico City, 1968), 1: 395 (chap. 128). C. Taylor, 'Homosexuality in Precolumbian and Colonial Mexico,' in S. Murray (ed.), *Male Homosexuality in Central and South America* (New York, 1987), 10f, records a Tlaxcalan tradition that the Mexicans surrendered to the Spaniards when Cortés threatened to take from Montezuma a blond page who, at Cortés's instigation, had successfully seduced the Aztec ruler. Cf. Chapter 2 for the tale that the Moors had often conquered the Spaniards with just such blandishments.

28 It is not said that these boys, clearly used sexually, were dressed as girls: 'Lo mismo habían criado a muchos muchachos para que no las conoscan mujeres; estos sirvieron despues para los soldados'; J. de Santacruz Pachacuti Yamqui, *Relación de Antigüedades deste reyno del Perú* (Madrid, 1968), BAE, 209: 290. My thanks to Jorge Urioste for help with this and other Santacruz passages.

29 'No solamente le hizo a los más sangrientos reproches, sino que les envió a él y a Guépanti, Huanca-Mayta y otros jefes, vestidos de mujer, *chumbis* y espejos de los que se sirven las mujeres y les ordenó terminantemente ponérselos y así vestidos entrar al Cusco'; M. Cabello Balboa (fl. 1576–86), *Historia del Perú bajo la dominación de los Incas* (pt 2 of *Miscelanea Austral*) (Lima, 1920), 155 (chap. 19). Note that the famous Inca dualism did not affect the culture's readiness to insult men as women. Some Eurasian corollaries of Huascar's action: the Florentine chronicler Giovanni Villani says under 1292 that the Tatar khan Abaga forced his defeated soldiers to wear women's clothes for life; *Croniche di Giovanni, Matteo e Filippo Villani* (Trieste, 1857), 1: 146 (bk 7, chap. 83 of GV); as punishment for their failed insurrection, the male peasants of sixteenth-century Raunau near Ulm were forced to wear a (woman's) veil for six weeks, both inside and outside of their domiciles; A. Bastian, *Der Mensche in der Geschichte*, vol. 3 (Leipzig, 1860), 313.

30 Friederici, 'Über die Behandlung,' 118; D. Schultz, *Month of the Freezing Moon: the Sand Creek Massacre, November 1864* (New York, 1990), esp. 138, 145. For the Pueblos, R. Gutiérrez, 'A Gendered History of the Conquest of America: the View from New Mexico,' in Trexler, *Gender Rhetorics*, 58f.

31 For the behavior of the Sienese women in the field after the 1260 battle of Montaperti, see Trexler, '*Correre la Terra*,' in *Dependence in Context*, 161. The behavioral structure of city children decimating condemned enemies of the people (Trexler, *Public Life*, 69, 367) probably echoes such

war behavior. Friederici, 'Über die Behandlung,' 80f. For comparison of human and animal triumphalism, see the literature in Fehling, *Ethologische Überlegungen*, 32.

32 Friederici, 'Über die Behandlung,' 71. The triumphant entry of the native Americans needs a separate study.

33 Gutiérrez, 'A Gendered History,' in Trexler, *Gender Rhetorics*, 53f. Cf. the behavior of Iroquois women and children toward entering enemy warriors in L. Morgan, *League of the Iroquois* (Secaucus, 1962), 342–3. For Lakota women castrating enemy warriors, see J. Dorsey, *Omaha Sociology* (Washington, DC: Report 3, Bureau of Ethnography, 1881–2), 313.

34 Further thinking on this problem can be found in my '*Correre la terra*,' in *Dependence in Context*.

35 E. Parsons, 'The Zuñi La'mana, '*American Anthropologist*, 18 (1916), 524. I have modernized the spellings, and substituted Kolhamana for Kokk'okshi, following today's conventions.

36 'No era inferior el valor de los americanos, sino desigual su forma de luchar'; 'Así, cuando los nuestros se hubieron dado cuenta, principalmente en aquella batalla adversa, de que se trataba no de hombres con espiritu femenino, sino de gente fuerte, capaces de despreciar la muerte, consideraron que nada habría de hacerse temerariamente, ni avanzar hacia el enemigo en plan de desprecio'; *Juan Ginés de Sepúlveda y su crónica indiana, en el IV centenario de su muerte, 1573–1973* (Valladolid, 1976), 442, (bk 7, chap. 26).

37 'Es nacion tan belicosa toda ella, que ha sido el crisol del esfuerço de los Españoles, y por esto los estiman mucho, y dizen, que solos los Españoles merecen el titulo de gente, y no las naciones de los Indios poblados'; *The Memorial of Fray Alonso de Benavides, 1630*, trans. E. Ayer (Chicago, 1916), 132; I follow the translation in Benavides' *Memorial of 1630*, trans. P. Forrestal (Washington, 1954), 42, where 'men' brings out the meaning better than the 'people' of Ayer. Thus, as regards the indigenous peoples, the nomadic Apache equated settlements with effeminacy. Tlaxcala's well documented determination to be the Spaniards' rather than others' friends led to similar sentiments; see Trexler, 'We Think, They Act: Clerical Readings of Missionary Theatre in Sixteenth-Century Mexico,' in *Church and Community*, 594–8.

38 'Asimismo les demandaban cada día, que se les diesen, de cada pueblo, dos niños; no supieron declarar los Indios, que dieron essa relación, si querían estos para sacrificar, o para comer, o para servicio'; Torquemada, *Monarchia Indiana*, 1: 332 (bk 3, chap. 40). On the taking hostage of young boys among the eighteenth-century Aleuts, and by Russians of Aleuts, all to the end of enforcing agreements, see L. Black, 'Russia's American Adventure,' *Natural History* (Dec. 1989), 50.

39 'Que en su lengua quiere decir donde mataron los putos mexicanos'; Díaz del Castillo, *Historia verdadera*, 1: 318 (chap. 103). F. Scholes and R. Roys equate this with Cuilonia ('the place of the passives'), which was

once an Aztec garrison; *The Maya Contal Indians of Acalan-Tixchel* (Norman, 1968), 91.

40 C. Klein, 'Fighting with Femininity,' in Trexler, *Gender Rhetorics*, 132f.

41 C. Callender and L. Kochems attempted to sever the institution to be described here from that of the berdache by claiming that the Iroquois did not have berdaches; 'The North American Berdache,' 451. To the contrary, Greenberg thinks he proves that they did; *The Construction of Homosexuality* (Chicago, 1988), 40f. Unfortunately, two of the sources he cites and probably the third as well, the eighteenth-century explorer Charlevoix, say nothing of the sort. Charlevoix: 'Dans les pays méridionnaux il gardent peu de mesure sur l'article des femmes, qui de leur côté sont fort lascives. C'est de-là qu'est venuë la corruption des moeurs, qui depuis quelques années a infecté les nations septentrionnales. Les Iroquois en particulier étoient assez chastes, avant qu'il eussent commerce avec les Illinois, & d'autres peuples voisins de la Louysiane: ils n'ont gagné à les fréquenter, que de leur être devenu semblables. Il es vrai que la molesse & la lubricité étoient portées dans ces quartiers-là, aux plus grand excès. On y voyoit des hommes, qui n'avoient point de honte d'y prendre l'habillement des femmes, & de s'assuivoit une corruption, qui ne se peut exprimer. On a prétendu que cet usage venoit, de je no sçai quel principe de religion; mais cette religion avoit comme bien d'autres, pris sa naissance dans la dépravation du coeur, ou si l'usage, dont nous parlons, avoit commencé par l'esprit, il a fini par la chair: ces effeminé ne se marient point, & s'abandonent aux plus infâmes passions; aussi sont-ils souverainement meprisés'; *Journal historique d'un voyage . . .* (Paris, 1744), 303. The term 'ces quartiers-là' evidently refers to a region not a people, and the only region mentioned is 'les pays méridionnaux,' which is *là* rather than *ici* in the north, where Charlevoix is. Perhaps the latter thought that the institution of the berdache had spread from Louisiana to the Iroquois by way of the Illinois, but he does not say that; my thanks to Alexander Fischler for his expert help with this passage. This berdache description has also been erroneously assigned to the 'Seven Nations, especially the Iroquois' [sic!] by J. Katz (ed.), *Gay American History* (New York, 1976), 290, and by Whitehead, 'Bow and Burden Strap,' 84. Despite this case of sloppiness, Greenberg is right when he says that berdaches do seem to turn up in any American tribe when a serious search is done. The burden of proof lies on one who would assert the non-presence of the berdache in a particular tribe, and not the opposite.

42 A. Wallace, *Teedyuscung: King of the Delawares, 1700–1763* (Syracuse, 1949), 99, 196. The Tuscarora and Tutelo 'were entertained within the bosom of the [Iroquois] Oneida,' the Delaware, as we shall see, within that of the [Iroquois] Mohawk; see the Cayuga memorandum of 17 July 1885, in the *Library of the American Philosophical Society*, ms. 1650 (Seth Newhouse [Da-Yo-De-Kane], *Traditional History and Constitution of the Iroquois Confederacy*), 176–7. My thanks to the APS for allowing me access to this manuscript.

43 C. Weslager, 'Further Light on the Delaware Indians as Women,' *Journal of the Washington Academy of Sciences*, 37 (1947), 303. Cf. Wallace, *Teedyuscung*, 35ff. I have been unable to trace the notion of multiple penises, but for the comparable Spanish notion of four testicles in America, see I. Clendinnen, *Ambivalent Conquest: Maya and Spaniard in Yucatan, 1517–1570* (Cambridge, 1987), 110.

44 'I still remember the time,' said the Delaware Chief Tamaqua, the Beaver, in 1754; P. Wallace, *Indians in Pennsylvania* (Harrisburg, 1961), 56. The Delaware word for woman is *gantowisas*, which Wallace insists was originally not abusive.

45 Weslager, 'Further Light,' 299ff. All of the sources of this institution are writings of colonists. This has occasionally led to an attempt to dismiss the whole matter as a figment of the European imagination.

46 C. Weslager, *The Delaware Indians: a History* (New Brunswick, 1972), 178–81.

47 I. Goddard, 'Delaware,' in *Handbook of North American Indians*, vol. 15 (Washington, 1970), 223; the Delaware as dependent children are in Wallace, *Teedyuscung*, 36; further L. Morgan, *League*, 338–9.

48 C. Weslager, 'The Delaware Indians as Women,' *Journal of the Washington Academy of Sciences*, 34 (1944), 381.

49 Weslager, 'Delaware Indians as Women,' 384.

50 Ibid., 387.

51 That is, by having 'castrated' them; Weslager, 'Delaware Indians as Women,' 385; Wallace, *Teedyuscung*, 91.

52 Weslager, 'Delaware Indians as Women,' 385; Wallace, *Teedyuscung*, 113, and 37 for the notion of the Iroquois' 'women' as prostitutes.

53 Weslager, 'Delaware Indians as Women,' 386. Note the important linkage of a kin language to a sexual one, a 'woman' apparently addressing an 'uncle.' See the incisive article regarding kin vocabulary by F. Speck, 'The Delaware Indians as Women: Were the Original Pennsylvanians Politically Emasculated?' *Pennsylvania Magazine of History and Biography*, 70 (1946), 377–89. Perhaps most important, cf. T. Zuidema's remarks on Andean relationships at the end of the present chapter: perhaps branding a tribe as women was, among other meanings, roughly equivalent to branding those in inferior kin relationships, like younger brothers, as women.

54 Wallace notes, however, that being 'women' did, inversely, also bring the Delaware a certain dignity as allies of the Confederacy; *Teedyuscung*, 36, 92, 99.

55 Wallace, *Teedyuscung*, 195. 'They shall always be in readiness to entertain the Confederate Lords in their wigwam, and give them corn-bread, and corn-soup with bear's meat in it'; see above, note 42, *Library of the APS*, 176.

56 As noted earlier, formalized gender notions were present on the borders of the old Spanish sphere of influence, among the Catawba of South Carolina. One author, in an article marred by errors, has tried (unsuccessfully) to

link conceptually the Confederacy institutions to those of Spanish America, specifically the categorical division male–female among the Keres-speaking Pueblos of New Mexico; J. Miller, 'The Delaware as Women: a Symbolic Solution,' *American Ethnologist*, 1 (1974), 520.

57 Wallace, *Teedyuscung*, 196.

58 On 'como llegaron los mexicanos a Tenuchtitlan, [y] se presentaron ante Itzcoatl vestidos a usanza mugeril,' see H. Alvarado Tezozomoc, *Crónica Mexicana* [and the] *Códice Ramírez* (Mexico City, 1975), 263f, 54, 57, and also 29; further in Klein, 'Fighting with Femininity,' in Trexler, *Gender Rhetorics*, 132f.

59 'Sono questi gentili grandi idolatri, uomini effeminati e soggetti'; the *Suma oriental* describing the kingdom of Cambay, cited in G. Ramusio, *Navigazioni e viaggi* (Turin, 1978–85), 2: 732.

60 On circumcision and infibulation, or the sewing up of the penis, in America, see the attempted summary in De Pauw, *Recherches philosophiques*, 134–7, 146–50.

61 R. T. Zuidema, *Inca Civilization in Cuzco* (Austin, 1990), 29.

62 On younger brothers becoming servants of older ones, e.g., in Samurai Japan, see G. Bleibtreu-Ehrenberg, 'Pederasty among Primitives,' *Journal of Homosexuality*, 20 (1990), 24. M. Brewster Wray has studied sons-in-law who dressed as women when in the presence of their fathers-in-law; *Kinship and Labor in the Structure of the Inca Empire* (diss.: SUNY, Binghamton, 1988). See my query above, at note 53.

63 *The Book of Chilam Balam of Chumayel*, ed. R. Roys (Washington, DC, 1933), 168f. For the term *mostradores del dorso*, see J. Imbelloni, 'La Essaltatione delle Rose,' *Anales de arqueología y etnología*, 4 (1943), 161; Requeña, 'Noticias y consideraciones,' 45ff. The political meaning of the terms older and younger brother in the Yucatan can be flavored in the word 'brother,' indexed in *The Ancient Future of the Itza: the Book of Chilam Balam of Tizimin*, ed. M. Edmonson (Austin, 1982).

CHAPTER 4 THE DOMESTIC BERDACHE: BECOMING

1 *The Book of Chilam Balam of Chumayel*, ed. R. Roys (Washington, DC, 1933), 168f.

2 Ovid, on the aged Hercules transvested and subordinated to Omphale, queen of Lydia; *Ovid's Heroines*, trans. D. Hine (New Haven, 1991), 30f (9).

3 'Huius reguli domus reperit Vaschus nefanda infectam Venere. Foemineo amictum reguli fratrem, pluresque alios comptos & vicinorum testimonio pathicos offendit. Iussit a canibus circiter quadraginta lacerari, canum opera nostri utuntur in praeliis contra nudas eas gentes … Audita nostrorum in obscoenum id genus hominum severitate, tanquam ad Herculem populi confluebant quoscumque morbidos ea peste sentirent trahentes, ut e medio tollerentur expuendo in illos inclamitabant. In

Palatinos quippe, in populum haud quaguam contagio fluexerat. In coelum oculos manusque tendentes deum insinuabant esse tanto scelere iratum, inde mitti fulgura, tonitruaque, crebris namque fulguribus vexantur, & aquarum frequentes alluviesquae sata omnia raptent, famesque & morbos inde provenire conquerebantur, licet nil aliud pro deo colant praeterquam solem'; *Opera* (Graz, 1966), 106 (dec. 3, chap. 1); B. Bucher, *La sauvage aux seins pendants* (Paris, 1977), 211. One would like to know if the brother dressed like a woman was a younger brother. Such slaughters were apparently legal after a decree of Ferdinand the Catholic (d. 1516) against the Caribs, 'tan inhumanos crueles sodomitas idolatras': 'si perseverasen en su idolatria y comida de hombres y en la enemistad, los captivasen y matasen libremente, que hasta entonces no se consentia'; López de Gómara, *Historia de las Indias* (Madrid, 1946), BAE, 22: 189. The Justinian Code's linkage of sodomy and natural catastrophe is in the Codex Iuris Civilis, Nov. 77 and 141; see the translations in D. Bailey, *Homosexuality and the Western Christian Tradition* (London, 1955), 73ff.

4 'Aunque los unos y los otros [free and unfree Mexicans] se pueden llamar bárbaros, pues hacían tantas cosas contra toda ley natural ... Frecuentaban el pecado de sodomía que entre los otros pecados, por su fealdad, se llama contra natura, y así, como dice Sant Pablo, Dios los traía en sentido reprobado, cegándoles el corazón, como a Faraón, para que por sus pecados viniesen a pecar aún contra lo que la razón natural vedaba, hasta que Dios fuese servido, por su oculto e inscructable juicio, de inviar los españoles a que, haciendo primero las diligencias debidas, como se verá en la conquista, les hiciesen justa guerra hasta traerlos a que por su voluntad oyesen y rescibiesen el Evangelio'; F. Cervantes de Salazar, *Crónica de la Nueva España*, 2 vols (Madrid, 1971), BAE, 244: 131 (bk 1, chap. 16). The Mayas were punished in the same way for the same sin, according to *The Book of Chilam Balam*; A. Requeña, 'Noticias y consideraciones sobre las anormalidades de las Aborígenes Americanos: sodomía,' *Acta Venezolana*, 1 (1945), 47. As for the Incas, De Pauw told how the Spanish king was convinced by sycophants that god had the Spaniards conquer the Americas because of the natives' homosexuality. Then he added: it was 'sans doute pour adoucir les remords des destructeurs du Perou que Garcilasso a soutenu que la sodomie y etoit punie de avant leur arrivee'; C. De Pauw, *Recherches Philosophiques sur les Americains* (London, 1770), 1: 67; F Guerra, *The Pre-Columbian Mind* (New York, 1971), 208. On this appraisal of Garcilaso de la Vega, see Chapter 7.

5 B. Sahagún, *Florentine Codex: General History of the Things of New Spain*, 13 vols (Santa Fe, 1975–82), bk 9: 14. Note that this question is raised regarding not an infant, but an older boy, perhaps 12 years of age.

6 Some modern work is by R. Green, *The 'Sissy Boy Syndrome' and the Development of Homosexuality* (New Haven, 1987); R. Stoller, *Presentations of Gender* (New Haven, 1985); J. Brody, 'Boyhood Effeminacy and Later Homosexuality,' *New York Times* (16 Dec. 1986). Many modern

authors studying North American tribes have recorded native fathers embarrassed by their sons exhibiting such behavior, how they tried to dissuade them, etc. A classic in this respect is the 1832–4 report of Maximilian, Prince of Wied, who at some length tells how Mandan berdaches (Mih-Dacka) insisted that they merely followed a dream-command as their medicine: unsuccessfully, 'many fathers,' says the prince, 'have tried to turn their children away from such convictions.' But others warn that awful things will happen if a berdache were to be forced from this practice; Maximilian Prinz zu Wied, *Reise in das innere Nord-America in den Jahren 1832 bis 1834* (Coblenz, 1841), 2: 132ff. Needless to say, already at that date, an overweening white society condemned such figures as 'sissies'; thus native apologies of this type are hardly reliable as evidence of pre-Columbian or pre-white attitudes.

7 The Laches 'no resista la ociosidad con que viven, y ambición que tienen de estar bien servidos, tienen por ley que si la mujer paría cinco varones continuados, sin parir hija, pudiesen hacer hembra a uno de los hijos a las doce lunas de edad, esto es, en cuanto a criarlo e imponerlo en costumbres de mujer, y como lo criaban de aquella manera, salían tan perfectas hembras en el talle y ademanes del cuerpo, que cualquiera que los viese no los diferenciaría de las otras mujeres, y a éstos llamaban Cusmos, y ejercitaban los oficios de mujeres con robustecidad de hombres, por lo cual en llegando a edad suficiente, los casaban como a mujeres y preferíanlos los Laches a las verdaderas, de que según se sigue que la abominación de la sodomía fuese permitida en esta nación'; L. Fernández Piedrahita, *Historia general del nuevo reino de Granada* (Bogotá, 1942), 1: 25. Among the Alaskan Kodiak, once this selection was made the berdache was actually trained for girlhood, so that at age 10 to 15, s/he could find a rich husband; E. Westermarck, *The Origin and Development of Moral Ideas* (London, 1917), 2: 457.

8 E. Blackwood, 'Sexuality and Gender in Certain Native American Tribes,' *Signs*, 10 (1984), 30.

9 At age 14 or 15, s/he was then married to some wealthy man; H. Bancroft, *The Works* (*The Native Races of the Pacific*, vols 1–5 [San Francisco 1883–6]), 1: 82. The only reference to female berdaches I have found in Central and South America in the early colonial period is to chaste warrior women in the Amazon by Pero de Magalhaes (fl. 1575), *The Histories of Brazil* (New York, 1922), 89f.

10 Westermarck, *Origin*, 2: 458.

11 'Puede haber sido en la tierra firme o parte de tierra firme que habemos comprendido dentro de la Nueva España, que el demonio, queriendo tener parte, como ya hemos dicho, en todo género de pecados, hubiese inducido y enseñado otro peor género de sacrificio, como fue aquel de que arriba en el capítulo [159] hecimos mención que ofrecían los moles y afeminados, porque se hallaron (según dijeron algunos españoles) algunos mozos vestidos como mujeres.' The cross-dressing was not for reasons of sodomy, 'sino solamente por hacerles sacrificio agradable'; B. de Las Casas,

Apologética historia Sumaria, 2 vols (Mexico City, 1967), 2: 232 (chap. 180).

12   'Si faceva descrizione di tutte le donne gravide che erano nella terra, e che la prima di esse che partoriva maschio, era deputato a dover far quell'esercizio muliebre ... Questi tali non possono aver commercio carnale con donna alcuna, ma sí ben con essi tutti i giovani della terra che sono da maritarsi.' Alarcón's main interest was in the males' prostitution, for he follows by describing the female prostitutes: this oldest text is in G. Ramusio, *Navigazioni e viaggi* (Turin, 1978–85), 6: 652.

13   A rarity in this regard, G. Bleibtreu-Ehrenberg speaks of 'willkürliche Umklassifizierungen von Jungen in Mädchen ... bereits *vor* der Geburt eines Kindes'; *Der Weibmann* (Frankfurt am Main, 1984), 104. Needless to say, W. Williams 'doubt[s] the validity of such written sources'; *The Spirit and the Flesh: Sexual Diversity in American Indian Culture* (Boston, 1992), xii (a new introduction to the paperback edition).

14   E. C. Parsons, 'The Zuñi La'mana,' *American Anthropologist*, 18 (1916), 521, 525f. Compare these protestations that a child exercised 'free will' to those in any traditional Catholic society that young girls married of their own free will, when of course they did not.

15   'Algunos de estos sacerdotes no tenían mujeres, sino en lugar de ellas muchachos de que abusaban; pecado tan común en estas regiones, que mozos y viejos le cometían, y hasta niños de seis anos solían hallarse infestados de el. Más ahora, gracias a Dios, han comenzado muchos a seguir el orden natural, y convertidos ya al cristianismo, piden con grande ansia el bautismo y confiesan sus pecados'; J. García Icazbalceta (ed.), *Bibliografía Mexicana del siglo XVI* (Mexico City, 1886), 398. Note the emphasis on older practitioners.

16   'Desde chequito lo havia acostumbrado'; see the full text at Chapter 3, note 21.

17   'Me respondieron: que ellos no tenían culpa, porque desde el tiempo de sus niñez los avian puesto allí sus caciques, para usar con ellos este maldito y nefando vicio, y para ser sacerdotes y guarda de los templos de sus Indios'; P. Cieza de León, *Crónica del Perú* (Lima, Universidad Católica del Perú), 1: 200 (bk 1, chap. 64).

18   This age would be decreased if, like the modern Hindu sect of boys called Jinras, children were prepared for passive reception by having their anuses widened with wooden or metal conical objects; G. Rattray Taylor, 'Historical and Methodological Aspects of Homosexuality,' in J. Marmor (ed.), *Sexual Inversion: the Multiple Roots of Homosexuality* (New York, 1965), 162.

19   A. Holder, 'The Bote: Description of a Peculiar Sexual Perversion Found Among North American Indians,' *New York Medical Journal*, 50, no. 575 (7 Dec. 1889), 624. See also F. Karsch-Haack, 'Uranismus oder Päderastie und Tribadie bei den Naturvölkern,' *Jahrbuch für sexuelle Zwischenstufen*, 3 (1901), 138. Significantly, not anal reception but fellation was the practice among the Crow berdache on whom Holder commented.

20 G. Devereux, 'Greek Pseudo-Homosexuality,' *Symbolae Osloenses*, 42
    (1968), 69–92, esp. 73. Devereux knew the American materials as well.
    See his 'Institutionalized Homosexuality of the Mohave Indians,' *Human
    Biology*, 9 (1937), 498–527. Devereux called this 'pseudo-homosexuality'
    because it had more to do with social than with psychological realities:
    adolescents sought out the companionship of older males because they
    lacked attention from their fathers. See further below on Devereux's
    important concept of 'sliding.'

21 M. Rocke, *Male Homosexuality and its Regulation in Late Medieval
    Florence* (diss.: SUNY, Binghamton, 1989), 257.

22 One wonders how often accusations of sodomy were based on little more
    than having seen men transvested and acting like women. Oviedo: 'Y así,
    habes de saber que el que dellos es paciente o toma cargo de ser mujer en
    aquel bestial e descomulgado acto, le dan luego oficio de mujer, e trae
    naguas como mujer'; *Historia general y natural de las Indias* (Madrid,
    1959), BAE, 117: 119 (bk 5, chap. 3); 'Entre los indios en muchas partes
    es muy común el pecado nefando contra natura, y públicamente los indios
    que son señores y principales que en esto pecan tienen mozos con quien
    usan este maldito pecado; y los tales mozos pacientes, asi como caen en
    esta culpa, luego se ponen naguas, como mujeres, que son unas mantas
    cortas de algodón, con que las Indias andan cubiertas desde la cinta hasta
    las rodillas, y se ponen sartales y puñetes de cuentas y las otras cosas que
    por arreo usan las mujeres, y no se ocupan en el uso de las armas, ni hacen
    cosa que los hombres ejerciten, sino luego se ocupan en el servicio comun
    de las casas; así como barrer y gregar y las otras cosas á mujeres
    acostumbradas. Son aborrecidos estos tales de las mujeres en extremo
    grado; pero como son muy sujetas á sus maridos, no osan hablar en ello
    sino pocas veces, ó con los cristianos. Llaman en aquella lengua de Cueva
    a estos tales pacientes Camayoa; y asi, entre ellos cuando un indio a otro
    quiere injuriar o decirle por vituperio que es afeminado y para poco, le
    llama camayoa'; *Sumario de la natural historia de las Indias* (Madrid,
    1946), BAE, 22: 508 (chap. 81), describing the province of Cueva
    (Panama). Note that, in both cases, being dressed like a woman followed
    after assuming the passive homosexual role.

23 Obviously, only boys approaching 12 years of age could safely receive a
    penis. Without specifying actives or passives, López de Velasco (1574)
    says natives of 'Florida' were 'shamed by being forced to dress in women's
    garments'; cited in Guerra, *Pre-Columbian Mind*, 130; Cieza says that, in
    the valleys and mountains around Puerto Viejo (Ecuador), sodomy was
    not widespread, but when it did occur, people began 'llamándole muger:
    diziéndole que dexase el habito de hombre que tenía'; *Crónica*, 1: 195 (bk
    1, chap. 62), and also 1: 235 (bk 1, chap. 80). Such punishments were
    used in Spain, and may have predisposed our sources to find them in the
    Americas; M. Perry, *Crime and Society in Early Modern Seville* (Hanover,
    NH, 1980), 142 (1585).

24 'Queriendo saber la cabsa por que traíe ábito de muger, confesó que desde

chequito lo havía acostumbrado y ganava su bida con los hombres al oficio'; see the full text at Chapter 3, note 21.

25 'Andaban vestidos en hábito de mujeres muchachos a ganar en aquel diabólico y abominable oficio'; *Historia verdadera de la conquista de la Nueva España* (Mexico City, 1968), 2: 359 (chap. 208).

26 Speaking of the time *before* the arrival of the Spaniards: 'Asimismo se prueba de oídas que en la provincia del Collao había algunos indios que cometían el pecado nefando, y que, para usar deste pecado, se vestían como mujeres y se afeitaban; algunos testigos dicen que los castigaban, y otros que no'; included in F. Montesinos, *Memorias antiguas historiales y políticas del Perú* (Madrid, 1882), 199f. These males were called *orua*; see the judicial testimony in 'Información de las idolatrias de los Incas e indios e de como se enterraban, etc.' in the *Colección de documentos inéditos . . . en América y Oceanía* (Madrid, 1874), 21: 131–220, questions 18 and 19; see also Guerra, *Pre-Columbian Mind*, 127. Recall that European female prostitutes sometimes dressed as males so as to seduce males; Trexler, *Dependence in Context in Renaissance Florence* (Binghamton, 1994), 394f.

27 See the text above at note 22.

28 See the text above at note 22. Oviedo's text is confirmed for Mexico as well by a ca. 1553 text: 'En [Mexico] avía hombres vestidos en ábitos de mugeres y estos eran someticos y h[a]zian los officios de mugeres como es texer y hilar y algunos s[eñores] tenían uno y dos para sus vicios'; F. Gómez de Orozco (ed.), 'Costumbres, fiestas, enterramientos y diversas formas de proceder de los Indios de Nueva España,' *Tlalocán*, 2 (1945), 58.

29 'Es gente muy viciosa, ociosa, de poco trabajo . . . [etc.]; son también idólatras, abujioneros, adúlteros, dados y acostumbrados á pecados nefandos y abominables: y cada uno de estos indios tenía una, dos ó tres mujeres, ó las que más podían sustentar, y no solo para el uso y ayuntamiento que naturalmente suelen tener los casados, mas para otros bestiales y nefandos pecados, de que se usaban en muchas maneras, así ellos como ellas, por ser como, en efecto eran, muy desordenados y sucio en lo que era este vicio de la carne en todos cuantos excesos se pueden pensar é imaginar; y el que de ellos tomaba cargo de ser mujer ó hacer su oficio en aquel bestial y descomulgado acto, luego se vestía en hábito de mujer y así trataba y le daban ofício como á tal'; Martín de Murúa, *Historia de los Incas, Reyes del Perú* (Lima, 1922), 122f (bk 2, chap. 4).

30 R. Trexler, *Public Life In Renaissance Florence* (New York, 1980), 370f.

31 Las Casas, *Apologética historia*, 2: 24f (chap. 139). For the exploitation of captive boys by the priests in the temples of Mexico during the feast of Xilomanaliztli, see Gómez de Orosco, 'Costumbres,' 39.

32 Devereux, 'Institutionalized Homosexuality,' 499f.

33 He accepted a pretty girl instead: 'Puerum annorum duodecim oblatum a Regulo recusavit Praetor [Grijalva], puellam admisit pulchre ornatam, sociis invitis puerum abiecit'; D'Anghiera, *Opera*, 150 (dec. 4, chap. 4).

For boys as sexual gifts from one Siwan father to another in Africa, see C. Ford and F. Beach, *Patterns of Sexual Behavior* (New York, 1951), 132.

34 'Cuando algunos hijos de señores se casaban con doncella muy pequeñas, los parientes de la desposada le daban una esclava para que gozase de ella hasta tanto que venía la edad para la desposada; pero los hijos que había de ella, nunca subían á ser señores, aunque no los tuviese de las mugeres legítimas, porque eran hijos de esclava'; F. Xímenez (fl. 1721), *Las historias del origen de los Indios de esta provincia de Guatemala* (Vienna, 1857), 208; partially cited in H. Bancroft, *Works*, 2: 664.

35 'Cerca del pecado nefando, lo que hay que con verdad decir es que nunca se vido entre aquellas gentes, antes se tuvo por grande y abominable pecado, hasta que les apareció un demonio en figura de indio, llamado Cu, y en otra lengua Chin, y en otras Cavil, y Maran, que los indujo a que lo cometiesen, como el lo cometió con otro demonio, y de aquí vino a que no lo tuvieron algunos dellos por pecado, diciendo que pues aquel dios o diablo lo cometía y lo persuadio, que no debía ser pecado'; Las Casas, *Apologética*, 2: 522 (chap. 239).

36 'De allí vino que daban algunos padres a los que eran mozos un niño para que lo tuviesen por mujer, y si algún otro llegaba al niño se lo mandaban pagar como hacen cerca de las mujeres el que violaba mujer ajena. Con toda esta corrupción, si alguno forzaba algun muchacho resistiéndolo el, lo castigaban con la pena del que forzaba mujer, y lo que más es, que todos los viejos y viejas reprehendían y reñían con los muchachos porque consentían en si aquellos malos actos, que eran gran pecado, y que se guardasen del, porque se morirían los que tal sufriesen y cometiesen. Finalmente, siempre había dellos quien murmuraba del y lo afeaban y abominaban'; Las Casas, *Apologética*, loc. cit. It is not specified, but I think implied, that the boy assumed female clothing.

37 For the Australian Aranda, see Ford and Beach, *Patterns*, 132. Devereux analyzes this period before heterosexual coition as one of 'sliding,' in which *inter alia* young Spartans were allowed by tribal customs to move from sexual passivity to activity with the least anxiety by using boys, girls dressed as boys, and the like; 'Greek Pseudo-Homosexuality,' 84f. This institution of a boy being bestowed by an elder on a pre-nuptial youth till the latter married, one type of 'marriage,' seems to be mentioned nowhere in the American literature but in Las Casas. Presumably he told of it from his experience as Bishop of Chiapas, hard on Guatemala, for he does not seem to have copied the same from an earlier writer, as was commonly the case. More generally, the phenomenon of parents because of need maintaining a culture in which they sell or rent out their young boys and girls to visitors is not difficult to document in today's world; see, e.g., S. Mydans, 'Philippine Town's Parents Battle Effort to Stop Their Children's Sex Trade,' *New York Times*, 2 Feb. 1989, where residents of Pagsanjan say: 'You're not going to get pregnant, and you get the money.'

38 Thus, in this Kimberley District of Western Australia, males rarely married until they were beyond forty years of age; Westermarck, *Origin*, 2: 460.

39   See Trexler, 'From the Mouths of Babes,' in *Church and Community* (Rome, 1987), *passim*.

40   'Por esta causa eran los padres muy solicitos de casallos cuan presto podían por los apartar de aquella corrupción vilísima, aunque casallos muchachos contra su voluntad y forzados y solamente por aquel respecto lo hacían; la razón es porque tenían de custubre de nunca casar los hijos hasta que pasaban de treinta años arriba'; Las Casas, *Apologética historia*, 2: 515 (chap. 237).

41   Medieval fathers were commonly accused of facilitating their sons' prostitution; see Trexler, *Public Life*, 379–82. Thus Giordano da Pisa preaching in Florence on 4 August 1303: 'Io ho trovato più volte che'l padre ha detto al figliuolo: "va, guadagna, e vestiti, e calzati"'; A. Bragaglia, *Degli 'Evirati Cantori'* (Florence, 1959), 17. On this market, see Rocke, *Male Homosexuality and its Regulation*. On poor Italian fathers having their sons castrated for operatic purposes (about 1500 onward) and then sometimes selling them, see A. Heriot, *The Castrati in Opera* (London, 1956), 38f.

42   The recently deceased Henry IV of Castile, for example, had perfected such an exchange mechanism; T. Miller, *Henry IV of Castile* (Philadelphia, 1972), 80–95 and *passim*. In Florence, preachers raged that the Medici (= 'doctors') healed sodomy; Trexler, *Public Life*, 381. The comic literature of this city is crammed with images of sexy boys processing behind unnamed politicos.

43   A. Kehoe, 'The Function of Ceremonial Sexual Intercourse Among the Northern Plains Indians,' *Plains Anthropologist*, 15 (1970), 99–103. Within tribes with graded men's societies, (presumably younger) men lent each other their wives for sex so as to pass power to them. Among the Mandan especially, this might 'purchase' entry into a society.

44   Pánuco: 'Son asimesmo grandísimos putos, y tienen mancebía de hombres públicamente, de se acogen las noches mil dellos'; López de Gómara, *Historia*, 22: 183 (pt 1). Speaking of the lords of Darién, Gómara says their boys dressed as women to avoid going to war: the 'señores' 'tienen mancebías públicas de mujeres, y aún de hombres en muchos cabos, que visten y sirven como hembras sin les ser afrenta, antes se excusan por ello, queriendo, de ir a la guerra'; *Historia*, 22: 199 (pt 1). For the South American coast, see Oviedo, *Sumario*, 22: 508 (chap. 81), cited above at note 22.

45   'Y que también habían de ser limpios de sodomías. Porque tenían muchachos vestidos en habitos de mujeres que andaban a ganar en aquel maldito oficio'; Díaz del Castillo, *Historia*, 1: 162 (chap. 52). Note the link between religion (the images) and male prostitutes.

46   See my hypothesis about Medici authority in Florence, in *Public Life*, 381, and the evidence that, as landlords of brothels, families of such standing were able to offer clients female prostitutes; Trexler, *Dependence in Context in Renaissance Florence* (Binghamton, 1994), 387–91.

47   W. Hammond, for example, got the Pueblan cacique to admit that, as a young man, he had had the use of berdaches; *Sexual Impotence in the*

Male and Female (Detroit, 1887), 169f. The best-known case of domestic service for white people is the Zuni berdache We'wha's acting as a domestic for Matilda Cox Stevenson, described in W. Roscoe, *The Zuni Man-Woman* (Albuquerque, 1991). Cf. to this language: 'One of them does "squaw" work . . . with such skill and good nature that he frequently finds employment among the white residents'; Holder, 'The Bote,' 624. This is almost a common statement among nineteenth-century travellers.

48   Compare this mechanism with that documented in Rwanda and Tahiti by D. Greenberg, *The Construction of Homosexuality* (Chicago, 1988), 118.

49   I. Silverblatt, *Moon, Sun and Devil* (Princeton, 1987).

50   'Por sólo aquello juzgaron ser de aquel pecado corrompidos'; Las Casas, *Apologética*, 2: 540f (chap. 243). Such caution in making this linkage does not appear again for two centuries, when the Jesuit Lafitau said that 'the ignorance of Europeans as to the [religious] causes of their [transvested] condition' might explain why early writers 'imagined the most disadvantageous things that could be imagined' about the berdaches, that is, sodomy; J. Lafitau, *Customs of the American Indians Compared with the Customs of Primitive Times*, trans. W. Fenton and E. Moore (Toronto, 1974), 1: 57f; cited in J. Katz (ed.), *Gay American History* (New York, 1976), 289.

51   Las Casas, *Apologética*, 2: 232f (chap. 180).

52   Thus as regards the berdache, Las Casas sharply distinguished a woman's other duties from her sexual role: 'Oficios digo, no los vicios nefandos'; Las Casas, *Apologética*, 2: 233 (chap. 180). Even berdaches were few and far between. While Oviedo proclaimed that 'todos son sodomitos,' Las Casas said that, in all his years in Cuba, he had only encountered one transvestite; Las Casas, *Apologética*, 2: 232f (chap. 180).

53   'Solamente por hacerles sacrificio agradable'; *Apologética*, 2: 232 (chap. 180).

54   See, e.g., Hammond, *Sexual Impotence*, 163, 168, who, apparently thinking the Castilian word *amujerado* indicated that some dramatic step had been taken to render a male 'womanized,' decided that this action (or punishment, or public ritual humiliation) of repeated masturbation was what was meant by his Pueblan informants. I found no early colonial source, however, referring to the masturbation of a berdache. See A. Edwardes, *Erotica Judaica* (New York, 1967), 161, for the ancient Jewish punishment of being repeatedly masturbated in public; the same author's *The Jewel in the Lotus* (New York, 1959), 190, refers to its use by harem women. Without clear references to time or place, the same Edwardes, along with R. Masters, *The Cradle of Erotica: a Study of Afro-Asian Sexual Expression and an Analysis of Erotic Freedom in Social Relationships* (New York, 1962), 201, describes relays of women masturbating a berdache-to-be to render him impotent. However, recall the phobic association of masturbation causing impotence in nineteenth-century medicine; A. Karlen, *Sexuality and Homosexuality* (New York, 1971), 182f.

55 'Son como eunucos, inhábiles para ser casados, por lo cual hacen todos los oficios de las mujeres, así en hablar como en obras, y llamánlos afeminados; oficios digo, no los vicios nefandos'; Las Casas, *Apologética*, 2: 233 (chap. 180); the same author's *Historia de las Indias*, 3 vols (Mexico City, 1965), 2: 518 (bk 3, chap. 47); *Galen's Commentary on the Hippocratic Treatise, Airs, Waters, Places* (Jerusalem, 1982) in fact contains no reference to Scythians, as Las Casas claims. Hippocrates' own fascinating and relevant text on the matter is, however, in that treatise; *Hippocrates*, trans. W. H. S. Jones (Cambridge, MA, 1957), 1: 125–31 (chaps 21, 22). Hammond, *Sexual Impotence*, 157ff, uses the same story of the Scythian equestrian impotents to partially explain the Pueblan *amujerado*, needlessly; Las Casas's term *afeminado* is obviously akin to the New Mexican term *amujerado*, both meaning 'having become womanly.'

56 Herodotus, *The Persian Wars* (New York, 1942), 59f (bk 1, chap. 105).

57 'Las orejas son de tal naturaleza que sangrándolas causan esterilidad ... No por andar a caballo, sino por la muncha sangre, quizá, che se sacaron de las orejas o de otras partes, o por otros accidentes que non sabemos'; *Apologética*, 2: 233 (chap. 180); *Historia*, 2: 518; cf. *Hippocrates*, 1: 125–31 (chaps 21, 22). Las Casas's 'other parts' could refer shamefacedly and among other things to the famous penile bloodletting of the Maya, on which see L. Schele and M. Miller, *The Blood of Kings* (New York, 1986).

58 Las Casas, *Apologética*, 2: 541 (chap. 243); *Historia*, 2: 518 (bk 3, chap. 47).

59 *Historia*, 2: 518 (bk 3, chap. 47). Las Casas's reasoning is strikingly similar to what Wikan found among the Omani xanith she studied – effeminate males, forbidden to cross-dress, who sometimes married. If as widowers they wished to resume that status, they announced it by some public act, like singing at a wedding, that indicated they were no longer men; U. Wikan, *Behind the Veil In Arabia* (Baltimore, 1982), chap. 9; M. Garber, *Vested Interests* (New York, 1992), 349.

60 Las Casas, *Apologética*, 2: 359, 540 (chaps 206, 243), and the long consideration of the goddess 'Berecintia' in 2: 122–33 (chap. 158–9). Though uncited, Las Casas's source is the description of the *cinaedos* in Apuleius, described in Chapter 1.

61 Cited in A. Bastian, *Der Mensch in der Geschichte* (Leipzig, 1860), 3: 313f. Needless to say, those who avoid men and live exclusively with women run no risk of homosexual behavior.

62 M. Eliade, *Shamanism* (Princeton, 1972), 350ff, citing Roth.

63 V. Tixier, *Travels on the Osage Prairies* (Norman, 1940), 234. Tixier explained his name *Bredache* was 'that of an hermaphrodite animal'!

64 'Sodomy is a crime not uncommonly committed; many of the subjects of it are publicly known, and do not appear to be despised, or to excite disgust; one of them was pointed out to us: he had submitted himself to it, in consequence of a vow he had made to his mystic medicine, which

obliged him to change his dress for that of a squaw, to do their work, and to permit his hair to grow. The men carefully pluck their chins . . .'; report of Thomas Say, in *From Pittsburgh to the Rocky Mountains: Major Stephen Long's Expedition, 1819–1820*, ed. Maxine Benson (Golden, CO, 1988), 93; cited by Karsch-Haack, 'Uranismus,' 133.

65 Bleibtreu-Ehrenberg, *Der Weibmann*, 100ff. This author is one of the few who sensed that elderly men made up a separate class of berdaches and that their number was perhaps underestimated.

66 Palou, the friend and biographer of Junipero Serra in California, was convinced that was the goal of the local berdaches: 'Y menos el meterse entre las mujeres, con quienes se presumía estaría pecando'; F. Palou, *Relación histórica de la vida y apostólicas tareas del venerable padre Fray Junípero Serra* (Mexico City, 1982), 152. The only hint of bisexualism I know of, in 1673, regards Araucanian berdaches; 'No usan el cabello largo, siendo que todos los demas andan trenzados; se ponen también sus gargantillas, anillos y otras alhajas mujeriles, siendo muy estimados y respetados de hombres y mujeres, porque hacen con estas oficio de hombres, y con aquellos de mujeres'; F. Núñez de Pineda y Bascuñán, *Cautiverio feliz y razón de las guerras dilatadas de Chile* (Santiago de Chile, 1863), cited in A. Métraux, 'Le shamanisme Araucan,' *Revista del Instituto de Antropología, Universidad Nacional de Tucuman*, 2 (1942), 311f.

67 It is unclear if permanent female clothing was still the rule in Mexico City in 1658, when 14 persons were burned for sodomy; S. Gruzinski, 'Las cenizas del deseo: homosexuales novohispanos a mediados del siglo XVII,' in S. Ortega (ed.), *De la santidad a la perversión, O de porqué no se cumplía la ley de Dios en la sociedad novohispana* (Mexico City, 1985), 255–81; C. Taylor, 'Homosexuality in Precolumbian and Colonial Mexico,' in S. Murray (ed.), *Male Homosexuality in Central and South America* (New York, 1987), 14–17. But generally, in colonial areas, the repression of transvestism in daily public life proved easier to enforce than bans on homosexual behavior. Today's Oman presents an interesting case. There, the *xanith* or effeminate sometimes reassumes male sexual activity, but this must be linked to the fact that s/he is prohibited by law from donning women's clothes; Wikan, *Behind the Veil*, 174ff.

68 'Estant encor jeunes prennent l'habit des femmes qu'ils gardent toute leur vie'; *The Jesuit Relations and Allied Documents: Travels and Explorations of the Jesuit Missionaries in New France, 1610–1791*, ed. R. Gold Thwaites, 59 (1959), 128ff, and 309f for references to other tribes.

69 See especially the cautionary tabulations of this literature made by W. Roscoe, 'Bibliography of Berdache and Alternative Gender Roles Among North American Indians,' *Journal of Homosexuality*, 14 (1987), 154–70.

70 That seems to be the view of scholars such as L. Mott ('Pagode português') and A. Richlin (*The Garden of Priapus*), who, on finding groups of

transvestites associating together, speak of 'homosexuals' as constituting a social 'sub-group.' Yet without *dedicated* actives as partners, that is a dubious formulation.

CHAPTER 5 THE RELIGIOUS BERDACHE

1   R. T. Zuidema, *Inca Civilization in Cuzco* (Austin, 1990), 33.
2   'Y diré cómo se puso una picota en la plaza y fuera de la villa una horca'; B. Díaz del Castillo, *Historia verdadera de la conquista de la Nueva España* (Mexico City, 1968), 1: 139 (chap. 42), describing the foundation of Vera Cruz on Good Friday, 1519; cf. F. Graziano, *Divine Violence* (Boulder, CO, 1992), 159f.
3   One may survey the impressive early literature, beginning with Pierre Bayle on the Incas, in R. Goodland, *A Bibliography of Sex Rites and Customs* (London, 1931), under the indexed term 'Sodomy, ritual.'
4   Hammond's observations date to 1850–1; he published them first as 'The Disease of the Scythians (Morbus Feminarum) and Certain Analogous Conditions,' *American Journal of Neurology and Psychiatry*, 1 (1882), 339–55, then more elaborately in his *Sexual Impotence in the Male and Female* (Detroit, 1887), 157–73. H. Hay has reprinted this latter text with commentary: 'The Hammond Report: a Deposition, with Subsequent Commentary, on the Conspiracy of Silence anent Social Homophilia,' *One Institute Quarterly*, 6 (1963), 6–21. The essentials: Like many people of his time, Hammond believed the Pueblo peoples were sun-worshippers who descended from the Aztecs and who were awaiting the reappearance of their former emperor Montezuma. West of Albuquerque at Laguna Pueblo, he interviewed a 35-year-old transvestite who had been coerced into becoming a berdache, or *amujerado* (cf. the common Castilian *afeminado*: become feminized), at age 28. He interviewed another berdache at nearby Acoma who was 36 years old and had been *amujerado* for ten years. Hammond was told that each pueblo had one berdache. Besides the sexual services he may have rendered males throughout the year, the berdache was 'the chief passive agent in the pederastic ceremonies [later called orgies] which form so important a part of the performances. These take place in the spring of each year'; Hammond, 'Disease of the Scythians,' 343; *Sexual Impotence*, 164–8; Hay, 'Hammond Report,' 9–12.
    Half a century later, Parsons found no evidence that the Zuni berdaches were involved in religion; E. Clews Parsons, 'The Zuñi La'Mana,' *American Anthropologist*, 18 (1916), 524. Yet still today, a man-woman katchina, Kolhamana, that is, a religious image, plays an important role in the sacred Sha'lako procession, and in the later nineteenth century the famed Zuni berdache We'wha played the role of Kolhamana; W. Roscoe, *The Zuni Man-Woman* (Albuquerque, 1991), 148.
5   Hay, 'The Hammond Report,' has summarized this matter, rightly center-

ing on the unwillingness of many subsequent students to recognize the important symbolic and behavioral position of these berdaches in native societies. Assertedly philo-native whites seem at times to dismiss Hammond as if those who link religion and sexuality, like Hammond, want to humiliate native peoples. In fact, of course, the berdaches, and their behaviors, were and, to the extent they still exist, still are a fascinating, highly creative, and worthy part of native cultures.

6 On castrati as gate-tenders of the nunneries, see P. Cieza de León, *Crónica del Perú* (Lima, 1984–6), 1: 146 (chap. 44). Also Blas Valera about 1590: 'Muchos destos se ofrecían desde mochachos y duraban, no solo en continencia hasta la vejez, pero en virginidad ... Muchos destos o los más eran eunuchos, que ellos dicen corasca, que, o ellos mismos se castraban, en reverencia de sus dioses, o los castraban otros cuando eran mochachos, para que sirviesen en esta manera de vivir'; B. Valera (attrib.), *Relación de las costumbres antiguas* (Madrid, 1968), BAE, 209: 168f; F. Guerra, *The Pre-Columbian Mind* (New York, 1971), 141, 258. About the same time, the historian Pedro Gutiérrez de Santa Clara wrote that the Incas mutilated the noses and lips of the servants in their temples of the sun to make them unattractive to the *acllas*, without specifying if they were berdaches or eunuchs: 'Capaban y cortaban las narices y labios a los indios que servían en estos templos y los mataban cruelmente si alguno dellos tenía deshonesta conversación con ellas, a los cuales colgaban de los pies dándoles humo a las narices con axiseco hasta que muría rabiando. Y después de muerto lo descolgaban y hacían pedazos y los cuartos echaban al campo como cosa maldita y descomulgada'; P. Gutiérrez de Santa Clara (ca. 1580), *Historia de las guerras civiles del Perú* (Madrid, 1965), BAE, 166: 215 (bk 3, chap. 50). These disfigurements may be linked to Moche figurines discussed below; see also Guerra, *Pre-Columbian Mind*, 141, 258. See further, I. Gareis, *Religiöse Spezialisten des zentralen Andengebietes zur Zeit der Inka und während der spanischen Kolonialherrschaft* (Hohenschäftlarn: K. Renner, 1987), 95.

7 Though, as we have seen, Las Casas denied the connection of sodomy with transvestism in Tierra Firme; *Apologética historia*, 2: 232 (chap. 180), text given above, chapter 4, note 11. See also Fernández de Oviedo, *Historia general y natural de las Indias* (Madrid, 1959), BAE, 119: 127 (bk 26, chap. 30), on boys sacrificed in what is today Colombia, but with no indication of sexual usage.

8 Rites which did not give a just title for conquest, according to J. Acosta, *De procuranda indorum salute*, in *Obras* (Madrid, 1954), BAE, 73: 432 (bk 2, chap. 3).

9 'Oh Titlacauan puto, hacéis burla de mi!'; Bernardino de Sahagún, *Historia general de las cosas de Nueva España*, 4 vols (Mexico City, 1956), 1: 277 (III, 2); Guerra, *Pre-Columbian Mind*, 69. See also another of his names, Telpochtli, 'the young man,' for Tezcatlipoca; J. Soustelle, *L'Univers des Aztècques* (Paris, 1979), 31. Probably only an insult was involved; C. Klein finds no literary representation of an Aztec male divinity as

effeminate; 'Fighting With Femininity,' in Trexler, *Gender Rhetorics* (Binghamton, 1994), 118–24.

10 'El demonio para más predominallos los cegó e hizo creer que entre sus dioses se usó y fue licito aqueste vicio. E no obstante que ansí se lo notificó e introdujo, segund sus historias lo manifiestan, como sea vicio tan repugnante a la naturaleza, siempre lo tovieron por malo ye en grand deshonra y enfamia'; Toribio, called Motolinía, *Memoriales e historia de los Indios de la Nueva España* (Madrid, 1970), BAE, 240: 142. See also J. de Torquemada, *Monarquia indiana* (Mexico City, 1969), 2: 392ff (bk 12, chap. 11); Las Casas, *Apologética historia*, 2: 522 (chap. 239). Satan, being a natural creature, hated sodomy even though he caused men to practice it; Bernardino of Siena, cited in Trexler, *Dependence in Context in Renaissance Florence* (Binghamton, 1994), 376 (1425); and in America: P. Ragon, *Les amours indiennes* (Paris, 1992), 54 (Rome, 1480s); J. Trevisan, *Perverts in Paradise* (London, 1986), 67 (1707 Bahía synodal constitutions).

11 See Klein's information in her 'Rethinking Cihuacoatl,' in J. K. Josserand and K. Dakin (eds), *Smoke and Mist* (Oxford, 1988). For Maya practices, see A. Stone, 'Aspects of Impersonation in Classic Maya Art,' *Sixth Palenque Round Table, 1986* (Norman, 1991), 194–202. I wish to thank Professor Stone for her help in this matter.

12 Both cited in M. Graulich, 'Ochpaniztli, la fête des semailles des anciens mexicains,' *Anales de antropología*, 18 (1981), 59–100, esp. 74.

13 G. Olivier, 'Conquérants et missionaires face au "péché abominable": essai sur l'homosexualité en Mésoamérique au moment de la conquête espagnole,' *C. M. H. L. B. Caravelle 55* (1990), 36f.

14 See the full text in Chapter 4, at note 15. Ragon, *Amours indiennes*, missed this crucial primary source.

15 That is, the duty to receive sodomites: 'Según decían y alcanzamos a saber, aquellos papas eran hijos de principales y no tenían mujeres, más tenían el maldito oficio de sodomías'; *Historia*, 1: 162 (chap. 52). Neither I nor A. Karlen can confirm the latter's statement that the younger sons of prominent Aztecs were at times castrated and sent to temples 'to serve as *bijanas*, "dedicated to the gods"'; Karlen, *Sexuality and Homosexuality* (New York, 1971), 236.

16 See the quotes in Chapter 4, at note 4.

17 Cited in Guerra, *Pre-Columbian Mind*, 125.

18 T. Bozio, *De signis ecclesiae dei*, 3 vols (Cologne, 1593), 1: 519 (bk 7, signum 29); cited in Ragon, *Amours indiennes*, 77.

19 'En dos o tres provincias bien lejos de Mexico sé que ovo sodomía causi permitida ... por carecer de ley de gracia y divina'; *Memoriales*, 240: 141f.

20 On such attitudes and insults, see Chapter 7.

21 It was for this reason fathers tried to marry the boys off even before they had reached thirty years of age: 'Por causa de que fuesen instruidos en la religion mandábanles dormir en los templos, donde los mozos mayores en

aquel vicio a los niños corrompían, y después salidos de allí mal acostumbrados, dificíl era librallos de aquel vicio. Por esta causa eran los padres muy solicitos de casallos cuan presto podían por los apartar de aquella corrupción vilísima, aunque casallos muchachos contra su voluntad y forzados y solamente por aquel respecto lo hacían; la razón es porque tenían de custubre de nunca casar los hijos hasta que pasaban de treinta años arriba'; *Apologética*, 2: 515 (chap. 237). Early in the present century, von Hahn described homosexual relations between passive Albanians 12 years old or older and active adolescents 16 and older. The lovers took communion together; cited in J. Bremmer, 'An Enigmatic Indo-European Rite,' *Arethusa*, 13 (1980), 289.

22 'Y es gran falsedad y testimonio pernicioso lo que algunos de los nuestros les levantan, que los mancebos que había en los templos cometían unos con otros el nefando pecado. Esto es gran maldad, porque (como abajo se verá) si tal cosa cometieran, luego fueran muertos ahorcados o quemados. Y desto estamos certificados de religiosos y personas seglares que lo han inquirido sabiendo la lengua, y aún que desde muchachos estando mucho tiempo entre ellos, los cuales ya son viejos, y de quien no se curaban de guardar, en cuya presencia hacían su bueno y su malo, y estos testifican que nunca tal cosa hallaron'; Las Casas, *Apologética historia*, 2: 24, no. 1 (chap. 139).

23 The earlier text remains, but the variant is appended: 'Algunos de los nuestros han dicho que los mancebos que en estos templos se criaban cometían el pecado nefando, no en todas, sino en algunas partes o provincias; pero siempre se tuvo por malo. En algunas, como en la que llaman de los mixes [Oaxaca], muy cruelmente los quemaban y celebraban el castigo desta manera: que se juntaban todos los sacerdotes y viejos y personas principales en una sala del templo, cada uno de los cuales tenía un tizón de fuego en la mano, y ponian el delincuente desnudo delante cada una dellos, y el primero le hacia una gran reprehension, diciendo: "Oh, malvado! Como osabas hacer en la casa de los dioses tan gran pecado?" y otras palabras muy asperas; y acabadas, dábale con el tizón un gran golpe, y así todos hacían cada uno; el que más podía lo reprehendía, y con el tizón lo lastimaba. Despues lo sacaban fuera del templo y lo entregaban a los muchachos que lo quemasen, y así lo quemaban'; *Apologética historia*, 2: 24f (chap. 139).

24 See Trexler, 'Ritual in Florence: Adolescence and Salvation,' in *Dependence in Context*, 296 seq., for the problem as experienced in Florence.

25 Torquemada, *Monarquia Indiana*, 2: 186f (bk 9, chap. 13). G. Freyre, on the contrary, believes that the 'big houses' where male youth lived explain native Brazilian homosexual comportment; *The Masters and the Slaves* (New York, 1971), 123. It should not escape the reader that this discourse about the purity of Aztec schools was a way to emphasize purity within their own friary schools; see Trexler, 'From the Mouths of Babes,' in *Church and Community, 1200–1600* (Rome, 1987).

26 'Son mintrosos, ladrones, crueles sométicos, ingratos, sin honora, sin

vergüenza, sin caridad ni virtud'; Lopez de Gómara, *Historia de las Indias* (Madrid, 1946), BAE, 22: 278 (pt 1).

27 Oviedo's phrase, in his *Historia*, 117: 119. Garcilaso de la Vega follows Cieza in this matter; see his *Comentarios reales de los Incas*, 3 vols (Madrid, 1960–3), BAE, 133: 24 (bk 1, chap. 14); ibid., 208 (bk 6, chap. 11); ibid., 218 (bk 6, chap. 19). I have generally used H. Livermore's translation (Austin, 1966). See Chapter 7 for a close study of Garcilaso's motivations.

28 'Los que an escrito generalmente de los yndios condenándolos en general en este pecado, afirmando que son todos sométicos,' is in the *Crónica*, 2: 74f (pt 2, chap. 25).

29 In chapter 25 of part 2 of the *Crónica*, the argument runs: 1) there is widespread sodomy at Puerto Viejo; 2) elsewhere there are only the occasional 'pecadores'; 3) 'porque los que tenían por sacerdotes en los templos, con quien es fama que en los días de fiestas se ayuntavan con ellos los señores, no pensavan ellos que cometían maldad ni que hazían peccado'; *Crónica*, 2: 74f. That is, Cieza thought that homosexual prac-titioners in civil life knew they sinned, but the (passive) temple ones did not. Note that Cieza casts the Andean priests as passives, whereas in Mexico the emphasis is upon priests who were actives.

30 'En la ysla de Titicaca, como en Hatuncolla, y en otras partes. Destos se tiene, que aborrescian el peccado nefando: puesto que dizen que algunos de los rústicos que andavan guardando ganado los usavan secretamente: y los que ponían en los templos por induzimiento del demonio'; *Crónica*, 1: 278 (pt 1, chap. 101). Gutiérrez de Santa Clara also has the fabled giants who once inhabited the Manta peninsula (Ecuador), as well as that area's contemporary inhabitants, sodomizing 'en sus ritos y cerimonias y en sus borracheras', *Historia*, 166: 259 (chap. 66).

31 'Generalmente entre los serranos et Yungas ha el demonio introduzido este vicio debaxo de specie de sanctidad. Y es, que cada templo o adoratorio principal tiene un hombre o dos, o más: segun es el ídolo. Los quales andan vestidos como mugeres dende el tiempo que eran niños, y hablavan como tales: y en su manera, trage y todo lo demás remedavan a las mugeres. Con estos casi como por vía de sanctidad y religión tienen las fiestas y días principales su ayuntamiento carnal y torpe: especialmente los señores y principales'; Cieza de León, *Crónica*, 1: 199 (pt 1, chap. 64). Domingo was an important lexicographer – he wrote the first Quechua–Spanish, Spanish–Quechua dictionary – a friend of Las Casas and an opponent of the historian of the Andes, Martín de Murúa.

32 One of many links of sodomy to drunkenness, by Gutiérrez, is cited in the penultimate note. See W. Taylor, *Drinking, Homicide, and Rebellion in Colonial Mexican Villages* (Stanford, 1979), 33. Following medieval authorities, A. de la Calancha sees gluttony as the mother of sodomy; *Crónica moralizada*, 6 vols, continuous pagination (Lima, 1974–81), 821. On a more-than-plausible link of enemas to sodomy, see M. Arboleda, 'Representaciones artísticas de actividades homoeroticos en la cerámica

Moche,' *Boletín de Lima*, 16 (1981), 102, 106. I turned up no such association in P. de Smet, *Ritual Enemas and Snuffs in the Americas* (Amsterdam, 1985).

33 'Me respondieron: que ellos no tenían culpa, porque desde el tiempo de su niñez los avían puesto allí sus caciques, para usar con ellos este maldito y nefando vicio, y para ser sacerdotes y guarda de los templos de sus Indios'; Cieza de León, *Crónica*, 1: 200 (pt 1, chap. 64).

34 'En los días de fiestas se ayuntavan con ellos los señores'; ibid., 2: 74f (pt 2, 25). Comparable evidence that, as late as Huascar, the *acllas* as well might be publicly raped is in J. de Santacruz Pachacuti Yamqui, *Relación de antigüedades deste reyno del Perú* (Madrid, 1968), BAE, 209: 312; see Chapter 7.

35 See the text above, at note 6. On fear of castration in the Andes at the hands of the demon *naqaq*, see B. J. Isbell, *To Defend Ourselves: Ecology and Ritual in an Andean Village* (Austin, 1978), 141, 164, 243; on castration fears among the Mehinaku, see T. Gregory, *Anxious Pleasures: The Sexual Lives of an Amazonian People* (Chicago, 1985), 131, who traces these fears to the Oedipal complex.

36 'En los oraculos y adoratorios donde se davan las respuestas, [el demonio] hazía entender que convenía para el servicio suyo que algunos moços desde su niñez estuviessen en los templos, para que a tiempos y quando se hiziessen los sacrificios y fiestas solemnes, los señores y otros principales usassen con ellos el maldito peccado de la sodomía'; Cieza de León, *Crónica*, 1: 199 (pt 1, chap. 64). Of course 'the devil' was a figment of the Christians' imagination, not the natives'; see Trexler, 'Das sprechende Bildnis: Versuch einer Typologie im Spiegel spanischer Quellen des 16. Jahrhunderts,' in *Laienfrömmigkeit im späten Mittelalter*, ed. K. Schreiner (Munich, 1992), 283–308.

37 This caption stems from the original edition of the work: 'Como el demonio hazía entender a los indios de estas partes que era ofrenda grata a sus dioses tener Indios que assistiessen en los templos, para que los señores tuviessen con ellos conoscimiento cometiendo el gravíssimo peccado de la sodomía; Cieza de León, *Crónica*, 1: 198 (pt 1, chap. 64).

38 'Porque a su grandeza y señorio no era decente hablar con hombres bajos y viles, sino con reyes y grandes señores, y que al ídolo Rimac, que era su criado, mandaría que hablase a la gente común.' This detail seems to be only in Garcilaso, *Comentarios*, 133: 235 (bk 6, chap. 31). See more in Trexler, 'Das sprechende Bildnis.'

39 Including the 'dog gesture'; K. Arnold, 'The Introduction of Poses to a Peruvian Brothel and Changing Images of Male and Female,' in *The Anthropology of the Body*, ed. J. Blacking (London, 1977), 179–97.

40 Providing some direction is R. Trexler, 'Den Rücken beugen: Gebetsgebärden und Geschlechtsgebärden im frühmodernen Europa und Amerika,' in *Verletzte Ehre: Formen, Funktionen und Bedeutungen in Gesellschaften des Mittelalters und der frühen Neuzeit*, ed. K. Schreiner and G. Schwerhoff (Cologne, 1995).

41 'Las espaldas vueltas al ídolo, andando hacia atrás, y doblando el cuerpo y inclinando la cabeza, ponianse en una postura fea, y asi consultaban'; J. Acosta, *Obras* (Madrid, 1954), 153 (*Historia*, bk 5, chap. 12). 'Iban las espaldas vueltas al dicho idolo, con los ojos bajos, llenos de turbación y temblor, y haciendo muchas humillaciones, se ponían a esperar el oráculo en una postura indecente y fea'; B. Cobo, *Obras*, 2 vols (Madrid, 1964), BAE, 92: 188 (*Historia del Nuevo Mundo*, bk 13, chap. 17). Paraphrasing Acosta, Herrera is more direct: 'La consulta era que entraban de noche los sacerdotes, andando la cara atrás, y haciendo una gran dobladura o inclinación pedían lo que querían'; Antonio de Herrera, *Historia general de los hechos de los castellanos en las islas y tierrafirme del mar Océano*, 17 vols (Madrid, 1934–57), 10: 290f (bk 4, chap. 5). Cf. this passage in Calancha: 'El modo de consultar dudas, o pedir respuestas los sacerdotes en casos futuros o mercedes presentes, era entrar a prima noche bueltas las espaldas al ídolo, agoviando el cuerpo'; Calancha, *Crónica*, 838f. On the sexual meaning of this greeting, I. Eibl-Eibesfeldt, *Love and Hate* (New York, 1971), 177f, 195, and especially the illustration on 178; and the section on the buttocks in D. Morris, *Body Watching* (New York, 1985), esp. pp. 205ff.

42 See the text in the previous note. Elsewhere, Calancha describes a village whose men worshipped succubuses: 'En el pueblo de Tauca adoravan a los duendes, que nosotros llamos sucubos, i ellos llaman Huaraclla ... Y toda el anima [penis?] tenían en aquellas duendas los varones, acrecentándose la adoración por la sensualidad'; *Crónica moralizada*, 1065. Calancha further defines incubus and succubus, ibid., 1435.

43 'Ah wawa tulupoob' or 'los que suelen mostrar su dorso,' the sin of Nacxit Xuchit; J. Imbelloni, 'La "Essaltatione delle Rose" ...,' *Anales de arqueología y etnología*, 4 (1943), 198, analyzing the Book of Chilam Balam of Chumayel. *The Book of Chilam Balam of Chumayel*, ed. R. Roys (Washington, DC, 1933), 169, apparently mistranslates the key phrase as 'backsliders.' In Greek Dionysian processions, one could find submissive males assuming buttock-presentation postures when the phallus was wheeled past; W. Burkert, *Homo Necans* (Berkeley, 1983), 69f.

44 'Entran donde está, vueltas asimesmo las espaldas, a recular; e sí entran cara a cara, es bajando mucho las cabezas, tanto que paresce que van a gatas, a cuando llega cerca para hablar a su señor, vuélvele las espaldas, porque en ninguna manera ha de hablar cara a cara'; Oviedo, *Historia*, 119: 126 (bk 26, chap. 31). Herrera picked this up: 'La reverencia que tienen los súbditos a los señores es muy grande, porque jamás los miran a la cara, aunque estén en doméstica conversación, y entran con las espaldas vueltas adonde está el señor'; Herrera, *Historia*, 12: 394 (dec. 6, bk 5, chap. 17). See Columbus's report in S. Morison, *Journals and Other Documents on the Life and Voyages of Christopher Columbus* (New York, 1963), 345.

45 On how the *acllas* represented submissive parts of the Inca Empire, see I. Silverblatt, *Moon, Sun, and Devil* (Princeton, 1987), 80–104. A

religious rite described as performed in Pomapampa by command of the Inca Huascar may be related to this complex; see Chapter 7, note 49.

46 The natives of Tierra Firme 'traían por joyel un hombre sobre otro, en aquel diabólico e nefando acto de Sodoma, hechos de oro de relieve'; Oviedo, *Historia*, 117: 118 (bk 5, chap. 3). Tabasco: 'E los cristianos que lo fueron a ver, dijeron que habian hallado entre aquellos cemis o idolos, dos personas hechas de copey (que es un arbol asi llamado), el uno caballero o cabalgando sobre el otro, en figura de aquel abominable y nefando pecado de sodomía, e otro de barro que tenía la natura asida con ambas manos, la qual tenía como circunciso'; ibid., 118: 144 (bk 17, chap. 17). Gómara rephrases the same report: 'un idolillo de oro y muchos de barro; dos hombres de palo cabalgando uno sobre otro a fuer de Sodoma, y otro de tierra cocida, con ambas manos a lo suyo, que le tenia retajado, como son casi todos los indios de Yucatan'; *Historia* 22: 184 (pt 1).

47 'Tenían muchos ídolos de barro, unos como caras de demonios, y otros como de mujeres, y otros de otras malas figuras, de manera que al parecer estaban haciendo sodomías los unos indios con los otros'; *Historia*, 1: 47 (chap. 2).

48 'Es toda la tierra desde Piastla, hasta el río de Culuacán ..., las casas estaban cubiertas de paja con gran artificio, y encima de los caballetes, algunas invenciones pintadas en especial hombres y mujeres que se juntaban, y hombres con hombres, porque tocaban mucho en el pecado nefando'; *Historia*, 9; 228 (dec. 4, bk 9, chap. 11); Guerra, *Pre-Columbian Mind*, 155.

49 Cf. Oviedo, 'Así que, ved si quien de tales joyas se prescia e compone su persona, si usara de tal maldad en tierra donde tales arreos traen, o si se debe tener por cosa nueva entre indios: antes por cosa muy usada e ordinaria e común a ellos'; Oviedo, *Historia*, 117: 119 (bk 5, chap. 3).

50 R. Larco Hoyle, *Checan: Essay on Erotic Elements in Peruvian Art* (Geneva, 1965), 112.

51 For the hypothesis that the prisoners' penises shown in Moche ceramics were being offered to a god, see E. Benson, *The Mochica: a Culture of Peru* (New York, 1972), 151. If this were true, castration would seem necessary to produce these penises.

52 Larco Hoyle, *Checan*, 110.

53 He allows one possible exception; Larco Hoyle, *Checan*, 110; further 117, 122, 127.

54 Larco Hoyle, *Checan*, 57.

55 Gómara is describing those in the area of modern Venezuela: 'Hay muchos sodométicos que no les falta para ser del todo mujer, sino tetas y parir'; *Historia*, 22: 202 (pt 1). M. Arboleda does consider this possibility in an exemplary fashion: 'Representaciones artísticas,' 102f. For example, one of the four subordinate figures he studied wears a female hair style but a male breechcloth; the conclusion is obvious. Further, some of the figures

on top (*figuras postradas*) are clearly supernaturals, those beneath terrestrials.

56 C. Donnan, *Moche Art and Iconography* (Los Angeles, 1976), 27f. A less elegant solution is to remain oblivious to possible meanings of such problematically gendered figures. Thus J. Marcos and M. de Manrique, 'De la dualidad fertilidad-virilidad a lo explicitamente femenino o masculino: la relación de las figurinas con los cambios en la organización social Valdivia,' in V. Miller (ed.), *The Role of Gender in Precolumbian Art and Architecture* (Lanham, MD., 1988), 35–51, analyzes certain sexless figures in statuettes of the pre-Moche Valdivia culture (Ecuador) without mentioning the berdache.

57 *Moche Art and Iconography*, 133f; Larco Hoyle was baffled because he could imagine fertility as the religious motivation for such figures, while anal intercourse was undertaken specifically to avoid conception; *Checan*, 112.

58 Oviedo assumed a link between vision-interpretation or divination on the one side, and healing on the other (Oviedo, *Historia*, 117: 110f [bk 5, chap. 1]), but of neither to the berdache. Some writers have gone even further, stating that Brazilian effeminates were and are often artists: Freyre, *Masters*, 118f. Without evidence, W. Williams makes such associations a fundamental argument of his work; *The Spirit and the Flesh* (Boston, 1986, 1992).

59 See Silverblatt, *Moon, Sun*, 99, on male priests assuming female voice. See Trexler, 'Das sprechende Bildnis,' esp. note 68, on the priest's changing of voices to fit the person speaking, not only in the Inca realm but in Christianity.

60 Peter Martyr d'Anghiera, *Opera* (Graz, 1966), 255–62 (dec. 8, chaps 8–9); Las Casas, *Apologética*, 2: 542–51 (chap. 244–5). On Tomás Ortiz talking to the *piaches*, see Trexler, 'Das sprechende Bildnis,' 296f.

61 G. Freyre associates the Brazilian berdaches with the *piaches* or soothsaying medicine men; *Masters and Slaves*, index, 'pajes,' while A. Requeña, 'Noticias y consideraciones ...,' *Acta Venezolana*, 1 (1945), 44, 57f, shows a picture of a modern traditional healer presumed to be homosexual. But any linkage of the two cannot be projected back to the time of the conquests. Without documentation, Trevisan, *Perverts in Paradise*, 22, says the *piaches* passed on medicine and their knowledge of it through anal intercourse with patients and students. If that were verified for our period, the question would need reopening.

62 A. Métraux, 'Le shamanisme Araucan,' *Revista del Instituto de Antropología, Universidad Nacional de Tucuman*, 2 (1942).

63 'Solo tienen por vil y vituperable el pecado nefando, con esta diferencia, que el que usa el oficio de varón no es baldonado por él, como él que se sujeta al de la mujer, y a estos los llaman *hueies*, que en nuestro vulgar lenguaje quiere decir nefandos y mas propiamente *putos* que es la verdadera explicación del nombre *hueies*. Y estos tales no traen calzones, sino es una mantichuela por delante que llaman *punus*; acomódanse a ser

machis o curanderos porque tienen pacto con el demonio'; F. Núñez de Pineda y Bascuñán, *Cautiverio feliz y razón de las guerras dilatadas de Chile* (Santiago, 1863) [Colección de Historiadores de Chile, vol. 3], 107. The other group 'verdaderamente no tienen pacto con el espíritu malo, como los otros que llaman *huyes*, que son nefandos, como queda dicho, y estos son los que causan mayor pavor y espanto.' Those without this pact were 'curanderos que hacen algunas ceremonias finjidas chupando al enfermo el estomago, y escupiendo sangre de la boca, dando a entender que se la sacan de adentro del pecho, y para esto dicen que suelen sajarse la lengua o picarse las encias, para hacer estas demostraciones; ibid., 164, and 157–9 on their ugliness.

64   W. Park, *Shamanism in Western North America* (Evanston, 1938), 21.

65   'Je ne scais par quelle superstition quelques Ilinois, aussi bien que quelques Nadoüessi, estant encor jeunes prennent l'habit des femmes qu'ils gardent toute leur vie. Il y a du mystère. Car ils ne se marient jamais, et font gloire de s'abbaisser a faire tout ce que font les femmes; ils vont pourtant en guerre, mais ils ne peuvent se servir que de la massue, et non pas de l'arc n'y de la flêche qui sont les armes propres des hommes, ils assistent a toutes les jongleriës et aux danses solemnelles qui se font a l'honneur du Columet, ils y chantent mais ils n'y peuvent pas danser, ils sont appelles aux Conseils, ou l'on ne peut rien decider sans leurs advis; Enfin par la profession quils font d'une vie Extreordinaire, ils passent pour des Manitous C'est a dire pour des Genies ou des personnes de Consequence'; *The Jesuit Relations and Allied Documents: Travels and Explorations of the Jesuit Missionaries in New France, 1610–1791* ed. R. Gold Thwaites, 59 (1959), 128ff.

66   Roscoe, *Zuni Man-Woman.*

67   As indicated by Charlevoix, *Journal historique d'un voyage ... dans l'Amerique* (Paris, 1744), 303. Several nineteenth-century accounts of other tribes allude to claims of religious legitimation of the berdache.

CHAPTER 6 ON THE GROUND

1   L. Fernández Piedrahita, *Historia general del nuevo reino de Granada* (Bogotá, 1942), 1: 25.

2   'And he being the only one of the tribe submitting to this disgraceful degradation, is looked upon as *medicine* and sacred, and a feast is given to him annually'; George Catlin, describing the Mandan berdache about 1840 and his painting *Dance to the Berdash* (see figure 9) in his *Letters and Notes on the Manners, Customs, and Conditions of North American Indians*, 2 vols (New York, 1973), 2: 15.

3   For We'wha, see W. Roscoe, *The Zuni Man-Woman* (Albuquerque, 1991).

4   A widespread insult regarding the Huayllas seems to have started in the military realm and stuck. See Chapter 7.

5   P. Cieza de León, *Crónica del Perú* (Lima, 1984–6), 1: 195 (pt 1, chap. 62).

6   The sodomy in which that area's residents 'gloriavan demasiadamente' was 'pública y descubiertamente' (*Crónica*, 1: 160 [pt 1, chap. 49]). 'De este gran reyno del Peru, solamente [en] algunos pueblos comarcanos a Puerto Viejo, y a la ysla de la Puna . . ., y no en otros'; ibid., 1: 199 (pt 1, chap. 64). Cieza also listed Andean peoples who, he said, did not practice sodomy except for isolated individuals; e.g., *Crónica*, 1: 147, 184, 199, 241. Note, however, the remarkable fact that the most Peruvian of all historians, F. Guaman Poma de Ayala, has all but nothing to say about homosexual activity in his massive *El primer nueva corónica y buen gobierno*, 3 vols (Mexico City, 1980), except to denounce the 'Sodom' that the colonial rulers had created (995).

7   *Crónica*, 1: 160 (pt 1, chap. 49). On the conquistador Francisco Pacheco, see ibid., 165 (pt 1, chap. 51). Details on Juan de Olmos, so selfless as to burn the sodomites 'aunque el pueblo estaba en su encomienda,' are in P. Gutiérrez de Santa Clara, *Historia de las guerras civiles del Perú* (Madrid, 1965), BAE, 166: 259 (bk 3, chap. 66).

8   'En especial los que vivián en llas costas y tierra caliente'; B. Díaz del Castillo, *Historia verdadera de la conquista de la Nueva España* (Mexico City, 1968), 2: 359 (chap. 208). He immediately added that those who assumed the female role in sodomy went dressed as women. And see Garcilaso de la Vega, *Comentarios reales de los Incas* (Madrid, 1960–3), BAE, 133: 343 (bk 9, chap. 8). Note that, in Europe, coastal areas (e.g., Valencia) were also thought to be given to homosexual behavior, because foreigners entered there and brought their habits with them.

9   A. de la Calancha, *Crónica moralizada* (Lima, 1974–81), 1249, 1158.

10 Ibid., 1158f.

11 Ibid., 1249f. For the Moche art, read further below.

12 The Latin phrase is in J. Trevisan, *Perverts in Paradise* (London, 1986), 22; Garcilaso, *Comentarios*, 133: 344 (bk 9, chap. 8); A. Zárate, *The Discovery and Conquest of Peru* (Baltimore, 1968), 32 (bk 1, chap. 4); cited in F. Guerra, *The Pre-Columbian Mind* (New York, 1971), 99.

13 J. Acosta, *Obras* (Madrid, 1954), BAE, 73: 393 (*De procuranda indorum salute*, proemio).

14 Opposed to private sins, see, e.g., the 'public and open' sodomy practiced in Guayaquil; Cieza, *Crónica*, 1: 159ff (pt 1, chap. 53). The Moors were said to 'practice sodomy in public'; E. W. Monter, *Frontiers of Heresy* (Cambridge, 1990), 293 (1584–5).

15 'Se juntaban hombre y muger como animales ponéndose la hembra en quatro pies públicamente'; *The Narrative of [P.] Castañeda*, in G. Parker Winship, *The Coronado Expedition, 1540–1542* (Washington: Fourteenth Annual Report of the Bureau of Ethnology, Part 1, 1986), 448.

16 Ibid., 448f. The natives of Suyo Valley (location unknown) revolted against the Spaniards in 1541. Was it in the light of this fact that Castañeda determined that they were sodomites?

17 Castañeda, *Narrative*, 451.

18   'Bersea la diferençia que ay de la una tierra a la otra para que meresca lo uno estar poblado de españoles y lo otro no abiendo de ser a el contrario quanto a cristianos, porque en los unos ay raçón de hombres y en los otros barbaridad de animales y más que de bestias'; Castañeda, *Narrative*, 447 (pt 2, introduction).

19   Cited in Guerra, *Pre-Columbian Mind*, 125.

20   Cieza de León, *Crónica*, 2: 74ff (pt 2, chap. 25).

21   In the province called Achira 'es jente muy bellaca son todos sométicos no ay principal que no trayga quatro o cinco pajes muy galanes Estos tiene por mancebos'; Juan Ruíz de Arce, *Servicios en Indias* (Madrid, 1933), 32. Ruíz claimed that this people was ruled by a woman.

22   G. Ramusio, *Navigazioni e viaggi* (Turin, 1978–85), 6: 652.

23   'Sólo en el tramo del canal de Santa Bárbara se hallan muchos Joyas, pues raro es el pueblo donde no se ven dos o tres'; F. Palou, *Relación histórica de la vida y apostólicas tareas del venerable padre Fray Junípero Serra* (Mexico City, 1982), 152 (chap. 46). To be sure of the sex, the missionaries checked the berdache's breasts and found them flat: 'sin pechos, teniendo bastante edad.'

24   This information is embedded in a significant text referring to just title: 'I have substantial evidence that those Indian men who, both here and farther inland, are observed in the dress, clothing, and character of women – there being two or three such in each village – pass as sodomites by profession (it being confirmed that all these Indians are much addicted to this abominable vice) and permit the heathen to practice the execrable unnatural abuse of their bodies. They are called *joyas*, and are held in great esteem. Let this mention suffice for a matter which could not be omitted – on account of the bearing it may have on the discussion of reduction of these natives'; *A Historical, Political, and Natural Description of California by Pedro Fages, Soldier of Spain*, trans. H. Priestley (Berkeley, 1937), 33; see also 48.

25   J. Tanner, *A Narrative of the Captivity and Adventures of John Tanner* (Minneapolis, 1956), 89f; also F. Karsch-Haack, 'Uranismus,' *Jahrbuch für sexuelle Zwischenstufen*, 3 (1901), 126ff.

26   A. B. Holder, 'The Bote,' *New York Medical Journal*, 50, no. 575 (7 Dec. 1889), 623. The possible significance of berdaches from one tribe knowing those of another relates to their potential diplomatic role, and to the link of the domestic berdache to the 'womanhood' of subordinate tribes within aboriginal confederations, like that of the Iroquois.

27   Unless otherwise stated, these ages were gathered by Karsch, 'Uranismus,' 121–44. For Kasinelu's and We'wha's ages, see Roscoe, *Zuni Man-Woman*, 29, 123, 197f.

28   E. Clews Parsons, 'The Zuñi La'Mana,' *American Anthropologist*, 18 (1916), 521; Roscoe, *Zuni Man-Woman*, 27.

29   W. Hammond, *Sexual Impotence in the Male and Female* (Detroit, 1887), 165ff; H. Hay, 'The Hammond Report,' *One Institute Quarterly*, 6 (1963), 9ff.

30 For the Crow, see Holder, 'The Bote,' 624. The Osage is referred to by Karsch, 'Uranismus,' 133.

31 See Chapter 5, note 6, Gutiérrez de Santa Clara (about 1580), translated in Guerra, *Pre-Columbian Mind*, 141f.

32 See the anonymous work (Valera?) cited in Chapter 5, note 6.

33 Presumably, in certain contexts it must have been necessary for the berdache to have been identifiable as such. Note also that at least one modern tribe's berdaches (Crow) 'never so far lose masculine qualities as to make it at all difficult to distinguish the bote from a woman'; Holder, 'The Bote,' 623.

34 'Hay muchos sodométicos que no les falta para ser del todo mujer, sino tetas y parir; adoran ídolos'; López de Gómara, *Historia de las Indias* (Madrid, 1946), BAE, 22: 202.

35 Palou, *Relación histórica de la vida*, 152. When the Franciscans went on to force this berdache to wear a man's clothing, that is, to go about all but naked, s/he 'quedó más avergonzado que si hubiera sido mujer'; ibid.

36 Roscoe, *Zuni Man-Woman*, 53-73.

37 See Oviedo's text in Chapter 4, note 22.

38 'Y estos tales no traen calzones, sino es una mantichuela por delante que llaman *punus*'; F. Núñez de Pineda y Bascuñán, *Cautiverio feliz y razón de las guerras dilatadas de Chile* (Santiago, 1863), 107.

39 Text in Chapter 4, note 22; Fernández de Oviedo, *Sumario de la natural historia de las Indias* (Madrid, 1946), BAE, 22: 508 (chap. 81); Gómara, *Historia*, 22: 201 (pt 1).

40 'Afeitados los rostros para usar este pecado de contra natura'; 'Información de las idolatrias,' in *Colección de documentos ineditos . . . en América y Oceanía*, 24: 131 (question 19); see also Toledo in Guerra, *Pre-Columbian Mind*, 127. The assessment that there were 'many' is in F. Pizarro, *Relación del descubrimiento y conquista de los reinos del Perú* (Lima, 1978), 282.

41 M. Cabello Balboa, *Historia del Peru* (Lima, 1920), 155.

42 R. de Lizárraga, *Descripción del Perú, Tucumán, Río de la Plata y Chile* (Madrid, 1986), 67 (chap. 6, which makes clear that they were called queer because of their hair style); see also Guerra, *Pre-Columbian Mind*, 166.

43 'Son muy putos y préciasen dello; ca en los sartales que traen al cuello ponen por joyel al dios Priapo, y dos hombres uno sobre otro por detrás, relevados de oro: tal pieza de aquestas hay que pesa treinta castellanos. En Zamba, que los indios dicen Nao, y en Gaira, crían los putos cabello y atapan sus verguenzas como mujeres, que los otros traen coronas come frailes; y así los llaman coronados . . .'; Gómara, *Historia*, BAE, 22: 201.

44 For the Kansan berdache, see M. Benson (ed.), *From Pittsburgh to the Rocky Mountains* (Golden, CO, 1988), 93. A Kodiak berdache depilated is in H. Bancroft, *The Native Races of the Pacific* (San Francisco, 1883–6), in his *Works*, 1: 82. And cf. the Aleuts' beards depilated; ibid., 92.

45 'Die Meinung einiger Schriftsteller, als wenn die Indianer, selbst in ihren reifsten Jahren blos Haare auf dem Kopfe hätten, und alle übrige Theile des Körpers davon frey blieben, ist ungegründet. Sie sind darinn von andern Menschen nicht verschieden. Weil sie aber den Auswuchs der Haare auf ihrem Körper für hässlich halten, so bringen sie es mit vieler Mühe dahin, daß fast keine Spur davon an ihnen zu sehen ist'; G. Loskiel, *Geschichte der Mission der evangelischen Brüder unter den Indianern in Nordamerika* (Hildesheim, 1989), 15f. On the general Amerindian absence of much of the body hair common to Caucasians, see Holder, 'The Bote,' 624.

46 Cited in P. Farb, *Word Play* (New York, 1973), 52–6.

47 B. de Sahagún, *Florentine Codex* (Santa Fe, 1975–82), 10: 89–90.

48 See Chapter 3.

49 See above, at note 21.

50 'Críanse allí unos niños dedicados al sol, que los tiene aquella gente como una reliquía e cosa consagrada y muy sancta; y desque son grandes, mátanlo y sacrifícanlos al sol. E los que van allá del Nuevo Reino, rescatan un niño de aquellos e tráenlo, e llámanle moja. No hay cacique que esté sin uno desos, e cacique hay que tiene dos y tres dellos por cosa muy religiosa y buena ... Y cuando los indios han cometido alguno pecado en que su ánima le acuse su maldad, no osan entrar en el templo o oratorio sin ese moja, e aquellos niños son los que cantan al sol e hacen la oración'; Fernández de Oviedo, *Historia general y natural de las Indias* (Madrid, 1959), BAE, 119: 127f (bk 26, chap. 30); see M. Helms, *Ancient Panama* (Austin, 1979), 159. One may speculate that this passage might shed light on the temple berdaches of the nearby Inca Empire. Note that, in Europe, testators paid friars to pray and sing aloud for their souls during the funerary procession, thus acting as retinue around the bier.

51 Oviedo obviously does not confuse these men with berdaches: 'Andaban un contrapás hasta sesenta personas, hombres todos, y entre ellos ciertos hechos mujeres'; *Historia*, 120: 413 (bk 42, chap. 11). While in nineteenth-century North American tribes the berdache commonly had a specific role in dances, I could find no such documentation in the period covered by this book. On Mexican temporal transvestism, see C. Klein, 'Fighting With Femininity,' in Trexler, *Gender Rhetorics* (Binghamton, 1994).

52 Bancroft, *Works*, 2: 337.

53 'Salían en esta fiesta, asimismo, los hombres afeminados, y mugeriles, en hábito, y trage de muger. Era esta gente mui abatida, y tenida en poco, y menospreciada, y no trataban estos, sino con las mugeres, y hacian oficios de mugeres, y se labraban y raiaban las carnes'; J. de Torquemada, *Monarquia Indiana* (Mexico City, 1969), 2: 299 (bk 12, chap. 35). I could find no evidence of berdache participation in the festivities associated with the divinity Xochipilli (or in his feminine appearance, Xochiquetzalli), said by some to be the very god of 'homosexuals'; C. Taylor, 'Homosexuality in Precolombian and Colonial Mexico,' in S. Murray (ed.), *Male Homo-*

sexuality in Central and South America (New York, 1987), 6f, with citations.

54 'En este mes llamado Quecholli, se manifestaban las mugeres públicas y deshonestas, y se ofrecían al sacrificio in trage conocido y moderado, que eran las que iban a las guerras, con la soldadesca, y las llamaban *maqui,* que quiere decir: las entremetidas, y se aventuraban en las batallas, y muchas de ellas se arrojaban à morir en ellas. Este genero de mugeres era mui deshonesto y desvergonçado; y quando se arrojaban à morir, se iban maldiciendo à sì mismas, y diciendo muchas deshonestidades, infamando à las mugeres buenas, recogidas, y honradas'; Torquemada, *Monarquia,* 2: 299 (bk 10, chap. 35). The description of these women as shock troops evokes the role of the medieval (male) ribalds in European armies; see Trexler, *Dependence in Context in Renaissance Florence* (Binghamton, 1994), 849–53. Whether these *maqui* are related to the *avianime* or courtesans-companions of young soldiers remains unclear; see J. Soustelle, *Daily Life of the Aztecs* (Stanford, 1961), 46, 131, 135, 171, 184.

55 For urban brothel prostitutes as a source of female (and male?) campfollowers in Morocco and France, see Chapter 2. Neither Klein's 'Rethinking Cihuacoatl' nor 'Fighting With Femininity' discusses this group.

56 See Chapter 4, notes 24, 25.

57 This was presumably one reason berdaches so often sought out anthropologists in North America, as indicated earlier; see Karsch, 'Uranismus,' 141.

58 G. García, *Origen de los Indios del Nuevo Mundo* (Mexico City, 1981), 115 (bk 3, chap. 6 [6]). This figure comes from Motolinía, who said that sodomy was *cuasi permitida* there; *Memoriales e historia de los Indios de la Nueva España* (Madrid, 1970), 141f.

59 Gómara, *Historia,* 22: 183.

60 Ibid., 22: 199.

61 'E não contentes estes selvagens de andarem tão encarniçoados n'este peccado, naturalmente cometido, são mui afeiçoados ao peccado nefando, entre os quaes se não tem por afronta; e o que serve de macho, se tem por valente, e contam esta bestialidade por proeza; e nas suas aldêas pelo sertão ha alguns que tem tenda publica a quantos os querem como mulheres publicas'; Gabriel Soares de Sousa, *Tratado descriptivo do Brasil em 1587,* in *Revista trimensal do Instituto historico e geographico do Brazil,* second edition, vol. 14 (Rio de Janeiro, 1879), 287 (bk 2, chap. 156).

62 'Pues aquestas tales [mujeriles] lupanarias moradas, entre cristiano se admiten por excusar otros daños mayores, no me paresce mal que las haya entre aquesta gente, pues que hay cuilones (que cuilon llaman al sodomita)'; Oviedo, *Historia,* 120: 421 (bk 42, chap. 12).

63 'Ni creo lo hacían porque los allegados de esta pestilencial miseria dicen que no son amigos de mujeres come eran éstos, que a esos lugares llevaban a las malas mujeres públicas y en ellos usaban de ellas, y las pobres que

entre esta gente acertaba a tener este oficio, no obstante que recibían de ellos galardón, eran tantos los mozos que a ellas acudían, que las traían acosadas y muertas'; D. de Landa, *Relación de las cosas de Yucatan* (Mexico City, 1959), 54 (chap. 30).

64 'Había mujeres públicas y adonde las había, apedreban a los sodomitas'; A. de Herrera, *Historia general de los hechos de los castellanos ...* (Madrid, 1934–57), 6: 394 (dec. 3, bk 4, chap. 7); F. Karsch-Haack, *Das Gleichgeschlechtliche Leben der Naturvölker* (New York, 1975), 377.

65 Cited without reference in R. Larco Hoyle, *Checan* (Geneva, 1965), 30.

66 For Europe, cf. Burgundy and the Rhone Valley, where the fear of females being raped was such a justification (J. Rossiaud, *Medieval Prostitution*, New York, 1988), with Florence, where it was not (Trexler, *Dependence in Context*), 374.

67 See the discussion of Las Casas and Alarcón in Chapter 4, at note 34.

68 Cristóbal Vaca de Castro (1542), cited in H. Brüning, 'Beiträge zum Studium des Geschlechtlebens der Indianer im alten Perú,' *Anthropophyteia*, 8 (1911), 200. Among others, Ramos Gavilan (1621) said that these peoples were lascivious and liked to dress as women; Guerra, *Pre-Columbian Mind*, 178.

69 One Portuguese source, intimating a dreadful lack of cultural development, says the Tupinambas of Brazil behaved 'nao admittindo diffrença entre agente e paciente; motivo por que com a mesma publicidade o executam.' Although the author of this text goes unstated, it is probably a variant text of Gabriel Soares de Sousa; *Revista do instituto historico e geographico do Brazil*, ser. 2, 1 (1856), 212.

70 Oviedo, *Historia*, 117: 118 (bk 5, chap. 3).

71 Holder, 'The Bote,' 623ff. The same fellation custom emerged in the same area, in a scandal in Boise, Idaho, in 1955–7; J. Gerassi, *The Boys of Boise: Furor, Vice and Folly in an American City* (New York, 1966).

72 The festive descriptions are in Diego Durán, *Historia de las Indias de Nueva España e Islas de la Tierra Firme*, 2 vols (Mexico City, 1967), 1: 146, 154f; trans. in *Book of Gods and Rites* (Norman, OK, 1971), 233–4, 244, where also the male is carrying the female instruments; see also M. Graulich, 'Ochpaniztli,' *Anales de antropología*, 18 (1981), *passim*.

73 'Barrer y fregar y las otras cosas á mujeres acostumbradas'; Oviedo, *Sumario*, 508 (chap. 81).

74 'El oficio de las mujeres, que es moler el maíz e hilar y guisar de comer'; Herrera, *Historia*, 8: 339 (dec. 4, bk 6, chap. 1); cited in Guerra, *Pre-Columbian Mind*, 155.

75 My italics. 'Porque ellas son las que cavan las tierras, y siembran los campos, y cogen las sementeras. Y muchos de sus maridos están en sus casas texendo y hilando, y adereçando sus armas, y ropa y curando sus rostros y haziendo otros oficios afeminados'; Cieza, *Crónica*, 1: 146f (pt 1, chap. 44), and the earlier quote in the *Crónica*, 1: 130 (pt 1, chap. 40).

76 Tanner, *Narrative of the Captivity*, 90; Karsch, 'Uranismus,' 126f. See a similar marriage among the Crow in Holder, 'The Bote,' 624 (1889).

77 See Chapter 4, at note 34. Other cultures also called these unions 'marriages.' For the Azande, see E. Evans-Pritchard, 'Sexual Inversion among the Azande,' *American Anthropologist*, 72 (1970), 1429.

78 Heterosexually, that is, 'elles ne se marient jamais.' Cited by C. De Pauw, *Recherches philosophiques sur les Americains* (London, 1770), 2: 98f; see J. Lafiteau's text in *Customs of the American Indians Compared with the Customs of Primitive Times* (Toronto, 1974), 1: 57f.

79 A. Núñez Cabeza de Vaca, *Naufragios* (Madrid, 1948), 538 (chap. 26). Gómara, *Historia*, 22: 182. He linked this behavior to native mistreatment of women; see the texts in Chapter 3, at notes 8, 13.

80 'Avía entre ellos hombres en ábito de mugeres que se casaban con otros honbres y les servían de mugeres'; Castañeda, *Narrative*, 447 (pt 2, chap. 1); trans. in Guerra, *Pre-Columbian Mind*, 109f.

81 Trevisan, *Perverts*, 23. About this time, Montaigne was reporting the marriage of a Portuguese male couple in Rome; see J. Spence, *The Memory Palace of Matteo Ricci* (New York, 1985), 226.

82 'Ejercitaban los oficios de mujeres con robustecidad de hombres, por lo cual en llegando a edad suficiente, los casaban como a mujeres y preferianlos los Laches a las verdaderas de que según se sigue, que la abominación de la sodomía fuese permitida en esta nación'; L. Fernández Piedrahita, *Historia general del nuevo reino de Granada* (Bogotá, 1942), 1: 25; Palou, *Relación histórica de la vida*, 151f.

83 See the text in the previous note; cited in A. Requeña, "Noticias y consideraciones sobre las anormalidades de los Aborígenes Americanos,' *Acta Venezolana*, 1 (1945), 54.

84 My italics. G. Boscana, *Chinigchinich* (Banning, CA, 1978), 54.

85 G. Shepherd, 'Rank, Gender, and Homosexuality,' in P. Caplan (ed.), *The Cultural Construction of Sexuality* (London, 1987).

86 Holder, 'The Bote,' 624. Note that such an arrangement might have afforded the husband a source of income or influence over those permitted to have intercourse with his wife.

87 Cieza, *Crónica*, 1: 146 (pt 1, chap. 44). On women *tamemes* in Central America, see W. Sherman, *Forced Native Labor in Sixteenth-Century Central America* (Lincoln, 1979), 322f. Unfortunately, Sherman does not raise the question of berdache load-bearers.

88 Typical is the 1775–6 report on the Yuma of the Jesuit Pedro Font: 'Among the women, I saw some men dressed like women, with whom they go about regularly, never joining the men. The commander called them *amaricados*, perhaps because the Yumans call effeminate men *maricas*'; *Font's Complete Diary of the Second Anza Expedition*, ed. H. Bolton (vol. 4 of *Anza's California Expedition*) (Berkeley, 1930), 105.

89 'I observed that he used the masculine pronoun *el* in referring to the individual,' Hammond concludes; 'The Disease of the Scythians,' *American Journal of Neurology and Psychiatry*, 1 (1882), 343f.

90 D. and J. Sherzer, 'Mormaknamaloe: the Cuna,' in P. Young and J. Howe (eds), *Ritual and Symbol in Central America* (Eugene, 1976), 28f, describing the *molas* made by the women and by *ome-kiit*, or women-like male homosexuals.

91 H. Whitehead, 'The Bow and the Burden Strap,' in S. Ortner and H. Whitehead, *Sexual Meanings* (Cambridge, 1981), 80–115.

92 On the primarily economic character of such marriages in Mombasa in East Central Africa, see Shepherd, 'Rank, Gender, and Sexuality.'

93 Gómara claims that Montezuma had 150 women pregnant at one time 'las cuales, á persuasion del diablo, movían, tomando cosas para lanzar las criaturas, é quizá porque sus hijos no habían de heredar'; Gómara, *Conquista de Mejico*, in BAE, 22: 344.

94 The author immediately attributes this to the fact that their husbands were sodomites: at their marriage rites they 'disponen de sus personas como quieren, ó porque son los maridos sodométicos'; Gómara, *Historia*, 22: 185; cited in Guerra, *Pre-Columbian Mind*, 86.

95 'Los naturales de Manta . . . casában debajo de condición, que los parientes y amigos del novio gozaban primero de la novia que no el marido'; Garcilaso, *Comentarios*, 133: 343 (bk 9, chap. 8).

96 'Fueron estos Indios de los valles muy inclinados a la sodomía, i oy no están libres deste contagio, siendo el cónplice muger, si en el tienpo de su gentilidad eran cónplices los onbres, oy muchos cubren con capa de matrimonio la traición echa a la naturaleza, quitando a la generación lo que dan a la sensualidad'; Calancha, *Crónica moralizada*, 1249f.

97 'Ay gran daño oy, i le a avido años antes en usar esta iniquidad, siendo los cónplices no varón i varón, sino India i India; I entre otros muchos Religiosos que me lo an asegurado, Dotrinantes que an sido en estos valles, me certificó el Bendito Padre fray Julián Martel, que llega la disolución a tanta publicidad, que en señal de que la India cometió la primera vez este delito nefando, le da el varón un vestido nuevo de gala, que llaman capuz con listas, siendo conocida su abominación por todos los que an advertido su maldita usança; con que se responde a todos los que buscan, quál será la causa porque están aniquilados los pueblos de los llanos, no llevando a sus Indios a minas de açoque, de oro ni de plata, multiplicándose los de la sierra, i no estando tan acabados como éstos aun los serranos que acuden a minas, i es, que la piedad de Dios ya que a nuestros ojos no los abrasa, a nuestra vista los consume, i tanbién porque si ay muchos destos asquerosos, es la mayor parte dellos linpia deste contagio, siendo los pueblos que dotrinan Religiosos más linpios, i los que se ensuzian menos descarados. En un pueblo destos llanos es constante tradición, que uvo cerca del un pueblo grande en que los más eran sodomitas, i que vino fuego del cielo, començando a quemar desde una casa en que se estava cometiendo el pecado, por muchos que avían echo borrachera para la junta, i que avían quedado solos unos pocos, i las mugeres destos que no eran conpreendidos en la abominación, los quales se salieron, del pueblo, i se fueron a abitar a otros lugares, muchos se quedaron en los canpos, i parte dellos fundaron

un lugarejo. Con gran cuydado trabajan nuestros Religiosos Dotrinantes en apagar estos fuegos, i es raro el que en los pueblos de nuestros dotrinas se alla encenegado; Dios los purifique, i se deula de todos.' Calancha, *Crónica moralizada*, 1158ff. This text covers the following translations.

98 'El Inga por remediar tan abominable inpulso puso ley, que sin piedad se ejegutó, que no solo quemavan los agentes, sino su rancho, casa, ganado, ropa, i quanto era suyo; i tal vez si lo avían entendido algunos de su sangre, o familia, abrasavan a todos sus descendientes, pagando los ignorantes a buelta de los sabidores. Entonces quando quemavan muchos avía a millares de millares los Indios, i aora que no matan ninguno, están sin Indios aniquilados los pueblos; Dios castiga quando las justicias no juzgan'; Calancha, *Crónica moralizada*, 1149.

99 'Algunos varones hay que no se quieren casar con mujeres mozas, diciendo no saben servir; casanse con viejas, porque les hacen la chicha y los vestidos ... Los indios de los Llanos, que llamamos Yungas, sobre todas desventuras, tienen otra mayor: son dados mucho al vicio sodomítico, y las mujeres estando preñadas facilmente lo usan. Entre los serranos, raros se dan a este vicio, por lo cual a los indios Yungas los ha castigado Nuestro Señor, que ya no hay casi en los valles, sino muy pocos'; R. de Lizárraga, *Descripción*, 244 (bk 1, chap. 112).

100 A. Zorita, *Life and Labor in Ancient Mexico: the Brief and Summary Relation of the Lords of New Spain* (New Brunswick, 1963), 228f.

101 Much as some Mexican migrant workers do today. A Public Broadcasting System special on the subject of Mexican migrant workers in Southern California was particularly illuminating in this regard.

CHAPTER 7 ATTITUDES AND ASSESSMENTS

1 'Tan vil y afrentoso, principalmente en los pacientes'; Pérez de Ribas, *Páginas para la historia de Sinaloa y Sonora* (Mexico City, 1944), 1: 132; see the whole relevant text below, at note 121.

2 Oviedo, cited without references in F. Guerra, *The Pre-Columbian Mind* (New York, 1971), 57.

3 F. de Alva Ixtlilxóchitl, *Obras históricas*, 2 vols (Mexico City, 1975), 1: 264ff, 529f; Bancroft, *Works*, 5: 198.

4 Thus in Cieza de Léon, *Crónica del Perú* (Lima, 1984–6), 1: 166ff (pt 1, chap. 52), followed by Garcilaso de la Vega, *Comentarios reales de las Incas* (Madrid, 1960–3), BAE, 133: 344ff (bk 10, chap. 9).

5 For the *mancebo hermoso*, see A. de la Calancha, *Crónica moralizada* (Lima, 1974–81), 1158f. Cieza's illustration for his chapter 52 is in the *Crónica*, 1: 169 (pt 1). Replications of Bible stories were common in early modern Europe; see, e.g., H. Trevor-Roper's chapter on 'The Fast Sermons of the Long Parliament,' which in the English Civil War specialized in uncovering such replications, in his *The Crisis of the Seventeenth Century* (New York, 1956), 294–344.

6   My italics; 'Como se hizo en Sodoma y en otras partes'; A. Zárate, *Historia del descubrimiento y conquista de la provincia del Perú* ... (Madrid, 1853), BAE, 26: 465 (bk 1, chap. 5). Seductive angels, whom Christians usually imagined as beardless young males, were ancient Christian lore.

7   B. Cobo, *Historia*, BAE, 92: 57 (bk 2, chap. 1). On the legendary Patagonian giants, who were also associated with sodomy, and circumcision, see J. Boon, *Other Tribes, Other Scribes* (Cambridge, 1982), 38, 165-8, and 274, note 11. And on giants in America in general, see P. Mason, *The Deconstruction of America* (London, 1993).

8   P. Gutiérrez de Santa Clara, *Historia de las guerras civiles del Perú* (Madrid, 1965), BAE, 166: 258 (chap. 66).

9   Cobo is especially good on this; *Historia*, 92: 57 (bk 2, chap. 1).

10 The word 'infection' is also found in the sources. See several such usages by Pedro Simón, *Noticias historiales de las conquistas de tierra firme en las Indias Occidentales* (Bogotá, 1882), 1: 93.

11 For Albert, see J. Boswell, *Christianity, Social Tolerance, and Homosexuality* (Chicago, 1980), 52.

12 Guerra claims Oviedo thought syphilis was passed through anal intercourse; *Pre-Columbian Mind*, 57. Today, we know that AIDS is.

13 'Para que los señores tuviessen con ellos conoscimiento cometiendo el gravíssimo pecado de la sodomia'; Cieza de León, *Crónica*, 1: 19, 198-201 (pt 1, chap. 64).

14 No chronicler suggests what jumped to my mind: that the 'obscene' reverence paid the god Pachacamac, for example, might have shown devotees that the gods approved of religious homosexual acts. For this prayer gesture, see Chapter 5, and see Trexler, 'Das sprechende Bildnis,' in K. Schreiner (ed.), *Laienfrömmigkeit im späten Mittelalter* (Munich, 1992), 245-70.

15 B. de Las Casas, *Apologética historia*, 2: 522 (chap. 239), and 2: 388 (chap. 213).

16 J. de Torquemada, *Monarquía Indiana* (Mexico City, 1969), 2: 392ff; see Chapter 4, at note 35.

17 Peter Martyr d'Anghiera, *Opera* (Graz, 1966), 106 (dec. 3, chap. 1); see the Latin text in Chapter 4, note 3.

18 Boswell, *Christianity*, 171f.

19 'Pues si deste rey o cacique Goacanagarí hay tal fama, claro está que no sería él sólo en tan nefando e sucio crimen; pues la gente común luego procuran (y aun todo el reino), de imitar al príncipe en las virtudes o mesmos vicios que ellos usan'; G. Fernández de Oviedo, *Historia general y natural de las Indias* (Madrid, 1959), BAE, 117: 118 (bk 5, chap. 3).

20 Letter of 28 October 1495; see the text in Chapter 3, note 6.

21 J. Trevisan, *Perverts in Paradise* (London, 1986), 41, 62.

22 'Están entregados a los más vergonzosos delitos de lujuria y sodomía. Tales se dicen ser los que los nuestros llaman Moscas en el Nuevo Reino, los de la campiña de Cartagena y toda su costa, los que habitan en las

costas del río Paraguay y los que pueblan las dilatadísimas regiones comprendidas entre los dos mares del Norte y del Sur todavía poco exploradas.' J. Acosta, *De procuranda indorum salute*, in *Obras* (Madrid, 1954), BAE, 73: 393.

23   F. Montesinos, *Memorias antiguas historiales y pólíticas del Perú* (Madrid, 1882), 53f, 56, 79, 85f.

24   Acosta, *De procuranda*, 73: 393.

25   Besides Oviedo and Gómara, Sarmiento de Gamboa (using the fact of Incaic usage as just title for conquest) and Murúa claimed sodomy was widespread throughout the Andean world; P. Sarmiento de Gamboa, *Historia Indica* (Madrid, 1960); Martín de Murúa, *Historia de los Incas* (Lima, 1922), 22f. Cieza condemns the exaggerators in his *Crónica*, 2: 74ff (pt 2, chap. 25).

26   'En muchas provinçias andavan los honbres como salvajes y los unos salían a se dar guerra à los otros y se comían como agora hazen los de la provinçia de Arma y otras de sus comarcas'; *Crónica*, 2: 75 (pt 2, chap. 25).

27   Ibid.

28   'Y aun por ventura podría ser que *los Yngas* ynorasen que tal cosa en los templos se cometiese, puesto que si disimulavan algo, era por no hazerse mal quistor y con pensar que bastava que ellos mandasen por todas partes adorar al Sol'; ibid.

29   This is developed in my 'Sprechende Bildnis.'

30   Garcilaso, *Comentarios*, 133: 218 (bk 6, chap. 19), narrating the punishment of Chinca sodomy, and *Comentarios*, 133: 101 (bk 3, chap. 13), punishment of the coastal natives' crime. Garcilaso cleverly proved his contention that, for the Incas as for the Judeo-Christian tradition, sodomy was an unmentionable sin, by stating that it was legally prohibited to hurl the accusation (of being a passive) against anyone in an argument. For such laws elsewhere, see further below.

31   Garcilaso, *Comentarios*, 133: 101 (bk 3, chap. 13).

32   Ibid., 133: 218 (bk 6, chap. 119).

33   See the text in Chapter 6, note 98.

34   John Rowe, in *Acta Americana*, 6 (1948), 49.

35   He is quoted in Anonymous, 'Les Incas condamnaient-ils l'homophilie?' *Arcadie*, 108 (Dec. 1962), 636. As I write this note (July 1992), the Nicaraguan government has passed draconian laws against homosexuality, and against speech favoring it.

36   For the text, see J. Hemming, *The Conquest of the Incas* (San Diego, 1970), 142; further F. Graziano, *Divine Violence* (Boulder, CO, 1992), 283. Pre-Columbian native American 'picotas' (Sillustani, Puno, Peru) are shown in F. Kauffmann Doig, *Comportamiento sexual in el antiguo Perú* (Lima, n.d.), 85ff.

37   'Por lo cual sea regla general que en toda la gentilidad no ha habido gente más varonil que tanto se haya preciado de cosas de hombres como los Incas, ni que tanto aborreciesen las cosas mujeriles; porque cierto todos

ellos generalmente fueron magnánimos y aspiraron a las cosas más altas de las que manejaron; porque se preciaban de hijos del sol, y este blasón les levantaba a ser heróicos'; *Comentarios*, 133: 226 (bk 6, chap. 25).

38   Jacopo da Voragine (fl. 1290s) cites Jerome as the source for the idea that the 'splendid light' of the Star killed off the sodomites, and Augustine of Hippo for the story that, nine months earlier, God almost scrubbed his incarnation when he discovered people practicing sins against nature; *Leggenda Aurea* (Florence, 1952), 54 ('La natività di N. S. Gesù Cristo'). See further S. Gruzinski, 'Las cenizas del deseo,' in S. Ortega (ed.), *De la santidad a la perversión* (Mexico City, 1985), 260. David Lindsay's early eighteenth-century English formulation is in A. Bray, *Homosexuality in Renaissance England* (London, 1982), 26. Curiously, accusations of bestiality are generally rare in the texts, and one writer said the natives had never heard of it; Guerra, *Pre-Columbian Mind*, 162.

39   'Quien más sentía esta desdicha eran las mujeres, por ver que a la naturaleza se la defraudaban aumentos y a ellas gustos. En sus juntas no trataban otra cosa sino del miserable estado de poca estimación a que habían llegado; ardíanse en celos, viendo entre los hombres comunicados los favores y halagos a ellas solamente debidos; daban y tomaban medios para el remedio; usaban de yerbas y artes, pero nada aprovechaba a tornar el libre alvedrio'; *Memorias*, 91f (chap. 16). The English translator in 1920 left this section out because it was 'not suitable for translation,' just as he omitted other passages because he 'thinks it best not to present them to the reader'; *Memorias antiguas historiales del Perú*, trans. P. Ainsworth Means (Nendeln, 1967), 68, 76. Needless to say, this translation is useless.

40   'Tan afeminado el valor, que lo más olvidado es la honda y la flecha'; *Memorias*, 99 (chap. 17).

41   'El que perdiese el sémen humano'; *Memorias*, 103 (chap. 18); mistranslated by Ainsworth Means, 77. Outlawing the spilling of semen 'out of the vase' betrays Christian influence, of course; that was a fundamental reason given for the canonic prohibition of sodomy, as we have seen.

42   Presumably because he spent so much time with passives: 'Este desbenturado Sinchichiruca dizen que siempre entendió en regalarse, el cual dizen los mandó buscar *chotarpo vanarpo*, para acostumbrar en las fornicationes, y assí an abido tantos *vacanquest* que los yndios los iban con aquellos presentes. Este desventurado ynga dizen que apenas tubo a un hijo llamado ynga Lluquiyupangui'; J. de Santacruz Pachacuti Yamqui, *Relacíon de antigüedades deste reyno del Perú* (Madrid, 1968), BAE, 209: 289, and read 285–90 for the Quechua linguistic context. The Quechua *arpa* means to sacrifice, *chot* to stand erect, *van* has the sense of receiving. *Vacanquest* = *guacanquis* [*cf. huaca*], meaning variously love charms, or the altars on which such charms were placed. The proposed reading is my own, but I am much indebted to Jorge L. Urioste for his help. See further F. Karsch-Haack, *Das gleichgeschlechtliche Leben der Naturvölker* (New York, 1975), 415, and especially the early seventeenth-century D. Goncalez Holguin, *Vocabulario de la Lengua general de todo*

el Perú, llamada lengua Qquichua o del Inca (Lima, 1952), 34, 125, 166. See further F. Guaman Poma de Ayala, *El primer nueva corónica y buen gobierno* (Mexico City, 1980), 249.

43 'Los reyes remediaban poco por no desabrir a sus vasallos; quien más lo sentian eran las mujeres, llegaron á tanto sus celos, que mandaban matar á muchos hombres con hechizos . . . Llegó esta á tanto rompimiento, que mataron á muchas personas principales. Mandó el Inga Sinchi Roca hacer junta . . .'; *Memorias*, 116 (chap. 20).

44 See the text in the previous note. 'Muy en su punto estaban las hechicerías en tiempo de Sinchi Roca, ocasionada de la sodomía, como hemos visto'; *Memorias*, 120 (chap. 21).

45 'Dizen que fue muy ayunador, que no abía querido conoçer mujeres hasta que fue muy biejo . . . Dizen que también los hordenó que todos los hombres de su señorio los pelasen las barbas y que fuesen como él lampeños . . . Y lo mismo habían criado a muchos muchachos para que no las conoscan mujeres; estos sirvieron despues para los soldados de guerra, principalmente los abía servido en tiempo de su hijo, &'; my italics; Santa Cruz Pachacuti, *Antigüedades*, 209: 290. Special thanks to Jorge Urioste for his insight into this passage.

46 Cited in Guerra, *Pre-Columbian Mind*, 187f.

47 Cited in Guerra, *Pre-Columbian Mind*, 189.

48 Cited in Guerra, *Pre-Columbian Mind*, 188; Calancha, *Crónica moralizada*, 220.

49 'Y estando assí en la plaza de Pomapampa, manda que sacaran a todas las *acllas*, de quatro maneras, a la plaça; y assi, estando todas, en medio de tantos números de *apocuracas* y todo el reyno de gente, hazen salir cien yndios *llamallamas* y *hayachucos*, y en el entretano que ellos hazian sus comedias, vessita a todas las donçellas, mirando a cada una, [y] manda a los *llamallamas* que los aremetieron a las donzellas cada uno, para usar la bestialidad en acto público, como los mismos carneros de la tierra; y por las donzellas viéndose assí forçados, haze esclamación, alsando los ojos al cielo; y desto todos los grandes del reyno siente grandemente'; Santacruz Pachacuti, *Antigüedades*, 209: 312; cf. Guerra, *Pre-Columbian Mind*, 170.

50 W. Williams, *The Spirit and the Flesh* (Boston, 1986, 1992), provides much evidence on this score.

51 See, e.g., Mohave forgetting in R. Stoller, *Presentations of Gender* (New Haven, 1985), 175.

52 This must be a reason why the mestizo Guaman Poma de Ayala says almost nothing about sexuality at all in his massive defense of native life; *Primer nueva corónica*. Note, however, that native peoples have resisted many less formidable aspects of Westernization that were linked, in the Iberian mind, with 'femininity.' I refer to men's long hair, earrings, bright colors, and the like.

53 'XX. Quien cometiere el pecado de sodomía, que muera arrastrado, y ahorcado, y luego sea quemado con todos sus vestidos, y lo mismo si se juntare con alguna bestia'; *Relación de las costumbres antiguas* (Madrid,

256   NOTES TO PAGES 156-158

1968), BAE, 209: 179. Sources do occasionally allude to bestiality with sheep or cameloids when describing Collasuyu, famed for such herding; see, e.g., Cieza, *Crónica*, 1: 278 (pt 1, chap. 101), who in the same breath mentions shepherds' bestiality and temple sodomy in Collasuyu; elsewhere he refers to cohabitation with monkeys in Antisuyu, that is, in the jungle, where 'estos usan con ellas como mugeres'; ibid., 1: 265 (pt 1, chap. 95). But G. Mendieta, *Historia eclesiastica indiana* (Mexico City, 1971), 137 f (bk 2, chap. 29), says the Mexicans were innocent of the same. As noted earlier, in peninsular Spain bestiality and sodomy often had the same punishments, and the words often comprised both meanings.

54 Cieza and others had already tried to explain why the Incas did not abolish temple homosexuality; cited above, note 28.

55 'Y en particular mando que con gran diligencia hiciesen pesquisa de los sodomitas ...'; *Comentarios*, 133: 101, 218 (bk 3, chap. 13; bk 6, chap. 19).

56 See above, notes 34, 35. De Pauw denies Garcilaso's 'fable' that Capac Yupanqui had ordered the extermination of sodomites as a 'fiction très-grossière.' Garcilaso made the claim of Inca anti-sodomy laws to one-up the Spaniards, who claimed they had conquered the Incas so as to put an end to sodomy; 'c'est d'après les loix romaines, que Garcilasso a imaginé le supplice du feu dont il parle tant, et qui etoit ignoré parmi les Peruviens'; *Recherches philosophiques sur les Americains* (London, 1770), 1: 63–70, esp. 67, 69.

57 Las Casas intimates that there was a law against sodomy there; *Apologética historia*, 2: 522 (chap. 239).

58 'Aunque algunos dicen que en Mexico morían los que cometían el pecado nefando; otros, que no se hacía caso del para castigarlo.' Herrera continues: 'pero es cierto que entre ellos era cosa afrentosa llamar a uno Cuylumpult que quiere decir, somético paciente; sobre lo cual combatían con espadas y rodelas y se permitía tal desafio'; A. de Herrera, *Historia general de los hechos de los castellanos ...* (Madrid, 1934–57), 6: 444 (dec. 3, bk 4, chap. 16); Guerra, *Pre-Columbian Mind*, 154.

59 'Pecado tan común en estas regiones, que mozos y viejos le cometían, y hasta niños de seis anos solían hallarse infestados de el'; J. García Icazbalceta, *Bibliografia Mexicana del siglo XVI* (Mexico City, 1886), 398. Peter was obviously surprised that *passivity* was practiced by elders, and by those six years and under.

60 This much discussed matter can be approached through J. Phelan, *The Millennial Kingdom of the Franciscans in the New World (1525-1604)* (Berkeley, 1956); B. Keen, *The Aztec Image* (New Brunswick, 1971).

61 'Y en las provincias de Mexico y Tezcoco, con lo a estos señorios subjeto, había pena de muerte, y no solo no lo permetían, más incurrían y buscaban los tales delincuentes para los punir con pena de muerte, como lo hizo el señor de Tezcoco llamado Nezahualpilzintli. E su hijo Conuanacothzin, que después subcedió en el señorio de Tezcoco, hizo lo mesmo que el padre, ca incurió y buscó los delincuentes de aquel crimen pèssimo é

justició é ahorcó públicamente muchos de ellos. Este alcanzó á los cristianos e fué baptizado . . ., donde colegimos que usaban del derecho natural é no tenían depravado ni ofuscado el seso natural, que ansí en esto como en todo lo que es contra los diez mandamientos de Dios, se tenia ser malo y habia leys . . .'; Motolinía, *Memoriales e historia de los Indios de la Nueva España* (Madrid, 1970), 142. The Tezcocans, living on the east side of the great lake of the Valley of Mexico, were, of course, Aztecs as well.

62 See Trexler, 'From the Mouths of Babes,' in *Church and Community, 1200–1600* (Rome, 1987).

63 'Ahorcaban al puto ó somético y al varón que tomaban en hábito de mujer'; found in 'Estas son leyes que tenían los indios de la Nueva España, Anáhuac ó México'; *Nueva colección de documentos para la historia de México*, ed. J. García Icazbalceta, vol. 3 (Mexico City, 1891), 311. At the end of the transcription of these alleged laws, Fray Andrés in Valladolid swears that everything above is true because he took it from the *Historia de los Mexicanos por sus pinturas*. That is not true, because the above 'law' is not in this *Historia*, as given here, 228–63; it, like another 'law' in this source allegedly punishing lesbians (310), is 'possibly not authentic,' to use García's generous language. However, for the afterlife of the anti-male 'law,' see Las Casas, *Apologética historia*, 2: 400 (chap. 215): 'Ahorcaban al que cometía el pecado nefando, y lo mismo al que tomaba el hábito de mujer'; see further along Las Casas's notion of aboriginal punishments for sodomy in the *Apologética historia*, 2: 388, where that consideration follows immediately after punishments for treason. P. Ragon recognizes that the *Historia de los Mexicanos por sus pinturas* is certainly closer to reality than these so-called laws because it does not ascribe any actual law to the natives; *Les amours indiennes* (Paris, 1992), 66f. Further on this complex matter in G. Baudot, *Utopie et histoire au Mexique: les premiers chroniqueurs de la civilisation mexicaine (1520–1569)* (Toulouse, 1977), 168, 194–202.

64 'Los que cometían el pecado nefando, agente y paciente, morían por ello. Y de cuando en cuando la justicia los andaba á buscar, y hacian inquisición sobre ellos para los matar y acabar: porque bien conocían que tan negando vicio era contra natura, porque en los brutos animales no lo veían. Más el de la bestialidad no se hallaba entre estos naturales. El hombre que andaba vestido en hábito de mujer, y la mujer que andaba vestida en hábito de hombre, ambos tenían pena de muerte'; Mendieta, *Historia*, 137f (bk 2, chap. 29). The homosexual behavior of animals was well documented since antiquity, of course; see Boswell, *Christianity*, 12f.

65 'El pecado nefando en dos maneras; el que servia de hembra, por las partes bajas le sacaban las entrañas, atado en un madero, y los muchachos de la ciudad lo cubrían de ceniza, de suerte que venía a quedar metido dentro de un monto hecho, y despues sobre esto ponian mucha leña y le daban fuego. Y el que servia de hombre lo cubrian vivo de ceniza, de suerte que venía a quedar atado a un madero hasta que allí moría; Ixtlilxóchitl, *Obras históricas*, 1: 405 (*Relación* 11). This is a late seventeenth-century

source, but authoritative for Texcoco; for similar information in earlier writers, see Mendieta, *Historia*, 137 (bk 2, chap. 29); Torquemada, *Monarquia*, 1: 166 (bk 2, chap. 52).

66 'La muger, que con otra muger tenia deleitaciones carnales, à las quales llamaban patlache, que quiere decir: Incuba, morían ambas por ello'; Torquemada, *Monarquia*, 2: 380 (bk 12, chap. 4).

67 See not only J. Offner, *Law and Politics in Aztec Texcoco* (Cambridge, 1983), 85, 151, who follows the apologists hook, line, and sinker. Other modern students, too numerous to mention, do the same.

68 Kindly brought to my attention by Cecelia Klein.

69 'Tenían por grande abominación el pecado nefando, y los sodomitas eran abatidos y tenidos en poco y por mujeres tratados. Más no los castigaban ... Aunque no había castigo para los tales pecados contra natura, eran de grande abominación y lo tenían por agüero y abusión. Ni menos casaban con madre ni con tía, ni con madrastra'; D. Muñoz Camargo, *Historia de Tlaxcala* (Mexico City, 1978), 138.

70 F. Clavijero, *Historia antigua de México* (Mexico City, 1987), 523. In the early twentieth century, Bancroft paraphrases this eighteenth-century conflict before coming down against Clavijero: as 'inexpressibly revolting as the sin must appear to a modern mind,' pederasty, he said, was common; *Native Races*, in his *Works*, 2: 467f. One does not know whether to cry or smile.

71 Such shame penalties are discussed in Herrera, *Historia*, 12: 394 (dec. 6, bk 5, chap. 6).

72 My italics. 'Que pena dan al que es puto, al cual vosotros llamais cuylón, si es el paciente?' 'Los muchachos lo apedrean e le hacen mal, e le llaman bellaco, e algunas veces mueren del mal que les hacen'; Oviedo, *Historia*, 120: 377 (bk 42, chap. 3).

73 See Trexler, 'We Think, They Act,' in *Church and Community*.

74 '... Anchora che conoscesse che il farlo gli potesse metter conto'; *Relatione di alcune cose della Nuova Spagna, e della gran Città di Temestitan Messico; fatta per uno Gentil'homo del Signor Fernando Cortese*, in *Colección de documentos para la historia de México*, ed. J. García Icazbalceta, 2 vols (Mexico City, 1858–66), 1: 397.

75 'Emborráchanse mucho, y entonces maltratan á las mujeres'; López de Gómara, *Historia de las Indias* (Madrid, 1946), BAE, 22: 182. Because of their sodomy, Peruvian men 'neglect their wives and pay them little respect'; Zárate, *The Discovery and Conquest of Peru: a Translation of Books I to IV of Agustin de Zárate's 'History'* ... (Baltimore, 1968), 32 (bk 1, chap. 4); cited in Guerra, *Pre-Columbian Mind*, 99. V. Tixier, *Travels on the Osage Prairies* (Norman, 1940), 182, linked sodomy and maltreatment as well. Coon found the presence of markets for boys coinciding with a low standing of women in twentienth-century Morocco; C. Coon, *Tribes of the Rif* (Cambridge, MA, 1931), 110f.

76 See Trexler, 'From the Mouths of Babes,' in *Church and Community*.

77 Among many such statements, see A. Núñez Cabeza de Vaca's description

of feminine work in his *Naufragios* (Madrid, 1946), BAE, 22: 538 (chap. 26). The classic text is the above-cited one of Cieza, *Crónica*, 1: 146f (pt 1, chap. 44), who contrasts the hard-working wives in the fields and the husbands indoors, weaving, painting themselves, and other 'oficios afeminados.'

78 On Hispaniola, 'este pecado abominable contra natura muy usado era, entre estos indios desta isla; pero a las mujeres aborrescible, por su interés mas que por ningún escrúpulo de conciencia, y aún porque, de hecho, había algunas que eran buenas de sus personas, sobre ser en esta isla las mayores bellacas e más deshonestas y libidinosas mujeres que se han visto en estas Indias o partes'; Oviedo, *Historia*, 117: 119 (bk 5, chap. 3).

79 'Si algún hombre hobiera maculado dello, las mujeres (dijo ella) a bocados lo comiéramos o lo matáramos, o otras semejantes palabras que me dijo'; Las Casas, *Apologética historia*, 2: 314 (chap. 198).

80 'Había mujeres públicas y adonde las había, apedreaban a los sodomitas'; 1522 data in Herrera, *Historia*, 6: 394 (dec. 3, bk 4, chap. 7); Guerra, *Pre-Columbian Mind*, 154.

81 'Son aborrecidos estos tales de las mujeres en extremo grado; pero como son muy sujetas á sus maridos, no osan hablar en ellos sino pocas veces, ó con los cristianos'; G. Fernández de Oviedo, *Sumario de la natural historia de las Indias*, in *Historiadores primitivos de Indias* (Madrid, 1946), BAE, 22: 508 (chap. 81).

82 'Como no serán abominables y notados de mujeres los hombres que descaradamente les hurtan el oficio acostumbrado, haciendo lo que ellas hacen?'; F. Núñez de Pineda y Bascuñán, *Cautiverio feliz y razón de las guerras dilatadas de Chile* (Santiago, 1863), 297. On the struggle to get men to choose women, see Trexler, *Dependence in Context in Renaissance Florence* (Binghamton, 1994), 373–6, and Trexler, *Public Life in Renaissance Florence* (New York, 1980), 379–82.

83 Gómara, *Historia*, 22: 185.

84 Montesinos, *Memorias*, 91f (chap. 16).

85 'Hazíanle grande afrenta, llamándole muger: diziéndole que dexase el hábito de hombre que tenía'; Cieza, *Crónica*, 1: 195 (pt 1, chap. 62). This rare case of a man dressed like a man being involved in homosexual behavior nonetheless conforms to our model: once practicing in that form, the male was expected to assume a woman's role and clothes.

86 'Hombres malditos y desventurados, hay (acaso) falta de mujeres en el mundo? Y vosotros que sois bardajas que tomáis el oficio de mujeres, no os fuera mejor ser hombres?'; Muñoz Camargo, *Historia*, 138. The curiosity about actives was that they chose other males when there were plenty of pretty women available. See also Cieza: 'Pues como estos fuesen malos y viciosos, no embargante que entre ellos avía mugeres muchas: y algunas hermosas, los más dellos usavan ... la sodomía'; Cieza, *Crónica*, 1: 160 (pt 1, chap. 49). For William of Auvergne criticizing the Moors in similar fashion, see Chapter 2, at note 71.

87 'Viven en esta ciudad [de Guayaquil] dos naciones de indios, unos llamados

Guamcavillcas, gente bien dispuesta y blanca, limpios en sus vestidos y de buen parecer; los otros se llaman Chonos, morenos, no tan politicios como los Guamcavillcas; los unos y los otros es gente guerrera; sus armas, arco y flecha. Tienen los Chonos mala fama en el vicio nefando; el cabello traen un poco alto y el cogote trasquilado, con lo cual los demas indios los afrentan en burlas y en veras; llamándolos perros chonos cocotados'; R. de Lizárraga, *Descripción del Perú* (Madrid, 1986), 216: 8 (chap. 5); 9 (chap. 6). Does this passage hint that Guayaquil was divided between 'men' and 'women' like the Iroquois, or, on the Inca model, between those living up (*hanan*) and down (*hurin*)?

88 The people of the province of Tarama 'es gente limpia del peccado nefando: tanto que entre ellos se tiene un refrán antiguo y donoso: el qual es, que antiguamente devió de aver en la provincia de Guaylas algunos naturales viciosos en esta peccado tan grave: tuviéronlo por tan feo los Indios comarcanos y vezinos a los que lo usaron, que por los afrentar y apocar dezían hablando en ello el refrán que no han perdido de la memoria, que en su lengua dize, Asta guaylas, y en la nuestra dirá, trás ti vayan los de Guaylas'; Cieza de León, *Crónica*, 1: 241f (pt 1, chap. 83). In his *Relación del descubrimiento y conquista de los reinos del Perú* (Lima, 1978) (73 [chap. 13]), Pedro Pizarro spelled out that the male Huaillas were also notorious for heterosexual cunnilingus: 'Guailas: hera xente çuçia, porque se dezía dellos que comían la semiente que la muger echava quando se ayuntavan con ella.' Garcilaso says that this tribe's homosexual behavior was a first for the mountains, though such comportment was already known along the coast; *Comentarios*, BAE, 133: 208 (bk 6, chap. 11). The word Huayllas is still used to designate a homosexual passive; H. Brüning, 'Beiträge zum Studium des Geschlechtslebens der Indianer im alten Perú,' *Anthropophyteia*, 7, (1911), 201.

89 Muñoz Camargo, *Historia*, 138.

90 'Era esta gente mui abatida, y tenida en poco, y menospreciada, y no trataban estos, sino con las mugeres'; Torquemada, *Monarquia*, 2: 299 (bk 12, chap. 35). Identical sentiments are found throughout the present work; see, e.g., below, notes 119, 121. See further Cieza, *Crónica*, 1: 235 (pt 1, chap. 80), and the same language, ibid., 1: 195 (pt 1, chap. 62).

91 'E o que serve de macho, se tem por valente, e contam esta bestialidade por proeza'; G. Soares de Sousa, *Tratado descriptivo do Brasil em 1587* ... (Rio de Janeiro, 1879), 287 (bk 2, chap. 156). 'En lo qual dizen que gloriavan demasiadamente'; Cieza de León, *Crónica*, 1: 160 (pt 1, chap. 49). Note that the Arabic term for an active, *nièk*, has a positive meaning at times, indicating virility; M. Chebel, *L'esprit de sérail* (Paris, 1988), 59.

92 'Solo tienen por vil y vituperable el pecado nefando, con esta diferencia, que el que usa el oficio de varón no es baldonado por él, como el que se sujeta al de la mujer'; 'Núñez de Pineda, *Cautiverio feliz*, 3: 107.

93 'Pues que hay *cuilones* (que *cuilón* llaman al sodomita)'; Oviedo, *Historia*, 120: 421 (bk 42, chap. 12).

94 'Pero es cierto que entre ellos era cosa afrentosa llamar a uno Cuylumputl, que quiere decir, somético paciente; sobre lo cual combatían con espadadas y rodelas y se permitía tal desafío; Herrera, *Historia*, 6: 444 (dec. 3, bk 4, chap. 16).

95 See also Seler's series of cognates, in Karsch-Haack, *Gleichgeschlechtliche*, 380. Karsch translates the word *tonmotlatlamachtia* as (active) 'sodomite.' However, William Christian warns me that the word could rather have a Latin root found in Spanish and Italian: 'culón,' 'culo' ('ass'), both commonly used in insulting expressions.

96 See Oviedo's text in Chapter 4, note 22. According to Brasseur, *camayoa* was the old Haitian word for passive; cited in Karsch-Haack, *Gleichgeschlechtliche*, 434.

97 'Se dice oura; y de los yndios de quien se tenían sospechas se reían y los llamaban oruas, que quiere decir hombre que hace de muger'; 'Información de las idolatrías,' 148.

98 Karsch-Haack, 'Uranismus,' *Jahrbuch für sexuelle Zwischenstufen*, 3 (1901), 153; Trevisan, *Perverts*, 55; G. Devereux, 'Institutionalized Homosexuality,' *Human Biology*, 9 (1937), 500. Antonio de Oliveira Cardonega, in his *Historia general das guerras Angolanas* (Lisbon, 1942), 259, has what, according to L. Mott ('Escravidão e homossexualidade,' in *História e sexualidade no Brasil*, ed. R. Vainfas [Rio de Janeiro, 1986], 27), is the earliest description of homosexuality in Black Africa, reading in small part: 'Há também entre o gentio de Angola muita sodomia, tendo uns com outros suas imundicies e sujidades, vestindo como mulheres. E lhes chamam pelo nome da terra *quimbandas* ... '

99 See the original text in Chapter 5, note 63.

100 Karsch-Haack, *Gleichgeschlechtliche*, 353–442; S. Gruzinski, 'Seis ensayos sobre el discurso colonial relativo a la comunidad domestica,' *Cuadernos de trabajo del departamento de investigaciones históricas, INAH*, 35 (Oct. 1980), 58f. An excellent vocabulary is in W. Roscoe, 'Bibliography of Berdache and Alternative Gender Roles Among North American Indians,' *Journal of Homosexuality*, 14 (1987).

101 Cited in G. Freyre, *The Masters and the Slaves* (New York, 1971), 124; Trevisan, *Perverts*, 21.

102 See Chapter 5, at note 49.

103 E.g., Karsch-Haack, *Gleichgeschlechtliche*, 353–442.

104 W. La Barre, e.g., exploits Bertonio's 1612 Aymara dictionary and found no such words, but many for passives; 'The Aymara Indians of the Lake Titicaca Plateau, Bolivia,' *American Anthropologist*, 50 (1948), 134.

105 According to Seler's information to Karsch-Haack, *cuiloni* means someone who can be taken. *Cuilónyotl* means a passive sodomite; the present tense of *cuilontia* is *ni-te-cuilontia* or 'I make someone into a passive; *tecuílontiani* is 'the one who makes passives'; Karsch-Haack, *Gleichgeschlechtliche*, 380.

106 See the various works of C. B. de Quirós: *La picota en América* (Havana, 1948); *Nuevas noticias de picotas Americanas* (Havana, 1952); *La picota:*

crimenes y castigos en el pais castellano en los tiempos medios (Madrid, 1907). For psychological readings of the same, see Graziano, *Divine Violence*, 158–63, and Quirós, *Nuevas noticias*, 61, and in Chapter 1 of the present work. An English cognate of *picota* is, of course, to prick or penetrate.

107 Herrera praised the natives of the New Kingdom of Granada in 1601 for using the *picota* against such crimes: 'La vida moral de estos indios es de gente de mediana razón, porque castigan los delitos, en particular el homicidio y el hurto y el pecado nefando, de que son muy limpios, y hay muchas horcas por los caminos'; *Historia*, 12: 394 (dec. 6, bk 5, chap. 6).

108 See Chapter 1.

109 Acosta implicitly does make the distinction with the term 'el pecado nefando con varones'; *Obras*, 432.

110 The Portuguese Inquisition records are certainly the earliest rich source for such vocabulary. Luis Mott has studied this language in his 'Pagode português,' *Ciencia e cultura*, 40 (1988), but unfortunately the author's zeal to make his point – that a 'gay sub-culture' (to use Boswell's term) already existed in Lisbon in the sixteenth century – leads to a certainly unintentional distortion of this invaluable documentation. Further, his undisciplined work procedures and apparatuses often make his results suspect and unusable.

111 See Chapter 2.

112 Torquemada, *Monarquia Indiana*, 2: 392ff (bk 12, chap. 10). The text is given above. Other references where the active is the one who 'commits' are: the 'law' in the Anonymous attributed to Blas Valera, *Relación*, 209: 179; the aggressive Arawaks in Michele di Cuneo; cited in Chapter 3, note 6.

113 'Información de las idolatrías,' 160; Calancha, *Crónica moralizada*, 1158f. Other examples are from Juan López de Velasco, cited in Guerra, *Pre-Columbian Mind*, 130. Cieza says the temple priests 'committed' sodomy; *Crónica*, 2: 74ff (pt 2, chap. 25).

114 Mott documents one 1652 use of the term *puto agente* in his Inquisition materials; 'Pagode,' 128. But without more text it is hard to say if the word *agente* here means 'acting as a passive,' or 'the active partner in the sodomitic act.' Mott unfortunately commonly uses the word 'sodomite' to refer indifferently to actives and passives.

115 Gómara, *Historia*, 22: 202.

116 B. de Sahagún, *Florentine Codex* (Santa Fe, 1975–82), 10: 89f; *Historia general de las cosas de Nueva España*, 4 vols (Mexico City, 1956), 3: 120. See the text of the latter further below.

117 Muñoz Camargo, *Historia*, 138. See the text above, at note 86.

118 'Estos yndios de estas provinçias del Collao es gente çuçia: tocan en muchos pecados abominables; andavan muchos varones en ábito de mugeres, usando mal y en muchas ydolatrías'; P. Pizarro, *Relación*, 111 (chap. 16).

119 'El somético paciente es abominable, nefando y detestable, digno de que

hagan burla y se rían las gentes. Y el hedor y fealdad de su pecado nefando no se puede sufrir, por el asco que da a los hombres. En todo se muestra mujeril o afeminado, en el andar o en el hablar, por todo lo cual merece ser quemado'; Sahagún, *Historia*, 3: 120 (bk 10, chap. 11).

120 See the text in the previous note. Esther Newton finds that, in contemporary US society, lower-class homosexuals tend to consider a passive partner gay and an active one sexually normal, and that, more than middle-class types, those of the lower classes insist on exclusive male or female role portrayals; 'Role Models,' in Janet L. Dolgin et al. (eds), *Symbolic Anthropology* (New York, 1977), 339.

121 My italics. 'Este vicio inmundo, que por su indecencia no se nombra, es así que en partes si hallaba entre estas gentes. Pero como el es mas que bruto pues no se halla en los brutos animales, era tenido entre estas naciones tan ciegas y ajenas de la luz de la razón por tan vil y afrentoso, principalmente en los pacientes, que estos eran conocidos y menospreciados de todos. Y los llamaban en su lengua con vocablo y palabra afrentosa, y los tales no usaban de arco ni flecha. Antes algunos se vestían como mujeres'; Pérez de Ribas, *Páginas*, 1: 132.

122 See above, at note 91.

123 L. Hanke, *All Mankind is One* (DeKalb, 1974), 107.

124 S. Brandes, *Metaphors of Masculinity: Sex and Status in Andalusian Folklore* (Philadelphia, 1980), 94–8, and 204, where themes of social status and sexual identity are seen as one basic issue, that of dominance and submission. For the Iberian insult word *fodidenculo* or passive ('fucked in ass'), see J. Corominas, *Diccionario crítico etimológico de la lengua castellana*, 4 vols (Madrid, 1954–7), 'joder.' Further on the Portuguese word, see W. Dyne's glossary in Murray, *Male Homosexuality*, 186.

125 S. Brandes, 'Like Wounded Stags: Male Sexual Ideology in an Andalusian Town,' in S. Ortner and H. Whitehead, *Sexual Meanings* (Cambridge, 1981), 233f. See further D. Gilmore, *Aggression and Community: Paradoxes of Andalusian Culture* (New Haven, 1987), and, by the same author, *Manhood in the Making: Cultural Concepts of Masculinity* (New Haven, 1990).

126 The news reports are in the *New York Times*, 11 May 1988, 47; ibid., 1 Feb. 1989; *International Herald Tribune*, 25 May 1989.

127 Graziano, *Divine Violence*, *passim*.

128 The interesting article by T. Almaguer, 'Chicano Men,' *Differences*, 3 (1991), 75–100, describes what happens when such attributes meet the more egalitarian notion of 'homosexuality' in North American society.

CHAPTER 8 YESTERDAY AND TODAY

1 The Dominican Palatino de Curzola in a 1559 treatise cited by L. Hanke, *All Mankind is One* (DeKalb, 1974), 125. This is the only extant statement of direct Iberian eye-witness observation I can find in the historical record.

2 Philip Wylie, paraphrasing the patriot of the Second World War; *Generation of Vipers* (New York, 1942), 56. Note also the title of chapter 8: 'Common Man: The Hero's Backside.'

3 *The New York Times* (5 Feb. 1989).

4 A. Scacco, *Male Rape* (New York, 1982), vii.

5 K. Arnold, 'The Introduction of Poses ...,' in J. Blacking (ed.), *The Anthropology of the Body* (London, 1977).

6 On the right to rape all virgin women on the lord's plantations, and the persistence of first-night rights, however, see S. Marcos, 'Indigenous Eroticism and Colonial Morality in Mexico: the Confession Manuals of New Spain,' *Numen*, 39 (1992), 165, and an unedited paper of 1977 cited by her: M. Olivera, 'El derecho de Pernada en las fincas cafetaleras de Chiapas.'

7 See further in Trexler, 'Correre la Terra,' in *Dependence in Context in Renaissance Florence* (Binghamton, 1994).

8 Examined in Chapter 5.

9 'The execution of anal intercourse always presupposes a certain degree of willingness on the side of the passive party'; M. Hirshfeld, *Sexual Pathology* (Newark, 1932), 180f.

10 *Phallós* (New York, 1972), 81 and 190–1 for how foreign the notion of phallic aggression is to today's world.

11 'Anal erotism is one of those components of the instinct which in the course of evolution and in accordance with our present civilizing education has become useless for sexual aims'; S. Freud, 'Character and Anal Erotism,' in *Collected Papers*, trans. J. Riviere, 2 (New York, 1959), 47.

12 The best antidote to such notions is K. Theweleit, *Männerfantasien* (Reinbek, 1986), which is not just about fantasies.

13 It has recently been re-edited as *The Other Balkan Wars, a 1913 Carnegie Endowment Inquiry in Retrospect*, intro. by G. Kennan (Washington, DC, 1993), esp. 368, 374.

14 An influential article on such brutality is by J. Burns, 'A Serbian Fighter's Trail of Brutality,' *The New York Times*, 27 Nov. 1992, A1, A12.

15 The accepted view is that sexual violations in the prisons of Nazi Germany were rare. But that view has no foundation; there has been no serious study of the records from this point of view.

16 In order: *The International Herald-Tribune*, 25 May 1989; *The Nation*, 17 Feb. 1992, p. 194.

17 M. Baker, *Nam* (New York, 1981), 174f, 199f, 206–13 and *passim*.

18 'A salient of non-European civilization that has continued to the present day to preserve many of its non-European characteristics, including some that fit even less with the world of today than they did with the world of eighty years ago'; *Other Balkan Wars*, intro., 13.

19 D. Finkelhor, *Child Sexual Abuse: New Theory and Research* (New York, 1984), esp. chapter 10: 'Boys as Victims. Review of the Evidence.' Father–daughter abuse as the dominant paradigm was established by D. Russell, 'The Incidence and Prevalence of Intrafamilial and Extrafamilial Sexual

Abuse of Female Children,' *Child Abuse & Neglect*, 7 (1983), 133–46; J. Herman with L. Hirschman, *Father–Daughter Incest* (Cambridge, MA, 1981).

20 Cf. with 38 per cent of women in the USA; *The New York Times*, 21 Nov. 1989, C1.

21 J. Berry, *Lead Us Not into Temptation* (New York, 1992).

22 Finklehor, *Child Sexual Abuse*, 150. Another reason was that the heterosexual father–daughter model was the only one around.

23 Freud's denials are analyzed by Herman, *Father–Daughter Incest*, 7–11, and J. M. Masson, *The Assault on Truth* (New York, 1984).

24 S. Freud, *New Introductory Lectures on Psychoanalysis*, ed. J. Strachey (New York, 1965), 86f, 129; further, A. Rich, *Of Woman Born* (New York, 1976), 197.

25 The writer was Domenico Cecchi; M. Rocke, *Male Homosexuality and its Regulation in Late Medieval Florence* (diss.: SUNY, Binghamton, 1989), 525.

26 Freud, *A General Introduction to Psychoanalysis* (New York, 1949), lecture 21.

27 *The Basic Writings of Sigmund Freud* (New York, 1977), 914–30 (*Totem and Taboo*, chap. 5).

28 Aristophanes describes these tense relations; K. Dover, *Greek Homosexuality* (Cambridge, MA, 1978), 143, and 192 for Sparta, where executive authority over the son was taken from the father by the polis. For intergenerational hatreds in Florence, see Trexler, *Public Life in Renaissance Florence* (New York, 1980), chapter 8. In Aztec culture, the hoarding of women by caciques helped the Spanish missionaries win young men's and women's support: the friars promised to find wives for young men and to protect wives through enforcing monogamy; Trexler, 'From the Mouths of Babes,' in *Church and Community, 1200–1600* (Rome, 1987).

29 G. Creed, 'Sexual Subordination,' *Ethnology*, 23 (1984), 166f.

30 On the former, see S. Gruzinski, 'Las cenizas del deseo,' in S. Ortega (ed.), *De la santidad a la perversión* (Mexico City, 1985); for the latter, I. Leonard, *Baroque Times in Old Mexico* (Westport, CT, 1981), 120.

31 One thinks, for example, of the recent revolution in Maya studies. Before, the Maya were philosophers who had no time for war, but now that their language is understood, the *Blood of Kings* stands revealed: L. Schele and M. Miller, *The Blood of Kings* (New York, 1986).

Bibliography

PRINTED SOURCES

Note: BAE: Biblioteca de Autores Españoles

Acosta, J., *De procuranda indorum salute*, in his *Obras* (Madrid: Atlas, 1954) [BAE, 73].

Acta Sanctorum, June V (Brussels, 1867–8).

Al-Muqaddasî, Muhammad Ibn Ahmad, *Description de l'Occident Musulman au IVe–Xe siècle*, ed. C. Pellat (Algiers: Editions Carbonel, 1950).

Alexander, M. (ed.), *Discovering the New World, based on the Work of Theodore de Bry* (New York: Harper & Row, 1976).

Alonso de Palencia, *Crónica de Enrique IV* (Madrid: Atlas, 1973) [BAE, 257].

Alvarus Pelagius, *Speculum regum*, ed. M. Pinto de Meneses, vol. 1 (Lisbon: Instituto de alta cultura, 1955).

Apuleius, L., *The Golden Ass* (Cambridge, MA: Harvard University Press, 1977).

——, *Opera Omnia*, ed. G. F. Hildebrand (Hildesheim: G. Olms, 1968).

Benavides, A. de, *The Memorial of Fray Alonso de Benavides, 1630*, trans. E. Ayer (Chicago, 1916).

——, *Benavides' Memorial of 1630*, trans. P. Forrestal (Washington, DC: 1954).

Benson, M. (ed), *From Pittsburgh to the Rocky Mountains: Major Stephen Long's Expedition: 1819–1820* (Golden, CO: Fulcrum, 1988).

Benzoni, G., *La historia del Mondo Nuovo* (Graz: Akademische Druck- und Verlagsanstalt, 1969).

Bianchi, Tommaso de', called de' Lanzalotti, *Cronaca Modenese*, vol. 1 (Parma, 1866).

Boccaccio, G., *Decameron*, in *Opere* (Milan: Mursia, 1966).

The Book of Chilam Balam of Chumayel, ed. R. Roys (Washington, DC, 1933).

The Book of Chilam Balam of Tizimin, The Ancient Future of the Itza, ed. M. Edmonson (Austin: University of Texas Press, 1982).

Boscana, G., *Chinigchinich* (Banning, CA: Malibi Museum Press, 1978).

Bozio, T., *De signis ecclesiae dei*, 3 vols (Cologne, 1593).

Bruce, J., *Travels to Discover the Source of the Nile in the Years 1768 . . . 1773*, vol. 6 (Edinburgh, 1813).

Burton, R., *The Erotic Traveler*, ed. E. Leigh (New York: Putnam, 1967).

Cabello Balboa, M., *Historia del Perú bajo la dominación de los Incas* (pt 2 of *Miscelanea Austral*) (Lima, 1920).

Caillaud, F., *Voyage à Méroé, au fleuve blanc, au delà de Fazoqul . . . 1819 . . . 1822* (Paris, 1824).

Calancha, A. de la, *Crónica moralizada*, 6 vols (Lima: Ignacio Prado Pastor, 1974–81).

Castañeda, P., *The Narrative of [P.] Castañeda*, in G. Parker Winship, *The Coronado Expedition, 1540–1542* (Washington, DC: Fourteenth Annual Report of the Bureau of Ethnology, Part 1, 1896).

Catlin G., *Letters and Notes on the Manners, Customs, and Conditions of North American Indians*, 2 vols (New York: Dover, 1973).

Cervantes de Salazar, F., *Crónica de la Nueva España*, 2 vols (Madrid, 1971) [BAE, 244].

Charlevoix, P.-F. *Histoire et description generale de la Nouvelle-France, avec le Journal historique d'un voyage fait par ordre du roi dans l'Amerique septentrionale* (Paris: Chez la veuve Ganeau, 1744).

The Chronicles of Michoacan, ed. E. Craine and R. Reindorp (Norman: University of Oklahoma Press, 1970).

Cieza de León, P. *Crónica del Perú*, 3 vols (Lima: Pontificia Universidad Católica del Perú, 1984–6).

Cobo, B., *Obras*, 2 vols (Madrid: Atlas, 1964) [BAE, 91–2].

Colección de documentos ineditos relativos al descubrimiento, conquista y organización de las antiguas posesiones españolas en América y Oceanía, vols 13, 21 (Madrid, 1870, 1874).

Colección de los viajes y descubrimientos que hicieron por mar los españoles, ed. M. Fernández de Navarrete, 5 vols (Buenos Aires, 1945–6).

Colección de documentos para la historia de México, ed. J. García Icazbalceta, 2 vols (Mexico City, 1858–66).

Cortés, H., *Cartas y documentos* (Mexico City: Porrua, 1963).

Les croniques valencianes sobre les Germanies de Guillem Ramon Català i de Miquel Garcia (Segle XVI), ed. E. Duran (Valencia, 1984).

De Pauw, C., *Recherches philosophiques sur les Americains*, 3 vols (London, 1770).

Díaz del Castillo, B., *Historia verdadera de la conquista de la Nueva España*, 2 vols (Mexico City: Porrua, 1968).

Diodorus of Sicily, trans. C. Welles, vol. 8 (Cambridge, MA: Loeb, 1963).

Du Cange, C., *Glossarium mediae et infimae latinitatis*, vol. 2 (Paris, 1937).

Durán, D., *Historia de las Indias de Nueva España e Islas de la Tierra Firme*, 2 vols (Mexico City: Porrua, 1967).

——*Book of the Gods & Rites and the Ancient Calendar* (Norman: University of Oklahoma Press, 1971).

Fages, P., *A Historical, Political, and Natural Description of California by Pedro Fages, Soldier of Spain*, trans. H. Priestley (Berkeley, 1937).

Fernández de Oviedo, G., *Historia general y natural de las Indias*, 5 vols (Madrid: Atlas, 1959) [BAE, 117–21].

——*Sumario de la natural historia de las Indias*, in *Historiadores primitivos de Indias* (Madrid: Atlas, 1946) [BAE, 22].

Fernández Piedrahita, L., *Historia general del nuevo reino de Granada*, vol. 1 (Bogotá, 1942).

'J. Flynt,' 'Homosexuality Among Tramps,' in *Sexual Inversion*, ed. H. Ellis and J. A. Symonds (eds) (New York: Arno Press, 1975), 252–7.

Freud, S., *The Basic Writings of Sigmund Freud* (New York: Modern Library, 1977).

——, *Collected Papers*, trans. J. Riviere, vol. 2 (New York: Basic Books, 1959).

——, *A General Introduction to Psychoanalysis* (New York: Perma Books, 1949).

——, *New Introductory Lectures on Psychoanalysis*, ed. J. Strachey (New York: Norton, 1965).

Galen's Commentary on the Hippocratic Treatise, Airs, Waters, Places (Jerusalem: Israel Academy of Science & Humanities, 1982).

García, G., *Origen de los Indios del Nuevo Mundo* (Mexico City: Biblioteca Americana, 1981).

Garcilaso de la Vega, *Comentarios reales de los Incas*, 3 vols (Madrid: Atlas, 1960–3) [BAE, 132–5].

Gautier le Leu, Le Jongleur, ed. C. Livingston (Cambridge, MA: Harvard University Press, 1951).

Gregory, Bishop of Tours, *Histoire ecclésiastique des Francs*, vol. 2 (Paris, 1837).

Guaman Poma de Ayala, F., *El primer nueva corónica y buen gobierno*, ed. J. Murra and R. Adorno, 3 vols (Mexico City: Siglo veintiuno, 1980).

Guerra, F. (ed.), *The Pre-Columbian Mind* (New York: Seminar Press, 1971).

Gutiérrez de Santa Clara, P., *Historia de las guerras civiles del Perú* (Madrid: Atlas, 1965) [BAE, 166].

Herodotus, *The Persian Wars*, ed. G. Rawlinson (New York: Modern Library, 1942).

Herrera, A. de, *Historia general de los hechos de los castellanos en las islas y tierrafirme del mar Océano*, 17 vols (Madrid: Real academia, 1934–57).

Hippocrates, trans. W. H. S. Jones, vol. 1 (Cambridge, MA: Loeb, 1957).

Ixtlilxóchitl, F. de Alva, *Obras históricas*, 2 vols (Mexico City: UNAM, 1975).

Jacopo da Voragine, *Leggenda Aurea* (Florence: Libreria Editrice Florentina, 1952).

The Jesuit Relations and Allied Documents: Travels and Explorations of the

Jesuit Missionaries in New France, 1610–1791, ed. R. Gold Thwaites, vol. 59 (New York: Pageant Book Co., 1959).

Katz, J. (ed.), *Gay American History* (New York: Harper & Row, 1976).

Kirk Grayson, A. and D. Redford (eds), *Papyrus and Tablet* (Englewood Cliffs, NJ: Prentice-Hall, 1973).

Krapf, J., *Reisen in Ostafrika ausgeführt in den Jahren 1837–1855*, vol. 1 (Stuttgart: F. A. Brockhaus, 1964).

Lafitau, J., *Customs of the American Indians Compared with the Customs of Primitive Times*, trans. W. Fenton and E. Moore, vol. 1 (Toronto: 1974).

Landa, D. de, *Relación de las cosas de Yucatan* (Mexico City: Porrua, 1959).

Las Casas, B. de, *Apologética historia Sumaria*, ed. E. O'Gorman, 2 vols (Mexico City: UNAM, 1967).

——, 'Entre los remedios', *Obras Escogidas*, vol. 5 (Madrid: Atlas, 1958) [BAE, 110].

——, *Historia de las Indias*, 3 vols (Mexico City: Fondo de cultura economica, 1965).

Laudonnière, R., *L'histoire notable de la Floride* (Paris, 1853).

Le Moyne de Morgues, Iacob, *Brevis narratio eorum quae in Florida Americae provincia Gallis acciderunt, secunda . . . Laudoniere . . . anno MDLXIII, quae est secunda pars Americae, additae figurae . . . auctore Iacobo de Moyne, cui cognomen de Morgues . . .*, ed. T. de Bry (Frankfurt am Main, 1591).

Lévi-Provençal, E. (ed.), 'Un document sur la vie urbaine et les corps de métiers à Séville au début du XIIe siècle: le traité d'Ibn Abdun,' *Journal Asiatique* (April–June 1934), 177–92.

Lichtheim, M. (ed.), *Ancient Egyptian Literature*, vol. 2 (Los Angeles: University of California Press, 1976).

Lithgow, W., *The Totall Discourse of the Rare Adventures and Painful Peregrinations of Long Nineteene Years Travayles* (Glasgow, 1906).

Livy, T., *History*, trans. B. O. Foster, vol. 1 (London: Loeb, 1988).

Lizárraga, R. de, *Descripción del Perú, Tucumán, Río de la Plata y Chile* (Madrid: Historia 16, 1986).

López de Gómara, *Historia de las Indias* (Madrid: Atlas, 1946) [BAE, 22].

Loskiel, G., *Geschichte der Mission der evangelischen Brüder unter den Indianern in Nordamerika* (Hildersheim: G. Olms, 1989).

Machiavelli, N., *Il Principe e Discorsi sopra la prima deca di Tito Livio*, ed. S. Bertelli (Milan: Feltrinelli, 1960).

Magalhaes, Pero de, *The Histories of Brazil* (New York, 1922).

Mansi, J.-D. (ed.), *Sacrorum Conciliorum . . . Collectio*, vol. 12 (Florence, 1766).

Maximilian Prinz zu Wied, *Reise in das innere Nord-America in den Jahren 1832 bis 1834*, vol. 2 (Coblenz, 1841).

Mendieta, G., *Historia eclesiastica indiana* (Mexico City: Porrua, 1971).

Modesti, J., 'Narrazione del Sacco dato alla terra di Prato dagli Spagnoli,' *Archivio Storico Italiano*, 1 (1842), 277–92.

Montesinos, F., *Memorias antiguas historiales y políticas del Perú* (Madrid, 1882).

Monumenta Germaniae Historica: Leges Visigothorum (Hannover, 1902).

——*Monumenta Germaniae Historia, Legum*, vol. 2, ed. G. Pertz (Hannover, 1837).

Motolinía, Toribio, called, *Memoriales e historia de los Indios de la Nueva España* (Madrid: Atlas, 1970) [BAE, 240].

Muñoz Camargo, D., *Historia de Tlaxcala* (Mexico City: Editorial Innovación, 1978).

Münzer, H., 'Itinerarium Hispanicum Hieronymi Monetarii, 1494–1495,' ed. L. Pfandl, *Revue Hispanique*, 48 (1920), 1–178.

Murúa, Martín de, *Historia de los Incas, Reyes del Perú* (Lima, 1922).

——, *Historia general del Perú* (Madrid: Historia 16, 1986).

Nueva colección de documentos para la historia de México, ed. J. García Icazbalceta, vol. 3 (Mexico City, 1891).

Núñez Cabeza de Vaca, A., *Naufragios* (Madrid: Atlas, 1946) [BAE, 22].

Núñez de Pineda y Bascuñán, F., *Cautiverio feliz y razón de las guerras dilatadas de Chile* (Santiago de Chile, 1863).

Oliveira Cardonega, Antonio de, *Historia general das guerras Angolanas* (Lisbon, 1942).

Ovid, *Ovid's Heroines*, trans. D. Hine (New Haven: Yale University Press, 1991).

Oviedo, *see* Fernández de Oviedo.

Palou, F., *Relación histórica de la vida y apostólicas tareas del venerable padre Fray Junípero Serra* (Mexico City: Porrua, 1982).

Pandolfi, V. and E. Artese (eds), *Teatro goliardico dell'Umanesimo* (Milan: Lerici editori, 1965).

Paulitschke, P., *Beiträge zur Ethnographie und Anthropologie der Somali, Galla, und Harari* (Leipzig, 1888).

Pérez de Ribas, A., *Páginas para la historia de Sinaloa y Sonora: triunfos de nuestra santa fe entre gentes las mas barbaras y fieras del Nuevo Orbe*, 3 vols (Mexico City, 1944).

Petronius, trans. M. Heseltine (London: Loeb, 1987).

Petrus Martyr d'Anghiera, *De orbe novo decades octo*, in his *Opera* (Graz: Akademischer Druck- und Verlagsanstalt, 1966).

Philippe de Vigneulles, *La Chronique de Philippe de Vigneulles*, ed. C. Bruneau, vol. 3 (Metz, 1932).

Pizarro, P., *Relación del descubrimiento y conquista de los reinos del Perú* (Lima: Pontificia Universidad Catolica del Perú, 1978).

Raccolta di documenti e studi pubblicati dalla r. commissione colombiana pel quarto centenario della scoperta dell'America, ed. C. de Lollis, pt 3, vol. 2 (Rome, 1893).

Ramusio, G. (ed.), *Navigazioni e viaggi*, 6 vols (Turin: Einaudi, 1978–85).

Rozmital, L. de, *Commentarius brevis et iucundus itineris atque peregrinationis, pietatis et religionis causa susceptae ab Illustri et Magnifico Domino, Domino Leone, libero barone de Rosmital et Blatna*, ed. K. Hrdina (Prague: Academia scientiarum et artium bohemica, 1951).

Ruíz de Arce, J., *Servicios en Indias* (Madrid, 1933).

Sahagún, B. de, *Florentine Codex: General History of the Things of New Spain*, 13 vols (Santa Fe, 1975–82).

——, *Historia general de las cosas de Nueva España*, 4 vols (Mexico City: Porrua, 1956).

Saikaku, I., *The Great Mirror of Male Love*, ed. P. Gordon Schalow (Stanford: Stanford University Press, 1990).

Santacruz Pachacuti Yamqui, J. de, *Relación de antigüedades deste reyno del Perú* (Madrid: Atlas, 1968) [BAE, 209].

Sarmiento de Gamboa, P., *Historia Indica* (Madrid: Atlas, 1960) [BAE, 135].

Say, T., in *From Pittsburgh to the Rocky Mountains: Major Stephen Long's Expedition, 1819–1820*, ed. Maxine Benson (Golden, CO: Fulcrum, 1988).

Sepúlveda, J. Ginés de, *Juan Ginés de Sepúlveda y su crónica indiana, en el IV centenario de su muerte, 1573–1973* (Valladolid: Seminario Americanista, 1976).

Simón, P., *Noticias historiales de las conquistas de tierra firme en las Indias Occidentales*, 2 vols (Bogotá, 1882).

Soares de Sousa, G., *Tratado descriptivo do Brasil em 1587*, in *Revista trimensal do Instituto historico e geographico do Brazil*, 2nd edn, vol. 14 (Rio de Janeiro, 1879).

Strabo, The Geography of, ed. H. Jones, vol. 5 (Cambridge, MA: Loeb, 1944).

Tanner, J., *A Narrative of the Captivity and Adventures of John Tanner* (Minneapolis: University of Minnesota Press, 1956).

Tezozomoc, H. Alvarado, *Crónica Mexicana* [and the] *Códice Ramirez* (Mexico City: Porrua, 1975).

Tixier, V., *Travels on the Osage Prairies* (Norman: University of Oklahoma Press, 1940).

Torquemada, J. de, *Monarquia Indiana*, 3 vols (Mexico City: Porrua, 1969).

Valera, B. (attrib.), *Relacíon de las costumbres antiguas* (Madrid: Atlas, 1968) [BAE, 209].

Varchi, B., *Storia fiorentina* (Florence: Salani, 1963).

Villani, Giovanni, Matteo e Filippo Villani, Chroniche di, 2 vols (Trieste, 1857).

Vitoria, Francisco, *Obras de, relaciones teológicas* (Madrid: Editorial Catolica, 1960).

Xímenez, F., *Las historias del origen de los Indios de esta provincia de Guatemala* (Vienna, 1857).

Zárate, A., *The Discovery and Conquest of Peru: a Translation of Books I to IV of Agustin de Zárate's 'History'* . . . (Baltimore: Penguin, 1968).

——, *Historia del descubrimiento y conquista de la provincia del Perú* . . . (Madrid: Atlas, 1853) [BAE, 26].

Zorita, A., *Life and Labor in Ancient Mexico: the Brief and Summary Relation of the Lords of New Spain* (New Brunswick: Rutgers University Press, 1963).

SECONDARY LITERATURE

Almaguer, T., 'Chicano Men: a Cartography of Homosexual Identity and Behavior,' *Differences*, 3 (1991), 75–100.

Anonymous, 'Les Incas condamnaient-ils l'homophilie?' *Arcadie*, 108 (Dec., 1962), 636–9.

Arboleda, M., 'Representaciones artísticas de actividades homoeroticos en la cerámica Moche,' *Boletín de Lima*, 16 (1981), 98–107.

Arjona Castro, A., 'Los eunucos y la cirugia de la castración en la España musulmana,' *Axerquia*, 3 (1981), 279–82.

Arnold, K., 'The Introduction of Poses to a Peruvian Brothel and Changing Images of Male and Female,' in *The Anthropology of the Body*, ed. J. Blacking (London, 1977), 179–97.

Bailey, D., *Homosexuality and the Western Christian Tradition* (London: Archon, 1955).

Bain, D., 'Aristophanes, *Ekklesiazousai*, 724,' *Liverpool Classical Monthly*, 7 (1982), 7–10.

Baker, M., *Nam* (New York: Morrow, 1981).

Bancroft, H., *The Native Races of the Pacific*, 5 vols (San Francisco, 1883–6) [vols 1–5 of his *Works*].

Barber, R., and Barker, J., *Tournaments: Joust, Chivalry and Pageants in the Middle Ages* (Woodbridge, Suffolk: Boydell, 1989).

Barton, C., 'All Things Beseem the Victor: Paradoxes of Masculinity in Early Imperial Rome,' in Trexler, *Gender Rhetorics*, 88–92.

Bastian, A., *Der Mensch in der Geschichte*, vol. 3 (Leipzig, 1860).

Baudot, G., *Utopie et histoire au Mexique: les premiers chroniqueurs de la civilisation mexicaine (1520–1569)* (Toulouse: Privat, 1977).

Bemont, C., *Simon de Montfort, Earl of Leichester (1208–1265)* (Oxford, 1930).

Bennassar, B. (ed.), *L'inquisition espagnole, XVe–XIXe siècle* (Paris: Marabout, 1979).

—, *The Spanish Character* (Berkeley: University of California Press, 1979).

Benson, E., *The Mochica: a Culture of Peru* (New York: Praeger, 1972).

Berlière, U., 'Le recrutement dans les monastères bénédictins aux XIIIe et XIVe siècles,' *Académie royale de Belgique, Mémoires de la Classe des lettres et des sciences morales et politiques*, 18 (1924), fasc. 6.

Bernis, C., 'Modas moriscas en la sociedad cristiana española del siglo XV y principios del XVI,' *Boletín de la Real Academia de la Historia*, 144 (1959), 199–228.

Berry, J., *Lead Us Not into Temptation: Catholic Priests and the Sexual Abuse of Children* (New York: Doubleday, 1992).

Bethe, E., 'Die Dorische Knabenliebe: ihre Ethik und ihre Idee,' *Rheinisches Museum für Philologie*, neue Folge 62 (1907), 438–75.

Biale, D., 'Ejaculatory Prayer: the Displacement of Sexuality in Chasidism,' *Tikkun* (July/August, 1991), 21–89.

——, *Eros and the Jews* (New York: Basic Books, 1992).

Binns, J., 'Women or Transvestites on the Elizabethan Stage?: an Oxford Controversy,' *Sixteenth-Century Journal*, 5 (1974), 95–120.

Black, L., 'Russia's American Adventure,' *Natural History* (Dec. 1989), 46–67.

Blackwood, E. (ed.), *The Many Faces of Homosexuality* (New York: Harrington Park Press, 1986).

——, 'Sexuality and Gender in Certain Native American Tribes: the Case of Cross-Gender Females,' *Signs*, 10 (1984), 27–42.

Bleibtreu-Ehrenberg, G., *Homosexualität: die Geschichte eines Vorurteils* (Frankfurt am Main: Fischer, 1981).

——, 'Pederasty among Primitives,' *Journal of Homosexuality*, 20 (1990), 13–30.

——, *Der Weibmann: kultischer Geschlechtswechsel im Schamanismus: eine Studie zur Transvestition und Transsexualität bei Naturvölkern* (Frankfurt am Main: Fischer, 1984).

Boon, J., *Other Tribes, Other Scribes* (Cambridge: Cambridge University Press, 1982).

Boswell, J., *Christianity, Social Tolerance, and Homosexuality: Gay People in Western Europe from the Beginning of the Christian Era to the Fourteenth Century* (Chicago: University of Chicago Press, 1980).

——, *The Kindness of Strangers* (New York: Pantheon Books, 1988).

Bradbury, G., 'Irregular Sexuality in the Spanish "Comedia",' *Modern Language Review*, 76 (1981), 566–80.

Bragaglia, A., *Degli 'Evirati Cantori'* (Florence: Sansoni, 1959).

Brandes, S., 'Like Wounded Stags: Male Sexual Ideology in an Andalusian Town,' in Ortner and Whitehead, *Sexual Meanings*, 216–39.

——, *Metaphors of Masculinity: Sex and Status in Andalusian Folklore* (Philadelphia: University of Pennsylvania Press, 1980).

Bray, A., *Homosexuality in Renaissance England* (London: Gay Men's Press, 1982).

Bremmer, J., 'An Enigmatic Indo-European Rite: Paederasty,' *Arethusa*, 13 (1980), 279–98.

Brewster Wray, M., *Kinship and Labor in the Structure of the Inca Empire* (diss.: SUNY, Binghamton, 1988).

Brody, J., 'Boyhood Effeminacy and Later Homosexuality,' *New York Times* (16 Dec. 1986).

Browe, P., *Zur Geschichte der Entmannung* (Breslau, 1936).

Brown, J., *Immodest Acts: the Life of a Lesbian Nun in Renaissance Italy* (New York: Oxford University Press, 1986).

Brundage, J., *Law, Sex, and Christian Society in Medieval Europe* (Chicago: University of Chicago Press, 1987).

——, 'Let Me Count the Ways: Canonists and Theologians Contemplate Coital Positions,' *Journal of Medieval History*, 10 (1984), 81–93.

Brüning, H., 'Beiträge zum Studium des Geschlechtlebens der Indianer im alten Perú,' *Anthropophyteia*, 7 (1911), 206–11; 8 (1911), 199–202.

Bucher, B., *La sauvage aux seins pendants* (Paris: Collection Savoir Hermann, 1977).

Bullough, V., 'Homosexuality as Submissive Behavior: Examples from Mythology,' *Journal of Sex Research*, 9 (1973), 283–8.

——, *Sexual Variance in Society and History* (Chicago: University of Chicago Press, 1976).

Bullough, V., and Bullough, B., *Cross Dressing, Sex, and Gender* (Philadelphia: University of Pennsylvania Press, 1993).

Burkert, W., *Homo Necans* (Berkeley: University of California Press, 1983).

Burns, J., 'A Serbian Fighter's Trail of Brutality', *The New York Times* (27 Nov. 1992).

Bynum, C. Walker, *Jesus as Mother* (Berkeley: University of California Press, 1982).

Callender, C., and Kochems, L., 'The North American Berdache,' *Current Anthropology*, 24 (1983), 443–70.

Cantarella, E., *Bisexuality in the Ancient World* (New Haven: Yale University Press, 1992).

Carrasco, R., *Inquisición y represión sexual en Valencia: historia de los sodomitas (1563–1785)* (Barcelona: Laertes, 1985).

Carrier, J., 'Cultural Factors Affecting Urban Mexican Male Homosexual Behavior,' *Archives of Sexual Behavior*, 5 (1976), 103–24.

Carroll, L., 'Machiavelli's Veronese Prostitute: *Venetia Figurata?*,' in Trexler, *Gender Rhetorics*, 93–106.

Carroll, M., 'The Erotics of Absolutism: Rubens and the Mystification of Sexual Violence,' *Representations*, no. 25 (1989), 3–30.

Cartledge, P., 'The Politics of Spartan Pederasty,' *Proceedings of the Cambridge Philological Society*, 207 (1981), 17–36.

Chebel, M., *L'esprit de sérail: perversions et marginalités sexuelles au Maghreb* (Paris: Lieu commun, 1988).

Chiffoleau, J., 'Dire l'indicible: remarques sur la catégorie du *nefandum* du XIIe au XVe siècle,' *Annales E.S.C.*, 45 (1990), 289–324.

Clavijero, F., *Historia antigua de México* (Mexico City: Porrua, 1987).

Clendinnen, I., *Ambivalent Conquest: Maya and Spaniard in Yucatan, 1517–1570* (Cambridge: Cambridge University Press, 1987).

Clover, C., 'Regardless of Sex: Men, Women, and Power in Early Northern Europe,' *Speculum*, 68 (1993), 363–87.

Cochrane, E., *Historians and Historiography in the Italian Renaissance* (Chicago: University of Chicago Press, 1980).

Cohen, D., 'A Note on Aristophanes and the Punishment of Adultery in Athenian Law,' *Zeitschrift der Savigny-Stiftung für Rechtsgeschichte, Romanistische Abteilung*, 102 (1985), 385–7.

Combs—Schilling, M., *Sacred Performances: Islam, Sexuality, and Sacrifice* (New York: Columbia University Press, 1989).

Constable, G., 'Aelred of Rievaulx and the Nun of Watton: an Episode in the Early History of the Gilbertine Order,' in *Medieval Women*, ed. D. Baker (Oxford: Blackwell, 1978).

Coon, C., *Tribes of the Rif* (Cambridge, MA: Harvard University Press, 1931).

Coser, L., 'The Political Functions of Eunuchism,' *American Sociological Review*, 29 (1964), 880–5.

Crapanzano, V., *Tuhami: Portrait of a Moroccan* (Chicago: University of Chicago Press, 1980).

Creed, G., 'Sexual Subordination: Institutionalized Homosexuality and Social Control in Melanesia,' *Ethnology*, 23 (1984), 157–76.

Daniel, N., *The Arabs and Medieval Europe* (London: Longman, 1979).

——, *Islam & the West* (Edinburgh: Edinburgh University Press, 1962).

De la Rosa y López, S., *Los seises de la catedral de Sevilla* (Seville, 1904).

De Oliveira Marques, A., *Daily Life in Portugal in the Late Middle Ages* (Madison: University of Wisconsin Press, 1971).

De Waal, F., 'The Relation between Power and Sex in the Simians: Socio-Sexual Appeasement Gestures,' in Trexler, *Gender Rhetorics*, 15–32.

Deleito y Piñuela, J., *La Mala Vida en la España de Felipe IV* (Madrid: Alianza Editorial, 1987).

Devereux, G., 'Greek Pseudo-Homosexuality and the "Greek Miracle",' *Symbolae Osloenses*, 42 (1968), 69–92.

——, 'Institutionalized Homosexuality of the Mohave Indians,' *Human Biology*, 9 (1937), 498–527.

Dillard, H., *Daughters of the Reconquest: Women in Castilian Town Society, 1100–1300* (Cambridge, Cambridge University Press, 1984).

Dines, W., and Johansson, W., 'London's Medieval Sodomites,' *The Cabirion and Gay Books Bulletin*, 10, nos 6 and 7 (1984), 5ff.

Dingwall, E., *Male Infibulation* (London, 1925).

Donnan, C., *Moche Art and Iconography* (Los Angeles: Museum of Cultural History, UCLA, 1976).

Dorsey, J., *Omaha Sociology* (Washington, DC: Report 3, Bureau of Ethnography, 1881–2).

Dover, K., *Greek Homosexuality* (Cambridge, MA: Harvard University Press, 1978).

——, 'Greek Homosexuality and Initiation,' in Dover, *The Greeks and their Legacy* (Oxford: Blackwell, 1988), 115–34.

Duerr, H. P., *Nacktheit und Scham* (*Der Mythos vom Zivilizationsprozess*, vol. 1) (Frankfurt am Main: Suhrkamp, 1988).

——, *Obszönität und Gewalt* (*Der Mythos vom Zivilizationsprozess*, vol. 3) (Frankfurt am Main: Suhrkamp, 1993).

Dupé, M.-O. (ed.), *Bizutages* (Paris: Panorama, 1992).

Duviols, P., *La lutte contre les religions autochtones dans le Perou colonial: 'l'extirpation de l'idolâtrie' entre 1532 et 1660* (Lima: Institut français d'études andines, 1971).

Edwardes, A., *Erotica Judaica: a Sexual History of the Jews* (New York: Julian Press, 1967).

——, *The Jewel in the Lotus: a Historical Survey of the Sexual Culture of the East* (New York: Julian Press, 1959).

Edwardes, A., and Masters, R., *The Cradle of Erotica: a Study of Afro-Asian*

Sexual Expression and an Analysis of Erotic Freedom in Social Relationships (New York: Bell, 1962).

Eibl-Eibesfeldt, I., *Love and Hate* (New York: Methuen, 1971).

Eliade, M., *Shamanism* (Princeton: Princeton University Press, 1972).

Engh, M. J., *Arslan* (New York: Tom Doherty Associates, 1976).

Evans-Pritchard, E., 'Sexual inversion among the Azande,' *American Anthropologist*, 72 (1970), 1428–34.

Farb, P., *Word Play* (New York: Knopf, 1973).

Fehling, D., *Ethologische Überlegungen auf dem Gebiet der Altertumskunde: phallische Demonstration-Fernsicht-Steinigung* (Munich: Beck, 1974).

Finkelhor, D., *Child Sexual Abuse: New Theory and Research* (New York: Free Press, 1984).

Flandrin, J.-L., *Le sexe et l'Occident* (Paris: Seuil, 1981).

Font, P., *Font's Complete Diary of the Second Anza Expedition* (vol. 4 of *Anza's California Expedition*), ed. H. Bolton (Berkeley, 1930).

Ford, C., and Beach, F., *Patterns of Sexual Behavior* (New York: Harper, 1951).

Forsyth, I., 'The Ganymede Capital at Vézelay,' *Gesta: International Center of Medieval Art*, 15 (1976), 241–6.

Foucault, M., *The History of Sexuality*, 3 vols (New York: Vintage, 1980–8).

Freyre, G., *The Masters and the Slaves* (New York: Knopf, 1971).

Friederici, G., *Skalpieren und ähliche Kriegsgebräuche in Amerika* (Braunschweig, 1906).

——, 'Über die Behandlung der Kriegsgefangenen durch die Indianer Amerikas,' in *Festschrift Eduard Seler*, ed. W. Lehmann (Stuttgart, 1922), 59–128.

Fry, P., 'Male Homosexuality and Spirit Possession in Brazil,' in Blackwood, *Many Faces*, 137–54.

Gade, K., 'Homosexuality and Rape of Males in Old Norse Law and Literature,' *Scandinavian Studies*, 58 (1986), 124–41.

Garber, M, *Vested Interests: Cross-Dressing & Cultural Anxiety* (New York: Harper, 1992).

García Icazbalceta, J. (ed.), *Bibliografía Mexicana del siglo XVI* (Mexico City, 1886).

Gareis, I., *Religiöse Spezialisten des zentralen Andengebietes zur Zeit der Inka und während der spanischen Kolonialherrschaft* (Hohenschäftlarn: K. Renner, 1987).

Gerard, K., and Hekma, G. (eds), *The Pursuit of Sodomy: Male Homosexuality in Renaissance and Enlightenment* (New York: Harrington Park, 1989).

Gerassi, J., *The Boys of Boise: Furor, Vice and Folly in an American City* (New York: Macmillan, 1966).

Gilmore, D., *Aggression and Community: Paradoxes of Andalusian Culture* (New Haven: Yale University Press, 1987).

——, *Manhood in the Making: Cultural Concepts of Masculinity* (New Haven: Yale University Press, 1990).

Girard, R., *Violence and the Sacred* (Baltimore: Johns Hopkins University Press, 1972).

Godelier, M., *La production des grands hommes* (Paris: Fayard, 1982).

Goffman, E., *Asylums* (New York: Anchor Books, 1961).

Goitein, S., 'The Sexual Mores of the Common People,' in *Society and the Sexes in Medieval Islam*, ed. A. Lutfi al-Sayyid-Marsot (Malibu: Undina Publications, 1979), 43–61.

Gómez de Orozco, F. (ed.), 'Costumbres, fiestas, enterramientos y diversas formas de proceder de los Indios de Nueva España,' *Tlalocán*, 2 (1945), 37–63.

Goodich, M., *The Unmentionable Vice: Homosexuality in the Later Medieval Period* (Santa Barbara: ABC-Clio, 1979).

Goodland, R., *A Bibliography of Sex Rites and Customs* (London, 1931).

Graulich, M., 'Ochpaniztli, la fête des semailles des anciens mexicains,' *Anales de antropología*, 18 (1981), 59–100.

Graziano, F., *Divine Violence: Spectacle, Psychosexuality, & Radical Christianity in the Argentine 'Dirty War'* (Boulder, CO: Westview Press, 1992).

Green, R., *The 'Sissy Boy Syndrome' and the Development of Homosexuality* (New Haven: Yale University Press, 1987).

Greenberg, D., *The Construction of Homosexuality* (Chicago: University of Chicago Press, 1988).

Gregory, T., *Anxious Pleasures: the Sexual Lives of an Amazonian People* (Chicago: University of Chicago Press, 1985).

Gruzinski, S., 'Las cenizas del deseo: homosexuales novohispanos a mediados del siglo XVII,' in *De la santidad a la perversión, O de porqué no se cumplía la ley de Dios en la sociedad novohispana*, ed. S. Ortega (Mexico City: Enlace/historia, 1985), 255–81.

——, 'Seis ensayos sobre el discurso colonial relativo a la comunidad domestica,' *Cuadernos de trabajo del departamento de investigaciones históricas, INAH*, 35 (Oct., 1980), 19–74.

Gutiérrez, R., 'A Gendered History of the Conquest of America: the View from New Mexico,' in Trexler, *Gender Rhetorics*, 47–64.

Gwyn Griffiths, J., *The Conflict of Horus and Seth* (Liverpool: Liverpool University Press, 1960).

Haberling, W., *Das Dirnenwesen in den Heeren und seine Bekämpfung: eine geschichtliche Studie* (Leipzig, 1914).

Hale, J., *War and Society in Renaissance Europe* (Baltimore: Johns Hopkins University Press, 1986).

Halperin, D., *One Hundred Years of Homosexuality and Other Essays on Greek Love* (New York: Routledge, 1990).

Hammond, W., 'The Disease of the Scythians (Morbus Feminarum) and Certain Analogous Conditions,' *American Journal of Neurology and Psychiatry*, 1 (1882), 339–55.

——, *Sexual Impotence in the Male and Female* (Detroit, 1887).

Hanke, L., *All Mankind is One: a Study of the Disputation between Bartolomé de Las Casas and Juan Ginés de Sepúlveda in 1550 on the Intellectual and Religious Capacity of the American Indians* (DeKalb: Northern Illinois University Press, 1974).

Hay, H., 'The Hammond Report: a Deposition, with Subsequent Commentary, on the Conspiracy of Silence anent Social Homophilia,' *One Institute Quarterly*, 6 (1963), 6–21.

Helms, M., *Ancient Panama* (Austin: University of Texas Press, 1979).

Hemming, J., *The Conquest of the Incas* (San Diego: Harcourt, Brace, Jovanovich, 1970).

Herdt, G., *Guardians of the Flutes: Idioms of Masculinity* (New York: McGraw-Hill, 1981).

Heriot, A., *The Castrati in Opera* (London: Da Capo, 1956).

Herman, J., with Hirschman, L., *Father–Daughter Incest* (Cambridge, MA: Harvard University Press, 1981).

Hess, A., *The Forgotten Frontier: a History of the Sixteenth-Century Ibero-African Frontier* (Chicago: University of Chicago Press, 1978).

Hinsch, B., *Passions of the Cut Sleeve* (Berkeley: University of California Press, 1990).

Hirschfeld, M., *Sexual Pathology* (Newark, 1932).

Hitzig, H., 'Castratio als Verbrechen,' in *Paulys Realencyclopädie der classischen Altertumswissenschaften, neue Bearbeitung*, vol. 3, pt 2 (Stuttgart, 1899), 1772–3.

Holder, A. B., 'The Bote: Description of a Peculiar Sexual Perversion Found Among North American Indians,' *New York Medical Journal*, 50, no. 575 (7 Dec. 1889), 623–5.

Hosken, F., *The Hosken Report: Genital and Sexual Mutilation of Females* (Lexington, MA: Women's International Network News, 1982).

Imbelloni, J., 'La "Essaltatione delle Rose" del Codice Vatican Mexicano 3738, el "Nictekatun" de las Fuentes Maya y el "Pecado Nefando" de la Tradición Peruana mas Remota,' *Anales de arqueología y etnología*, 4 (1943), 161–205.

Isaac, B., 'Aztec Warfare: Goals and Battlefield Comportment,' *Ethnology*, 22 (1983), 121–31.

Isbell, B. J., *To Defend Ourselves: Ecology and Ritual in an Andean Village* (Austin: University of Texas Press, 1978).

Johansson, W., 'Ex Parte Themis: the Historical Guilt of the Christian Church,' in *Homosexuality, Intolerance, and Christianity: a Critical Examination of John Boswell's Work* (New York: Gay Academic Union, 1981), 1–4.

Kadish, G., 'Eunuchs in Ancient Egypt?,' in *Studies in Honor of John A. Wilson* (Chicago: University of Chicago Press, 1969), 55–62.

Karlen, A., *Sexuality and Homosexuality: a New View* (New York: Norton, 1971).

Karsch-Haack, F., *Das gleichgeschlechtliche Leben der Naturvölker* (New York: Arno Press, 1975).

——, 'Uranismus oder Päderastie und Tribadie bei den Naturvölkern,' *Jahrbuch für sexuelle Zwischenstufen*, 3 (1901), 72–201.

Kauffmann Doig, F., *Comportamiento sexual en el antiguo Perú* (Lima: Kompaktos, n.d.).

Keen, B., *The Aztec Image* (New Brunswick: Rutgers University Press, 1971).

Kehoe, A., 'The Function of Ceremonial Sexual Intercourse Among the Northern Plains Indians,' *Plains Anthropologist*, 15 (1970), 99–103.

Kennan, G. (intro.), *The Other Balkan Wars, a 1913 Carnegie Endowment Inquiry in Retrospect* (Washington, DC: Carnegie Endowment, 1993).

Keuls, E., *The Reign of the Phallus: Sexual Politics in Ancient Athens* (Berkeley: University of California Press, 1985).

Kilmer, M., 'Genital Phobia and Depilation,' *Journal of Hellenic Studies*, 102 (1982), 104–22.

Klein, C., 'Fighting with Femininity: Gender and War in Aztec Mexico,' in Trexler, *Gender Rhetorics*, 107–46.

——, 'Rethinking Cihuacoatl: Aztec Political Imagery of the Conquered Woman,' in *Smoke and Mist: Mesoamerican Studies in Memory of Thelma D. Sullivan*, ed. J. K. Josserand and K. Dakin, vol. 1 (Oxford: B.A.R., 1988), 237–77.

——, 'Snares and Entrails: Mesoamerican Symbols of Sin and Punishment,' *Res*, 19/20 (1990–1), 81–104.

Koch-Harnack, G.,*Knabenliebe und Tiergeschenke: ihre Bedeutung im päderastischen Erziehungssystem Athens* (Berlin: Gebrüder Mann, 1983).

Krekic, B., '*Abominandum crimen*: Punishment of Homosexuals in Renaissance Dubrovnik,' *Viator*, 18 (1987), 337–45.

La Barre, W., 'The Aymara Indians of the Lake Titicaca Plateau, Bolivia,' *American Anthropologist*, 50 (1948), Memoir 68.

Lang, S., *Männer als Frauen–Frauen als Männer: Geschlechtsrollenwechsel bei den Indianern Nordamerikas* (Hamburg: Wayasbah, 1990).

Larco Hoyle, R., *Checan: Essay on Erotic Elements in Peruvian Art* (Geneva: Nagel, 1965).

Luritsen, J., '"Culpa Ecclesiae": Boswell's Dilemma,' in *Homosexuality, Intolerance, and Christianity: a Critical Examination of John Boswell's Work* (New York, 1981), 18–22.

Le Goff, J., and Schmitt, J.-C (eds)., *Le Charivari* (Paris: Mouton, 1981).

Leonard, I., *Baroque Times in Old Mexico* (Ann Arbor: University of Michigan Press, 1981).

Lerner, G., *The Creation of Patriarchy* (New York: Oxford University Press, 1986).

Lévi-Strauss, C., *The Raw & the Cooked* (New York: Harper, 1975).

Lewis, B., *The Political Language of Islam* (Chicago: University of Chicago Press, 1988).

Linehan, P., *History and the Historians of Medieval Spain* (Oxford: Oxford University Press, 1993).

Lynch, J., *Simoniacal Entry into Religious Life from 1000 to 1260* (Columbus: Ohio State University Press, 1976).

Mantegazza, P., *The Sexual Relations of Mankind* (New York, 1935).

Marchello-Nizia, C., 'Amour courtois, société masculine et figures du pouvoir,' *Annales E.S.C.*, 36 (1981), 969–82.

Marcos J., and Manrique, M. de, 'De la dualidad fertilidad-virilidad a lo explícitamente femenino o masculino: la relación de las figurinas con los cambios en la organización social Valdivia,' in *The Role of Gender in Precolumbian Art and Architecture*, ed. V. Miller (Lanham, MD: University Press of America, 1988), 35–51.

Marcos, S., 'Indigenous Eroticism and Colonial Morality in Mexico: the Confession Manuals of New Spain,' *Numen*, 39 (1992), 157–74.

Mason, P., *The Deconstruction of America* (London: Routledge, 1993).

Masson, J. Moussaieff, *The Assault on Truth: Freud's Suppression of the Seduction Theory* (New York: Farrar, Straus & Giroux, 1984).

McKendrick, M., *Women and Society in the Spanish Drama of the Golden Age: a Study of the Mujer Varonil* (Cambridge: Cambridge University Press, 1974).

Mernissi, F., *Le harem politique: le prophète et les femmes* (Paris: Albin Michel, 1987).

Métraux, A., 'Le shamanisme Araucan,' *Revista del Instituto de Antropología, Universidad Nacional de Tucuman*, 2 (1942), 309–61.

——, 'Warfare, Cannibalism, and Human Trophies,' *Handbook of South American Indians*, vol. 5 (New York, 1963), 383–409.

Meulengracht Sørensen, P., *The Unmanly Man: Concepts of Sexual Defamation in Early Northern Society* (Odense: University Press, 1983).

Mez, A., *The Renaissance of Islam* (Patna, 1937).

Miller, J., 'The Delaware as Women: a Symbolic Solution,' *American Ethnologist*, 1 (1974), 507–24.

Miller, T., *Henry IV of Castile, 1425–1474* (Philadelphia: University of Pennsylvania Press, 1972).

Monter, E. W., *Frontiers of Heresy: the Spanish Inquisition from the Basque Lands to Sicily* (Cambridge: Cambridge University Press, 1990).

Morgan, L., *League of the Iroquois* (Secaucus: Citadel, 1962).

Morison, S. (ed.), *Journals and Other Documents on the Life and Voyages of Christopher Columbus* (New York: Heritage, 1963).

Morris, D., *Body Watching* (New York: Grafton, 1985).

Mott, L., 'Escravidão e homossexualidade,' in *História e sexualidade no Brasil*, ed. R. Vainfas (Rio de Janeiro: Ediçoes Graal, 1986), 19–40.

——, 'Pagode português: a subcultura *gay* em Portugal nos tempos inquisitoriais,' *Ciencia e cultura*, 40 (1988), 120–39.

Muir, E., *Mad Blood Stirring: Vendetta and Factions in Friuli During the Renaissance* (Baltimore: Johns Hopkins University Press, 1993).

Murray, S. (ed.), *Male Homosexuality in Central & South America* (New York: Gai Saber Monograph 5, 1987).

——, *Social Theory, Homosexual Realities* (New York: Gay Academic Union, 1984).

Mydans, S., 'Philippine Town's Parents Battle Effort to Stop Their Children's Sex Trade,' *New York Times* (2 Feb. 1989).

Newton, E., 'Role Models,' in *Symbolic Anthropology*, ed J. Dolgin et al. (New York: Columbia University Press, 1977).

Nichols Barker, N., *Brother to the Sun King: Philippe, Duke of Orléans* (Baltimore: Johns Hopkins University Press, 1989).

Noonan, J., *Contraception* (Cambridge, MA: Harvard University Press, 1966).

O'Connor, T., 'Sexual Aberration and Comedy in Monroy y Silva's *El Caballero Dama*,' *Hispanófila*, 80 (1984), 17–39.

Offner, J., *Law and Politics in Aztec Texcoco* (Cambridge: Cambridge University Press, 1983).

Olivier, G., 'Conquérants et missionaires face au 'péché abominable': essai sur l'homosexualité en Mésoamérique au moment de la conquête espagnole,' *CMHLB Caravelle* 55 (1990), 20–40.

Ortner, S., and Whitehead, H. (eds), *Sexual Meanings* (Cambridge: Cambridge University Press, 1981).

Panagopoulos, A., *Captives and Hostages in the Peloponnesian War* (Athens: Hakkert, 1978).

Park, W., *Shamanism in Western North America* (Evanston: Northwestern University Press, 1938).

Parker, G., *The Army of Flanders and the Spanish Road, 1567–1659* (Cambridge: Cambridge University Press, 1972).

Parsons, E. Clews, 'The Zuñi La'mana,' *American Anthropologist*, 18 (1916), 521–8.

Paz, O., *Labyrinth of Solitude* (New York: Grove, 1961).

Pellizer, E., and Zorzetti, N. (eds), *La paura dei padri nella società antica e medievale* (Rome: Laterza, 1983).

Penzer, N., *The Harem* (London: Spring Books, 1965).

Perella, N., *The Kiss Sacred and Profane* (Berkeley: University of California Press, 1969).

Perry, M., *Crime and Society in Early Modern Seville* (Hanover, NH: Dartmouth College Press, 1980).

——, *Gender and Disorder in Early Modern Seville* (Princeton: Princeton University Press, 1990).

——, 'The "Nefarious Sin" in Early Modern Seville,' in Gerard and Hekma, *Pursuit of Sodomy*, 67–89.

Peschel, E., and Peschel, R., 'Medical Insights into the Castrati in Opera,' *American Scientist*, 75 (1987), 578–83.

Phelan, J., *The Millennial Kingdom of the Franciscans in the New World (1525–1604)* (Berkeley: University of California Press, 1956).

Phillips, W., Jr., *Enrique IV and the Crisis of Fifteenth-Century Castile* (Cambridge, MA: Harvard University Press, 1978).

Powers, J., 'Townsmen and Soldiers: the Interaction of Urban and Military Organizations in the Militias,' *Speculum*, 46 (1971), 655–71.

Praetorius, N. [pseudonym], 'Ueber gleichgeschlechtlichen Verkehr in Algerien und Tunis,' *Anthropophyteia*, 7 (1910), 184–6.

Quinn, P., *Better than the Sons of Kings* (New York: Lang, 1989).

Quirós, C. B. de, *Nuevas noticias de picotas Americanas* (Havana: J. Montero, 1952).

——, *La picota: crimenes y castigos en el pais castellano en los tiempos medios* (Madrid, 1907).

——, *La picota en América* (Havana: J. Montero, 1948).

Rabinowitz, D., 'Arms and the Man: a Sex Scandal Rocks Princeton,' *New York* (17 July 1989), 31–6.

Ragon, P., *Les amours indiennes, ou l'imaginaire du Conquistador* (Paris: Armand Colin, 1992).

Rattray Taylor, G., 'Historical and Methodological Aspects of Homosexuality,' in *Sexual Inversion: the Multiple Roots of Homosexuality*, ed. J. Marmor (New York: Basic Books, 1965).

Reeves Sanday, P., *Fraternity Gang Rape: Sex, Brotherhood, and Privilege on Campus* (New York: New York University Press, 1990).

A. Requeña, 'Noticias y consideraciones sobre las anormalidades de los Aborígenes Americanos: sodomía,' *Acta Venezolana*, 1 (1945), 44–73.

Rich, A., *Of Woman Born* (New York: Norton, 1976).

Richlin, A., *The Garden of Priapus: Sexuality and Aggression in Roman Humor* (New Haven: Yale University Press, 1983).

——, 'Not Before Homosexuality: the Materiality of the *Cinaedus* and the Roman Law against Love between Men,' *Journal of the History of Sexuality*, 3 (1993), 523–73.

Rocke, M., *Male Homosexuality and its Regulation in Late Medieval Florence* (diss.: SUNY, Binghamton, 1989).

——, 'Sodomites in Fifteenth-Century Tuscany: the Views of Bernardino of Siena,' in Gerard and Hekma, *Pursuit of Sodomy*, 7–31.

Rogers, F., *The Quest for Eastern Christians* (Minneapolis: University of Minnesota Press, 1962).

——, *The Travels of the Infante Dom Pedro of Portugal* (Cambridge, MA: Harvard University Press, 1961).

Rollison, D., 'Property, Ideology and Popular Culture in a Gloucestershire Village, 1660–1740,' *Past and Present*, no. 93 (1981), 70–97.

Rondeau, J., 'Prayer and Gender in the *Laude* of Early Italian Confraternities,' in Trexler, *Gender Rhetorics*, 219–34.

Roscoe, W., 'Bibliography of Berdache and Alternative Gender Roles Among North American Indians,' *Journal of Homosexuality*, 14 (1987), 154–70.

——, *The Zuni Man-Woman* (Albuquerque: University of New Mexico Press, 1991).

Rosselli, J., 'The Castrati as a Professional Group and a Social Phenomenon, 1550–1850,' *Acta Musicologica*, 60 (1988), 143–79.

Rossello Vaquer, R., *L'Homosexualitat a Mallorca a l'Edat Mitjana* (Barcelona: J. J. de Olañeta, 1978).

Roth, N., ' "Deal Gently with the Young Man": Love of Boys in Medieval Hebrew Poetry in Spain,' *Speculum*, 57 (1982), 20–51.

Rowson, E., 'The Categorization of Gender and Sexual Irregularity in Medieval Arabic Vice Lists,' in *Body Guards: The Cultural Politics of Gender Ambiguity*, ed. J. Epstein and K. Straub (New York: Routledge, 1991), 69–72.

——, 'The Effeminates of Early Medina,' *Journal of the American Oriental Society*, 111 (1991), 671–93.

Ruggiero, G., *The Boundaries of Eros: Sex Crime and Sexuality in Renaissance Venice* (New York: Oxford University Press, 1985).

Runciman, S., *The Fall of Constantinople 1453* (Cambridge: Cambridge University Press, 1965).

Russell, D., 'The Incidence and Prevalence of Intrafamilial and Extrafamilial Sexual Abuse of Female Children,' *Child Abuse & Neglect*, 7 (1983), 133–46.

Sandoval, A. de, *Un tratado sobre la esclavitud* (Madrid: Alianza Editorial, 1987).

Saxonhouse, A., *Women in the History of Political Thought: Ancient Greece to Machiavelli* (New York: Praeger, 1985).

Scacco, A. (ed.), *Male Rape: a Casebook of Sexual Aggression* (New York: AMS Press, 1982).

Schele, L., and Miller, M., *The Blood of Kings: Dynasty and Ritual in Maya Art* (New York: Braziller, 1986).

Schirmann, J., 'The Ephebe in Medieval Hebrew Poetry,' *Sefarad*, 15 (1955), 55–68.

Scholes, F., and Roys, R., *The Maya Contal Indians of Acalan-Tixchel* (Norman: University of Oklahoma Press, 1968).

Schreiner, K., ' "Er küsse mich mit dem Kuß seines Mundes," ' in *Höfische Repräsentation: das Zeremoniell und die Zeichen*, ed. H. Ragotzky and H. Wenzel (Tübingen: Niemeyer, 1990), 89–132.

Schultz, D., *Month of the Freezing Moon: the Sand Creek Massacre, November 1864* (New York: St Martin's Press, 1990).

Sergent, B., *L'homosexualité initiatique dans l'Europe ancienne* (Paris: Payot, 1986).

Shepherd, G., 'Rank, Gender, and Homosexuality: Mombasa as a Key to Understanding Sexual Options,' in *The Cultural Construction of Sexuality*, ed. P. Caplan (London: Tavistock, 1987), 240–70.

Sherman, W., *Forced Native Labor in Sixteenth-Century Central America* (Lincoln: University of Nebraska Press, 1979).

Sherzer, D., and Sherzer, J., 'Mormaknamaloe: the Cuna,' in *Ritual and Symbol in Central America*, ed. P. Young and J. Howe (Eugene: University of Oregon Anthropological Papers no. 9, 1976).

Silverblatt, I., *Moon, Sun, and Devil: Inca and Colonial Transformations of Andean Gender Relations* (Princeton: Princeton University Press, 1987).

Simons, P., 'Alert and Erect: Masculinity in some Italian Renaissance Portraits of Fathers and Sons,' in Trexler, *Gender Rhetorics*, 163–86.

Smet, P. de, *Ritual Enemas and Snuffs in the Americas* (Amsterdam: CEDLA, 1985).

Soustelle, J., *Daily Life of the Aztecs* (Stanford: Stanford University Press, 1961).

——, *L'Univers des Aztècques* (Paris: Hermann, 1979).

Speck, F., 'The Delaware Indians as Women: Were the Original Pennsylvanians Politically Emasculated?' *Pennsylvania Magazine of History and Biography*, 70 (1946), 377–89.

Spence, J., *The Memory Palace of Matteo Ricci* (New York: Viking, 1985).

Stoller, R., *Presentations of Gender* (New Haven: Yale University Press, 1985).

Stone, A., 'Aspects of Impersonation in Classic Maya Art,' *Sixth Palenque Round Table, 1986* (Norman: University of Oklahoma Press, 1991), 194–202.

Striedter, J., 'Erzählformen als Antwort auf den Schrecken in der Geschichte, oder: Wie Drakula überlebte,' in *Geschichte als Literatur: Formen und Grenzen der Repräsentation von Vergangenheit*, ed. H. Eggert et al. (Stuttgart: J. B. Metzler, 1990), 104–27.

Taylor, C., 'Homosexuality in Precolumbian and Colonial Mexico,' in *Male*

Homosexuality in Central and South America, ed. S. Murray (New York: Gai Saber, 1987), 4–21.

Taylor, W., *Drinking, Homicide, and Rebellion in Colonial Mexican Villages* (Stanford: Stanford University Press, 1979).

Tentler, T., *Sin and Confession on the Eve of the Reformation* (Princeton: Princeton University Press, 1977).

Theweleit, K., *Männerfantasien* (Reinbek: Stroemfeld/Roter Stern, 1986).

Thompson, E. P., '"Rough Music": le charivari anglais,' *Annales ESC*, 27 (1972), 285–312.

Tiger, L. *Men in Groups* (New York: Random House, 1969).

Torres Fontes, J., *Estudio sobre la 'Crónica de Enrique IV' del Dr Galíndez de Carvajal* (Murcia: Sucesor de Nogres, 1946).

Tov Assis, Y., 'Sexual Behaviour in Mediaeval Hispano-Jewish Society,' in *Jewish History: Essays in Honour of Chimen Abramsky*, ed. A. Rapoport, A. and S. J. Zipperstein (London: P. Halban, 1988), 25–59.

Trevisan, J., *Perverts in Paradise* (London: GMP, 1986).

Trevor-Roper, H., *The Crisis of the Seventeenth Century* (New York: Harper & Row, 1956).

Trexler, R., *Church and Community, 1200–1600: Studies in the History of Florence and New Spain* (Rome: Storia e Letteratura, 1987).

——, 'Correre la Terra: Collective Insults in the Late Middle Ages', in Trexler, *Dependence in Context*, 113–70.

——, *Dependence in Context in Renaissance Florence* (Binghamton: MRTS, 1994).

——, 'Follow the Flag: the Ciompi Revolt Seen from the Streets,' *Bibliothèque d'humanisme et Renaissance*, 46 (1984), 357–92.

——, 'From the Mouths of Babes: Christianization by Children in Sixteenth-Century New Spain,' in Trexler, *Church and Community*, 549–73.

—— (ed.), *Gender Rhetorics: Postures of Dominance and Submission in History* (Binghamton: MRTS, 1994).

——, 'Celibacy in the Renaissance: the Nuns of Florence,' in Trexler, *Dependence in Context*, 343–72.

——, 'Florentine Prostitution in the Fifteenth Century: Patrons and Clients,' in Trexler, *Dependence in Context*, 373–414.

——, *Public Life in Renaissance Florence* (New York: Academic Press, 1980; Ithaca: Cornell University Press, 1991).

——, 'Den Rücken beugen: Gebetsgebärden und Geschlechtsgebärden in frühmodernen Europa und Amerika,' in *Verletzte Ehre: Formen, Funktionen und Bedeutungen in Gesellschaften des Mittelalters und der frühen Neuzeit*, ed. K. Schreiner and G. Schwerhoff (Cologne, 1995).

——, 'Ritual in Florence: Adolescence and Salvation in the Renaissance,' in Trexler, *Dependence in Context*, 259–325.

——, 'Das sprechende Bildnis: Versuch einer Typologie im Spiegel spanischer Quellen des 16. Jahrhunderts,' in *Laienfrömmigkeit im späten Mittelalter*, ed. K. Schreiner (Munich: Oldenbourg, 1992), 283–308.

——, 'We Think, They Act: Clerical Readings of Missionary Theatre in Sixteenth-Century Mexico,' in Trexler, *Church and Community*, 575–614.

Trumbull, R., 'Gender and the Homosexual Role in Modern Western Culture: the 18th and 19th Centuries Compared,' in *Homosexuality, Which Homosexuality?*, ed. D. Altman et al. (Amsterdam: An Dekker Schorer, 1989), 149–69.

Van der Kroef, J., 'Transvestism and the Religious Hermaphrodite in Indonesia,' *Journal of East Asiatic Studies*, 3 (1959), 257–65.

Van Dülmen, R., *Theater des Schreckens* (Munich: Beck, 1985).

Vanggaard, T., *Phallós* (New York: International Universities Press, 1972).

Veyne, P. (ed.), *A History of Private Life*, vol. 1 (Cambridge, MA: Harvard University Press, 1987).

——, 'L'homosexualité à Rome,' *Communications*, 35 (1982), 26–33.

Viñas y Mey, C., *El problema de la tierra en la España de los siglos XVI–XVII* (Madrid: Instituto Jeronimo Zurita, 1941).

Wagner, K., 'La Inquisición en Sevilla (1481–1524),' in *Homenaje al profesor Carriazo*, vol. 3 (Seville: Publicaciones de la Universidad, 1973), 439–60.

Wallace, A., *Teedyuscung: King of the Delawares, 1700–1763* (Syracuse: Syracuse University Press, 1949).

Wallace, P., *Indians in Pennsylvania* (Harrisburg: Pennsylvania Historical and Museum Commission, 1961).

Watt, W. Montgomery, *A History of Islamic Spain* (Edinburgh: Edinburgh University Press, 1965).

Wentersdorf, K., 'The Symbolic Significance of *Figurae Scatologicae* in Gothic Manuscripts,' in *Word, Picture, and Spectacle*, ed. C. Davidson (Kalamazoo: Medieval Institute, 1984), 1–20.

Weslager, C., *The Delaware Indians: a History* (New Brunswick, NJ: Rutgers University Press, 1972).

——, 'The Delaware Indians as Women,' *Journal of the Washington Academy of Sciences*, 34 (1944), 381–8.

——, 'Further Light on the Delaware Indians as Women,' *Journal of the Washington Academy of Sciences*, 37 (1947), 298–304.

Westermarck, E., *The Origin and Development of Moral Ideas*, 2 vols (London, 1917).

——, *Ritual and Belief in Morocco*, 2 vols (London, 1926).

Whitehead, H., 'The Bow and the Burden Strap: a New Look at Institutionalized Homosexuality in Native North America,' in Ortner and Whitehead, *Sexual Meanings*, 80–115.

Wickler, W., *The Sexual Code* (Garden City, NY: Doubleday, 1973).

Widstrand, C., 'Female Infibulation,' *Studia ethnographica Upsaliensia*, 20 (1964), 95–122.

Wikan, U., *Behind the Veil in Arabia: Women in Oman* (Baltimore: Johns Hopkins University Press, 1982).

Williams, W., *The Spirit and the Flesh: Sexual Diversity in American Indian Culture* (Boston: Beacon Press, 1986; repr. with new introduction, 1992).

Winkler, J., *Constraints of Desire: the Anthropology of Sex and Gender in Ancient Greece* (New York: Routledge, 1989).

Wylie, P., *Generation of Vipers* (New York, 1942).

Zuidema, R. T., *Inca Civilization in Cuzco* (Austin: University of Texas Press, 1990).

Index

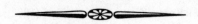

Abd al-Rahman, 43
abduction, 27–9
Abu-Muslim, 52
abuse, child, 49, 58–9, 92, 178–80
    clerical, 178
Acagchemem, 136
acllas, 103, 110, 127, 154
Acoma, 126
Acosta, J., 110, 122, 147
activity and passivity, sexual, attitudes
    toward, 35–7, 43, 44, 45, 50,
    155–72
adultery, 22
Afonso, King of Portugal, 45
Africa, 136
ages, 56, 81, 84–101, 124–7, 131, 133,
    176, 203
Al-Jadiz, 52
Al-Katib, 51–2
Al-Muqaddasî, Muhammad Ibn Ahmad,
    39
Al-Mu'tamin, King of Saragossa, 42
Al-Ramadi, 42
Alarcón, H. de, 87, 92, 124, 133
Albert the Great, 145
Alexander, M., 67
Alfonso I, King of Aragon, 42
Alfonso X, King of Aragon, 45
Almería, 57
Alvarez Chanca, D., 65, 82

Ammianus Marcellinus, 24
Andalusia, 171
Andrés de Alcobiz, 158
Angola, 166
Apaches, 73–4
Apuleius, 34
Aquinas, Thomas, 17
Araucanians, 115, 128, 163, 165, 166
Arawaks, 65, 147
Ardian, 180
Aristophanes, 20, 21
Aristotle, 17
Arizona, 123
arms, gendered, 66–7, 116
Arnold, K., 109
Atahualpa, 71, 154
Australia, 93
Aymara, 80

Baja California, 123
Balboa, V. N. de, 82, 146
Balkans, 177
Barbosa, D., 61
Barton, C., 34
Benavides, A. de, 73–4
Benevento, 39
Bennassar, B., 57
berdaches, female, 6, 86, 159
berdaches, male, 6, 8–9, 40, 53–4,
    64–180

representations of women, 84
  space of, 137
  strength of, 86, 118, 137
bestiality, 17, 44, 46, 56, 156, 159, 256
Bethe, E., 30
Bianchi, T. de', 52
birth control, 140
bisexuality, 32
Borneo, 98
Boscana, G., 136
Boswell, J., 5–6, 42, 43, 48, 49, 56
Bozio, T., 104
Bracton, H. de, 19
Brazil, 132, 147, 165, 171
Browe, P., 21
Bucendo, 180
Burkert, W., 17, 18
Burton, R., 12
butchering, 17–18, 23, 58
Bynum, C. Walker, 50
Byzantine Empire, 39, 50, 62

Calancha, A. de la, 110, 122, 138, 143,
  149–50, 154, 169
Cañari, 134, 136
cannibalism, 148–9
Cantarella, E., 24, 28
Cape Catoche, 111
Cape San Mateo, 124
Caribs, 65, 147
Carnegie Report, 177–8
Cartagena, 122
Cartledge, P., 28
Castañeda, P., 123, 135
castration, 17–21, 39, 41, 45, 48, 57,
  58, 64, 65, 76, 78, 108
Catawba, 76
Cavil, 146
Cervantes de Salazar, F., 104
Cevallos Saavedra, H., 150
Cha'kwena, 73
Chan, 93, 146, 168
charivari, 29
Charles V, Emperor, 1, 2
Chichimeca, 68, 88, 90
Chilam Balam, Books of, 81, 175
Chimu, 122
China, 12, 17
Chincha, 107, 149
Chipewa, 126, 134
Chiribichi, 4, 115
Chivington, J., 72
Chonos, 128, 164

Chukchi, 123
Cibola, 123
Cieza de León, P. de, 3, 4, 106–7, 108,
  121, 122, 124, 134, 136, 143, 145,
  146, 148, 154, 156, 164
Cihuacoatl, 71, 79
cinaedos, 34, 98
circumcision, 18, 20, 31
Cistercians, 50
Clavijero, F. J., 160
Cleisthenes, 33
Clement VII, Pope, 46
clergy
  American, 102–17
  European, 3–4, 47–8, 51
  Muslim, 47–8
clothing and cosmetics, 32, 67, 77–8,
  79, 80, 90–1, 100, 127–8
Coaunacothzin, 158
Cobo, B., 10, 145
codpieces, 60
Collasuyu, 133, 157, 166, 169
Colombia, 86, 110, 122, 129
Colorado River, 87, 123, 124
Columbus, C., 110
contagion, 46–7, 65, 83, 145–7
Conti, N. de', 61
contra naturam, 17, 145
Coronado, F., 127
Cortés, H., 95
Cox Stevenson, M., 127
Coyohuacan, 80
Creed, G., 179–80
Crete, 27–8, 30
Crow, 88, 125, 126, 133, 136
Cu, 146
Cueva, 91, 165
Culiacan, 123
Cuylonemiquia, 74
Cuzco, 71, 79, 91, 109, 147, 151–2,
  156, 173, 175

Dakota, 125
Darién, 95, 132
Darius III, King of Persia, 34
De Pauw, C., 156, 160
Delaware (Lenape), 76–9, 81, 100, 129
Demosthenes, 33
Denver, 72
dependency, 33–4, 79, 85, 86, 131
depilation, 20, 38, 56, 98, 128
development, theories of, 3, 4, 147–55,
  167, 176, 248

Devereux, G., 30, 89, 92, 99, 128
Díaz del Castillo, B., 90, 95, 104, 111,
   121, 122, 131
diplomacy, 79–81
Domingo de Santo Tomas, 107, 111
Donnan, C., 113, 114
Dover, K., 28, 30, 31, 35
Durán, D., 105

Ecuador, 4, 124, 138, 148
Edward II, King of England, 19
Edwardes, A., 20
effeminacy, 3, 4, 8, 13, 25, 31–5, 60,
   152, 155, 161, 169, and *passim*
Egica, King of the Visigoths, 43–4
Egypt, 12, 18, 27, 39
Eliade, M., 114
Elvira, Council of, 43
enemas, 107
England, 21
entries, 72
Ephoros, 27–8
eros and seduction, 3, 6
eunuchs, 25–6, 39, 41, 61–2, 65–6,
   103, 108, 127, 180
   see also castration
Eurymedon, 14
evisceration, 19, 68, 159

Fages, P., 124
falsettists, 41, 114
fathers, 49, 178–80
Fehling, D., 22
fellation, 26, 33, 87, 88, 111, 133–4
Fellini, F., 174
Ferdinand and Isabella, monarchs of
   Spain, 46, 58
Fernández de Oviedo, G., 1, 4, 66, 84,
   90–1, 92, 94, 96, 110, 127–8, 129,
   130, 132, 133, 134, 147, 148, 161,
   162–3, 165, 166, 171
Fernández Piedrahita, L., 86, 135–6
Ferrara, 52–3
Fez, 53–5, 57
Flatheads, 125
Florence, 53, 58, 61
Forsyth, I., 49
France, 5, 55, 67–8, 77–8
Francisco de León, 59
Freud, S., 11, 177, 178–9, 205–6
Freyre, G., 147
Foucault, M., 2–3
Fuera real, 45

Galen, 97
gangs, *see* youth groups
Ganymede, 49
Garcilaso de la Vega, 106, 109, 122,
   132, 138, 148–50, 154, 156, 157
Germany, 21, 24
gestures, 32
   see also postures
giants, 142–5, 157
Golden Ass, The, 19, 22
Gómara, *see* Lopez de Gómara
Greece, 12–13, 20, 23–4, 28, 30, 31, 35
Greenberg, D., 220
Gregory, Bishop of Tours, 36, 48
Grijalva, J., 92, 94
Gros Ventres, 125
Guaicuru, 166
Guaman Poma de Ayala, F., 74
Guarmey, 122
Guatemala, 74, 93, 104, 105, 121, 133,
   157
Guayaquil, 164
Guerra, F., 5
Gutiérrez de Santa Clara, P., 145
Guzman, N. de, 68, 88, 131

Halperin, D., 33
Hammond, W., 102, 127, 133, 137
Hammurabi, Code of, 26
Hanke, L., 171
harems, 23, 25, 51, 55, 61, 179, 265
Henry III, King of France, 34
Henry IV, King of Castile, 45, 55
Hercules, 82
hermaphrodites, 67
Herodotus, 17–18, 97
Herrera, A. de, 111, 132, 134, 157, 159,
   160, 162, 165
Hippocrates, 97–8
Hirschfeld, M., 176–7
Hispaniola, 147, 162
Holder, A., 88, 125, 133, 136
'homosexuals' and 'homosexuality,' 6,
   10, 85, 176, 232–3
Honduras, 97
Hormuz, 61–2
hostages, 14, 74
Huánuco, 107
Huascar, 71, 79, 128, 154
Huayllas, 121, 164
Huitzilopochtli, 71, 104

Ibn 'Abdun, 47, 48
Ibn Khaldun, 52
Illinois, 66, 116
Inca, realm of the, 4, 71–2, 106, 124, 148–55, 156
incest, 81, 91–2
India, 12, 61
infection, see contagion
initiation, male, 26
Inquisition, 46, 55, 58
insults, 65, 71, 80, 165–6
Iroquois, 75–9, 80
Islam, 50, 51
Israel, 12, 18, 19, 20
Italians, 5, 57, 58, 147
Itzá, 81
Itzcoatl, 80
Ixtlilxóchitl, F. de Alva, 159

Japan, 24

Kansans, 98, 128
Kasinelu, 128
Kaska, 86
Kennan, G., 178
Kia'nakive, 73
Klein, C., 71, 79
Koch-Harnack, G., 28
Kodiak, 86
Kolhamana, 73
Kon Tiki, 145
Koran, 39, 47

La Carpintería, 125
Laches, 86, 135–6
Lactantius, 44
Lafitau, J., 135, 230
Laguna Pueblo, 126, 137
Lampuna, 164
Landa, D. de, 132
Larco Hoyle, P., 111–12, 114
Las Casas, B. de, 2, 4, 84, 86–7, 91, 92, 93, 94, 96–9, 100–1, 105–6, 108, 115, 124, 135, 146, 148, 159, 162, 171
Lasbeke, 126
Laudonnière, R., 67
laws, sexuality, 10, 43–7, 149–50, 152, 156–61
Le Moyne de Morgues, J., 2, 67
Leo Africanus, 53–4
Lerner, G., 6–7, 13–14, 21, 23–4
Lery, J. de, 166

lesbianism, 7, 138–9, 160
lex talionis, 21
Lima, 109, 122
Liutprand, Bishop of Cremona, 39
Livy, 14
Lizárraga, R. de, 139–40
Lloque Yupanqui, Inca, 153
Lopez de Gómara, F., 66, 67, 106, 112, 127, 132, 135, 138, 162, 169
López Medel, T., 104, 124
Loskiel, G., 128

Machiavelli, N., 34
macho, see manliness
Madrid, 57
Mahicans, 76
Mama Ciuaco, 152
manliness, 3, 25, 26–7, 32, 60, 150, 155, 173–4, 175
Manuel, King of Portugal, 46
Maran, 146
Marchello-Nizia, C., 51
markets, sex, 39–42
Marquette, J., 66, 100, 116, 135
marriages, 24–7, 29–31, 40, 59, 66–89, 93–4, 134–6, 152
Mary, mother of Jesus, 122
masturbation, 20, 97, 152
Maya, 74, 81, 93–4, 132
Mayta Capac Amaro, Inca, 154
Medina, 32
Mehmet, Sultan, 62
Melanesia, 6
Mendieta, G., 159
Mesopotamia, 12, 22, 26, 103, 109
Metz, 58
Meulengracht Sørensen, P., 14
Mexico, 5, 71–172
Mexico City, see Tenochtitlan
Michael, Archangel, 143
Michele di Cuneo, 65, 80, 147
Michoacán, 68
Midrash, 18
military, 52–5, 64–81
Mixtecs, 105
Moche, 111–14, 122
Mohave, 92, 166
Mohawk, 77
monasticism, 3, 7, 48, 49
Montesinos, F., 147, 151–3, 163
Montfort, S. de, 58
Moors, 5, 7, 47

Morocco, 41
Moscas, 122
Motolinía, T., called, 103–4, 106, 158–9
Mott, L. 55–6, 262
Muhammad Ibn Malike, 42
Muisca, 129
Muñoz Camargo, D., 164, 169
Münzer, T., 57
Murúa, M. de, 91
mutilation, of guards, 127

Nadoüessi, 116
Nanticoke, 76
Nebuchadnezzar, 20
Nez Percés, 125
Nezahualcoyotl, 159
Nezahualpilzintli, 158
Nicaragua, 130, 132, 134, 161
Nóbrega, M. de, 135
Noriega, M., 172
Notaras, L., 62
Nuñez Cabeza de Vaca, A., 66, 67, 135, 136
Nuñez de Pineda y Bascuñan, F., 115, 116, 163, 165, 166

Oliva, G. Anello, 154
Olmecs, 74, 143
Olmedo, 57
Olmos, J. de, 122
Ortiz, D., 68, 70
Osage, 68–9, 98, 126
Oviedo, see Fernández de Oviedo

Pacasmayo, 138
Pacaxes, 123
Pachacamac, 109–10, 111
Pachacuti, Inca, 154
Pacheco, F., 122
pages, 55
Pagsanjan, 173
paideia, 26
Palladius, Count, 36
Palma de Mallorca, 56
Palou, F., 124–5
Panama, 66, 82, 146, 172, 177
Pánuco, 95, 132
Papua New Guinea, 6, 26, 145
Park, W., 115
Parsons, E. Clews, 87, 126
Parthenius, Bishop of Gévaudan, 36
Passau, 122

Payta, 122
Pechina, 39
Pedro de León, 58
Pelagius, St, 43
Pennsylvania, 59, 76–9
Pérez de Ribas, A., 66, 170–1
Persia, 61
Peru, see Inca, realm of the
Petatlan, 123
Peter Martyr d'Anghiera, 59–60, 82, 92, 115, 146
Peter of Ghent, 88, 100, 104, 105, 158, 160
Peter the Chanter, 44
Philip II, King of Spain, 46
piaches, 114, 115
picota, 102, 140, 150, 167
pimping, 94–5
Pires, T., 61
Pizarro, F., 124, 150
Pizarro, P., 170
Plutarch, 28
poetry, Hebrew, 41–2
polygyny, 93, 136, 163–4
Pomapampa, 154
Pompeii, 22
poor, the, 33–4
portage, 66, 67, 68
Portugal, 59, 135, 147
postures, 17, 20, 32, 109–10
power, 23–31, 148, and passim
Prato, 53
pregnancy, 52
Priapus, 21, 23, 167–8
property, 13–23, and passim
prostitution, female, 31, 51, 52, 54, 61, 130, 131–3
   male, 32, 57, 61, 62, 90, 128–9, 131–3
Pueblo peoples, 72
Puerto Viejo, 122, 142–3, 145
Puna, 121
punishment, 7, 14, 17, 22, 24, 43–7, 55–60, 71, 90–1, 139, 149, 157, 158–61, and passim
Punta de los Pedernales, 125

Quaraca, 82
Quaregua, 146
Quinatun, map of, 160
Quinones, 143
Quito, 134

Ragon, P., 214
rape
  of females, 7, 13–14, 92, 143, 154
  of males, 7, 14, 20–3, 27–8, 29, 38,
    50, 53, 56, 57, 65, 68–9, 91, 129,
    171
retinue, 27, 62, 64, 92, 94, 129
ribalds, 55
Richlin, A., 34
Rio de Palmas, 162
Rio Paraguay, 122
Roca, Inca, 152
Rocke, M., 58
Rome, 17, 19, 22, 28, 35
Rossello Vaquer, R., 56, 57
Rowe, J., 150
Rowson, E., 32
Rozmital, L. de, 57
Ruíz de Arce, J., 124, 129
Rwanda, 177

sacrifice, 17, 68, 86–7, 97, 103, 104,
    108, 117, 129, 146, 148, 154, 175
Sahagún, B. de, 85, 104, 128–9, 169,
    170
Salinas y Córdoba, B. de, 154
San Antonio, 125
San Cristóbal de las Casas, 105
San Luís Obispo, 125
Sancho IV, King of Castile, 52
Santa Barbara, 125
Santa Cruz Pachacuti, J. de, 153, 154
Scandinavia, 18, 48
Scythians, 97–8
Seler, E., 71
semen, 26, 49
Seneca, 34, 35
Senecas, 78
Sepúlveda, J. G. de, 73
Serra, J., 124–5
Seth and Horus, 27
Seville, 58
Sforza, 59
shamans, 114–15, 166
Shepherd, G., 136
Shoshone, 125
Silverblatt, I., 7, 95
Sinaloa, 111, 123, 135, 170–1
Sinchi Roca, Inca, 153
Sioux, 98–9, 125
slavery, 13, 22, 24, 40, 49, 92, 171
Soares de Sousa, G., 132, 165, 171
Sodom and Gomorrah, 23, 45, 143

sodomy
  in art, 110–14
  and decline of the collectivity, 84,
    104, 139, 147, 150–5
  denied by Amerindians, 155–6
  and geography, 107, 121–3
  heterosexual, 9, 91, 138, 139, 140
  'sodomy' and 'sodomites,' 23, 168–9
Sofali, 59
Spain and Spaniards, 5, 38–63, 81, and
    passim
state building, 23, 24, 25, 27, 30, 81,
    94–5, 102
status, 108, 146–7, 165, 167
Suetonius, 35
Suyo Valley, 123
syphilis, 141

Tabasco, 110
Tahus, 123
Tanner, J., 125, 134
Tatars, 98
Teedyuscung, 78
Templars, 45–6
temples, 103–17
Tenochtitlan, 71, 80, 103–4, 105, 106,
    130, 160, 175, 180
Tepaneca, 80
testicles, 17–18, 58
Texas, 66, 135
Texcoco, 68, 158, 159
Tezcatlipoca, 103
theft, 14, 21
Tierra del Fuego, 145
Tierra Firme, 92, 95, 110, 128,
    133, 147
Titicaca, lake, 80, 90, 107, 128, 170
Tixier, A., 98
Tlaxcala, 130, 164
Toledo, Council of, 43
Toledo, F. de, 90
Toltecs, 71
Torquemada, J., 74, 106, 130, 146, 160,
    164, 168
transvestism, passim
  link to sodomy, 84, 89, 96–7, 99–100
  temporary, 71, 79, 130, 134
tribute, 76–7
Tristan and Lancelot, 51
Trujillo, 122

Tsalatitse, 126
Tumucua, 67–8
Tupinamba, 132, 166
Turkey, 50
Tuscaroras, 76
Tutelos, 76

U'k, 126
United States of America, 29, 172,
    177–8, 205
Uzbek, 39

vagabonds, 209
Valencia, 46, 57, 58, 147
Valera, Blas, 108, 151, 156
Vanggaard, T., 177
Venezuela, 127, 169
Veracruz, 1
Veragua, 110
Verdun, 39
Vezelay, 49
Vietnam War, 178
Vitoria, F. de, 5
vocabularies, gender-specific, 128

Washington, DC, 127
We'wha, 116, 118, 126, 127
William of Adam, 40
William of Auvergne, 51
William of Tripoli, 39–40

William Rufus, King of England, 34
Winnebago, 68
women, 6, 22–3, 30, 50–5, and passim
    attitude of, toward male homosexual
        behaviour, 10, 62, 91, 138, 151–2,
        153, 161–4
    'castration' of, 23, 30
    character of, 32, 163
    manly (mujer varoníl), 209
    military, 52–5, 130
    occupations of, 32, 34, 53, 64, 66, 78,
        79, 86, 91, 97, 116, 134–6, 137,
        150
    shamed, 72
    transvested, 52, 56, 142, 159
    treatment of, by males, 122, 162
    triumphant, 72–3
    see also berdaches, female;
        prostitution, female; rape, of
        females

Xenophon, 23

youth groups, 27, 29
Yucatan, 110
Yuma, 92, 124

Zárate, A., 122, 143, 162
Zempoala, 95
Zorita, A. de, 3
Zulus, 19